STAR-SPANGLED BANNER

STAR-SPANGLED BANNER

The Unlikely Story of America's National Anthem

MARC FERRIS

JOHNS HOPKINS UNIVERSITY PRESS

Baltimore

© 2014 Johns Hopkins University Press
All rights reserved. Published 2014
Printed in the United States of America on acid-free paper
2 4 6 8 9 7 5 3 1

Johns Hopkins University Press
2715 North Charles Street
Baltimore, Maryland 21218-4363
www.press.jhu.edu

Ferris, Marc, 1963–
Star-spangled banner : the unlikely story of America's national anthem / Marc Ferris.
pages cm
Includes bibliographical references and index.
ISBN 978-1-4214-1518-5 (hardcover : alk. paper) — ISBN 978-1-4214-1519-2
(electronic) — ISBN 1-4214-1518-6 (hardcover : alk. paper) —
ISBN 1-4214-1519-4 (electronic) 1. Star-spangled banner (Song)
2. National songs—United States—History and criticism. I. Title.
ML3561.S8F47 2014
784.7′1973—dc23
2014002572

A catalog record for this book is available from the British Library.

*Special discounts are available for bulk purchases of this book. For more information,
please contact Special Sales at 410-516-6936 or specialsales@press.jhu.edu.*

Johns Hopkins University Press uses environmentally friendly
book materials, including recycled text paper that is composed of at least
30 percent post-consumer waste, whenever possible.

To my parents,
Alan and Helene Ferris

Contents

Illustrations follow page 133

Acknowledgments

SPECIAL THANKS to Jonathan Ferris and Suzanne Ferris.

Thanks to Nicholas Albicelli, Kathi Ash, Paula Baker, Jan Benzel, Winfred E. A. Bernhard, Don Bracken, Robert J. Brugger, Sidney A. Burrell, Kathleen M. Capels, Hank Cash, Lisa Cesarano, Judy Codding, Bob D'Aprile, Michael Dardano, Diane Davis, Peter Eisenstadt, Amelia Ferris, Conrad Ferris, Jackie Levi Ferris, Lilah Ferris, Mary Ferris, Reuben Ferris, Mia Ferris Freeman, Andy Gates, Peter Giles, John Giriat, Eva Havas Gonzales, Matthew Gonzales, Michael Gonzales, Pancho Gonzales, Peter Goodman, Yvonne Y. Haddad, Eric Hagemann, Trevor Hochman, Regina Holmes, Becky Hornyak, Kenneth T. Jackson, Andy Jacobs Jr., Kim Johnson, Jack Kadden, Fred Kameny, Susan Key, Robert Kolker, Jeff Korman, Jennifer Krauss, Richard F. Kuisel, Michael LaPick, Calvin Lawrence, Sandra Loureiro-Mato, Lou Malcomb, Joseph H. March, Gerald W. McFarland, Wilbur R. Miller, Ann-Marie Nieves, Regula Noetzli, Ron Pearcey, Kathy Peiss, William J. Pencek Jr., Jaclyn Penny, Cora Provins, Susan Rabiner, Leonard L. Richards, Jeffrey Richter, Julie Ades Richter, Roland Sarti, Helena Schwarz, Scott S. Sheads, Ann Shepardson, Evan Siegel, Jeanne Siegel, Max Siegel, Ralph Siegel, Dick Sine, Linda Smith, Andrew Szabo, Lonn Taylor, Barbara L. Tischler, Nancy Tomes, Nancy Toth, Rich Triblets, Anna Von Lunz, Gregory Weidman, Stephen Williams, and Doug Wright.

ACKNOWLEDGMENTS

This book began in a Department of History graduate seminar at Stony Brook University. A Smithsonian Institution fellowship allowed research at the National Museum of American History, the Library of Congress, the National Archives, the New York Public Library, the Enoch Pratt Free Library, the Fort McHenry National Monument and Historic Shrine, the Maryland Historical Society, and the Historical Society of Frederick County.

STAR-SPANGLED BANNER

Prologue

THE NATIONAL ANTHEM of the United States of America is no laughing matter, but an old wisecrack tells of a child who thinks the last words of *The Star-Spangled Banner* are "play ball." More than one quip takes advantage of the song's oft-misunderstood first five words. For example, a young boy attends his first ballgame, and when he comes home his mother asks how things went. "I had such a great time and everyone was so nice," he replies. "A man showed us to our seats and people kept bringing us hot dogs and sodas. Then this song started and every person in the stadium stood up and asked me, 'Jose, can you see?'" But the real national inside joke about *The Star-Spangled Banner* is the widespread lack of familiarity with the actual words of even the first verse—and few Americans realize that there are four in all. Alluding to the country's amnesia regarding the lyrics, in one yarn that dates to World War I, a doughboy approaches an outpost at night after patrolling enemy territory and is challenged by the guard on duty:

SENTINEL: Who goes there?
   SOLDIER: An American.
SENTINEL: Then come forward and recite the first verse
            of *The Star-Spangled Banner.*
   SOLDIER: I can't remember it.
SENTINEL: Then pass, American.

Besides sometimes serving as an object of mirth, *The Star-Spangled Banner* is also the most controversial musical composition in United States history. Written during the War of 1812, when Francis Scott Key coined the phrase to honor the massive American flag that withstood the British bombardment of Fort McHenry in Baltimore harbor, the song rocketed to prominence but also attracted criticism. Detractors decried the hard-to-sing melody and denounced the alleged militarism of the words. In time, Anglophiles chafed at the lines in the third verse that insulted the British, who turned from foe to friend in the late 1800s. Anti-alcohol crusaders also condemned the composition that inspired Key, *To Anacreon in Heaven*, which celebrated the pursuits of a gentlemen's drinking, dining, and music club in London. Many Americans revere the anthem due to its legal status and long history—rarely do they gush over the song itself. Recurring debates over the merits and the meaning of *The Star-Spangled Banner* during the past two hundred years reflected the use of music for propaganda purposes, the intersection between religion and patriotism, and the rise of liberal and conservative political factions after the Revolutionary War.

The core issues in the song's long journey center on why it took Congress 117 years to pass a national anthem law and what finally prompted them to act in 1931. With all the negativity heaped on *The Star-Spangled Banner* and with so many other viable rivals for anthem status in the United States—including *Yankee Doodle*; *Hail, Columbia*; *My Country, 'Tis of Thee* (*America*); *Columbia, the Gem of the Ocean*; *America the Beautiful*; and *God Bless America*—it is a wonder that Francis Scott Key's composition rose to the top and remained there. Beginning in the 1700s, many countries sanctioned certain anthems as ploys to create compliant citizens or reinforce a particular ruler's power, but the world's most influential and enduring national songs, including *God Save the Queen*, *The Marseillaise*, and *The Star-Spangled Banner*, achieved instant popularity during times of crisis. On the surface, given the year that Congress took action, legislation to designate the country's official anthem seems to reflect efforts by an overwhelmed federal government to manufacture patriotism by decree and bolster national unity in the early years of the Great Depression. The real story is much more complicated.

Anthem before a Nation, 1814–1860

BECAUSE CONGRESS TOOK SO LONG to single out *The Star-Spangled Banner* as the national anthem, the song could have easily faded into obscurity. A handful of other contenders arose in the interim, and elected representatives in the United States avoided selecting a signature composition, even as other newly formed nations announced their arrival with flags flying and bands blaring. In popular culture, Americans generally celebrate newfangled fads, so it is even more remarkable that ordinary citizens and government actors held on to such an old-fashioned song for so long. Key's creation gained instant popularity and remained cherished by enough people over time to earn its spot as the sonic embodiment of nationhood. Key himself is rarely mentioned in school history lessons outside his home state, but his gift to the nation continues to exert a strong cultural and emotional pull.

The term "anthem" refers to a type of song popular in the Church of England and is derived from the word "antiphone," or voices singing against each other, connoting a call and response. Pop songs are referred to as anthemic when they inspire fist pumping during a catchy chorus. Sports anthems encourage mass participation. Colleges have fight songs, many sports teams adopt signature tunes, and each branch of the armed forces in the United States is represented by anthems, including the

Marines' Hymn, Anchors Aweigh, The Army Goes Rolling Along, and *The U.S. Air Force Song.*

The people of England adopted the first modern-day "anthem of anthems" seemingly overnight during the mid-1700s. Born of war, as most lasting national anthems are, *God Save the King* (or queen, depending on the monarch's gender) gained instant popularity. The origin of the music and lyrics for *God Save the King* is largely obscure, though portions of the tune appeared in works by Henry Purcell and other composers in the 1600s. Long before the advent of any melody, "God save the king," a phrase lifted from the Bible, became commonplace in England as a salutation uttered when departing the company of others or toasting the nation and its fortune. First published in 1744, the song catapulted to national fame during the Jacobite uprising the following year, when Prince Charles Edward Stuart landed troops in Scotland, intent on toppling King George II and reclaiming the throne in the name of his grandfather, James II.[1]

As the rebel army marched toward London, a newspaper notice announced that "Mr. Lacy, Master of his Majesty's Company of Comedians, at the Theatre-Royal in Drury-lane, has applyd for Leave to raise 200 Men, in Defence of his Majesty's Person and Government; in which the whole Company of Players are willing to engage." That evening, after the presentation of a play entitled "The Alchemist," three soloists, backed by a choir, strolled onto the stage and sang a rousing rendition of *God Save the King* in support of the sitting monarch. One account reported that the audience was "agreeably surpriz'd" by the performance of "the Anthem of God save our noble King," which met with "universal Applause" and "encored with repeated Huzzas." This group of actors pledging loyalty to their then-current monarch started a chain reaction that led to the spontaneous spread of *God Save the King* from the heart of London to the rest of the country. The first publication of it in the provinces also referred to the song as an anthem.[2]

The words of *God Save the King* initially applied to the Stuart dynasty, in power during the early 1700s, and a circa 1725 wine cup identified the lyrics as the Jacobite Anthem. The first line of the first printing in 1744 extolled "God save our Lord the King / Long Live our noble King." The following year, as the Stuarts and Hanovers battled for the throne, the Drury Lane actors changed it to "God save great George our king" to clarify which side the performers supported. At the height of his rebellion, Bonny Prince Charlie's forces reached to within a hundred miles of London, but George II prevailed. By 1748, the chimes at Westminster Abbey rang out the tune's notes and church poets borrowed the melody to construct hymns and songs of praise. *God Save the King*, taken up by the royal family and hawked on the streets as a ballad sheet by music publishers, never needed official recognition, since it "soon acquired a status close to sacred through its incorporation in civic and military ceremonies." The informal yet forceful adoption of an official song in England inspired other nations to follow suit. "Every civilized country had for long had its national flag and when Britain had led the way, every civilized country wanted also a National Anthem," wrote one musicologist.[3]

The melody of *God Save the King* served as the basis for almost two dozen interim national anthems across Europe over the next seventy-five years, beginning with Denmark in 1790. Ludwig von Beethoven, who composed seven variations on the theme, called it a "godsend." Franz Joseph Haydn also adapted musical and lyrical motifs for his composition *Gott Erhalte Franz der Kaiser* (God Save Emperor Francis) after visiting London in the 1790s. Stately and somewhat pompous, yet simple enough for children to sing, *God Save the King* crossed over to North America as a symbol of civility and order. Before 1776, it served as the unofficial anthem of the thirteen colonies. During the Revolutionary War, loyalists to the crown sang it in defiance of the rebels, and English forces played it to celebrate battle victories. In 1780, after a six-week siege, British troops reached the gates of Charleston, South Carolina, and the company's oboists struck up the anthem.[4]

England's enemies sometimes recast the words in mocking tones, participating in the accepted practice, known as a parody, of writing new, topical verses to existing music, a church tactic dating back to the Reformation. Song parodies document history from the bottom up, revealing the feelings and beliefs of ordinary folk. Commentators on the day's events found it much easier to create memorable rhymes and phrases by fitting their words to well-known compositions, often listed underneath the title of the parody to help singers along. The instant popularity of *God Save the King* led to a "never-ending flood" of poems matched to the melody that "has not yet ceased."[5] In England, Jacobites congregated in secret societies and continued to sing versions venerating antiestablishment heroes long after the failed 1745 rebellion, and one revolutionary-era poet in North America repurposed it as *God Save Our States*: "God save our thirteen states / Long rule the United States / God save our states / Make us victorious, happy and glorious, no tyrants over us / God save our states."[6]

The world's second national anthem, *La Marcha Real* (The Royal March of Spain), never resonated beyond the borders of Spain. First published in 1761 and performed during Catholic masses to augment the communion-wafer ceremony, this solemn march lacks lyrics, for one thing. King Carlos III declared it the nation's Honor March in 1770, and the composition aired during patriotic and royal ceremonies. *La Marcha Real*, the first official song ever designated by government fiat, also exerted a limited influence outside the country, due in part to its imposition from above. Over time, the song evolved into the recognized national anthem of Spain, and a royal decree made it official in 1997. Attempts to add lyrics to the melody engendered controversy through the centuries and never met with lasting success.[7]

Semisacred national songs like *God Save the King* and *La Marcha Real* offer revealing insights into the give-and-take between individuals and top-down, officially sanctioned efforts to foster patriotism. Religious allusions often fuse with rituals and symbols honoring national glory. Throughout history, true believers in many causes—especially nationalism—overtly invoked the sanction of the divine, a tendency that French philosopher Jean-Jacques Rousseau identified as "civil religion" in *The Social Contract*. When "codified in a single country," this phenomenon "gives it its gods, its own tutelary patrons; it has its dogmas, its rites, and its external cult prescribed by law." Civil religion runs amok, Rousseau wrote, when it "becomes tyrannous and exclusive, and makes a people bloodthirsty and intolerant, so that it breathes fire and slaughter, and regards as a sacred act the killing of every one who does not believe in its gods."[8] Throughout United States history, many public events, inaugurations, and official holiday commemorations unfolded with the cadence of religious ceremonies. Usually accompanied by a benediction, these secular prayer sessions often employed *The Star-Spangled Banner* to leave listeners with a heightened sense of belonging to the national family—or to reinforce the interests of the dominant group—depending on one's perspective.

During the late 1700s, when the American Revolution inspired ethnic minorities around the globe to consider themselves as nations-in-waiting, civil religion replaced the cross with the flag, the apostles with the Founding Fathers, and the Bible with the Declaration of Independence and the Constitution. The Declaration, which referred to "nature's God," the "Creator," and the "Supreme Judge of the world," assumed the "protection of Divine Providence" for the revolutionary endeavor. Civil War battlefields are often referred to as sacred ground, and the sacrifices of soldiers and other martyrs became fodder for five national holidays (a variant of the term "holyday"), including Martin Luther King Day, Memorial Day, Independence Day, Veterans Day, and Christmas. Pilgrims flock to the patriotic temples of Boston, New York, Philadelphia, and Washington, D.C. In Baltimore, Fort McHenry, the epicenter of *The Star-Spangled Banner*, is the only landmark in the entire national park system designated as a "national monument and historic shrine." This tendency to solemnize nationalistic sentiments runs counter to what is otherwise a revered tenet in the United States, the concept of the separation of church and state. Like the nebulous term "patriotism," the word "God" is one that "means so many different things to different people that it is almost an empty sign," according to one sociologist.[9] Another effective catchphrase, referencing "the people," evokes the idea of a mythical consensus. Other terms with interchangeable interpretations that have saturated the American political lexicon include "republic," "democratic," "freedom," "liberty," and "progress." One person's freedom to own slaves or monopolize a sector of the economy, for example, can be another's oppression.

Symbols surrounding patriotism display a similar ambiguity, but songs are particularly open to interpretation. Musical compositions carry an emotional punch and play a vital role reinforcing the creed of almost every institution, with national anthems serving as primary conduits for the crossover from religion to patriotism. *God Save the King* makes a plea for direct divine intervention in the country's earthly affairs. The Canadian anthem, *O Canada*, asks God to "keep our land glorious and free." The French dismantled vestiges of clericalism in the 1790s, but their cherished musical symbol, *The Marseillaise*, acknowledges a "sacred love of our native land." With the exception of *Yankee Doodle*, other songs in contention for the national anthem of the United States equate patriotism with godliness. By the early 1800s, *God Save the King* became synonymous with the monarchy, yet it also nestled into the consciousness of ordinary people: "Every British man, woman, and child, whether in the mother country or overseas, looks upon that tune as part of his or her personal inheritance."[10]

In addition to the language and the legal system passed down to its American colonies, England also supplied the main musical mold (influenced considerably by Africans and others). English ballads and the volley of competing parodies helped gird the colonists for war in 1776. One of the first compositions published in the embryonic United States, *The Liberty Song*, fused original lyrics with the music of the Royal Navy anthem, *Heart of Oak*, and stuck a finger in the mother country's eye. Written in 1768 by John Dickinson, a prominent Pennsylvania lawyer and colonial propagandist, the lyrics invoked God's blessing for the protests against the Townshend Duties, imposed by the British on tea, glass, paint, lead, and paper in 1767. This policy prompted violent nonimportation protests, whipped up by the very newspapers and magazines subject to the tax. One verse included a slogan that resurfaced in subsequent songs: "Then join hand in hand brave Americans all / By uniting we stand, by dividing we fall / In so Righteous a cause let us hope to succeed / For Heaven approves of each generous deed."

Yankee Doodle, the most popular musical emblem during the revolutionary period, remained in the national anthem conversation through the end of the 1800s. The origins of this song are mysterious, but according to legend, the English used the word "Yankee" to mock a ragtag regiment of Connecticut troops that served alongside British regulars during the French and Indian War, which broke out in 1754. The term's first instance in print, from the pen of General James Wolfe in 1758, merely mentioned "two companies of Yankees," suggesting that it referred to all Americans. No matter what Yankee applies to, a "doodle" is a fool. The song *Yankee Doodle* appeared in "The Disappointment," a 1767 stage presentation known as a ballad opera or comic opera, which featured parodies of popular period melodies instead of original compositions. Eventually, American colonists used the term Yankee for "the inhabitants of some colony other than their own," according to one historical account. Early in the Revolution, Americans embraced the nickname and flipped it into a badge of honor that blunted "the point of the joke, and indeed used it in rebuttal by appropriating the tune with all its associations for their patriotic field music." Played with fife and drum, *Yankee Doodle* served as a peppy march, especially when embellished with snappy drum rolls, and it could be heard wherever armies on both sides of the battle lines assembled. The continentals and the British engaged the melody as a vehicle for innumerable lyrical jousts that provided a running commentary on the progress of the war. Long before the American Revolution magnified its popularity, a character in "The Disappointment" called it the song with 199 verses.[11]

Eventually the word Yankee came to specify and ridicule New Englanders, although after the Civil War it signified all Northerners. It is possible to play a heartfelt, catchy version of *Yankee Doodle*, but getting past the lyrics can be difficult. The words "Yankee Doodle went to town, riding on a pony / Stuck a feather in his cap and called it macaroni" probably date to the period between 1764 and 1767. They most likely satirize lower-class strivers who aped one of the fashionable sets of the day, known as "macaronis." The standard Revolutionary War version began: "Father and I went down to camp along with Captain Gooding / There they saw the men and boys as thick as hasty pudding." Other verses from around 1776 recount events and sights encountered at the military encampment. After the Revolution, the song served as the de facto national anthem when it came time to establish the new country's symbols, since the fledgling federal government never designated an official song. Congress did settle on the general design of the flag in 1777, modifying the pattern in 1794, and in 1782 they approved the Great Seal, featuring a bald eagle. Popular custom recognized Independence Day, which featured wild displays of patriotic fervor and a day off from work. Congress took almost one hundred years to designate July 4 as the first federal holiday, and the selection of an official national anthem took even longer. While later displaced, *Yankee Doodle* still remains a favorite school selection and is the official state song of Connecticut.

In 1789, when George Washington took office as the first president of the United States, the revolutionary spirit rippled to France, and those repercussions rebounded to the New World. The most enduring byproduct of the French Revolution, *The Marseillaise*, experienced a tumultuous history since its creation, and it eventually evolved into the preeminent radical and antiestablishment song throughout the world, a position it held into the 1900s. In 1792, army engineer and amateur musician Joseph

Rouget de Lisle attended a party at the home of the mayor of Strasbourg. Responding to the host's request that he write a song to support the French revolutionary government's declaration of war on Austria, de Lisle took about twenty-four hours to craft from scratch what would become one of the most repeated melodies in human history (including by the Beatles in the beginning of *All You Need Is Love*).

First titled *War Song for the Army of the Rhine*, de Lisle's composition appeared like a lightning bolt permanently etched into the sky, as one historian wrote. Composer André Grétry called it "music out of the mouth of a cannon." The tune accompanied a squadron from Marseilles as they marched to Paris, and it spread by bayonet point with the mobs that stormed the Tuilleries palace. Individuals sang it in the streets, actors bellowed it in the theaters, printers dashed off copies, and the song accompanied every state function (including executions). Recognized as the French national anthem by government proclamation in 1795, *The Marseillaise* eventually became associated with a revolutionary spirit, no matter the country or situation, the " 'song of songs' of revolt," rivaled only by *The Internationale* (with lyrics first intended to fit *The Marseillaise*). During the seesaw fight for power between monarchists and republicans in the early 1800s, several rulers of France attempted to ban the song and decree other selections as official anthems. Eventually *The Marseillaise* became what one historian called "the obligatory accompaniment to Bastille Day celebrations," the French equivalent to July 4.[12] Unlike *God Save the King*, *The Marseillaise* downplayed the Deity and extolled blood sacrifice in defense of the motherland. The vivid scenario in the first verse is typical:

Come, children of the nation
Our day of Glory has arrived
Against us stands tyranny
The bloody flag is raised
The bloody flag is raised
Listen, in the countryside
The roar of these ferocious soldiers
They are coming into our midst
To cut the throats of your sons, your compatriots
To arms, citizens!

Form your battalions
March! March!
Let their impure blood
Water our fields.

The French Revolution and its fallout spawned the War of 1812 and *The Star-Spangled Banner*. Turmoil in France split the United States into two main factions, both of which claimed to be the legitimate heirs of the revolutionary legacy. As president, George Washington remained neutral, and his farewell address warned against "passionate attachment" to foreign countries. Appalled at the bloodshed and excesses of the French Revolution, Federalists John Adams and Alexander Hamilton backed England and its monarchy. Jeffersonian Republicans sought to export the freedoms unleashed by the Spirit of 1776 and aligned with revolutionary France. As the battle in Europe moved from the continent to the high seas, England and France, the two naval superpowers at the time, affronted American pride by seizing sailors, stealing cargo, and confiscating United States vessels. Until the XYZ Affair became public knowledge in April 1798, the new country lacked the ability to stop the harassment. This incident centered on the demand for a bribe by three French ministers, identified as X, Y, and Z in official correspondence to shield their identities. Congress strengthened the American navy and embarked on what became known as the Quasi-War with France. Federalist Anglophiles, led by President John Adams, passed the Alien and Sedition Acts in June and July to squelch opposition from the Republicans and tar any opposition as treasonous.

Music emerged as another weapon in the Federalist arsenal. *Adams and Liberty*, a parody that became one of the country's first popular campaign songs, employed the melody that would later become *The Star-Spangled Banner*. Written in 1798, the lyrics hailed the country's founders, promoted free trade, and denounced the French for threatening worldwide stability. A revealing verse invoked the Almighty:

Let fame to the world sound America's voice
No intrigue can her sons from the government sever
Her pride is her Adams—his laws are her choice
And shall flourish till liberty slumber forever!

Then unite, heart and hand, like Leonidas' band
And swear to the God of the ocean and land
That ne'er shall the sons of Columbia be slaves
While the earth bears a plant or the sea rolls its waves.

The word "Columbia" in the second to last line referenced a popular term for the Americas through the 1800s, derived from the last name of Christopher Columbus. It also signified a female figure—usually dressed in flowing robes and akin to Marianne in France and Britannia in England—that personified the nation and rivaled the eagle as the preeminent national symbol for the United States.

In the late 1790s, the composition *Hail, Columbia* created a political firestorm and bypassed *Yankee Doodle* as a popular national song. The music dates to 1789, when Philadelphia-based violin virtuoso and music teacher Philip Phile composed an instrumental piece called *The President's March* to commemorate the inauguration of George Washington. In 1798, downtrodden actor Gilbert Fox requested his acquaintance Joseph Hopkinson to write lyrics for Phile's tune, since "the poets of the theatrical corps had been trying to accomplish it, but could not succeed." First bearing the undistinguished title *New Federal Song*, in honor of the Federalist political faction, it later became known as *Hail, Columbia* after the lyric's first words. When Fox introduced the tune at a Philadelphia theater, the audience demanded a dozen encores, and it spread to playhouses in New York and Baltimore. Newspapers and magazines carried the song to the masses, taking Hopkinson by surprise: "Its public reception has at least equaled anything of the kind. The theatres here [Philadelphia] and at New York have resounded with it night after night; and men and boys in the streets sing it as they go." The lyrics celebrated the Founding Fathers and, of course, the icon itself.

Hopkinson, a lawyer, congressman, and federal judge, identified with the Federalists, and the song generated controversies over its lyrical nuances. One early critic dismissed it as an "aristocratic tune," and the first sheet music issue included a portrait of President Adams. During one early airing, a Philadelphia magazine reported that inside the theater, the Federalist admirers of the British "loudly vociferated" to hear it. "When the wished for song came, which contained, amidst the most ridiculous bombast, the vilest adulation to the anglo-monarchical party, and the two Presidents, the extacy of the party knew no bounds, they encored, they shouted, they became Mad as the Priestress of the Delphic God." In 1840, Hopkinson disavowed any partisan intentions. He had simply attempted "to get up an American spirit which should be independent of, and above the interests, passion, and policy of both belligerents, and look and feel exclusively for our honour and rights." Hopkinson later contended that the song's popularity rested on its impartiality: "No allusion is made to France or England, or the quarrel between them, or to the question [of] which was most at fault in their treatment of us." The composition "endured infinitely beyond the expectation of the author, as it is beyond any merit it can boast of except that of being truly and exclusively patriotic in its sentiment and spirit."[13]

Hail, Columbia introduced the often-repeated term "band of brothers" and claimed that the country's founders enjoyed the blessings of God. The first verse has aired the most throughout the years:

Hail, Columbia, happy land
Hail, ye heroes, heaven-born band
Who fought and bled in freedom's cause
Who fought and bled in freedom's cause
And when the storm of war was gone
Enjoyed the peace your valor won
Let independence be our boast
Ever mindful what it cost
Ever grateful for the prize
Let its altar reach the skies
Firm, united let us be
Rallying round our liberty
As a band of brothers joined
Peace and safety we shall find.

The last four lines, seemingly conciliatory toward the Republican opposition, can also be interpreted as a Federalist rallying cry. Civil religion saturates the lyrics of the three other verses. George Washington figured in the divine plan ("With equal skill, with God-like power / He governs in the fearful hour"), as did Adams, who focused his hopes "on heaven and you."

Largely because two Americans wrote it, *Hail, Columbia* remained popular as an unofficial national anthem, the coequal of *The Star-Spangled*

Banner through the late 1800s. A well-written song that carries a hint of regal pomp, its stanzas feature three distinct parts and a rousing finale. Drawbacks include several lyric lines that require awkward phrasing to execute. To put it over well, instrumental accents must be precise, but brass bands and wind ensembles occasionally performed clunky arrangements, with jarring rests that impeded the song's flow. It is also debatable if "find" rhymes with "joined." For a song with so few words, getting through it is something of a high-wire act. Written in the high key of C, *Hail, Columbia* became a showpiece for tenor singers. Though long forgotten, nowadays it serves as period music for films set in the past and as the vice-presidential counterpart of *Hail to the Chief,* the presidential anthem and entrance march.

Hail, Columbia represented a product of the Founding Sons, the second generation of American revolutionaries. The lyricist's father, Francis Hopkinson, signed the Declaration of Independence, helped design the flag and the Great Seal, wrote what is considered to be the first American opera, and accepted President Washington's appointment as a federal judge. *The Star-Spangled Banner*'s creator, Francis Scott Key, also represented this next generation of American patriots, as did Joseph Hopkinson. Key's family came to America in 1726. Less accomplished than Francis Hopkinson, Key's father, John Ross Key, a lawyer and state-level judge, served as a captain in the Continental Army during the Revolutionary War. The family plantation, known as Terra Rubra for the soil's reddish hue, later evolved into the hamlet of Keysville.

Despite *Hail, Columbia* and their other musical triumphs, the Federalists lost the White House from 1800 to 1816. Republicans Thomas Jefferson and James Madison sympathized with the French and steered the country toward war with England. Though considered an insignificant conflict, the War of 1812 came at a pivotal time. Many Americans called it the Second War of Independence and believed that the conflict imperiled United States sovereignty and commercial freedom. In 1807, the British warship HMS *Leopard* fired at the USS *Chesapeake*, an American navy vessel, killing six and hauling off four alleged deserters from the British navy. In response, President Madison imposed an embargo that alienated the Federalists of New England, who responded by assaulting pro-war officials, trading with the enemy, and threatening to secede from the union. The British continued to harass the burgeoning American merchant marine fleet and forcibly impressed sailors into the Royal Navy. They also fomented Indian rebellions in Ohio, Illinois, Indiana, and Michigan. Southern War Hawks seeking to annex Florida, then in the hands of England's ally Spain, also backed the war effort. In 1812, after Madison declared war on a foreign nation for the first time in United States history, American troops unsuccessfully invaded Canada twice and surrendered Detroit to the British in August of that year. The burning of Toronto, then Canada's capital, in April 1813 left a lingering sting. In May, English forces exacted revenge by sacking Havre de Grace, Maryland, and other towns along the Chesapeake Bay. The Americans ended the Indian threat in the Midwest and won several naval battles, but the British imposed an effective blockade of the Atlantic coast south of New England.

When Napoleon abdicated for the first time in April 1814, signaling an end to the fighting in Europe, England deployed seasoned troops and sailors to launch a three-pronged assault on the United States. Replicating their same failed strategy from the Revolutionary War, the British planned to split the country apart by taking control of Lake Champlain and moving south toward New York City, conquering the Chesapeake Bay area, and capturing New Orleans. English authorities sought to punish the new nation for daring to challenge Britain's monarchy and for exporting rebellion around the world, but they never expected to regain political control over the United States. Vice Admiral Alexander Cochrane, in charge of a fleet of twenty warships and support vessels that sailed from Bermuda to the Chesapeake in August 1814, wrote that "I have it much at heart to give [Washington, D.C., and Baltimore] a complete drubbing before peace is made." Later that month, the British landed a raiding party on the western shore of Chesapeake Bay and marched on Washington, D.C., a soft, symbolic target. On August 24, army troops under the command of Major General Robert Ross brushed off American defenses at Bladensburg and burned the White House, the Capitol, and other government buildings to the ground. The English also moved on Alexandria, Virginia, where its mayor surrendered and then let the enemy plunder the town. The incident, known as the "rape of Alexandria," preoccupied the British navy for several days.[14]

Rather than march north by land toward Baltimore, Ross and his troops retreated to the fleet anchored in Chesapeake Bay. Many Marylanders

count the land and sea battles that began on September 12, 1814, and lasted for two days as the proudest legacy in the state's history. September 12,
known as Defenders Day, remains a holiday in Maryland and continues to
be celebrated in Baltimore like a localized July 4. Maryland, founded as a
haven for Catholics by Lord Baltimore in 1632, is known as the Old Line
State for its soldiers' gallant showing in the Revolutionary War. During the
pivotal Battle of Long Island in New York, the Maryland Line helped keep
the British at bay and allowed George Washington to escape. By the War
of 1812, Baltimore bustled as the country's third-largest city and earned its
reputation as a rough seafaring town. In 1814, England held particular ill
will for the city and its 50,000 inhabitants, because of the privateers that
called its deep natural harbor home and sailed with the blessing of the
federal government. The "nest of pirates" in Baltimore, as the British called
them, routinely disrupted English shipping on the high seas and captured
or sank more than five hundred enemy vessels.

The English took about three weeks to mount their assault on Baltimore,
a tactical blunder that saved the city. As news from Washington, D.C.,
filtered north, residents scrambled to build defenses and muster volunteers
to fight. Reinforcements also arrived from Pennsylvania. Earthworks from
the period are still visible on Hampstead Hill in Patterson Park. During
the lull, a random chain of events created the conditions that led to *The
Star-Spangled Banner*. As British troops returned to their ships after sacking
the nation's capital, several stragglers during the disorderly retreat harassed
residents in Upper Marlboro, Maryland, just east of the city. William Beanes, a sixty-five-year-old doctor and the town's most prominent citizen, led a
posse to capture them. One soldier escaped and alerted British authorities,
who arrested Beanes on August 28 and took him aboard the HMS *Tonnant*,
the fleet's flagship.

Influential friends of Beanes sought help from Francis Scott Key, a
well-connected thirty-five-year-old lawyer practicing in Georgetown,
then a suburb of Washington, D.C. On September 5, with the blessing
of President Madison, Key and John Skinner, a federal agent in charge of
prisoners, sailed from Baltimore under a white flag of truce to the mouth
of the Potomac River in an attempt to free Dr. Beanes. They boarded the
HMS *Tonnant* and dined with Ross and Cochrane, who entertained their
guests while hatching the plan of attack on Baltimore. Key carried several

letters from British soldiers attesting to the doctor's upright conduct in treating their wounded after the Battle of Bladensburg and convinced Ross to release Beanes, rather than bring him to Halifax, Nova Scotia, for a trial. But because Beanes, Key, and Skinner became privy to British strategy, Cochrane transferred the trio to another ship—probably anchored near Old Road Bay—and kept them under guard, though he may have moved them farther upstream during the firefight. On September 12, a raiding party of around five thousand English soldiers landed at North Point, a neck of land twelve miles southeast of the city. With the ultimate goal of burning Baltimore to embers and looting its banks and stock houses, the invaders intended to fight their way downtown, despite being outnumbered two to one by the local militia. Things went awry almost immediately, when a sniper killed General Ross. The British fought on, setting up camp on the outskirts of town. Planning to raid the city center during the night of September 13, in conjunction with a naval attack, the redcoats probed for weaknesses, but the defenders stood their ground. English troops camped out as rain pounded their tents.

Foiled by land, the British unleashed an attack by sea. Baltimoreans took extreme measures to prevent the British fleet from getting close enough to inflict direct damage on the city, sinking several vessels and stretching a chain of ship masts across the narrow entrance to the inner harbor. On one side of this passage, the Whetstone Point peninsula juts into the Patapsco River. At the tip of this land mass stood star-shaped Fort McHenry, guarded by a thousand soldiers. The defenders stationed gunboats in the mouth of the harbor and installed several batteries of cannon along the shoreline, including a large array at Lazaretto Point, across the river from Fort McHenry. The fort remained the only target in range of British fire. At 6:30 a.m. on September 13, Cochrane launched a daylong bombardment, using anywhere from 1,500 to 1,800 Congreve rockets. These terrifying weapons, which weighed more than 200 pounds, whistled through the air and exploded overhead, raining shells and shrapnel onto the soldiers at the garrison and shaking buildings throughout Baltimore. The fragments often caused fires where they landed, and a direct hit on the fort's gunpowder magazine most likely would have killed many men and made the fort indefensible. Around four hundred hissing missiles fell on the defenders, whose commander likened their situation to that of "pigeons tied by the legs to be shot at."[15]

Unable to force the surrender of Fort McHenry, the British assembled a raiding party aboard twenty barges, which attempted to make landfall just west of the garrison at 2:00 a.m. on September 14. But eleven of the vessels took a wrong turn, and the others attracted the attention of American soldiers manning two battery positions along the coastline. Once the raiders returned to the fleet, Cochrane unleashed more rockets through the night as Key, Beanes, and Skinner watched and listened from afar. They could see that the fort's storm flag "was still there," but they had no idea whether anyone remained alive to haul it down. Then, at around 7:00 a.m. on the morning of September 14, everything stopped. "The awful stillness and suspense were unbearable," wrote Key. "You may imagine what a state of anxiety I endured." When the Americans pulled the storm flag down and replaced it with the massive 42 by 30 foot garrison flag, the banner impressed a British midshipman, who wrote that "the Americans hoisted a splendid and superb ensign on their battery, and at the same time fired a gun of defiance." One soldier at Fort McHenry recorded his perspective: "at dawn on the 14th, our morning gun was fired, the flag hoisted, 'Yankee Doodle' played, and we all appeared in full view of a formidable and mortified enemy." Key and his companions rejoiced when the mammoth flag flapped over the fort atop a 90-foot pole. This "manifest deliverance" provided "a higher idea of the 'forbearance, long-suffering, and tender mercy' of God than I had ever before conceived," Key wrote, quoting the Bible. The attack on Fort McHenry left five Americans dead and twenty-four wounded. The city stayed on the alert, since the British fleet remained in the harbor, but the Battle of Baltimore essentially ended the War of 1812. Weary of fighting, English officers abandoned the war effort. The Battle of New Orleans, which transpired in January 1815 after dignitaries from the two nations had signed a peace treaty, delivered another morale boost to the emboldened United States.[16]

Born in 1779 in Frederick (now Carroll) County, Francis Scott Key spent almost his entire life of privilege in Maryland, attending St. John's College in Annapolis, practicing law in Frederick and Georgetown, and regularly visiting Baltimore. Deeply religious, Key considered entering the Episcopal ministry and helped found the American Bible Society, dedicated to distributing copies of the revered book around the world. A descendant of John Key, poet laureate of England under King Edward IV in the 1400s,

Francis fancied himself a lyricist and often wrote song parodies. He contributed the words of two selections in the Episcopal Church hymnal. Though opposed to the War of 1812 on conscientious grounds, Key volunteered in the Georgetown Field Artillery Company and saw action at Bladensburg in defense of Washington, D.C. He cultivated friends in high places, and his sister married his law partner, Roger B. Taney, who became Chief Justice of the United States Supreme Court in 1836. Key fathered eleven children and one of his daughters, Elizabeth, married into the family of John Eager Howard, a Revolutionary War hero, governor, congressman, senator, and the namesake of Howard County, Maryland.

When Key saw the flag rise above Fort McHenry on the morning of September 14, 1814, he began scribbling the words of the composition almost every American knows as *The Star-Spangled Banner*—four verses in all—on the back of a letter. After the shelling in Baltimore's harbor ceased that day, the British fleet prepared to set sail. Key probably came ashore on September 16 with a rough draft of his lyrics and sat down to complete the final copy at an undetermined hotel, a version that served as the template for the first printing. In the surviving manuscript, Key changed the phrase "through the dawn's early light" to "by the dawn's early light" and crossed out the words "They have wash'd out," replacing them with "Their blood has wash'd out."

Key's first verse asks an open-ended question, which the second stanza resolves. Both recap the dramatic events in Baltimore's harbor. Over the years, the song's opponents bashed its allegedly warlike qualities, yet the lines "rocket's red glare" and "bomb bursting in air" (as written by Key) are observations. In the second and especially the third verses, Key taunted the British, claiming that "their blood has wash'd out their foul footstep's pollution" and that "no refuge could save the hireling & slave / From the terror of flight or the gloom of the grave," references to the soldiers and mercenaries who served England's monarch. Still, his position toward the enemy is much milder than the one taken by *The Marseillaise*. In the final verse, a low-key prayer, Key exalts the victory as one approved from on high. Referring to the country as a "heav'n rescued land" and praising "the power that hath made and preserved us a nation," he also justified American participation in armed conflicts, but with a condition: "Then conquer we must, when our cause it is just / And this be our motto—'In God is our trust.'" The forward-looking orientation of the fourth verse sets it apart from many other national anthems. Key used inclusive pronouns like "ours," "us," and "we" when referring to the nation. The catchphrases "freemen" and "peace" further broaden its appeal. Through at least the early 1900s, when attention spans began to constrict, Americans typically learned and sang all four verses. Educators and publishers began to drop the third verse after England became an ally in the late 1800s.

Major George Armistead, commander of Fort McHenry, had commissioned the large flag seen throughout the harbor, the star-spangled banner glorified in the song. In 1813, anticipating that Baltimore might become a target, Armistead hired local flagmaker Mary Pickersgill to create an emblem so large that "the British would have no difficulty in seeing it from a distance." Pickersgill and several female relatives started sewing the garrison flag in her home and assembled it at a nearby brewery. (They also completed the smaller storm flag that flew over the fort during the battle.) Possession of this memento passed down to Armistead's daughter, Georgina Appleton, who allowed it to be unfurled at select patriotic gatherings, including many Defenders Day celebrations in Baltimore. Over the years, souvenir seekers cut pieces from the fly end, shortening the flag's length to 33 feet. Appleton apparently sewed part of the letter *A*, for Armistead, onto one of the white stripes, a common practice at the time. Her son, Eben Appleton, inherited the fragile artifact and, weary of being badgered over the relic, kept it in a Manhattan safe-deposit box until he gifted it to the Smithsonian Institution.

God Save the King celebrated monarchy as the embodiment of the country. Key, however, distilled the essence of nationhood to the flag, a more ambiguous and democratic symbol. Uncle Sam, the other enduring emblem to emerge from the War of 1812, personified the state and kept the relationship between Americans all in the family. In addition to coining the phrase "star-spangled banner," which appears in each stanza, in the fourth verse Key included the line "In God is our trust," later parsed to "In God We Trust" and first printed on the nation's currency in 1864.

Though the flag endured as a symbol of patriotic resilience, the song that it inspired exerted a much more vital impact on United States history. Francis Scott Key served as a journalist—an eyewitness to history—and never intended to create a lasting ode. For years, scholars debated whether Key wrote his verses to stand alone as a poem or if he purposely fit them to a particular melody. Subsequent generations perpetuated the myth that Baltimore actor Ferdinand Durang paired Key's words with the music. Despite much conjecture regarding his intentions, there is no question that Key deliberately intended the lyrics to match a melody first used in England for *The Anacreontic Song*, also called *To Anacreon in Heaven*. The tune, a bawdy, boozy ballad written around 1775, served as the anthem, or "constitutional song," of the convivial gentlemen's club known as the Anacreontic Society, which met at the Crown and Anchor Tavern in London. The name derived from Anacreon, once referred to by a detractor of *The Star-Spangled Banner* as the "Dirty Old Man of Greek poetry." The original lyrics of *The Anacreontic Song* concocted a fable populated by Greek gods to justify the club's stated passion for bending the elbow and bellowing lusty songs:

> To Anacreon, in Heav'n, where he sat in full glee
> A few sons of harmony sent a petition
> That he their inspirer and patron would be
> When this answer arriv'd from the jolly old Grecian
> Voice, fiddle, and flute, no longer be mute
> I'll lend ye my name, and inspire ye to boot
> And, besides, I'll instruct ye, like me, to intwine
> The myrtle of Venus with Bacchus's vine.

Over five more verses, several characters consider whether to join in or condemn the proceedings, including Jupiter, Apollo, and Momus, all of whom eventually sanctioned the revelry as the group toasted, "May our Club flourish happy, united and free!" The society, along with several other gentlemen's clubs, emerged in London during the 1760s and became known for the quality of its musical offerings. Composer Franz Joseph Haydn visited it once, and Johann Hummel, at age twelve, performed a piano piece for its members. Supper sometimes attracted two hundred people and the musical programs lasted for hours.[17]

Despite its wide, octave-and-a-half range and odd meter, the melody of *To Anacreon in Heaven* attained widespread popularity in the United States, undergirding at least eighty-four other compositions written before 1820. In addition to the well-known 1798 campaign song, *Adams and Liberty*, other parodies include *The Fourth of July*, *Union of the Gods*, and a lyric that began

"To the Gods who preside, o'er the nation below."[18] By the early 1800s, the tune evolved into a standard for "poetically inclined patriots," according to one musicologist. Francis Hopkinson also mated original words with the song.[19] Key never wrote a musical composition during his life and, like many amateur poets in the days before copyright enforcement, he relied on existing songs to animate his muse. In 1805, he paired the melody of *To Anacreon in Heaven* with his poem *When the Warrior Returns (from the Battle Afar)*, a tribute to the naval victories of fellow Marylander Stephen Decatur during the Barbary Coast War, first published in the *Frederick-Town Herald*. In its verses he also experimented with his famous phrase: "And pale beam'd the Crescent, its splendour obscur'd / By the light of the star-spangled flag of our nation." There is no doubt that Key also tailored the words of his more famous later composition to that particular melody.

Anacreontic Society president Ralph Tomlinson received universal credit as the author of the lyrics of *To Anacreon in Heaven* since its inception, but the composer of the music remained unidentified through the 1800s. Sheet music and songbook collections usually failed to include a songwriter for *The Star-Spangled Banner* and even left out or misspelled Key's name. In 1841, a Baltimore newspaper singled out another president of the Anacreontic Society, Samuel Arnold, as a possible composer and his name appeared on many editions, though scholars remained skeptical. In the twentieth century, William Lichtenwanger at the Library of Congress discovered a document establishing John Stafford Smith as the composer. Smith and Key, who lived on different sides of the ocean, shared an exceeding modesty throughout their lives. Smith died at age eighty-six in 1836, more than fifty years after he wrote the melody, yet he never took credit for it. Key also eschewed any fame or fortune concerning *The Star-Spangled Banner*.

It is unclear who took the manuscript of *The Star-Spangled Banner* to the *Baltimore American and Commercial Daily Advertiser*, which had suspended publication during the battle. Early accounts identified Key's friend and brother-in-law, Judge Joseph Nicholson, who commanded the artillery at Fort McHenry and eventually came into possession of the document. But Nicholson may have remained on duty at the fort. John Skinner, Key's fellow captive, probably made the visit to the printing office. After completing the verses, Key returned to Frederick, Maryland, since he had been held incommunicado for eleven days. "We were becoming uneasy about him, when, to our great joy, he made his appearance at my house, on his way to join his family," wrote Roger B. Taney, his brother-in-law. In passing, Key mentioned that "under the excitement of the time, he had written a song."[20]

At the *Baltimore American*, fourteen-year-old apprentice Samuel Sands typeset Key's handwritten poem in less than an hour and struck off a broadside, a sheet of paper printed on one side that many Americans cherished as a keepsake or used as a poster. Sands and his overseer made fifty-nine editorial changes to Key's manuscript, including grammar, punctuation marks, and capitalization. In one of the verses, for example, they dropped the hyphen in the phrase "star-spangled," though Key used it all four times in his written version. They also capitalized the word "Power" in the last verse to signify the deity, a change that caused a tiff in the 1950s. Key never designated an official title for the song, and there is no standard usage in print. The *Baltimore American* initially called it *The Defence of Fort M'Henry* and, like many parodies, listed the melody on which it was based (in this case "Tune—Anacreon in Heaven") underneath the title.

The Defence of Fort M'Henry became an instant hit in Baltimore and all the troops at the fort received a copy. Even before publication, Key's creation had "already been extensively circulated," according to the printer, who predicted that it would be "destined long to outlast the occasion, and outlive the impulse which produced it." On September 20, the *Baltimore Patriot and Evening Advertiser* published the broadside, followed the next day by the *Baltimore American*. The *Frederick-Town Herald* reprinted it on September 24. Two days later, it appeared in Washington, D.C., then spread to Georgetown and New York City on September 27. By early October, the lyrics made it as far as New Hampshire and Savannah, Georgia. In November, they first turned up in a Maryland magazine.[21] At least twenty songbooks included it between 1814 and 1842, mostly in the Northeast. In 1816, *The Star Spangled Banner: Being a Collection of the Best Naval, Martial [and] Patriotic Songs*, published in Delaware, included a fifth verse for the first time in print. The addition praised Andrew Jackson for his victory in battle at New Orleans and carried as its final sentence, "Where the Star Spangled Banner in triumph still waves / In proudest defiance of Britain's vile slaves." In several patriotic songbooks—including editions issued in New Haven, Connecticut (1819); Newark, New Jersey (1834); and Philadelphia (1835 and 1845)—*The Star-Spangled Banner* appeared as the first selection, signaling its prominent position in the pantheon of patriotic music. In 1836, Key's song made it to Cincinnati, then the far western frontier, and the book *National Hymns*, published in Boston, also included it. An entry in prominent Manhattan lawyer and music patron George Templeton Strong's 2,250-page diary provided an interesting insight into its widespread appeal. On December 22, 1837, Strong wrote that "a lot of tipsy loafers are just going past, screaming out 'The Star-Spangled Banner' at the top of their lungs, and in all sorts of diabolical discords. But it sounds gloriously. It's a glorious thing altogether—words and music—no matter how it's mangled."[22]

As the popularity of *The Star-Spangled Banner* remained robust for years after the Battle of Baltimore, an inevitable backlash ensued. On July 3, 1821, an editorial in the *Charleston Courier* in South Carolina referred to the phrase "star-spangled" as "the vilest combination that ever speech was guilty of" and protested its use in July 4 oratory. "To connect a star, a mighty luminous orb, a world of light and beauty, with a Spangle, diminutive, insignificant tinsel, worthless ornament of a dirty kid slipper . . . is a most degrading association. Let us maintain, if we can, the elevation of the stars, but God deliver us from the objectives of the spangles." The rival *City Gazette* retorted that renowned literary figures Dryden, Addison, and Milton used the term "spangle." Shakespeare also paired it with stars in "A Midsummer Night's Dream" ("by spangled star-light sheen") and "The Taming of the Shrew" ("what Stars do Spangle heaven with such beauty?"). As the *Courier's* objections indicated, Key's song became a mainstay at patriotic ceremonies and testimonial dinners, where participants offered long-winded toasts into the night.[23]

Many songbooks of the period, mostly in New England, omitted *The Star-Spangled Banner*, prompting future scholars to underestimate its role before the Civil War. In 1909, Oscar Sonneck at the Library of Congress claimed that the tune did not rush "to the front of our national songs" until the War between the States. Before then, "its progress as a national song had been steady, but comparatively slow." Yet the composition diffused aurally much faster than it did in print and instantly joined *Yankee Doodle* and *Hail, Columbia* in the country's patriotic hit parade. That it lasted intact through the tumultuous pre–Civil War era is remarkable, given the numerous parodies written to the same melody, along with the appearance of other frequently played nationalist numbers that served as powerful cohesive symbols at a time when a local orientation and regional fragmentation dominated the daily lives of most Americans.

Popular histories identify stage actor Ferdinand Durang as the first person to sing the lyrics before an audience. As Francis Scott Key retreated into the background, Durang inserted himself into the historical record and, although the song definitely aired in a formal fashion at a Baltimore theater in mid-October 1814, the actor's involvement is dubious. Thomas Carr, who owned a Baltimore music store, published the initial sheet music version around the same time and astutely changed the title to *The Star Spangled Banner*, sans hyphen. Today Americans sing the words "O say" in the first line with three different, descending notes, but in Carr's version (along with the first two syllables in *The Anacreontic Song*), the words are assigned to two notes, both the same. The first modern version appeared in 1843, although the original rendition remained in print for decades. In the Carr version the phrase "proudly we hailed" consists of four descending notes divided into equal beats, which differs from the current practice of holding the first syllable of the word "proudly." The publisher also changed a phrase in Key's original manuscript, pluralizing the line "Rockets' red glare, the Bombs bursting in air." Curiously, Carr's music sheet included the wrong date of the Fort McHenry bombardment and mistakenly credited the words to "B. Key Esqr," the first time any part of Key's name became associated with the song. The first edition also included a prominent typo in the subtitle, calling it "A Pariotic Song." This error appeared in at least eighteen other editions published by music houses across the country, since Carr never enforced his copyright.

The nation's flag, also dismissed by some scholars as a minor symbol until the Civil War, grew in stature because of Key's creation. The term "star-spangled banner" evolved into a popular nickname for the flag, like Old Glory and the Stars and Stripes. Patriotic fervor, which increased after the Battle of Baltimore, helped the American flag attain cultlike status as the nation entered the Era of Good Feelings after the War of 1812. The original star-spangled banner that flew over Fort McHenry contained fifteen stars and fifteen stripes. In 1818, Congress froze the number of stripes at thirteen to symbolize the original colonies and added a star for every new state admitted to the union, a tangible way to measure the country's growth. The official issue of each new flag served as an excuse to hold public celebrations. Flag worship after the War of 1812 grew slowly, but it gained particular prominence during the election of 1840, when candidates bought voters drinks, bands blared during all-day campaign rallies, and political parties unfurled the Red, White, and Blue. One songbook promoting War of 1812 hero and presidential candidate William Henry Harrison included eight different partisan parodies set to the familiar melody, including *The Harrison Banner*. Hijacking *The Star-Spangled Banner* for political purposes became commonplace during elections through the rest of the 1800s.

Americans have long complained about the stiff quality of Key's verses. For example, Key used the word "doth" instead of "does," and, like *The Anacreontic Song*, he relied on apostrophes to shoehorn words into the melody, a common practice at the time. He also used an ampersand instead of the word "and" in eleven places, including each time he wrote the line "O'er the land of the free & the home of the brave," a phrase that appears in all four verses. In later years, especially after *America the Beautiful* rose to popularity, Americans also criticized the music of Key's song, calling it difficult to sing. Yet the widespread early adoption of *The Star-Spangled Banner* attested to its appeal. Each verse includes a solo portion, probably a part sung by the president of the Anacreontic Society, and a chorus, consisting of the last two lines. The notorious high notes—corresponding to the words "red glare" in the solo section and "free" in the chorus—hardly daunted audiences that sang in unison, though the original is written in the key of C, quite high for trained voices, even today. Many defenders of Key's creation tried to deny that *The Anacreontic Song* represented a dirty ditty suitable for taverns, yet the melody embodies a lusty, hoist-the-tankard quality. The tune, written in 6/4 time, with the emphasis on the first beat, also became adapted to 3/4 time. Military bands transformed its steady meter into 4/4 time, suitable for marching. The popularity of the song with the armed forces proved pivotal in its eventual adoption as the national anthem. Key's hybrid composition attracted additional criticism for being only half American. The English provenance of the tune so rankled New York composer and music publisher James Hewitt that he wrote original music to fit Key's lyrics in 1816.

Parodies of English songs remained popular, and in 1831, Samuel Francis Smith, a divinity student in Andover, Massachusetts, lifted the melody of the patriotic song *My Country, 'Tis of Thee*, also known as *America*, from *God Save the King*. Smith worked with songbook pioneer Lowell Mason to spread religious and patriotic music throughout the schools. After Mason handed his acolyte a German songbook and asked him to identify suitable melodies for hymns and other songs, Smith became enamored with a parody of *God Save the King* and crafted the words of *My Country, 'Tis of Thee* in about a half hour. More than fifty years later, Smith wrote that "I did not design it for a national hymn, nor did I think it should gain such notoriety." After sending it to Mason, the young tunesmith forgot about the song. To his surprise, "on the succeeding 4th July, he [Mason] brought it out on occasion of a Sunday school celebration in Park St. church, Boston." Smith wrote later, "If I had anticipated the future of it, doubtless I would have taken more pains with it."

Smith claimed that he unwittingly borrowed the anthem of the nation's chief enemy, England. Despite this obvious feature, *My Country, 'Tis of Thee* seamlessly entered the canon of national airs. Smith paid homage to "freedom" and "liberty" and lionized the New England landscape. His words also attested to the role of music in spreading nationalist sentiment: "Let music swell the breeze / And ring from all the trees / Sweet freedom's song." Like *The Star-Spangled Banner*, the final verse serves as a prayer that places God above earthly rulers:

> Our fathers' God to thee
> Author of liberty
> To thee we sing
> Long may our land be bright
> With freedom's holy light
> Protect us by thy might
> Great God, our King!

Smith also penned a forgotten fifth verse that criticized the British and borrowed imagery from Key's lyrics: "No more shall tyrants here / With haughty steps appear / And soldier bands / No more shall tyrants tread / Above the patriot dead / No more our blood be shed / By alien hands."[24]

In 1843, as the territory and influence of the United States expanded, the naval ode *Columbia, the Gem of the Ocean* became the final song to vie for the title of unofficial national anthem in the 1800s, the others in the patriotic "Big Five" being *Yankee Doodle*; *Hail, Columbia*; *The Star-Spangled Banner*; and *My Country, 'Tis of Thee*. Philadelphia actor David T. Shaw is generally recognized as the song's composer, yet some evidence points to a fellow thespian, credited as Thomas à Becket on some sheet-music scores. It is also uncertain whether a similar tune, *Britannia, the Pride of the Ocean*, appeared before or after *Columbia, the Gem of the Ocean*. The latter composition is also known as *The Red, White, and Blue* from its participatory chorus section at the end of each verse, claiming that "thy banners make tyranny tremble / when borne by the red, white, and blue." The song enjoyed instant appeal. With a robust melody, the tune blended patriotism and religion, referring to the country as the "ark" of "freedom's foundation." It also appropriated several phrases from *The Star-Spangled Banner*, beginning with the first verse:

> O Columbia! The gem of the ocean
> The home of the brave and the free
> The shrine of each patriot's devotion
> The world offers homage to thee.

Another verse borrowed Key's title phrase: "The star spangled banner bring hither / O'er Columbia's true sons let it wave / May the wreaths they have won never wither / Nor its stars cease to shine on the brave." Curiously, it became the "favorite song" of the Baltimore and Washington Battalion, know as "Baltimore's Own." Aboard a transport ship sailing from Vera Cruz, Mexico, to New Orleans in 1848 at the end of the Mexican-American War, "the voices of five hundred men swelled the anthem, 'To the shrine of each patriot's devotion.'"[25]

The Star-Spangled Banner also inspired poems with the same title that shared little in common with the song, other than a desire to worship the flag. In 1846, a play entitled "The Star Spangled Banner" received favorable reviews in New York City. Newspaper publishers used the phrase as the title of their dailies and weeklies. During the 1830s, an age dominated by Andrew Jackson (D-Tenn.), the first president of the common man, partisan discourse became shriller. Jackson's patrician opponents, known as Whigs, fiercely fought the rise of the rabble. As both factions battled, French visitor Alexis de Tocqueville, who toured the United States for nine months in 1831, observed that patriotism functioned as "a kind of religion" that "does not reason, but acts from the impulse of faith and sentiment."[26] One Philadelphia newspaper, named the *Star-Spangled Banner* and subtitled *Liberty or Death*, published its first issue in 1834 and sounded the alarm against Jacksonian policies, stating that "in such a crisis, an association of gentlemen have resolved to unfurl the flag of our Country—the Banner of the Free." The editorial referred to the "Temple of Freedom" built by Washington: "Alas! Its foundations have been shaken; its massive columns have been broken; its spire has fallen; its alter is in ruins, and but a few faithful votaries still offer their sacrifices there." Another partisan periodical (based in Nashville, Tennessee), also called the *Star Spangled Banner,* lasted from April 8, 1844, through the aftermath of the November presidential election and stumped hard for the eventual winner, James K. Polk (D-Tenn.), a Jackson ally. "We shall wage a fierce and determined war upon the errors and dangers of whigism," according to one editorial. "We have a right, then, to appeal to the advocates of democratic principles to rally to our Banner."[27]

Between 1847 and 1854, Bostonian Justin Jones published a racist, nativist newspaper called *Star Spangled Banner*. Jones, under the pseudonym Harry Hazel, also issued inexpensive novels that associated the flag with territorial expansion and pilloried African Americans, Irish Catholic immigrants, the Chinese, Muslims, Mexicans, and the French. He supported the Mexican-American War, which lasted from 1846 to 1848 and added almost two million square miles to United States territory. An early edition of Jones's newspaper recounted the nation's major battles—from Lexington, Massachusetts, to Buena Vista, Mexico—coupled with profiles of John Hancock, Ben Franklin, and generals Washington, Lafayette, Jackson, Taylor, and Scott. By 1854, anti-Catholic nativism, along with discrimination against blacks, expanded across the Northeast as the secret fraternal organization known as the Order of the Star-Spangled Banner spread from New York to Boston and other cities. The nativist movement evolved into the influential American Party, better known as the Know-Nothing Party, since members would routinely reply to outsiders that they "know nothing" about the platform or operations of the movement.[28]

With the popularity of musical parodies rife in the bustling United States during the 1830s and 1840s, interest groups across the political spectrum rewrote the lyrics of *The Star-Spangled Banner* and other national numbers. Playing rousing patriotic songs became the musical equivalent of waving the flag. Songbooks identified *The Star-Spangled Banner* as a "popular National Air," and it eventually landed abroad in an 1842 London compilation that identified it as the "National American Song." In 1847, a New York publisher offered a "new and beautiful steel plate engraving" of *The Star-Spangled Banner*, "representing an American mother teaching her children to sing THE NATIONAL AIR." At Niblo's Garden, a popular New York City entertainment center, the 1850 season opened with what the program referred to as "the National Ode of 'The Star Spangled Banner.'" As the song rose to singular prominence, the battle to interpret its symbolic meaning embroiled Americans of all political persuasions. Many of these adaptations mimicked the words "O say can you see" to evoke familiarity. The easy-to-rhyme phrases "land of the free" and "home of the brave" provided important thematic threads for numerous compositions, newspaper headlines, and speeches throughout United States history.[29]

Before the Civil War, evangelists, slavery abolitionists, temperance crusaders, territorial expansionists, and even volunteer firefighters used the melody of Key's creation to write new verses derived from his lyrics and wrap their causes in the folds of the flag. The church-based antislavery movement that emerged in the 1830s chose the song to underscore the contradiction between the real and the ideal.[30] From the founding of the movement, abolitionists circulated parodies of many nationalistic songs: *My Country, 'Tis of Thee*; *The Marseillaise*; *Auld Lang Syne*; *Hail, Columbia*; and, especially, *The Star-Spangled Banner*. The first verse of *The Patriot's Banner* ended with the lines "'Tis the star-spangled banner, while it doth wave / O'er the land no more free—'tis the home of the slave!" Another parody of *The Star-Spangled Banner*, a "New Version of the National Song," highlighted slavery's cruelty:

> Oh, say do you hear, at the dawn's early light
> The shrieks of those bondmen, whose blood is now streaming
> From the merciless lash, while our banner in sight
> With its stars mocking freedom, is fitfully gleaming?
> Do you see the backs bar? Do you mark every score
> Of the whip of the driver trace channels of gore?
> And say, doth our star-spangled banner yet wave

O'er the land of the free, and the home of the brave?

During a July 4, 1840, ceremony at the Philadelphia Museum, anti-alcohol crusader Catharine Waterman sang a *National Temperance Ode* that identified teetotaling with God, the Founding Fathers, liberty, and the flag. From 1843 to 1853, temperance societies published texts to the melody of *The Star-Spangled Banner* in at least five magazines and songbooks, delighting in the irony of reconfiguring a ribald bacchanalian ballad to serve the "Cold Water Army."[31] One 1843 parody began: "Oh! Who has not seen by the dawn's early light / Some poor bloated drunkard to his home weakly reeling." The last verse followed the meter and lyric of Key's third verse:

> But thanks to that band who so faithfully swore,
> That the havoc of rum and the bottle's confusion
> Our home and our country should ravage no more
> It aught might o'ercome the foul curse & pollution
> They are striving to save the victim and slave,
> From th' horrors of guilt & th' drunkard's dark grave
> And the temperance banner in triumph shall wave,
> O'er the land of the free and the home of the brave.[32]

Evangelical groups also appropriated the song's melody. Around 1850, Baltimore music publisher F. D. Benteen praised the Lord with "O! say, can you see, by the truth's holy light?" and claimed that the "banner unfulr'd . . . shall conquer the world." The chorus intoned: "O the Cross is that banner—and long may it wave / 'Till Jesus lead capture both death and the grave."[33]

Jingoists gung-ho for the Mexican-American War in 1846 circulated a version of *The Texas War Cry*:

> Up Texians, rouse hill, and dale with your cry,
> No longer delay, for the bold foe advances,
> The banners of Mexico tauntingly fly,
> And the vallies are lit, with the gleam of their lances,
> With justice our shield, Rush forth to the field.[34]

A second verse exhorted able-bodied men to "Grasp rifle and blade, with hearts undismayed / And swear by the temple brave Houston has made / That the bright star of Texas shall never be dim / While her soil boasts a son to raise rifle or limb." Another lyric, *The Texian Banner*, invoked God's grace over the undertaking and referenced the Lone Star flag: "Then the sweet star of hope, like a heavenly isle / On the banner of Texas with triumph shall smile."[35]

Volunteer firemen in New York City also flaunted their patriotism. *The Fireman's Song*, written in 1858, celebrated the presentation of a "prize trumpet," which served as sirens at the time:

> Oh! Say, can you hear amid terror and flight
> When ruin lurks daily round love's peaceful dwelling?
> Where the red fire glows on the dark brow of night
> As it bursts 'mid the gloom in full chorus swelling?
> Now it catches the ear, With a melody clear
> Now breaks through the crowd with a strong, manly cheer:
> 'Tis the Firemen's trumpet, And long may it wave
> When blown by the free, and cheer'd on by the brave.

Despite numerous alternatives circulating in popular culture, Francis Scott Key's original version of *The Star-Spangled Banner* sold briskly and, in practice, evolved into the national anthem long before the Civil War, though his name continued to be misspelled (often as Francis S. Keys). Key spent most of his time in Georgetown and Frederick but, although he hobnobbed with the nation's powerbrokers, he never ran for office. Between 1833 and 1841, Key served as the United States District Attorney in Washington, D.C., an appointed position, and argued several cases before the Supreme Court. On occasion, he sought to uphold the rights of free blacks, but he also used the office to fight abolitionists, defend the rights of slaveholders, and suppress free speech.

Throughout his life, Key retained an unusual modesty regarding *The Star-Spangled Banner*. He commented publicly on the song only once, at a dinner to honor his brother-in-law, Roger B. Taney, held in Frederick on August 6, 1834. During a round of toasts, Key downplayed and deflected his achievement: "I was but the instrument in executing what you have been pleased to praise; it was dictated and inspired by the gallantry and patriotism of the sons of Maryland. The honor is due not to me who made the song, but to the heroism of those who made me make it." Toward the end of his life, Key wrote out signed copies of his song for friends and acquaintances. Four of these later souvenirs, which included inadvertent changes from the original document of 1814, have been located. In 1843, Key died in Baltimore at the age of sixty-three. Chief Justice Roger B. Taney contributed an introduction to the collection *Poems of the Late Francis S. Key, Esq.*, published in 1857, which recounted the events leading up to the writing of *The Star-Spangled Banner*. Taney touted Key's composition as the preeminent "national ballad," and his book helped solidify the song's reputation. Thanks to Taney's publicity efforts, Key became universally associated with *The Star-Spangled Banner*.[36]

But no song or national emblem could keep the nation together as the union of states spiraled out of control, and the relatively peaceful times enjoyed by Key and his generation after the Era of Good Feelings devolved into the Civil War.

American Dischord, 1860–1865

IN OBVIOUS CONTRADICTION to the phrase "land of the free," Francis Scott Key owned slaves. The quandary, a "dischord" for the song's author, gnawed at Key's conscience, since he helped found the American Colonization Society in 1816, which advocated an end to the slavery problem by sending blacks back to Africa. The movement established the Republic of Liberia in 1822; its capital, Monrovia, is named after President James Monroe, who occupied the office at the time. Liberia's flag, with eleven stripes and one white star in a field of blue, resembles Old Glory. At one time, Key's family owned "scores" of slaves. The number of bound servants Key himself owned is undetermined, and he could have set them free at any time. His will, written in 1837, provided for his "slaves to serve my wife during her life, and then to be free unless (which I wish she would do) she should chuse sooner to manumit them." By 1838, Key had emancipated seven people, expressing anxiety over their future.[1]

Slavery and issues related to the future of the vast western territory added to the United States after the Mexican-American War tore the North and the South apart. In April 1861, three days after Confederate troops fired the first shots of the Civil War at Federal soldiers in Fort Sumter, *London Times* correspondent William Howard Russell traveled by train through North Carolina. Riding with the engine crew, he spied the Stars and Bars, the first Rebel emblem, fluttering on a tall pine tree stripped of its branches. "That's our flag!" the engineer said. "And long may it wave—o'er the land of the free and the home of the ber-rave!"[2] Since Americans had subjected the meaning of the flag and *The Star-Spangled Banner* to various permutations for almost fifty years, it seemed natural to mix and match symbols during this grave crisis.

Once secession became inevitable in the South, the war effort to safeguard the breakaway Confederate States of America took precedence. Officials sanctioned the basic tokens of nationhood on the fly. In the conflict's early days, many Southerners suggested seizing Old Glory and its premier anthem as war booty and forcing the North to search for a suitable substitute. The defection of Francis Scott Key's entire family from the Union clouded the ownership of an already ambiguous symbol and validated the Confederates' claim to *The Star-Spangled Banner*. "In 1861 there were upwards of sixty descendants living, and I think of them also every man, woman, and child was Southern," though none owned slaves, wrote Key's grandson McHenry Howard, who served in the Confederate army from the Battle of Manassas until two days before Appomattox.[3]

Other Rebels disavowed the song and the flag it praised. In Maryland, the ancestral home of the Key family, the Civil War played out in microcosm. Unionists, led by Governor Thomas Holliday Hicks, battled followers of Baltimore's Mayor George W. Brown, a Rebel sympathizer. In the mid-1800s, Baltimore served as a pivotal port and rail hub. Explosive population growth heightened tensions, and the city acquired the nickname Mobtown, due in part to a rash of riots and gang violence in the 1840s and 1850s. Fire scenes often erupted into street brawls between rival volunteer firefighting companies. On April 19, 1861, seven days after the bombardment on Fort Sumter, as the Sixth Massachusetts Regiment passed through Baltimore on their way to protect Washington, D.C., a gang of Rebels attacked their train. Battling for a mile across town in order to meet a connection at Camden Station, the Union soldiers shot into the crowd and shed the war's first blood at a place and time they least expected to encounter a fight. Four Yankees and a dozen rowdies died in the brawl. Confederates called it the Lexington of 1861, referencing the anniversary of the famous Revolutionary War battle.

Reading about the melee, James Ryder Randall, a Baltimorean teaching English at tiny Poydras College in Louisiana, dashed off nine pro-Southern stanzas that meshed with the melody of the German folksong *O Tannenbaum* and called his piece *Maryland! My Maryland!* First published in the *New Orleans Delta* newspaper, it then appeared in the *Baltimore South* on May 31. New Orleans music publisher Armand Edward (A. E.) Blackmar referred to the composition as "a Patriotic Song" and Randall's plea for Maryland to join the Rebels glorified the pro-Southern "patriotic gore / That flecked the streets of Baltimore." The song's original lyrics contained a controversial line that referred to the contested status of *The Star-Spangled Banner* with a wry pun: "Come to thine own heroic throng, that stalks with liberty along / And give a new KEY to thy song, Maryland! My Maryland!"[4] Union parodists immediately responded to Randall's plea with some wordplay of their own: "April the 19th '61, in Maryland, my Maryland / Those traitorous acts were first begun, in Maryland, my Maryland / But lo! behold, it was not long, the Union men said this is wrong / We'll give a new key to the song, of Maryland, my Maryland."[5]

President Abraham Lincoln clamped down on Baltimore by declaring martial law. Union troops mounted Gatling guns atop what is now known as Federal Hill. In September, as the Maryland state legislature prepared to cast its vote, Lincoln ordered the arrest of pro-Southern legislators and newspaper editors, to ensure that the state stayed within the Northern orbit. The dragnet snagged Mayor Brown of Baltimore and Key's grandson, Francis (Frank) Key Howard, editor of the anti-Lincoln *Baltimore Exchange*, who spent the night of September 13, 1861, imprisoned at Fort McHenry. "When I looked out in the morning, I could not help but being struck by an odd, and not pleasant coincidence. On that day, forty-seven years before, my grandfather, Mr. F. S. Key . . . had witnessed the bombardment of Fort McHenry" and "wrote the song so long popular throughout the country, the 'Star-Spangled Banner.'" Howard "could not but contrast my position with his," writing that "the flag which he had then so proudly hailed, I saw waving, at the same place, over the victims of as vulgar and brutal a despotism as modern times have witnessed." Union agents also jailed his father, Charles Howard, and three of his brothers: John Eager Howard, Charles Howard Jr., and Edward Lloyd Howard.[6] Maryland officially sided with the Union, but the state remained the quintessential "house divided" as significant pockets of resistance smoldered throughout the war.

Musical disputes, like those fought over *Maryland! My Maryland!*, captured the passions on both sides of the divide. The North and the South wrestled over which region could lay legitimate claim to *The Marseillaise*, the French revolutionary anthem. In November 1860, when South Carolina redesigned its Palmetto state flag, praised in song and rhetoric after Fort Sumter, *The Marseillaise Hymn* accompanied the proceedings. A version called the *Southern Marseillaise* aired during the unveiling of Louisiana's and Alabama's new flags, and the lyrics to *The Virginia Marseillaise* rang the alarm: "Virginia hears the dreadful summons / Sounding hoarsely, from afar / On her sons she calls and calmly / Bids them now prepare for war." As the underdogs, and with Louisiana being home to a large French-speaking enclave, the Rebels appeared to have dibs on *The Marseillaise*, but sheet music publishers in Boston, New York, Philadelphia, Cleveland, and Cincinnati included the song in sets of complete editions or in medleys, alongside *Hail, Columbia*; *The Star-Spangled Banner*; *Yankee Doodle*; and *My Country, 'Tis of Thee*. Some Northern publishers adorned music covers with color lithographs depicting crossed flagstaffs of Old Glory and the French tricolor, which is also red, white and blue.[7]

The rush to adopt the musical representation of the French Revolution epitomized the divergent interpretations of the revolutionary legacy taken by each side. The Rebels used the song to cast their uprising as an enlightened revolt against newfangled Northern despots whose oppression made Old World tyrants tolerable, and who, through guile, cunning, and hypocritical moralizing, would force the weaker Southern states into serfdom by absolving their political rights and confiscating their property. The legitimacy of their revolution rested on the right of a breakaway territory to fulfill its national destiny. Confederates contended that the North subverted the credo of the nation's founders by preventing a popular uprising in a region that considered itself to be abandoned by the federal system after the election of Lincoln. Designers of the Great Seal of the Confederacy deliberately featured George Washington, dressed in his Revolutionary War uniform and riding a white steed, above the motto *Deo Vindice* (Vindicated by God). The date on the seal, February 22, 1862, in addition to reflecting the month and day of Washington's Birthday, commemorated the inauguration of Jefferson Davis as the elected president of the Confederate States of America.

Northern propagandists depicted the South as a corrupt fiefdom inimical to republican values. Unionists dismissed their adversary's attempt to scuttle the colonies' democratic experiment, which inspired the French Revolution. Slavery threatened to choke economic opportunity throughout the nation. If plantations took root in the newly acquired western territories, wages would shrivel and land better used for individual homestead plots would disappear. Some Northerners decried the hypocrisy of slavery, but they remained marginalized. The Union justification for employing *The Marseillaise* centered on its claim to be the rightful caretakers of the Spirit of 1776, crystallized by Lincoln's line in the Gettysburg Address, "that government created of the people, by the people, for the people shall not perish from this earth." Though George Washington hailed from Virginia, a Confederate state, one New York music publisher released the song *The Last Words of Washington* in 1862. The lyrics claimed that on his deathbed, the general blessed the Union: " 'Sheath'd be the battle blade, And hush'd the cannon's thunder / The glorious Union God hath made, Let no man rend asunder!' "

Outside of France, where *The Marseillaise* still aroused bitter passions, the song degenerated into a generic call-to-arms. From the early 1800s, aggrieved parties around the world employed it to rally the troops, reveling in its alarmist tone and lust for blood. In a circa 1861 version of *The Marseilles Hymn*, which appeared in the *Nashville Gazette*, E. F. Porter of Alabama paraphrased the original words:

> Sons of the South, arise! awake! be free!
> Behold! the day of Southern glory comes
> See where the blood-stained flag of tyranny
> Pollutes the air that breathes around your home
> Pollutes the air that breathes around your home
> Rise! Southern men, from villages and farms
> Cry vengeance! Oh! Shall worse than pirate slaves
> Strangle your children in their mother's arms
> And spit on dust that fills your fathers' graves?
> To arms! sons of the South! Come like a mountain-flood
> March on! let every vale o'erflow with the invaders' blood.[8]

In the North, words rarely accompanied sheet music of the song, leaving the symbolic interpretation up to each listener or performer. Nevertheless, one collection, published in New York, included lyrics to *The Union Marseillaise* printed beneath a picture of bombs bursting over Fort Sumter at the mouth of Charleston Harbor, a scene reminiscent of the Battle of Baltimore during the War of 1812. References to the lyrics of *The Star-Spangled Banner*, along with calls to God, expanded the Union's pedigree to include the patriots of 1814:

Arise! Arise! ye sons of patriot sires!
A Nation calls! and Heaven speed your way
Now freedom lights anew her waning fires
And spreads her banner to the day
And spreads her banner to the day
While to His Throne our hearts are swelling
Freedom, and Law, and Truth, and Right
May God defend by his own might
By his right arm the treason quelling
Ye loyal sons, and true
Sons of the brave and free
Join hearts, join hands, to strike anew
For God and Liberty.[9]

Despite the tug-of-war over *The Marseillaise*, *The Star-Spangled Banner* remained the most contested and influential tune throughout the war. Even before the incident at Fort Sumter, some Southerners argued that their new nation should adopt the song and the flag it commemorated. "I never could learn to get entirely over a certain moisture of the eyelids that always comes to me listening to the sweet and stately melody of 'The Star Spangled Banner,'" wrote a correspondent from Louisiana in *Dwight's Journal of Music* in January 1861. The reporter also lauded *Hail, Columbia* and *Yankee Doodle*. "These tunes and anthems of right belong to the South" and dated to a time when slavery operated legally in the whole country. "Instead of abandoning [the songs], let us claim them as our legitimate property." Southerners "would almost as soon fight for their retention as they would for the protection of their section—so strong is their reverence for, and powerful their attachment to, the grand old tunes they have admired and loved from earliest boyhood to the present moment."[10] Other Rebels tried to flip Northern songs and strip them of their former meaning, as the colonists had done with *Yankee Doodle*. Lyricist Virginia L. French recast *Hail, Columbia* as *A Southern Gathering Song* and gushed in the head note that "we shall *never* give up 'Hail, Columbia' to the Abolitionists. It is *ours* and we mean to hold, as one of our dearest rights, this, the grandest march ever composed by mortal man."[11] Southerners also laid claim to *Yankee Doodle*, recasting it as *Dixie Doodle* or the *Southern Yankee Doodle*.[12]

At the February 1861 Montgomery Convention, when the upstart Confederacy ratified its constitution and established a provisional government, delegates debated the pattern for their flag and, by extension, the would-be country's anthem. The decision fell to the Committee on Flag, Seal, Coat of Arms, and Motto, chaired by William Porcher Miles of South Carolina, which never singled out an official anthem. The committee considered several configurations, but Mississippi delegate Walker Brooke called for the final version to be "as similar as possible to that of the United States.... Sir, let us preserve it as far as we can; let us continue to hallow it in our memory, and still pray that 'Long may it wave, O'er the land of the free, and the home of the brave.'" Miles retorted that ever since his childhood, he regarded the Stars and Stripes as "the emblem of oppression and tyranny." In March, to coincide with Lincoln's inauguration, the committee announced its adoption of the Stars and Bars. This compromise design featured three broad bars—two red, one white—and a blue square in the upper left corner containing seven white stars arrayed in a circle, with others to be added as states joined the breakaway confederacy. The final report, drafted by Miles, declared that despite an "attachment to the Stars and Stripes" among some committee members, "it is manifest that, in inaugurating a new government, we cannot retain the flag of the government from which we have withdrawn. Something was conceded by the committee to what seemed so strong and earnest a desire to retain at least a suggestion of the old stars and stripes," including the colors and the basic motif. The resolution alluded to *The Star-Spangled Banner*, adding that "if adopted, long may [the Stars and Bars] wave over a brave, a free, and a virtuous people."[13]

During the war's early days, the degree of flag worship and exuberance on both sides of the conflict astonished an English traveler in North Carolina, who wrote that "these pieces of coloured bunting seem to twine themselves through heart and brain." Southerners remained torn over Old Glory. After music publisher J. W. Davies in Richmond, Virginia, issued the song *Farewell to the Star Spangled Banner: Respectfully Dedicated to the Army & Navy of the C.S.A.*, disappointed editors at the *Savannah [Ga.] Republican* called for the new nation to "re-erect the stars and stripes as their national flag, and resume upon the Southern lyre those glorious old tunes, 'Hail, Columbia' and the 'Star-Spangled Banner.'" In April 1861, the *Richmond Examiner* wrote, "Let us never surrender to the North the noble song, the 'Star-Spangled Banner.' It is Southern in origin, in sentiments, in poetry, and song; in its association with chivalrous deeds, it is ours."[14]

Some Rebels most likely found solace in the fact that the Stars and Bars never took hold. Hanging limp around a pole, it resembled the Stars and Stripes and caused considerable confusion at the First Battle of Bull Run in July 1861. In September, the Confederate Congress decided to model a new flag after the one borne by the Army of Northern Virginia, a blue St. Andrew's cross studded with thirteen white stars on a crimson background, now universally recognized as the preeminent Confederate icon. No one could mistake it for Old Glory, and it generated songs with patriotic and religiously influenced titles, including *The Stars of Our Banner* and *The Southern Cross*. The emblem never received official sanction, however, and it carried one major flaw: the flag's symmetrical pattern meant that it could not be flown upside down, the universal shipping signal of distress in the days before radio.[15] As late as December 1861, the *Richmond Dispatch* rehashed the flag issue, lamenting the loss of the Stars and Stripes. "We were maintaining the principles it was intended to represent, and the North had abandoned them," the reporter wrote. "We were honestly entitled to the whole flag. And we should either have ... kept the flag as a whole, or else we should have abandoned it as a whole and adopted another," reiterating the South's equal right to seize *Hail, Columbia* and *Yankee Doodle*. In May 1863, the Confederate Congress designed a new flag, placing the battle banner in the top left corner of a white background, an act commemorated by the song *The Star-Spangled Cross and the Field of Pure White*.[16] This pattern resembled a flag of truce or surrender, and legislators considered adding a red stripe along the right border, but they never officially ratified the change.

Technically, all of the Confederate flags qualified as star-spangled banners. In the war's early stages, when it became clear that the Union refused to relinquish the Stars and Stripes, many "Southrons" burned, buried, or otherwise defiled Old Glory and heaped hatred upon Key's tune. In 1861, lyricist Ella D. Clark published *Adieu to the Star Spangled Banner for Ever*. Vermont-born A. E. Blackmar, who moved to New Orleans in 1860 and became known as the "Voice of the South," released the more prosaic *Farewell to the Star Spangled Banner*. *The Banner of the South*, published in Mobile, Alabama, in 1861, cried: "Up with 'Our Flag' / Come one, come all / We'll rally where 'tis seen / 'God and our Right' 'tis Freedom's call."[17] All three compositions abandoned the standard tune.

Public opinion in the Confederacy seesawed over Key's song, and vitriolic parodies pegged to the melody poured from Southern music presses, particularly in New Orleans, deep within Rebel territory. *The Stars and Bars*, published in 1861, asked: "Oh! say has the star-spangled banner become / The flag of the Tory and Vile Northern scum?"[18] One version of *The Southern Cross*, the title of several songs with different combinations of words and music, fused religious and patriotic imagery, highlighted sectional divisions, and portrayed Dixie's army as freedom fighters:

> How peaceful and blest was America's soil
> 'Til betrayed by the guile of the Puritan demon
> Which lurks under Virtue, and springs from its coil
> To fasten its fangs in the life blood of Freemen
> Then loudly appeal, to each heart that can feel
> And crush the foul Viper 'neath Liberty's heel
> And the Cross of the South shall for ever remain
> To light us to Freedom and Glory again.

Another parody published in New Orleans, the song *Confederate Flag*, replaced the chorus with the line: "For this flag of my country in triumph shall wave / O'er the Southerners' home and the Southerners grave."[19]

The status of *The Star-Spangled Banner* as the nation's most revered and renowned patriotic song aroused hostility in the North as well. An early anthem contest dated to 1806. Master showman P. T. Barnum also held a national song competition in the 1850s, yet he never awarded a prize, due to lackluster entries. In the absence of any official anthem in 1861, it seemed like a good idea to jettison *The Star-Spangled Banner*, with its musical roots in the previous century, its lyrical focus on a battle from a bygone era, and its author's ownership of slaves. Among the first of many futile attempts during this period to supplant Key's creation, after the rebels fired on Fort Sumter, a group of wealthy New Yorkers sponsored a national hymn contest, offering $250 for the words and $250 for the music. One advertisement placed by the group exclaimed: "Wanted, by the American Nation, a Marseillaise." Another sought "$250 worth of Genius and Inspiration embodied in Patriotic Music and Words." But the press savaged the presumptuous project (one newspaper called it "that insane Committee") and contest judge George Templeton Strong admitted in his diary that he subjected himself to scrutiny and ridicule for no good reason. "This is among the funniest things ever undertaken by mortal man," he wrote. "We stand a good chance of being consumedly laughed at."[20]

The project sought to replace *The Star-Spangled Banner*, a song "growing in favor in the loyal States from the beginning of the secession movement" and "played continually by all military and orchestral bands, and sung often at concerts and private musical gatherings," wrote committee spokesman Richard Grant White. Then, contradicting his initial observation, White concluded that "as a patriotic song for the people at large, as the National Hymn, it was found to be almost useless." White, an editor, music critic, Shakespeare scholar, and father of renowned architect Stanford White, wrote a book about the contest that carried the condescending title *National Hymns: How They Are Written and How They Are not Written*. He grumbled about the rhythm of *The Star-Spangled Banner*, griped about the lyrics, and groused over the song's wide vocal range. White recalled watching large groups of people stand mute, "while in some instances it was sung by a single voice or in most cases it was only played by a band." The words are "too long and the rhyme too involved for a truly patriotic song. They tax the memory." He dismissed Key's song as being "so utterly inadequate to the requirements of a national hymn."[21]

Still, wrote White, it trumped *Yankee Doodle*, which "no sane person would ever dream of regarding" as a national hymn. "Its words, as all know who have ever heard them, are mere childish burlesque; and its air, if air it must be called, is as comical as its words, and can hardly be regarded as being properly music." He considered *Hail, Columbia* to be "worse than 'Yankee Doodle,'" also calling it comical and contending that "it is respectable because it makes no pretence. But both the words and music of 'Hail, Columbia' are common-place, vulgar, and pretentious; and the people themselves have found all this out." To remedy this, White and his cohorts established ground rules for their contest. Submissions should be "purely patriotic, adapted to the whole country—not a war-song, or only appropriate to the present moment." The ideal song "should be of the simplest form and most marked rhythm; the words easy to be retained by the popular memory, and the melody and harmony such as may be readily sung by ordinary voices." *God Save the King* represented the model. White expected that the winner would "proclaim, assert, and exult" in freedom; "be brimful of loyalty to the flag, which is our only national symbol"; and "let its allusions be to our fathers' struggle for national existence." The committee would hold the copyright and remit all proceeds to the local Patriotic Fund.[22]

The judges collected 1,275 entries from as far away as Italy and California and, White stated, gleefully tossed one after another into a giant washing basket, "the temporary tomb of these extinguished hopes. . . . Alas, for the hapless writers!" His book, an attempt to justify the preposterous proceedings, presented several pages of logical criteria and traits of successful national hymns. The committee glossed over the near impossibility of ordering a ready-made musical composition, intended to exert a lasting impact, as if it were some kind of widget. White lambasted the contestants in print and complained about those "who talked and fumed, who wearied the members of the committee with calls and letters of remonstrance and inquiry, who waylaid them in the streets, who entered the office of the publishers big with bombast and terrible with threats."[23]

In the end, no one won and the committee disbanded. White took out his frustration on the contestants. Most of the composers, he wrote, remained "ignorant of the very first principles of harmony, and who to their ignorance added utter lack of native musical capacity." Richard Storrs Willis's *National Hymn* included two dubious rhymes: "God for Our banner / Union forever! / Once and again! / Union forever! / God it maintain!" A clumsy moon-June-spoon passage marred a submission by John H. Hopkins: "God Save Our Fatherland, True home of freedom! . . . / One in her hills and streams, One in her glorious dreams, One in love's noblest themes! / One evermore!" White delighted in denigrating the worst lyrics, beginning one chapter with a selection entitled *A National Hymn*: "All hail our country great / May she never falter / But every damn'd secessionist / Be hung up by a halter!" He also criticized Reverend John Pierpont's *E Pluribus Unum*, which fitted original words to the melody of *The Star-Spangled Banner*, as being "a model of what a song intended for a national hymn ought not to be."[24]

Despite White's scorn and his futile effort to mold public opinion, *The Star-Spangled Banner* endured in the North. Confederates, denied the ability to claim Key's song as their own, scrambled to find a suitable substitute. In the months before the war, Southerners adopted *The Bonnie Blue Flag* as the aspiring nation's first unofficial anthem. The title refers to an influential banner of the Confederacy, consisting of a large white star amid a blue background, which first flew over the Mississippi state house during the January 1861 convention that ratified secession. England-born Harry B. Macarthy, billed as the "Arkansas Comedian," had become popular through his "Personation Concerts," where he mimicked various ethnic groups. Macarthy penned original words that he wedded to the tune of *The Irish Jaunting Car*, which featured a rousing sing-along chorus. His lyrics quoted the "band of brothers" line from *Hail, Columbia* and referred to the flag as "the banner of the right." The song's refrain elevated it into the most popular flag song in the South: "But now, when Northern treachery attempts our rights to mar / We hoist on high the Bonnie Blue Flag that bears a single star / Hurrah, hurrah, for Southern rights, hurrah / Hurrah for the Bonnie Blue Flag that bears a single star." Mississippi officials distributed a thousand copies. Macarthy tirelessly performed the song throughout the Confederate states and scored other hits during the war, including *Our Flag and Its Origins*; *A Tribute to the Stars and Bars*; and *Missouri, or, a Voice from the South*, a knockoff of *Maryland! My Maryland!* intended to sway the divided western border state toward the Confederacy. New York City–born composer and poet John Hill Hewitt, nicknamed the "Bard of the Stars and Bars," sniped at his rival's success. Macarthy "gave the patriotics several wishy-washy songs which became extremely popular for the reason that he was continually singing them at his public entertainments," Hewitt wrote. "There was very little originality in them and they were of the clap-trap order." History ratified Hewitt's critique, as the popularity of *The Bonnie Blue Flag* began to fade even before Macarthy dodged the draft and fled to Philadelphia in 1864, and his song exerted a limited cultural impact.[25]

The Southern adoption of *Dixie* represented a circumstance as ironic as the Union capture of *The Star-Spangled Banner*. Ohio-born blackface entertainment pioneer Daniel Decatur Emmett wrote *I Wish I Was in Dixie's Land* in 1859 for his band, Bryant's Minstrels, during an engagement in New York City. Emmett may have learned the sentimental song from African American musicians in his hometown. Although Emmett was the first person to publish the phrase "Dixie's Land," whose origin is obscure, he claimed that it was "but another name for home among the Southern negroes." Known as *Dixie*, the song became an instant hit in New York. Beginning in April 1860, after the producer of the play "Pocahontas" performed it onstage at the New Orleans Varieties Theatre, *Dixie* spread spontaneously among supporters of the rebellion. Its airing at the inauguration of Jefferson Davis as the appointed president of the Confederacy in February 1861 gave it a hint of official sanction. The *Richmond Dispatch* called it the "National Anthem of Secession" in March 1861, though the Confederate government never designated an official anthem.[26] Roger B. Taney, Francis Scott Key's brother-in-law, presided over the inauguration of Abe Lincoln in March 1861, where bands performed *The Star-Spangled Banner* and *Dixie* for the new president, a fan of minstrelsy.

Like Key's song a generation earlier, *Dixie* rose to popularity without any artificial prompting, either from above or from its author. Emmett renounced the song after it became associated with the Southern cause. In one of the great paradoxes of American history, an antislavery Northerner composed the Southern anthem, while a slave owner, whose entire line of descendants joined the Confederacy, had created the Union hymn. Southerners printed pirated copies of *Dixie* by the thousands, and the song spread with "wild-fire rapidity," wrote London-based Confederate propaganda agent Henry Hotze in his diary. "Considered as an intolerable nuisance when first the streets re-echoed it from the repertoire of wandering minstrels, it now bids fair to become the musical symbol of a new nationality, and we shall be fortunate if it does not impose its name on our very country." Emmett's verses, written in dialect that demeaned southern blacks, ended up representing the Confederate cause by chance. Only a Rebel sympathizer could appreciate the lines, told from the perspective of a freed slave longing for "home": "Way down south in the land ob cotton / Old times there are not forgotten" and "In Dixie Land whar I was born in / Early on one frosty mornin / Look away, look away, look away, Dixie Land." The song's chorus inadvertently captured the South's defiant spirit and provincial pride: "Den I wish I was in Dixie, Hooray! Hooray! / In Dixie land, I'll take my stand / To lib and die in Dixie / Away, away, away down South in Dixie." The popularity of *Dixie* baffled the Swiss-born Hotze. "What magic potency is there in those rude, incoherent words, which lend themselves to so many parodies, of which the poorest is an improvement over the original? What spell is there in the wild strain that it should be made to betoken the stern determination of a nation resolved to achieve its independence? I cannot tell."[27]

Shortcomings notwithstanding, *Dixie* "became spontaneously the *national* tune" below the Mason-Dixon Line, wrote John Hill Hewitt. "The words are uncouth and unmeaning; some patriotic verses have however been wedded to the mongrel melody, and have proved stirring. The children in all sections of the Confederacy were taught to sing it, while at the North to do so was treason." Few lyrical rewrites of *Dixie* in the South exerted any lasting impact, except for verses completed by Albert Pike, Indian Commissioner for the Confederacy. Published by the *Natchez [Miss.] Courier* in April 1861, *Pike's Dixie*, also known as *The War Song of Dixie*, began: "Southrons, hear your country call you! / Up! lest worse than death befall you! / To arms! To arms! To arms, in Dixie." Though taboo in Union-controlled areas, the song crossed enemy lines with such ease that Northern bands sometimes forgot proper protocol. In 1865, the Second United States Artillery Band from Washington, D.C., visited the Union prison at Point Lookout, Maryland, to perform for the Confederate captives. George Neese, who served with the Army of Northern Virginia, reported that "after playing a few pieces some Rebel called for 'Dixie,' and the band at once struck up old 'Dixie' as well as I ever heard it. As the first sweet strain swelled over the listening throng the prisoners all over camp gave a regular Rebel yell that shook the prison wall." As soon as the band finished *Dixie*, "they quickly covered it up with 'Hail, Columbia.'"[28]

The Star-Spangled Banner, the preeminent song of the conflict, aired continuously before fighting broke out. During the 1860 presidential campaign, Lincoln squared off with southern Democrat John Breckenridge.

Reminiscent of the 1798 campaign tune *Adams and Liberty*, the song *Lincoln and Liberty* borrowed the melody of *The Star-Spangled Banner* and proclaimed: "Then up with the banner so glorious, the star-spangled red, white, and blue / We'll fight 'til our banner's victorious, For Lincoln and Liberty, too." At a January 1861 rally in Philadelphia, Key's creation went over as "the greatest favorite, and the people seemed never to tire listening to and applauding it. Again and again it was called for and given by the musicians." After a couple of speeches, the crowd demanded an encore, and "the band in the gallery struck up 'The Star Spangled Banner,' which was listened to in breathless silence, and vociferously applauded at its conclusion."

After the attack on Fort Sumter, music rallied the martial spirit above the Mason-Dixon Line as Northerners erupted into what the *Detroit Free Press* called "Star-Spangled fever." Unionists battled their foes with ballads as well as bullets. Early in the war, *Dwight's Journal of Music*, published in Boston, reported that Northerners heard *The Star-Spangled Banner* "at concerts, declaimed with fiery energy by accomplished singers, in the streets and in the public meetings by the sonorous tones of brass bands, often sung in spontaneous chorus by all who had heart to feel or a voice to sing." A profusion of songbooks and sheet music, along with public airings at solemn ceremonies, draft inductions, and troop musters, helped Lincoln's minions consolidate control over Old Glory and its chief ode. Repetition drowned out the opposition and provided more evidence that the song served as the true and accepted national anthem long before the 1860s.[29] Musical performances typically punctuated patriotic proceedings for maximum symbolic effect. On May 1, 1861, almost three weeks after Fort Sumter, several prominent Bostonians held a "Consecration of the Flag of the Union" at the Old South Meeting House, the staging point for the Boston Tea Party. Renowned bandleader Patrick Gilmore's group opened the ceremony with a solemn version of *Hail, Columbia*. After Reverend Dr. George W. Blagden asked God to bless the Union endeavor, "the Flag was unfurled amid the cheers of the crowd. The Band saluted it, playing the 'Star Spangled Banner.' "[30]

In 1862, Union Leagues emerged in the North. The rituals of the Maryland chapter included three pro-Union parodies of *Auld Lang Syne*, one of which included the line "in God we put our trust." The proceedings ended with either *The Star-Spangled Banner* or *Hail, Columbia* "or such other patriotic hymn as may be determined," along with a prayer: "May the blessing of Almighty God rest upon our Country and our cause forever.—Amen." In Baltimore, at a Grand Union Concert to benefit the Ladies Union Relief Association, the program included *The Union Forever*, a song written by a local high school student: "Hurrah for our forefathers true! / Down with each flag that is new! / Raise higher the Red, White, and Blue!" The event ended with a rendition of *The Star-Spangled Banner* and a pro-Union parody of *Maryland, My Maryland*, called *The Traitors' Feet Are on the Shore of Maryland, My Maryland*. When news of the Union victory at Gettysburg reached the White House on July 4, 1863, wild cheers broke out. After they subsided, the band played *The Star-Spangled Banner*. Sometimes, the constant blare of patriotic songs led to overkill. The night before Lincoln delivered the Gettysburg Address in November 1863, the *New York World* wrote that the barrage of music in town "was all done without malicious intention, but seemed in bad taste and out of place."[31]

Though Northerners revered Key's verses, wordsmiths knew that many Southerners despaired at losing the tug-of-war over *The Star-Spangled Banner* and gleefully tweaked the tune's lyrics to denigrate their adversaries. One broadside, *The Flag of Fort Sumter*, commemorated the war's first skirmish: "O say have you heard how the flag of our sires, is insulted by traitors in boastful alliance / When for Union's dear cause over Sumter's red fires, in front of Rebellion it waved its defiance."[32] Almost immediately, Key's song became the "musical seal of condemnation of sympathizing traitors," according to a Philadelphia newspaper.[33] Through the early 1900s, textbooks in several Northern states included a fifth verse, written by future Supreme Court Justice Oliver Wendell Holmes in 1861:

When our land is illumined with Liberty's smile
If a foe from within strikes a blow at her glory
Down, down with the traitor that dares to defile
The flag of her stars and a page of her story!
By the millions unchained, when our birthright was gained
We will keep her bright blazon for ever unstained
And the star spangled banner in triumph shall wave
While the land of the free is the home of the brave.

Other songs channeling Union fervor and paying homage to the flag poured from the presses. Approximately ten thousand titles circulated in the North during the war, including a large number of lesser compositions. These remain interesting regardless of their limited influence, since the songwriters attempted to attract as wide an audience as possible and publishers banked on their success. In works of commercial art, the "chicken-or-the-egg" question is central: are hit songs or books (and movies or television shows) popular because they give the people what they want and reflect the fantasies and realities of a broad range of the population, or is their influence so strong that they shape public opinion and behavior? During the Civil War the public demanded songs dripping with flag imagery, appeals to God, and gore-filled passages aimed toward civil religious purposes. Many of these patriotic songs quoted lines from *The Star-Spangled Banner*, underscoring its monumental status and intensifying Northern flag worship.

One tune, cowritten by a member of the renowned Hutchinson Family musical group, tried to institute the awkward phrase *The Triple Hued Banner*. Many songs revered Old Glory as a religious totem. In *God and Our Union*, published in Philadelphia in 1860, one verse stated: "Then shall thy sons 'neath thy star-lighted banner, One in their purpose, a brotherhood be / Chanting the anthem of Freedom: 'Hosanna! God and our Union!'" In 1861, the song *Union, God, and Liberty (Our National Flag)* proclaimed love for the Stars and Stripes. Another tune, *Down with the Traitors Serpent Flag*, took a more negative approach: "Death to the wretch o'er which it waves! And let our heaven born banner float / O'er freemen's Homes and Traitors' Graves!" The second verse of *The Flag of Our Union: National Song* proclaimed that "God in his Wisdom and Mercy design'd" Old Glory. A ceremony held in New York City on April 20, 1861, raised the venerated flag taken down from Fort Sumter and inspired *God Save Our Country's Flag*. The song *Our Banner of Glory!*, published in Cincinnati, hailed "the flag of the brave and the free" and called the star-spangled banner a "sign and a promise from God."[34]

Other compositions referenced standard slogans of freedom and liberty and equated death in the service of patriotism with martyrdom. In *The Stars and Stripes: A National Song*, the emblem "marked the spot where heroes stood, It was baptized in heroes' blood." *The Union Forever: A National*

Anthem contained the lines "our country; blest land, the favor'd of nations, Baptized in the blood of the brave and the free / To Him whose right hand sustains thy foundations, Our pray'rs shall ascend, O, our country, for thee!" and "To die for our flag the honor we'll covet, Our lives for our country, our souls to our God."

Northern publishers issued elaborate keepsakes, including a sheet music edition of *The Star-Spangled Banner* that featured color illustrations accompanying each of the four verses. The same New York City publisher also released *The Boy's Banner Book*, an illustrated collection of verse.[35] Union poets contributed to the fluid musical culture by reworking Southern anthems as parodies. Colonel J. L. Geddes of the Eighth Iowa Infantry wrote *The Bonnie Flag with the Stripes and Stars*. In Philadelphia, "Johnson, Song Publisher," released a Union parody of *The Bonnie Blue Flag*:

> We're in the right and will prevail, The Stars and Stripes must fly
> The "bonnie blue flag" be hauled down, And every traitor die
> Freedom and peace enjoyed by all, As ne'er was known before
> Our Spangled Banner wave on high, With stars just thirty-four
> Hurrah, hurrah, for the union, boys, hurrah!
> Hurrah for our forefathers' good old flag
> That glitters with many a star.

The reference to thirty-four stars represented the number of Northern and Southern states in 1860 and reflected the policy of officials in Washington, D.C., to keep the design of Old Glory intact. Almost every Northern state promoted its own version of *Dixie*. Calling the South a home of traitors, "rattlesnakes, and alligators," one lyric pledged that "where cotton's king and men are chattles, Union-boys will win the battles."[36] *Michigan Dixie* used the past to inspire the present:

> Away down South where grows the cotton
> Seventy-six seems quite forgotten
> Far away, far away, far away, Dixie Land
> And men with rebel shout and thunder
> Tear our good old flag asunder
> Far away, far away, far away, Dixie Land
> Then we're bound for the land of Dixie, Hurray! Hurray!

In Dixie land we'll take our stand, And plant our flag in Dixie
Away, away, away down South in Dixie.[37]

Only a handful of Northern songs endured beyond the Civil War. *The Battle Hymn of the Republic*, a schoolroom favorite, remained on the short list as a possible replacement for *The Star-Spangled Banner* through the 1920s. The tune, first known as *Grace Reviving in the Soul* and published in an 1807 hymnal, became better known on the camp meeting circuit as *Say Brothers, Will You Meet Us*. Just before the war, a regiment in Massachusetts popularized new lyrics for the song, turning it into *John Brown's Body*, an ode to the radical slavery abolitionist. During a visit to Washington, D.C., New York City–born poet, travel writer, and Union sympathizer Julia Ward Howe heard a group of troops sing it. Her original words for *The Battle Hymn of the Republic*, influenced by biblical passages, appeared on the cover of *Atlantic Monthly* in February 1862. Howe, who lived in Boston at the time, clearly sought to tap wartime sentiment. A year earlier, she had submitted an entry to Richard Grant White's farcical national hymn contest in New York City. Another popular war song, *The Battle Cry of Freedom* (also known as *Rally Round the Flag*), written by professional songwriter George F. Root in 1861, remained a staple at veterans' and patriotic gatherings through the early 1900s. Another Root hit, *Tramp! Tramp! Tramp! (The Prisoner's Hope)*, which refers to the "starry flag," retained its popularity after the conflict, when overseas military ventures helped bind the divided nation back together. An enterprising Chicago preacher borrowed the melody for the popular parody *Jesus Loves the Little Children*. In a sequel, *On, On, On, the Boys Came Marching! Or the Prisoner Free*, Root included the line "On, on, on the boys came marching, like a grand majestic sea / And they dashed away the guard, from the heavy iron door, and we stood beneath the starry banner free."[38] Another professional songwriter, Henry Clay Work, scored a hit with *Marching through Georgia*, which celebrated General George Sherman's Savannah Campaign, popularly known as the March to the Sea. *We Are Coming, Father Abraham* followed Lincoln's troop call-up in July 1862 and referred to "the spangled flag." *When Johnny Comes Marching Home*, composed in 1863 by Patrick Gilmore, is still played and sung today (inspiring *English Civil War* by The Clash in 1978).[39]

In the South, sheet music resembled the drab uniforms of the Confederate army, especially after paper became scarce and the government went bankrupt. The output in the South—estimated at around six hundred titles—represented a tiny fraction of the songs published up North, and original tunes remained scarce. *The Yellow Rose of Texas*, a minstrel-influenced number, dated to the 1830s. Confederate patriotic poetry often placed the Rebel cause at the right hand of God. In one of the many songs simply titled *National Hymn*, the chorus repeated the line "God save our land" six times. Sung in 1863 at a gathering in Houston for Major General John Magruder, the tune *God Bless Our Southern Land*, a parody of *God Save the King*, appealed to God for freedom, liberty, and victory. *The Land of King Cotton*, a song popular in Tennessee, borrowed the melody of *Columbia, the Gem of the Ocean* and promoted Dixie as "the home of the brave and the free." A version of *The Star-Spangled Cross*, published in Virginia toward the war's end, declared: "Our trust is in God, who can help us in fight / And defend those who ask Him in prayer."[40] The silly ditty *Goober Peas* referred to peanuts, a staple of the Rebel soldiers' diet toward the war's end. Several sentimental numbers popular with both sides evoked home and hearth, Mom or sweetheart, especially *Lorena*, written a few years before the war. Other marches and ballads commemorated battle victories and camp life in songs so temporal that consumers discarded them like day-old newspapers.

Music, especially when used as a symbol of domination, stirred intense passion. In April 1862, after pacifying battling Baltimore, Union General Benjamin Butler occupied New Orleans, the largest Southern port and the gateway to the Mississippi River. Butler banned *The Bonnie Blue Flag* and ordered fines of twenty-five dollars for "every man, woman, or child who sang, whistled, or played it on any instrument." Underscoring his intentions, the general arrested publisher A. E. Blackmar, destroyed his stock of the song, and fined him $500. Still, according to the *North American Review*, "defiant citizens in New Orleans sang the 'Bonnie Blue Flag' day and night and nurtured their children on it in kindergartens." One Union observer wrote that "so vindictive and morose was the secesh feeling that managers of the theaters refused to permit the orchestra to play any of our national airs." During a performance at an unnamed New Orleans theater, vociferous Northerners in the audience requested *Hail, Columbia* and *The Star-Spangled Banner*. The manager declined. Then "a single man arose in the boxes and cried out that the American national airs should be played, and called upon loyal Union men to second him. The house became at once a scene of fierce excitement. But the brave loyalist stood his ground. He demanded the 'Star-Spangled Banner' and the 'Red, White, and Blue' [*Columbia, the Gem of the Ocean*] should be given, and the manager was forced to yield." After Union troops evacuated the city, someone allegedly murdered the local resident who requested the Union songs, Dr. A. P. Dostie.[41]

Despite their inevitable enmity, soldiers and sailors from the North and the South sometimes bonded over music. In January 1863, the CSS *Alabama* sank the USS *Hatteras* off the coast of Galveston, Texas, but the Rebel seamen saved around a hundred of the enemy sailors. After the *Alabama* reached the island of Jamaica, the city of Kingston became "a constant scene of revelry," wrote Commander Raphael Semmes. Locals plied all the Americans with rivers of alcohol, and the crews performed endless "break down" and "double shuffle" dances, which helped ease tension between the combatants. "In these merry-makings, and debaucheries, the Confederate sailors and the Yankee sailors harmonized quite capitally together." The admiral reported that the men "sailed as amicably together, up and down the contradance . . . as though the *Alabama* and *Hatteras* had never been yard-arm and yard-arm, throwing broadsides into each other."[42]

Lieutenant W. J. Kinchelos wrote to his father about a musical round-robin in Virginia. As the armies encamped within earshot of each other on the banks of the Rappahannock River, "our boys will sing a Southern song, [and] the Yankees will reply by singing the same tune to Yankee words." In 1863, the night before the bloody Battle of Murfreesboro in Tennessee, the Northern band played *Yankee Doodle* and the Confederate band responded with a Rebel tune. The musicians alternated back and forth until they all played *Home, Sweet Home* together. The next morning, they slaughtered each other by the thousands. During Pickett's Charge at the Battle of Gettysburg, *The Bonnie Blue Flag* fortified the Rebels; Union forces countered with *The Star-Spangled Banner*. And, when opposing armies met at Greenville, Alabama, a Union band played *Yankee Doodle* and *Hail, Columbia* and *The Star-Spangled Banner*, while Southern musicians responded with *Dixie* and *The Bonnie Blue Flag*. Music also helped prisoners endure their ordeals. Joseph Ferguson, captain of the First New Jersey Volunteers, recalled the time one of his comrades pulled a concealed American flag out of a hat on July 4, 1864, at a Confederate prison in Macon, Georgia: "No sooner was the banner displayed than it was welcomed with three hearty cheers, which said, 'We still love our country; there are no traitors here.' An officer struck up the 'Star-Spangled Banner,' which was sung in a fine, manly voice, with artistic taste, every one present joining in the chorus, with the full power of the lungs."[43]

In the 1864 presidential election, held only in the North (except for Union-occupied areas of Tennessee and Louisiana), Lincoln faced off against his former general, Democrat George McClellan. At the Democratic Convention in Chicago, the party created a commotion by laying claim to *The Star-Spangled Banner*, since McClellan's running mate, George Pendleton, had married one of Francis Scott Key's daughters. The *New York News* asked, "What will the Lincolnites who use this song as a cover for their want of patriotism now do?" *The Star-Spangled Banner*, which the paper called "that best of national songs," belonged to the "Democratic Party; and when again in power, they will end the war, restore the white man to liberty, and then once more: 'The Star Spangled Banner in triumph shall wave / O'er the land of the free and the home of the brave.'" At a postconvention Republican rally in Philadelphia, one newspaper noted the performance of a girls' glee club, "a novel feature at political meetings," which sang *The Battle Cry of Freedom* and *The Star-Spangled Banner*. Ten days later at a Democratic extravaganza, thirty-four young ladies dressed in red, white, and blue outfits appeared on the platform as the band played Key's composition.[44]

Later that year, Union troops adopted scorched-earth tactics and hammered home their inevitable triumph with music. In his account of General George Sherman's arrival in Savannah, Georgia, Colonel Adin B. Underwood of Massachusetts recalled how the general let his band loose in the city center to deliver the ultimate slap in the face. "Christmas day, according to promise, it was playing 'John Brown,' 'Yankee Doodle,' 'The Star Spangled Banner,' [and] 'Dixie,' in Pulaski Square, to an over-joyed crowd of darkies of all ages, sizes, and colors, swarming to hear the 'Linkum band'; singing, crying, and dancing for joy, that 'De day of de Lord hab come.' They swarmed in to the number of thousands, and there was such a mass that Sherman, reluctantly, had to order the square cleared, finally."[45] After the fall of Richmond in April 1865, the last stand of the Lost Cause, music played a central role in the choreography of defeat. With the city in ruins, bands turned onto Main Street and marched toward Capitol Square, the heart of the Confederacy, playing *The Battle Cry of Freedom* and *Yankee Doodle.* Forlorn eyewitness Sallie Putnam wrote that as troops stacked their arms in the street, "the strains of an old familiar tune floated upon the air—a tune that, in days gone by, was wont to awaken a thrill of patriotism. But now only the most bitter and crushing recollections awoke within us, as upon our quickened hearing fell the strains of 'The Star Spangled Banner.' For us, it was a requiem for buried hopes."[46] On April 3, 1865, George Templeton Strong described the scene in downtown New York City: "Never before did I hear cheering that came straight from the heart, that was given because people felt relieved by cheering and hallooing," he said. "These were spontaneous and involuntary and of vast 'magnetizing' power. They sang 'Old Hundred,' the 'Doxology,' 'John Brown,' and 'The Star-Spangled Banner,' repeating the last two lines of Key's song over and over, with a massive roar from the crowd and a unanimous wave of hats at the end of each repetition." The "rude, many-voiced chorale" made a lasting impression and "seemed a revelation of profound national feeling, underlying all our vulgarisms and corruptions, and vouchsafed us in their very forms and centre in Wall Street itself."[47]

Flags, songs, and displays of military might are the basic symbols of countries striving to be taken seriously. The Confederate States of America stumbled over its flag design as control over *The Star-Spangled Banner* slipped from its statesmen's grasp, and Southern composers and musicians contributed few lasting musical monuments to their legacy. At the end of the war, publisher A. E. Blackmar issued a hastily composed piece, *The Conquered Banner.* New York publishers heralded victory with topical tunes, including *The Peace Jubilee* and *The Nation's Jubilee,* which featured the verse: "Fling out the nation's starry flag, In glory on the air! The ancient flag of freedom still; No star is missing there / The Lord of hosts has giv'n the word the people all are free."[48]

Both sides carried *The Star-Spangled Banner* like a security blanket through trying times. Considering the status of the major patriotic songs during the Civil War, William Lichtenwanger at the Library of Congress called *Yankee Doodle* "too frivolous for a national anthem." *Hail, Columbia* he referred to as "too old-fashioned and not sufficiently exciting to a nation about to tear itself apart." *My Country, 'Tis of Thee* and *Columbia, the Gem of the Ocean* suffered from their use of melodies that originated in England. *The Battle Hymn of the Republic* remained "enmeshed with the earlier gospel song and 'Jon Brown' uses of the tune." Thus *The Star-Spangled Banner* emerged as "an almost inevitable choice." In 1865, when General Robert Anderson raised the same tattered flag at Fort Sumter that he lowered in defeat four years earlier, booming cannon fire from warships docked in Charleston Harbor punctuated the strains of the song. The War between the States vastly eclipsed the single battle glorified by Francis Scott Key, yet *The Star-Spangled Banner*, bound with the sacred swath of cloth it described, cemented itself in the country's consciousness. The tune also comforted the victors and the vanquished, since the flag and the song evoked a time when the North and the South together ousted a foreign foe and created a dynamic nation. With both sections legitimately claiming possession of the song at the outset of the war, Key's creation made a smooth transition from celebration ode to olive branch after the guns fell silent.[49]

Recounting an incident in Richmond soon after General Robert E. Lee's surrender on April 9, 1865, Richard Wentworth Browne wrote that after touring the town, he and three colleagues returned to their quarters, sat down at the piano, and harmonized. In deference to a group of Confederate officers staying in the house next door, they avoided patriotic songs. The Southerners soon sent a note asking if they could come over and listen. Wentworth and his companions assented, performing glees and college songs for their guests. But the former enemies insisted on hearing Union music. The quartet "gave them the army songs with unction, the 'Battle Hymn of the Republic,' 'John Brown's Body,' 'We're Coming Father Abraham,' 'Tramp, Tramp, Tramp, the Boys are Marching,' through the whole catalogue, to the 'Star-Spangled Banner'—to which many a foot beat time as if it had never stepped to any but the 'music of the Union.'" After closing the impromptu concert with *The Battle Cry of Freedom*, a "tall, fine-looking fellow in a major's uniform exclaimed, 'Gentlemen, if we'd had your songs we'd have licked you out of your boots! Who couldn't have marched or fought with such songs? While we had nothing, absolutely nothing, except a bastard 'Marseillaise,' the 'Bonny Blue Flag,' and 'Dixie,' which were nothing but jigs." As the group disbanded, a high-ranking general identified as standing "second only to Lee or Jackson, in the whole Confederacy," showed less enthusiasm. Shaking Browne's hand, he said: "Well, the time *may* come when we can *all* sing the 'Star-Spangled Banner' again."[50]

Striving to Reunify, 1865–1900

THE DAY AFTER Confederate General Robert E. Lee surrendered at Appomattox, a large crowd, accompanied by a band, stood outside Abraham Lincoln's window at the White House. Noticing the musicians, the president requested *Dixie*, which he called "one of the best tunes I have ever heard. Our adversaries over the way attempted to appropriate it, but I insisted yesterday that we fairly captured it. I presented the question to the Attorney General, and he gave it as his legal opinion that it is our lawful prize." The statement angered some vanquished Confederates. "Many embittered Southerners . . . believed, that he meant to say that 'Dixie' belonged to the North by right of conquest," wrote Kentucky native John Lair. "I believe he meant that here on the common ground of admiration for a good song the North and South could find a unity, a fellowship, of enjoyment and appreciation."[1]

Former Confederates harbored sore feelings, but many of them turned to *The Star-Spangled Banner* as a familiar and comforting totem. In June 1865, at an amateur concert in Charlestown, South Carolina, the *Columbia Daily Record* reported that "the 'Star Spangled Banner' brought down the house." In 1867, the *Star-Spangled Banner*, a Hinsdale, New Hampshire, mail order catalogue that masqueraded as a newspaper, took out advertisements in the Fayetteville, Tennessee, *Observer*. The ads listed the title twice in capital letters, betting that a reference to the song would attract, rather than repel, Southerners so soon after the war's end. And, at an 1868 Democratic Party campaign rally in Memphis, Tennessee, attended by ten thousand people, "on the arrival of the officers on the stand, the band played the 'Star Spangled Banner.' "[2]

Key's tune and other national songs that predated the Civil War eventually helped heal the enmity between belligerents, who rediscovered their common bonds by engaging in commerce, subjugating African Americans, and fighting foreign wars. After the South surrendered, several popular Union numbers lost their controversial trappings and evolved into broad-based songs that transcended lines on a map. Still, some Northerners subtly gloated. New England clergyman and author Elias Nason wrote that instead of discarding the country's pre–Civil War musical heritage and forging a new future, as some people suggested, the "grand old songs must still roll on" to "draw the eye to the dear old flag; to repeat the story of the men of 1776; to rehearse the glory of the braves who placed the flag upon the domes of Richmond;" and "to consolidate us into one vast free people." Songs seared in the heat of battle aired at ceremonies that included schoolchildren and veterans. By the end of the 1890s, sheet music reflected reconciliation between the Blue and the Gray.

After the war, an accessible civil religion welcomed newcomers into the fold. Like most belief systems, patriotic practices in the United States gave rise to a raft of colorful dissenters. Even the Founding Fathers bickered after they broke free from the British yoke and split into two political factions. Their heirs, broadly defined as militant patriots and liberal patriots, battled to institute competing interpretations of the national narrative into local, state, and federal statutes and to influence rituals in schools and town squares. They also fought over the meaning of the flag and *The Star-Spangled Banner*, especially when talk about seeking to designate an official anthem increased in the late 1890s.[3]

In their extreme guise, often peaking during wartime, militant patriots extolled battlefield sacrifice, God, and country. Tracing their lineage to the Federalist Party, which favored an active centralized government and generally supported law and order, they regarded the Revolutionary War as a conservative movement that delivered a far superior outcome than the bloody chaos that emerged in France and elsewhere. Any rebellion represented treason. The Federalist political party imploded in 1800, but its heirs sought to Americanize immigrants, support foreign incursions, hold military drills in schools, and enforce lockstep conformity during flag rituals and performances of *The Star-Spangled Banner*. Liberal patriots also defied simple classification. This faction claimed to represent the revolutionary legacy precisely because they questioned society's sacred tenets. To them, the events of 1776 obliged Americans to try to perfect society rather than accept the new status quo. Thomas Jefferson captured it best in a 1787 letter, when he proposed that "a little rebellion now and then is a good thing." Liberal patriots chafed at the conformity that characterized prescribed patriotic rituals ostensibly celebrating freedom and individual rights. This camp traced its origins to the rural-rooted mistrust of authority among the Jeffersonian Republicans and influenced crusading pre–Civil War reformers, labor unions, immigrants, African Americans, and the Populist Party. Yet, despite this fundamental ideological divide, patriots across almost the entire political spectrum expressed loyalty toward the United States.

Both sides also pledged allegiance to the almighty dollar. The Civil War put into motion the most colossal, freewheeling economic engine in world history and accelerated the commercialization of patriotism. During the 1800s, flimflam artists and legitimate businesses alike flaunted the flag at vaudeville theaters in the big cities and at medicine shows on the prairies, making it difficult to discern the difference between nationalistic exuberance and the urge to make a quick greenback. Prompted by the perception of political and commercial abuse of the Red, White, and Blue, in 1880 the first attempt to regulate the use of the flag stalled in Congress, since politicians feared that they would be unable to fly the colors at their rallies. Hucksters of all stripes used national symbols to promote their goods and services. In the introduction to his lackluster collection of *Star-Spangled Banner Poems, Consecrated to Union and Liberty*, published in 1862, James Homer Kennedy of Lenni, Pennsylvania, promised that his book "will fire your patriotism, invigorate your loyalty, and help you kindle a bonfire to Freedom." He sought "Patriotic Local Agents" to buy copies in bulk and influence "the People to scatter broadcast this Patriotic Work among our half million and upward Soldiers." All orders, he wrote, "must be 'Cash.'" Like a songwriter repeating chord sequences, Kennedy's hackneyed poems included recurrent rhymes with the words "star," "banner," "free," "brave," "red," "white," and "blue." In the selection *Our Land Is in Tears*, he wrote "God shall Columbia save!" and in *The Banner of the Sun*, he asked, "Oh! Is it not, also, the Banner of Heaven?" In Chicago during the Civil War, Charles Heck, a manufacturer and dealer in Union goods, jewelry, stationery, and maps, inserted a broadside with his Champion Prize Package that featured seventeen patriotic union songs.[4]

As corporations began to build mass markets after the Civil War, a growing national identity overshadowed local and regional affiliations, with the help of generic patriotic appeals. Businesses took advantage of the printing revolution to silently scream their messages, distributing inexpensive pamphlets and calling cards that featured lyrics and sometimes music. "Learn to sing your country's songs," admonished the cover of the modest 1889 booklet, *Our National Songs: American Patriotic Melodies with Words*, which included *Hail, Columbia*; *The Star-Spangled Banner*; *My Country, 'Tis of Thee*; and *Columbia, the Gem of the Ocean*. Sponsored by the White Sewing Machine Company in Cleveland, Ohio, ad copy inside this booklet tied into the grand theme: "A National Song, The White is King, Sung Everywhere By Everybody that Owns a White Machine." Another advertising vehicle, *Our Country's Songs: A Collection of American National Airs*, consisted of a template that included the patriotic Big Five and sometimes an original song or two printed on other pages, with custom copy provided by different companies. In one issue, published for the Valley City Milling Company in Grand Rapids, Michigan, purple prose promoted "the songs of our country, inspired by devotion, Reflecting the joy of our heart's deep emotion / We love them, and sing them with joyful acclaim / 'Till the blood coursing quickly becomes all aflame." Patriotic songs "thrill us and move us as nothing else will, Unless when we're hungry we go to the mill / And exchanging our wheat for 'Lily White Flour' / We sing of its praises from that very hour."

In the late 1800s, another national advertiser, Piso's Cure for Consumption, issued an almanac, a puzzle in the shape of the United States, and collections of musical scores featuring national airs. English author Samuel Johnson's contention that "patriotism is the last refuge of a scoundrel" may apply to E. T. Hazeltine and Company, makers of Piso's in western Pennsylvania. Though it originally contained opiates, the formula eventually settled on a strange brew of cannabis, chloroform, and alcohol. Consumption, now known as tuberculosis, affected the urban poor, and in the mid-1890s the federal government cracked down on patent medicines like Piso's. The company also issued a pamphlet featuring *The Star-Spangled Banner* and five pages of testimonials, along with a series of booklets about the size of a business card that, when folded, included the words and music of patriotic songs on the front and purported customer testimonials on the back.[5] On July 4, 1897, the American Electrical Works in Providence, Rhode Island, which sold bare and insulated wire, created a thick booklet tied with a ribbon that included all four verses of *The Star-Spangled Banner*, along with a rendering of the fifteen-star banner hovering over smoke-shrouded Fort McHenry. Baltimore businesses, including Bromo Seltzer, also used the song to generate goodwill. Newspapers routinely included sheet music inserts, and when advertisers realized that readers held on to them, the sponsors' names began to dominate the song titles. In addition, Bromo Seltzer issued several editions of popular song collections with piano and organ accompaniment, including the top patriotic numbers, Stephen Foster songs, and frivolous ditties like *De Gal I Dream About* and *I Love My Love*.

In such a freewheeling era, the lure of writing a big hit remained irresistible. Composers, both lofty and lowbrow, attempted to craft songs intended to vault to the top of the patriotic song heap—or at least earn some money. One of them, George M. Vickers, achieved a degree of popularity with his original patriotic, minstrel, and sentimental tunes. He pushed *Guard the Flag* as a "new National song," which included the line "God save the banner of the free!" and appeared in several schoolbooks. Vickers claimed that it "is sung in Public Schools, Concerts, in the Home Circle; its stirring strains are played by bands everywhere: in short, it has won the hearts of the American people." He also penned *Columbia, My Country* and *God Bless Our Land*, the latter presented as a national anthem, and contributed to commercial songbooks. Songwriting contests continued to proliferate. Frederick J. Nelson, a lawyer in Frederick, Maryland, and a proponent of *The Star-Spangled Banner*, prepared a paper in the late 1800s ridiculing the folly of "blind, darkened souls, mousing around, still hunting for a national anthem, and proposing prizes for one yet to be written. . . . As though a nation's song-writer ever drew his inspiration from the jingle of coin, like a competitor for a prize at a country fair!" Comparing Key's song to the French anthem, *The Marseillaise*, Nelson argued that national songs "come from the heart of genius, glowing, sincere, interpreting the heart of the nation. It comes as the lightning of Heaven."[6]

Sheet music and songbook editions featured *The Star-Spangled Banner* arranged for brass band, piano, and vocals, including solos and quartets. Beyond the reams of paper pouring from printing presses, other industrial advancements spread music more rapidly and helped consolidate the country's culture. By 1870, improved designs and manufacturing techniques generated a boom in the brass-instrument business. A widespread movement helped promulgate *The Star-Spangled Banner* nationwide and instituted a military band craze. In 1889, almost ten thousand towns, schools, and fraternal organizations across the country sponsored at least one brass band. These groups featured musicians from all over Europe, especially Germany. Also, no upper- or middle-class parlor in the mid-1800s could be complete without a piano, the "first machine used to disseminate a mass-music culture," and the number of instruments produced in the country jumped from 9,000 in 1850 to 360,000 in 1910.[7]

With the ability to create grand spectacles, thanks to the development of theatrical pyrotechnics, Victorian performance styles in the Gilded Age exposed millions of people to *The Star-Spangled Banner*. At the Great National Peace Jubilee, held in Boston in 1869, renowned bandleader Patrick Gilmore arranged the song for a chorus of ten thousand, plus "Organ, Orchestra, Military Band, Drum-Corps, Chiming of Bells, and Cannon Accompaniment," with effects triggered by the "touch of an electrician." Gilmore believed that music could heal the world, and he held a second extravaganza in 1872, the World's Peace Jubilee and International Music Festival, the largest concert in the world up to that time. In addition to a 2,000-member orchestra and 20,000-voice choir, Gilmore also employed a "battery of cannon to emphasize the rhythm" of *The Star-Spangled Banner*, which played every day during the nearly three-week-long festival.[8]

As the nation turned toward commerce and the promise of progress, *The Star-Spangled Banner* graced numerous bridge and railroad dedications and aired at anniversaries large and small. On July 4, 1876, at the national celebration of the centennial of the Declaration of Independence in Philadelphia, pipe organs seemed to magically repeat *The Star-Spangled Banner*, along with *Hail, Columbia* and *Yankee Doodle*, all day long.[9] During a commemoration of the centennial of the Battle of Groton Heights, Connecticut, held in 1881, a band played Key's creation and Matthias Keller's 1866 composition, *American Hymn*, which remained popular through the 1920s.[10] In 1886, the state of Michigan celebrated its fiftieth anniversary at Lansing, where participants heard a parody verse of *The Star-Spangled Banner* by Reverend John T. Oxtoby of Saginaw that paid homage to the Wolverine State.[11]

At the 1893 World's Columbian Exposition in Chicago, a massive tribute to the landing of Columbus in North America, the state of Maryland budgeted $60,000 to construct an elaborate exhibit hall. This building contained a reading room stocked with publications from across the state, and a fact book distributed by the *Baltimore Sun* doted on Key, his song, and the flag. One and a half million visitors walked through the exhibition's doors. On Maryland Day at the fair, held on Defenders Day (September 12), the black, gold, red, and white colors of the schizophrenic state banner mingled with the Stars and Stripes to create a bouquet of local and national pride. Civil War veterans who fought for the Union led a procession from the Maryland Building to the Music Hall. When the Cardinal and Archbishop of Baltimore entered, all 2,500 people in attendance stood up. The band played a special composition, *The Armistead March*, written by James M. Deems of Baltimore in honor of the officer in charge of Fort McHenry in 1814. After a version of *Maryland, My Maryland*, Miss Martha Ford sang *The Star-Spangled Banner*.[12]

Featured speaker John V. L. Findlay waxed rhapsodic over Maryland's charms before recounting the role *The Star-Spangled Banner* played in the state's and the country's history. Findlay went on record as one of the first to suggest a national holiday to honor the song. "We look at the cross, and all that it stands for—the universal sacrifice, the bloody agony, the long struggle for supremacy, the final triumph, and the still more splendid fruitions beyond the grave—in an instant are present to the mind." Americans abroad might gaze at the flag floating over a ship in a foreign port "and our veins tingle with a warmer glow." But no one feels "the full force of those associations until, in a sort of rapture and ecstacy, he has been caught up in those billowing strains of the 'Star-Spangled Banner' . . . and borne away into the seventh heaven of sentiment and emotion." Findlay claimed that "greater than constitutions, stronger than laws, enduring as time, this splendid lyric binds a nation together with cords stronger than steel in a union not visible, but eternal as the stars." At the governor's reception held after the concert, "the Maryland Building was illuminated for the evening's festivities. Chinese lanterns and lamps were placed all about the grounds and the word 'Maryland' in lights was displayed on the grass of the north front. The fire-works came off according to programme," with displays illustrating the bombardments of Fort McHenry and a design of the national flag. So many people jammed the hall that "it was hardly possible to move through the rooms with ease."[13] The presentation attempted to affirm Maryland as a faithful star within the constellation of states and as a conduit of progress.

It is no coincidence that when Maryland dignitaries paraded to their grand concert at the Columbian Exposition, they chose a group of Union veterans to escort them. The former soldiers represented the Grand Army of the Republic, a national organization founded in Decatur, Illinois, in 1866. Known as the G.A.R., they lobbied Congress for pensions, kept wartime memories alive, and participated in annual state and national encampments. At first their platform expressed unease over the South's apparent lack of repentance, but these objections faded. In 1888, G.A.R. membership peaked at 361,779. The following year, Southerners established a similar organization, the United Confederate Veterans. G.A.R. departments (state level) and posts (community level), precursors to the Veterans of Foreign Wars and the American Legion, served as political powerbrokers through the 1920s. They also instituted Decoration Day, when members and their families visited Union cemeteries and left flags and other mementos on the headstones. Southerners participated in Confederate Memorial Day ceremonies soon after the war ended, and both holidays eventually merged into Memorial Day.[14]

Music played a major role in the G.A.R. encampments, where Southern songs rarely aired. An 1870 compilation of patriotic speeches and poems for the Union Veterans' Camp included a stanza by Charles H. Tiffany: "Sweet music's power! One chord doth make us wild / But change the strain, we weep as little child / Touch yet another, men charge the battery gun / And by those martial strains, a victory's won."[15] Religious imagery influenced their patriotism. A *G.A.R. Memorial Hymn* sought to bring "glory to God who our victories gave," to "hallow the dead hero's tomb," and to honor the martyrs of freedom whose "souls rest in heaven."[16] In 1883, department historian Samuel Peters of Ohio compiled an official G.A.R. songbook containing thirty-six selections, including *Hail, Columbia*; *The Star-Spangled Banner*; and *Columbia, the Gem of the Ocean*. The melody of *My Country, 'Tis of Thee* obtained new lyrics in the national organization's *Muster In Ode*. Peters included Northern hits from the war, along with a special *Hymn for Decoration Day*: "God of the living and the dead, We bow before thy face. . . . Our strength was in Thy mighty arm—Thy guardian love our shield." Peters also included a few Southern numbers, though these rarely crossed the Mason-Dixon Line. The *Closing Ode* vowed never to forget "the honored dead / That sleep beneath the sod / Who gave their lives for liberty / Our country and our God." Other song collections contained the standard national tunes, along with the sentimental numbers *Hymn for a Dead Comrade* and *Sleep, Sacred Dust of Noble Dead*.[17] Traveling troubadours, including John Hogarth Lozier, G.A.R. department chaplain in Iowa, sold his act and his music books at encampments and gatherings of all kinds, including the collection *40 Rounds from the Cartridge Box of the Fighting Chaplain*, "for the benefit of posts of the G.A.R., and the Women's Relief Corps, and Sons of Veterans."[18] Lozier borrowed lyrical imagery from Francis Scott Key. The cover of *O, Guard That Banner while We Sleep*, published in 1891, featured two sentinels flanking a podium containing a bust of Washington and an open bible beneath an American Flag. Maudlin words about dead heroes and nameless graves helped sell his "patriotic entertainments."[19] The rousing chorus of *My Father's Flag and Mine* also appealed to patriots: "O, the beauty! O, the glory! That in radiant splendor shine / In the old Star-Spangled Banner, . . . My father's flag and mine!"[20]

At G.A.R. encampments, veterans and their families found themselves on the receiving end of pointed advertisements drilled home with music. First published in 1886 by a Syracuse, New York–based veteran, J. C. O. Redington, the *Acme Haversack of Song and Patriotic Eloquence* served as the cornerstone of a publishing enterprise that also included special edition songbooks, leaflets of sheet music, and compilations for G.A.R. encampments held in Northern cities. Redington filled each bimonthly issue with music, poems, articles, and long lists of nationwide G.A.R. posts and Civil War battles. The Howard W. Spurr Coffee Company advertised its April 19 Patriots' Coffee brand with a woodcut of the "Midnight Ride of Paul Revere."[21] Other advertisers sometimes adopted a more tactless approach. A full-page ad for Fould's Wheat Germ Meal, which appeared

that revered the Anglo-Saxon contribution to the nation's history. Music played a pivotal role in their attempt to assert control over the country's historical and national symbols, a drive that eventually culminated with the ratification of *The Star-Spangled Banner* as the national anthem. To counter social instability, hereditary and nationalist organizations worked to introduce the study of American history and civics in the schools, supplemented with elaborate flag ceremonies and music featuring *The Star-Spangled Banner*. Less-benevolent interest groups also formed as a backlash to the influx of immigrants, including the secret anti-Catholic American Protective Association (1887) and the Immigrant Restriction League (1894), heirs to the Order of the Star-Spangled Banner from the 1850s, all of whom became aggressive stewards of patriotic rituals and instituted loyalty tests.[25]

Unease rippled, especially through the schools—the prime incubators of civil religion, where *My Country, 'Tis of Thee* and *The Star-Spangled Banner* wormed their way into youthful minds. The first flag to fly over a schoolhouse purportedly occurred in Colrain, Massachusetts, in 1812 to show support for the war effort. In the mid-1840s, the Patriotic Order Sons of America attempted to institute patriotic education among young men between ages sixteen and twenty-one. After the Civil War, state-level education officials began to introduce patriotic studies, and the battle over *The Star-Spangled Banner* moved into the schools. Education officials in Maryland, like their counterparts in other states, pushed patriotic topics for decades, helping to create a large constituency that supported legislation on behalf of *The Star-Spangled Banner*. In 1876, Baltimore educators advocated "the use of the history of Maryland in the schools" to instill pride in the state's past. In 1887, Andrew S. Draper, superintendent of public instruction in New York, lamented the nation's lack of patriotic backbone: "If I had my way, I would hang the flag in every school-room, and I would spend an occasional hour in singing our best patriotic songs, in declaiming the masterpieces of our national oratory, and in rehearsing the proud story of our national life." In 1892, another prominent educator claimed that at least a dozen state education superintendents, along with other pedagogues in charge of colleges, teacher-training schools, city schools, high schools, and grammar schools, "have actively entered upon the plan of making the inculcation of patriotism a special function of their work."[26]

The G.A.R pushed to influence the schools and add the Civil War to the history curriculum. In 1889, at their national encampment, held in Milwaukee, Commander in Chief William Warner praised posts in New York City that delivered flags to select schools on Washington's Birthday: "The future citizens of the Republic are being educated in the public schools. . . . Let them learn to look upon the American flag, 'By angels' hands to valor given,' with as much reverence as the Israelites look upon the ark of the covenant." Only then would the nation's future be assured, and "that flag shall forever wave 'O'er the land of the free / And the home of the brave.' "[27] In 1896 in Auburn, Maine, the G.A.R. Burnside Post distributed pamphlets to public school pupils that included the G.A.R. badge and two crossed flags on the cover. Inside, a poem read: "May the colors of our precious Flag for which so many have suffered, and for which so many of our loved ones have died, be immortal. . . . May its stars stand aloft as long as the stars of God."[28]

One of the country's most prominent instigators of patriotism in the schools, New York City Board of Education auditor George Balch, vigorously promoted methods to influence immigrant children with strategically orchestrated flag rituals, buttressed by a reward system. Balch attended his first patriotic ceremony at a New York City school in 1888. Sounding the alarm against "fifteen million aliens" that he feared "diluted our civilization," he contracted with the Children's Aid Society to introduce his program to five thousand students in twenty-one schools. Balch favored regimented exercises, writing that nothing "impresses the youthful mind and excites its emotions more forcibly or permanently than the observance of form and ceremony." Music played an integral role in his elaborate rituals, which singled out *The Star-Spangled Banner* and *Hail, Columbia*: "The music and songs chosen and the addresses delivered . . . shall stamp indelibly on the hearts of all present, the real meaning and significance of the occasion." Balch suggested that "if there should be in the school either a boy or girl who can drum, or play the fife, the bugle, the horn, or the cornet, I would have them present to assist in the ceremony," yet probably few immigrants or their offspring would have been proficient on instruments so closely related to the Revolutionary Era. During ceremonies, he recommended that a drum roll or a flourish of wind instruments accompany the dipping of the flagstaff. Balch understood that instilling patriotism by the "point of the bayonet" or by decree would fail, since "neither patriots nor saints can be created by statute."[29]

Balch triggered a trend. In 1890, New Jersey and North Dakota adopted regulations requiring public schools to prominently display Old Glory. By 1908, twenty-nine states followed their lead. Balch also devised the first oath to the flag: "I give my heart and my hand to my country—one country, one language, one flag," which later became overshadowed by the Pledge of Allegiance. In 1900, two years after New York State mandated that every public school fly a flag during school days, state superintendent of public instruction Charles Skinner published a *Manual of Patriotism* that incorporated many of Balch's suggestions. Referring to music, poetry, and prose as the "gateways beautiful into the mind of the child," Skinner recommended that "school be opened by a patriotic song and salute to the flag" and reminded teachers to ensure that the emblem should "at all times [be] sacredly cared for." To support his agenda, he included thirty-nine songs and singled out *The Star-Spangled Banner* as a selection that every student should know. "In the sweet and strong music of the book you may feel your young spirits strengthened to fight, in years to come, in peace or in war, the noble battles of Patriotism and the Flag." Skinner acknowledged the G.A.R, the D.A.R., and allied groups for helping to spread the word in the schools. In order to promote the militant patriot viewpoint, readings in his book doted on grand battles and heroes of the past, including "Dirge for a Soldier" and "The Bivouac of the Dead." The selection "Uncover to the Flag," by E. C. Cheverton, helped reinforce popular customs and included a verse honoring Francis Scott Key.[30]

As schools instituted civics into the curriculum, publishers aggressively marketed elaborate songbooks, plays, and stage settings to mold young patriots. One cantata for soloists and a choir, *Our Flag with the Stars and Stripes*, published in 1896 by celebrated Civil War composer George F. Root, offered costume patterns, in cooperation with the Butterick Company, a worldwide distributor of home-sewing patterns. The program directed students to sing "praise be God for our dear old flag."[31] *Songs of Flag and Nation*, a schoolbook filled with more than twenty flag songs, including *The Star-Spangled Banner*, mentioned "the host of patriotic compilations with which the market swarms."[32] In an 1899 collection, *Patriotic Songs for School and Home*, John Carroll Randolph wrote: "The past decade has been marked by a deepening and quickening of the national consciousness. Nowhere has this revealed itself as in the common schools." The spirit of patriotism "has found expression in new and stirring music, and has brought into renewed favor melodies of earlier days." Of the eighty-two songs in the collection, seventeen contained overtly religious overtones, including *God Bless Our Native Land* and *God of Our Fathers*, written for the 1876 centennial and also known as *The Prayer for the Republic*. Many new songs, arranged for four-part harmony and piano, illustrated a lack of imagination regarding patriotic themes, including *Flag of the Constellation*, *Flag of the Free*, *Our Flag Is There*, *Our Victorious Banner*, *Unfurl the Glorious Banner*, *Banner of the Sea*, and *Columbia's Banner on the Sea*.[33] Reinforcing the religious realm of patriotism, the Hope Publishing Company of Chicago issued *Uncle Sam's School Songs*, two volumes that blended responsive bible readings with hymns and patriotic tunes. The song *America, Pride of the World* included the lines: "Her flag is the emblem of freedom, On ev'ry broad ocean and shore / baptized in the blood of her heroes, Who died 'neath the colors they bore." The collection also included *The Star-Spangled Banner*; *Hail, Columbia*; *Columbia, the Gem of the Ocean*; *The Battle Hymn of the Republic*; and *God, and Home, and Liberty*, the slogan of the D.A.R.[34]

Just as the Colonial Revival movement influenced architecture and music, the 400th anniversary of the landing of Columbus and his ships in the New World revitalized the term "Columbia" for a new generation. In *Columbian Selections: American Patriotism for Home and School*, published in 1892, a chapter about breeding patriotism in the schools included essays entitled "The American School System of the Future—Character and Patriotism to Be Inculcated" and "The Problem of Today—Patriotism the Great School Lesson." The book straddled the new and the old by including updates of *Columbia, the Gem of the Ocean* (parodied as *Song of the Flag*) and *The New Hail Columbia*. The anthology suggested programs for Washington's Birthday, July 4, Forefathers' Day (marking the Plymouth Rock landing), and the "Anniversary of the Discovery of America" (presumably Columbus Day), and it recommended *The Star-Spangled Banner* as either the first or the last musical selection in every ceremony.[35]

With *The Star-Spangled Banner* emerging as the chief aural symbol of national identity, Americans developed rituals to distinguish the song from other compositions. During this period, many groups and individuals took credit for introducing the custom of removing hats and standing when Key's song aired, including G.A.R. members attending the 1891 encampment in Detroit, Michigan. A plaque affixed to the Bostwick Building in downtown Tacoma, Washington, placed by the local D.A.R. chapter in 1970, honors Rossell G. O'Brien. It stated that in 1893, "during a regular session of the Washington Commandery of the Military Order of the Loyal League of the U.S.A. [O'Brien] did originate the custom of standing during the rendition of the 'Star Spangled Banner.'" At O'Brien's grave in Oakland, California, a small marker, placed by another D.A.R. chapter, also credits him with starting the practice, which spread to other league chapters. The Tacoma Loyal League, an offshoot of the G.A.R., passed a resolution requiring "that in the future and for all time," each member "shall immediately rise to his feet and uncover and remain standing until the music of its inspiring strains shall have ceased." They also instructed their female counterparts to "encourage the same patriotic observance of the grand old song," and, according to lore, the practice spread nationwide. Though the story about O'Brien enjoys widespread credence, the likelihood of it being true is almost nil.[36]

Pinpointing the very first time someone removed a hat and stood for *The Star-Spangled Banner* or other venerated patriotic songs is impossible, but an undocumented story claims that Daniel Webster initiated the practice in 1851, when he attended a concert by the "Swedish Nightingale," Jenny Lind, at Castle Garden in New York City. New York City resident George Templeton Strong's diary recorded a trip he took to Governor's Island in April 1861, three days after the attack on Fort Sumter. The band's program included "that jolliest of tunes, 'Dixie Land,' and 'Hail, Columbia.' We took off our hats while the latter was played. Everybody's patriotism was rampant and demonstrative now." And, when the CSS *Alabama* unfurled the Confederate flag on deck for the first time in 1862, Admiral Raphael Semmes recalled that everyone assembled uncovered their heads "in deference to the sovereign authority, as is the customary on such occasions." The band then launched into *Dixie*, "the soul-stirring anthem of the new-born government." In 1864, Abe Lincoln, a music lover who often joked that he had trouble recognizing one tune from the next, told young singer Lillie de Hegermann-Lindencrone that he only knew two songs. One of them had to be *Hail, Columbia*, she said. Lincoln replied, "Oh yes, I know that, for I have to stand up and take off my hat." The other one?, she asked. "The

other one! The other one is the other when I don't have to stand up!"[37]
In another eyewitness account, when Liliuokalani, the future queen of
Hawaii, visited Washington, D.C., in 1887, she took a steamer to George
Washington's plantation at Mount Vernon. As the vessel drew near to the
grounds, the band "changed to more solemn cadences; and, as the edifices
which mark the sacred spot came in sight, the American flag was lowered,
the steamer's bell was tolled, the gentlemen removed their hats, and the
air of the 'Star-Spangled Banner' was rendered with impressive effect."[38]

Schoolchildren also helped institute the rituals of standing and removing
headgear. In New York City, Balch's treatise instructed teachers that during
flag ceremonies, "the whole school will rise . . . in military fashion." At other
times, following the custom in the navy, pupils should show their respect by
the "boys uncovering the head by taking off their hat or cap for an instant,
the girls by a respectful and graceful bending of the head and upper part
of the body," he wrote. In the 1892 collection *Columbian Selections*, aimed
at educators, directions for an assembly honoring Washington's Birthday
suggested that thirteen young ladies, representing the thirteen original
states, enter the stage or platform, escorted by a female teacher or older
pupil bearing the American flag and symbolizing Columbia. "The audience
[should] rise and stand during the singing" of either *Hail, Columbia* or *The
Star-Spangled Banner*. The program for celebrating July 4 included instructions for a flag tableau, a fancy name for the staged popular entertainment
of the era. In this presentation, after representatives of the colonies left
the stage and moved to the rear of the audience or into an anteroom, they
joined with representatives of the added states, marched down the aisles,
and ascended the stage in the order of the various states' admission to the
Union, each responding " 'Here am I,' as called. Upon being grouped by
Columbia, the audience rising, all unite in singing 'The Star-Spangled
Banner,' " followed by a hymn, either *Praise God from Whom All Blessings
Flow* or a benediction, "as may be preferred."[39] The script for "Salute to the
Flag," a ritual for public school students, "or by any Assemblage," directed
that "after the flag has been run to the top of its flag staff, or as it is unfurled
in the room, or brought to the front by a color guard of either boys or girls,
let all rise and salute the colors."[40]

In 1891, the children's periodical *St. Nicholas* published an article detailing the veneration shown to the flag by the military and urging children to

emulate these practices. The author, when aboard the USS *Yantic*, heard the bugle call for an evening flag lowering. "The moment he [the bugler] sounded the first note, the officers rose from their chairs, faced the colors, took off their caps, and stood silent, in respectful attitudes." When the colors reached the deck, "the last note of the bugle died away, the officers put on their caps, resumed their seats, and went on with their conversation. Removing the cap in honor of the colors is the common form of salute in the navy." Six years later, the magazine published a detailed account of the evening color ceremony at Camp Smith, training ground for the New York National Guard, noting the central role of *The Star-Spangled Banner* in the ceremony. The writer added that "gradually the Army and the National Guard are educating thought-less or ignorant people who have never re-alized what the Flag stands for. A few years ago, when *St. Nicholas* told of 'Honors to the Flag,' a man or woman in New York who rose in an armory at 'retreat,' [the evening flag ceremony] or who saluted a regimental flag, would have been remarked. Now, anyone who does not do these things will soon be considered as unmannerly as a man who should wear his hat in the house or in church."[41]

At the army-navy football contest in 1899, the *New York Sun* noted another instance where military duty influenced civilian behavior. At the time, War Department regulations required all uniformed personnel to stand and salute during *The Star-Spangled Banner*. The reporter lamented that too few people knew the words to the song, which he erroneously referred to as "officially our national air or national hymn." Americans "are sometimes lacking in their show of respect for national symbols. Apparent indifference in pose and manner when the national air is played or sung, or when the national colors are displayed, is shown too frequently," especially in comparison with practices in other countries. The increased presence of the song in the schools ensured that the rising generation would know the words, but "unfortunately, the children are not always taught to stand when they sing this hymn or hear it played." Indeed, the great majority of people "have not been taught to uncover as the flag is carried by in processions or displayed on formal occasions." At the football game, when the band that had "come with the sailor lads" began to play *The Star-Spangled Banner*, "at once every cadet within sound of the music, whether sailor or soldier, stood at attention and uncovered, as he was bound to do by regulation.

Every other military man present obeyed the instincts of his training immediately. Then all present followed this example and the assemblage of nearly 25,000 persons stood in silence in the attitude of respect until the stirring sounds ceased."[42]

Besides ceremonies in the schools, the armed forces, and patriotic societies, sporting events—mainly baseball games—served as the prime incubator for flag and national anthem rituals. The date of the first airing of *The Star-Spangled Banner* before a baseball game is undetermined, just as the definitive origins of the game are lost in the mists of history. The earliest documented performance occurred on May 15, 1862, during the opening game played at Union Base Ball and Cricket Grounds in Brooklyn, New York—the first stadium enclosed by a fence, which allowed the owner to charge admission. The promoters hired a band, and "at 3 o'clock, the music arrived, and the proceeding commenced, opening by playing the 'Star Spangled Banner.' "[43] The practice of performing the song on the opening day of the baseball season became established by the mid-1890s. Baseball historian Peter Morris referenced a rendition at the start of the 1892 season in San Francisco. Another early account of this practice appeared in April 1897, when the New York Giants played the Phillies in Philadelphia. Before the game, "the players paraded across the field company front, and then raised the new flag, while the band played 'The Star-Spangled Banner.' "[44] The next year, at the Polo Grounds, the *New York Times* wrote that the opening ceremonies unfolded as they had in previous years. The two teams lined up in front of the clubhouse and participated in the "opening march to victory. The teams fell in line behind Meyer's Seventh Regiment Band and began marching to the grand stand." As soon as the music began, the crowd began to applaud. "As the players neared the stand the enthusiasm burst into an uproar. The teams parted at the home plate, and then, doffing their caps, retired to the bench. The band, however, stopped at the home plate, and when the enthusiasm had subsided, rendered 'The Star Spangled Banner.' This was a signal for another display of enthusiasm."[45]

The 1898 season opened during the midst of the Spanish-American War, and in Brooklyn, team owner Charles Ebbets held a flag raising on opening day. "After the teams had lined up on each side of the plate the Twenty-third Regiment Band began the National Air. At the first strains of 'The Star-Spangled Banner,' " Ebbets's four-year-old daughter tugged at a halyard that hoisted the flag. "The thousands of persons forgot baseball at this stage and stood up with uncovered heads. The wildest enthusiasm prevailed, thousands of small flags were waved by the crowd in the grand stand. The din was great and did not subside until the flag was spread to the breeze on top of the staff."[46] The following year, Brooklyn visited Boston for their season opener: "The players received a grand ovation as they came down the field to the home plate headed by a brass band playing 'The Star Spangled Banner.' "[47] Fans of the Chicago White Sox cheered on opening day in 1901 as the players marched to center field and stood beneath the flagpole as the band played the song.[48] The following year, a band played it in Pittsburgh on opening day, and at the Polo Grounds in New York, Giants and Phillies players shook hands before their first game of the season. "Then the Seventh Regiment Band came down from its perch in the grandstand and lined up in front of the players, who had formed a column." The teams marched around the grounds. "When the phalanx came in front of the grandstand, a halt was called and the band struck up 'The Star Spangled Banner.' It was a noticeable fact that nearly all of the 18,000 rooters rose to their feet, and many of them uncovered when the National anthem was played." Before the seventh game of the 1903 World Series, a band representing the Boston Americans played *My Country, 'Tis of Thee*, eliciting wild cheers. The ensemble backing the Pittsburgh Pirates responded with *The Star-Spangled Banner*, and the Boston band then played a medley of *Yankee Doodle* and *Dixie*.[49]

The blaring of bands, the plinking of pianos, the roars in the ballpark, and the pyrotechnic spectacles drowned out the plight of African Americans below the Mason-Dixon Line. Federal troops could only patrol the South for so long, and after the disputed presidential election in 1876, the country's political leaders agreed to ignore racial injustices in exchange for accepting the victory of Republican president Rutherford B. Hayes, a capitulation known as the Compromise of 1877. Not all Northerners or Union veterans overlooked the issue, but peace and relative prosperity mitigated any lingering enmity. At Amboy, Illinois, in 1879, Union veterans organized Our Country's Defenders, which mimicked the G.A.R. but took a hard-line approach toward the South. Claiming that the Civil War represented a clash between right and wrong, the organization took issue with the intimidation of African Americans and the inability of citizens to adhere to the Fourteenth and Fifteenth Amendments to the Constitution. With the supremacy of national sovereignty over the states "again assailed," the situation "involves the whole question over which we fought. We must settle this finally and forever at the polls or else we must again settle it on the field of battle."[50] Yet this militant resolve eventually thawed, and relations between the former enemies drew closer in part as the South promoted tourism designed to attract Union veterans interested in revisiting the battlefields. Ironically, *Dixie* and *The Star-Spangled Banner* endured as the Civil War songs least likely to stir nettlesome feelings. Key's song predated the upheaval, of course, and instead of using it to taunt the South, Northerners referred to it and the rest of the patriotic Big Five as national songs that encompassed the entire country. *Dixie*, with its rousing chorus, became popular throughout the nation, including up north. By the late 1800s, music publishers often paired the tunes in sheet music editions.

The song *A Knot of Blue and Gray*, published in Boston in 1876, centered on a woman with two brothers, one of whom fought for the Union and the other for the Confederacy. It arrived at a time when Americans celebrated the centennial of the Declaration of Independence and foreshadowed the coming reconciliation. In 1886, the cover of *The Blue & the Gray*, published in St. Joseph, Missouri, depicted Ulysses S. Grant and Robert E. Lee shaking hands.[51] One of the earliest collections of Civil War music spanning both sides, *Our War Songs North and South*, published in Chicago in the mid-1880s, included more than four hundred tunes and served the needs of patriotism and commerce: "The book contains all the songs sung by both Armies during the Rebellion. The only book of its kind ever published. This book is sold by subscription only. Good agents can make handsome profits."[52] Former Yankees and Rebels filled the ranks of the U.S. Army and battled Native Americans on the high plains through the early 1890s. By 1898, when United States troops began to muster for the Spanish-American War, the approach of a new century helped to accelerate reconciliation, as reflected (or shaped) by music.

A catalog of *G.A.R. Songs for Memorial Day*, issued in 1896, included a tune called *The Blue and the Gray* by W. W. Weaver, along with the maudlin selections *Heroes Were They* and *Angels Guard Our Comrades' Graves*.[53] The collection *Patriotic Songs*, published in Boston in 1898, included two versions of *The Star-Spangled Banner* and an arrangement of *Dixie's Land*.

That same year the *Atlanta Constitution* announced that the "'Star-Spangled Banner' Is Better Thought Of in the South Now." In 1899, *The Blue and the Gray March* combined *The Star-Spangled Banner* and what it called *Dixey*, while the *Buffalo [N.Y.] News* reported that a performance of the Confederate anthem at the Pan-American Exposition in 1901 evoked "the most spontaneous, enthusiastic bursts of applause."[54] *Patriotic Songs for School and Home*, a vocal and piano book released by a large northern publishing house in 1899, featured variations on national patriotic themes and included a version of *Dixie*.[55] One topical song, *He Laid Away a Suit of Gray to Wear the Union Blue*, told of "a southern soldier fighting for his country's stars and stripes," who vowed to "show that Dixie's sons, will to the flag prove true."[56] With the turn of the century, the ranks of war survivors began to thin. The song *The Boys in Blue Are Turning Gray* claimed: "The foes of yore are foes no more, The gray oats mingle with the blue / One flag floats proudly over all, The emblem of a nation true . . . / The men of Gray are now true blue, And boys in blue are turning gray," symbolizing the dissipation of hostilities engendered by the War between the States.[57]

Duties and Customs, 1880–1910

DURING THE 1800s, empires crumbled, nationalist fervor rumbled, and new boundaries laced the globe, spurring the use and abuse of history and culture for political ends. In the United States, post–Civil War industrial buildup established the infrastructure for a dynamic domestic economy and also created the capacity to undertake more ambitious naval operations. The United States Navy patrolled the high seas to secure trade routes, scout potential colonies, and redress the mistreatment of shipwrecked sailors. Increased contact with other countries led American officials to revamp their notoriously informal diplomatic practices. As military bands exported the nation's popular and patriotic songs, the lack of a designated anthem became part of that issue. Treaty signings and state visits generally featured the ceremonial airing of national anthems, and, on such occasions, when asked to play the country's official song, United States diplomats picked whatever suited them, usually *The Star-Spangled Banner* or *Hail, Columbia*, confounding their counterparts. In the late 1800s, the military appeased foreign diplomats and singled out Key's creation, but confusion reigned at home.

Faster ships and advances in geographic knowledge increased the interactions between countries. Though American culture celebrated technology, particularly at the 1876 Centennial International Exposition in Philadelphia, the romantic movement in Europe provided a humanistic counterbalance to this mechanistic worldview. From the early 1800s on, Romantics celebrated "the folk" and advocated organic nationhood rather than the top-down imposition of monarchical power over territory. Across the globe, determined cultural nationalists forged new countries as grand empires began to dissolve. The persistent question of minorities and their rights, along with the instinct to build empires, continued to foment disorder. Europe experienced hypernationalism in the 1800s, and, as hereditary rulers began to disappear, the Romantics rushed to fill the power vacuum with what they considered to be historically homogeneous nations. Then and now, successful countries foster a familial sense of belonging, a feeling tapped by schools, sports teams, voluntary organizations, and fans of bands, movies, comic books, and TV shows. And every country typically adopts at least three identifying emblems—a flag, an official seal, and an anthem—that theoretically convey the values and culture of a particular people.

New nations responded to the Romantic impulse and routinely adopted songs that allegedly embodied the folk, especially in Europe and its New World colonies. Official anthems often shifted over time. With the model already set in the 1700s by England, Spain, and France, the Austrian Empire adopted the temporal *Gott Erhalt Franz Den Kaiser* (God Save Emperor Francis) in 1804. Holland selected its first anthem in 1815 but swapped it for another song in 1932. In 1816, the Russian royal family adapted the lyrics of its anthem to the music of *God Save the King*, though they switched to *God Save the Tsar* in 1833. This song, featuring original music known as *The Prayer of Russians* and fitted to a rough translation of *God Save the King*, lasted until the Bolshevik revolution in 1917. Other early anthem adopters in Europe included Poland (unofficially in 1795, officially in 1927), Belgium (1830), Portugal (1834), Denmark (first using the melody of *God Save the King*, then adopting a different tune in 1835), and Greece and Hungary (1844). Once divided into hundreds of principalities, Italy decreed an anthem upon declaring nationhood in 1861, and Germans sang the militaristic *Watch on the Rhine* after their unification in 1871. Both tunes have since been replaced.

South and Central Americans, also swept by revolutionary fervor in the United States and France, overthrew colonial rule and adopted anthems to announce their independence. The oldest anthem in the region dates to the early 1800s in Venezuela, when the people took *Gloria al Bravo Pueblo* to heart. Their government granted formal sanction to the song in 1881. Argentina declared its official air in 1813. Peru held an anthem competition and chose their winner in 1821. Soon thereafter, Brazil, Chile, and Uruguay also adopted national songs. The first Honduran anthem dates to 1838, and Costa Rica selected its national air in 1853, to be played when the country hosted visiting delegates from England and the United States. In Africa, Liberia (mid-1840s) and the South African Republic (1875), precursor to the present-day Republic of South Africa, established that continent's first anthems. Other countries decreed official songs after overthrowing colonialism in the 1950s and 1960s. Most Middle Eastern and Asian countries designated national anthems in the twentieth century. A round-robin of rulers imposed anthems from above and, in many cases, changed selections throughout the years, including China after the Communist Party came to power in 1949, and North Korea and South Korea after World War II.[1]

In the United States, geographic isolation influenced a laissez-faire attitude toward officially adopting the musical trappings of nationhood. In the late 1800s, officials took a low-key approach toward diplomatic formalities. "For many years in our service, confusion existed as to the identity of the national air of the United States," wrote Admiral George Dewey. "Characteristic instances of the embarrassment, in the exchange of international courtesies, which naturally resulted from the circumstances, had frequently come to my notice." He recalled an incident in Hong Kong aboard a German ship when the band honored the president of the United Sates by playing *Hail, Columbia*. "As the guests were reseating themselves after this toast, I reminded the Prince [Henry of Prussia] that 'Hail Columbia' was not our national air. 'What is it?' His Highness asked. 'The Star-Spangled Banner,' I told him." That night, Dewey sent a copy of the song to the prince; the very next morning, the band performed it at colors.[2]

Though derided for being provincial, United States citizens expressed interest in the rest of the world. One book, *The Maritime Flags and Standards of All Nations*, published in 1856, included color depictions of South American national and city flags, along with the banners of European, Middle Eastern, and Asian countries. A "Geographical Sketch" showed "at one view the situation of every empire, kingdom, and republic; Also, the principal sea-ports of every nation in the world," which often served as the nucleus of burgeoning countries. "Haddock's Cards of the Nations," printed with commercial messages from various businesses on the front and back of the cards, included a dozen designs of girls dressed in native garb and each nation's flag and coat of arms. Egyptienne Straights cigarettes sponsored a series of flag silks, small keepsakes featuring the names and flags of foreign lands. In 1879, "Carter, Decorative Painter, Haverhill, Mass.," issued a complete set of *Carter's Forty Flags, Emblematical Colors, representing Banners and Ensigns of FORTY CHIEF NATIONS OF THE WORLD.* Allen & Ginter, makers of Dixie Dainties and other cigarette brands in Richmond, Virginia, published *Flags of All Nations* in the 1880s, which gave Old Glory top billing and also included the banners of American states, territories, and even the District of Columbia. In New York, the Simonds Soap Company offered a series of forty-eight cards depicting "National, Maritime & Signal Flags of the World" if customers sent in ten cents' worth of stamps and three product wrappers. In 1899, apothecary manufacturers C. I. Hood & Company of Lowell, Massachusetts, published a sixteen-page booklet, *The Flags of All Nations.*[3]

Other marketing ploys tapped an interest in international anthems. In 1890, the advertising department of the Woolson Spice Company in Toledo, Ohio, offered a full-color collection of *Songs of All Nations,* printed on hard cardboard pages and tied together with a ribbon. The illustrations placed each nation's flag and anthem title within a backdrop of military and historical scenes. An 1896 issue of the *Boston Weekly Journal of Sheet Music,* a subscription service, arranged "Eight National Anthems" for the piano, including selections from the United States, Austria, England, France, Germany, Russia, Spain, and Sweden. In 1903, the journal compiled the "National Songs of America," consisting of the patriotic Big Five. The book *Flags of the Principal Nations* used a Japanese-style font for the last two words.[4]

International events and competitions, including the America's Cup yachting race (founded in 1851), bicycle tournaments, automobile races, art exhibitions, and polo matches also generated Americans' interest in other countries. The modern Olympic movement dates to 1896, though the playing of national anthems during medal ceremonies began in 1924. As explorers raced to the North Pole in 1909 and the South Pole in 1911, their quest to plant the first flag at each landmark captivated the world. At home, Americans interacted with representatives of other nations and cultures at extravagant world's fairs, including the 1893 Columbian Exposition in Chicago; the 1901 Pan-American Exposition in Buffalo, New York; and the Louisiana Purchase Exposition, held in St. Louis in 1904. Maryland representatives appropriated $65,000 to attend the St. Louis event, claiming that "the principal value of a great exposition lies in the fact that it is a superb advertising medium." Maryland also sent a delegation to the 1915 Panama-Pacific Exposition, held in San Francisco, where they displayed historical exhibits detailing the settlement of the colony and Francis Scott Key. Though exposition organizers and exhibitors inevitably presented a distorted view of the world, they at least tried to expose fairgoers to other cultures. A "grand medley" written for the 1893 Chicago fair, entitled *A Trip through the Midway Plaisance*, started with excerpts from *Yankee Doodle*, *The Star-Spangled Banner*, *The Blue Danube*, the *Radetzky March* (the Austro-Hungarian anthem), *In Cairo* (with a note reading "Arab on Camel"), *Watch on the Rhine*, a Turkish tune, and an Irish melody. The final selections included *The Marseillaise*, *God Save the King*, *Home Sweet Home*, and the festive popular ditty *Ta-Ra-Ra Boom-De-Ay*.[5]

In a strange historical irony, England and the United States engaged in two wars—the American Revolution and the War of 1812—that killed tens of thousands of combatants and civilians, and then became inseparable on the world stage. Additional direct contact with the British on the high seas occurred as the United States Navy became involved in dozens of small-scale, little-known skirmishes abroad. The first war in which Americans fought on foreign soil, the Barbary Coast War, raged off the coast of northern Africa from 1801 to 1805. In addition to policing the Atlantic Ocean after Congress outlawed the slave trade in 1808, the U.S. Navy embarked on the Second Barbary War in 1815. American ships also patrolled the Caribbean from 1817 to 1825 to thwart pirates. The Monroe Doctrine of 1823 warned European powers against attempting to establish any new colonies in the Americas. The U.S. Navy fought ten battles in the waters off Central and South America, from the 1820 Callao Affair in Peru through the 1894 skirmish in Rio de Janeiro, when three United States merchant ships suffered damage during a Brazilian naval revolt. Responding to the crisis, the USS *Detroit* exchanged gunfire with a Brazilian gunboat, guided the American vessels out of harm's way, and reopened the port. In 1863, the United States took control of the Swan Islands, located in the northwestern Caribbean Sea (turning them over to Honduras in 1971).[6]

Beginning in the 1820s, the United States Navy crisscrossed the vast Pacific Ocean to protect American whalers and spice traders, who sought to establish outposts on remote islands. Merchant mariners often came in contact with hostile tribes, which sometimes cannibalized the visitors. When loss of life or property occurred, U.S. Navy ships arrived to rescue survivors, demand compensation from local chieftains, and sometimes burn villages or fire on forts. In 1832, the United States dispatched a warship to Sumatra after natives attacked the USS *Friendship*, killing three American pepper traders and looting the ship's cargo. Naval vessels returned there under similar circumstances in 1838. That same year, Congress dispatched an Exploring Expedition to chart the Pacific Ocean, which lasted four years and whose collection of natural specimens formed the core collection of the Smithsonian Institution. The United States signed a trade pact with China in 1844 and Commodore Matthew Perry's first trip to Japan in 1853 sought to open that nation's ports to American vessels, establish a coaling depot, and assure favorable treatment for shipwrecked sailors. Perry's hulking "black ships" terrified the Japanese by steaming into Tokyo harbor and firing their cannons. As Perry went ashore, the band played *Hail, Columbia*. Since he was unable to visit the royal family then, the commodore returned the following year and, as he disembarked, his musical ensemble played *The Star-Spangled Banner*. The United States annexed the remote Johnson Atoll in the Pacific Ocean in 1858, and in 1861, the USS *Saginaw* fired on a fort at Qui Nhon, Vietnam, to protect a United States merchant ship. In 1871, Americans killed two hundred Koreans during the Battle of Ganghwa, after a naval party came to search for a missing vessel and negotiate a trade treaty. After a clash with Hawaii, the United States claimed sovereignty over the Midway Islands, Wake Island, and the Palmyra Atoll in 1898.

These forays brought United States sailors into frequent contact with English seamen, and hostility between the two nations began to dissipate. In 1845, thirty years after the Battle of New Orleans, the USS *St. Louis* helped evacuate British citizens from New Zealand during the Battle of Kororareka, after the native Maori took down the Union Jack from Flagstaff Hill and routed British forces and civilians on the island. During the Battle of Ty-ho Bay in 1855, English and American ships scrapped with

Chinese pirates near Hong Kong. In the Second Opium War, the U.S. Navy fought alongside England and France against Chinese forces at the Battle of the Pearl River Forts. English and American forces joined to quell the 1874 Honolulu Court House Riot in Hawaii and both navies guarded against seal poachers in the Bering Sea during the 1890s. One parody of *The Star-Spangled Banner*, written by London lawyer George Spowers and published in 1871, reflected these newfound ties:

> But hush'd be that strain! They our foes are no longer
> Lo Britain the right hand of Friendship extends
> And Albion's fair Isle we behold with affection
> The land of our Fathers—the land of our Friends.
> Long, long may ye flourish, Columbia and Britain,
> In amity still may your children be found
> And the Star-Spangled Banner and Red Cross together
> Wave free and triumphant the wide world around.[7]

Despite the détente, each country sought to gain strategic advantage over the other. In the 1890s, Germany, England, and the United States clashed over Samoa and eventually divided the islands between Germany and the United States in 1899. The rise of the German and Japanese juggernauts helped drive former enemies Britain and America into an alliance that solidified in the years leading up to World War I. The lyrics of the symbolic 1906 song, *When Tommy Atkins Marries Dolly Gray*, declared that "the English speaking race against the world will stand."[8]

Increased interaction with other countries pressured United States naval officials to designate an official song for state occasions. Secretary of the Navy Benjamin Tracy, known as the father of the modern fleet, initiated a standardization drive that included General Order No. 374 of 1889: "To insure uniformity, the following routine will be observed at morning and evening colors on board all men-of-war in commission, and at all Naval Stations. When a band is present it will play—At morning colors: 'The Star Spangled Banner.' At evening colors: 'Hail, Columbia.'" The rather polite regulation mandated decorum during the song: "All persons present, belonging to the Navy, not so employed as to render it impracticable, will please face towards the colors and salute as the ensign reaches the peak or truck in hoisting." The following year, Tracy referred to *The Star-Spangled*

Banner as "the National Air of the United States" and requested that the Marine Band play it at the close of every performance, since "this is a custom strictly observed in other countries."[9]

The navy recognized that designating two official songs led to confusion. In 1893, as *Hail, Columbia* faded in popularity, officials directed that morning and evening flag ceremonies begin with three drum rolls and three trumpet flourishes: "At the third roll the ensign shall be started from the deck and hoisted slowly to the peak or truck, during which the band shall play the 'Star Spangled Banner.' When the ensign leaves the deck or rail all sentries shall salute and remain at a salute until the band ceases to play the national air; all officers and men present shall stand facing the ensign and shall salute when it reaches the peak or truck."[10] In 1895, the army directed that every military post or station hoist the flag at the first note of *Reveille* and in the evening, "while the flag is being lowered, the band will play 'The Star Spangled Banner.' "[11]

As an adjunct to his 1889 initiative, Tracy directed John Philip Sousa, leader of the United States Marine Band, "to compile for the use of the Department the National and Patriotic airs of all Nations," a project completed within a year. The marine band served as the primary point of contact with foreign dignitaries. During trips from Washington, D.C., to Mount Vernon, the ensemble performed aboard the *Despatch*, the presidential yacht. On one visit, representatives of seventeen countries climbed aboard and Tracy asked Sousa to play the anthems of every country present. Sousa began with *God Save the Queen*, "at which the English Ambassador immediately rose, followed by the rest of the guests." He continued with "the airs of France, Germany, Spain, Italy, Russia, Sweden, Denmark, etc., ending with *The Star Spangled Banner*." Navy regulations also encouraged playing the national anthems of other countries after morning colors when ships docked at foreign ports. Just in case a navy ship visited a remote atoll in the Pacific Ocean, or Fogo Island off the coast of Newfoundland in Canada, and wanted to perform a familiar air for their hosts, Sousa collected songs from 121 countries, colonies, and principalities—from Abyssinia to Zanzibar—in the volume *National, Patriotic, and Typical Airs of All Lands*. The book included selections that "are indigenous to the soil, or to the people," songs used for patriotic purposes and airs that "by official decree or by the voice of the people, are known as the principal patriotic airs of their respective countries." Sousa represented the United States with the music, the lyrics, and historical sketches of the patriotic Big Five, as well as songs from nine Native American tribes.[12]

As director of the U.S. Marine Band from 1880 to 1892, and later with his own ensemble, Sousa confused matters at official functions by flip-flopping between *Hail, Columbia* and *The Star-Spangled Banner*. In 1891, during the band's first national tour, a reporter at the *Daily Nebraska State Journal* in Lincoln asked Sousa to single out the national air. The bandleader "replied without hesitation that it was 'Hail Columbia.'" Sousa recalled receiving a letter from the French minister of war asking for a score of the national air of the United States. "I gave the matter a great deal of attention and finally settled upon 'Hail Columbia'" because two Americans wrote it, as opposed to Francis Scott Key's hybrid. After Sousa passed this information to the minister in France and authorities in England, *Hail, Columbia* served as "the national air of America" at the jubilee celebration of Queen Victoria's rule in 1887. An indication of Sousa's influence abroad includes the observation by music historian Louis C. Elson that "on state occasions abroad, when music plays its part in festivities . . . the European bands play 'Hail, Columbia' in homage to the United States." Other instances when *Hail, Columbia* served this role include the passage of the first American warship through the canal at Kiel, Germany, and the entrance of Thomas Edison into the Paris Grand Opera House in 1889.[13]

Despite Sousa's public endorsement of *Hail, Columbia*, at the U.S. Marine Band's performance in Lincoln, Nebraska, during 1891, he encored with *The Star-Spangled Banner*, as he did the following evening in Omaha. In 1898, when the marine band returned to Nebraska, the *Omaha World Herald* reported that Sousa's successor as band director, William H. Santelmann, "has educated Omaha people in one respect. The Marine band always ends its concerts by playing 'The Star Spangled Banner.'" At the concert, members of the band stood for the song, and "when the strains of the national anthem floated out upon the breeze the entire audience arose and remained standing until the anthem was concluded. The time may come when Americans whether indoors or out, will show their patriotism by standing unnerved when the national anthem is rendered." During a tour with his own band in 1903 at Windsor Castle, Sousa received word that the king of England was "very anxious to hear, at the end of our performance, the American national anthem." Sousa obliged with a rousing rendition of *The Star-Spangled Banner* and segued into *God Save the King*. In Russia, he played Key's tune again, and wrote that the band "never heard more sincere or lasting applause for any musical number."

As the nation's first musical superstar and undisputed "March King," Sousa might have single-handedly made *Hail, Columbia* the country's official song by declining to play *The Star-Spangled Banner*. He also refused to champion his own composition, *The Stars and Stripes Forever*, which achieved widespread popularity at a time when military band music became fashionable. Published in 1897, the song's lyrics referred to the flag as "the banner of the right," though they rarely aired, and the tune almost never came up for consideration during anthem debates. In 1915, Sousa wrote: "The Music Teachers' Association of California adopted a resolution petitioning Congress to make 'The Stars and Stripes Forever' and 'Dixie' the official airs of the United States. The idea did not appeal to me for, though Congress is a powerful body, it cannot make the people sing what they don't want to sing. If 'The Stars and Stripes Forever' ever becomes a national air it will be because the people want it and not because of any congressional decree."[14]

The military helped elevate *The Star-Spangled Banner* to the status of national anthem, yet sometimes regulations backfired as enlisted men and officers tried to subvert the rules. In 1901, Captain Richard Leary, commander of the League Island Navy Yard in Philadelphia, insisted that his charges know how to sing *The Star-Spangled Banner*, referred to as the national anthem in a *New York Times* write-up. The men dismissed the order as a joke, but when fifty sailors applied for shore leave, Leary denied thirty requests and required them to stay on the base until they learned the song. Several responded that they "will not sing it whether they know it or not."[15] In the early 1900s, the army and navy debated the merits of the country's national songs and revised their regulations in an attempt to establish uniform rituals of respect at flag ceremonies. In 1903, the navy ordered all officers to "stand at attention whenever 'The Star Spangled Banner' is being played, unless engaged in a duty that will not permit them to do so. The same respect shall be observed towards the national air of any country, when played in the presence of official representatives of such country." The regulations also required that the flag "be started up and hoisted smartly to the peak or trunk and the band shall play 'The Star-Spangled Banner,' at the conclusion of which all officers and men shall salute, ending the ceremony." The following year, Henry Clay Taylor, chief of the Bureau of Navigation, suggested that the secretary of the navy notify foreign governments of the adoption of *The Star-Spangled Banner* as the national air. Through an underling, the secretary replied that such a directive fell beyond the department's scope, claiming that the anti-British third verse rendered it unsuitable as a national air and contending that *Hail, Columbia* or *Columbia, the Gem of the Ocean* would make a better choice.[16]

The War Department also modified its flag etiquette regulations for the army in 1904, ordering that whenever a band played *The Star-Spangled Banner* "on a formal occasion at a military station, or at any place where persons belonging to the military service are present in their capacity, all officers and enlisted men present will stand at attention." The new orders also required personnel with no arms in hand to salute the flag by uncovering their heads. Drill regulations, which sometimes conflicted with other orders, prescribed that when service personnel did not bear arms, they should render a salute by holding their headgear "in the right hand opposite the left shoulder, right forearm against the breast." That same year, the army mandated that officers and enlisted men not shouldering arms keep their hats on and salute throughout the entire airing of *The Star-Spangled Banner* during evening colors. Major H. L. Roberts of Fort Brown in Texas, inquired about the propriety of playing the bugle call *To the Colors* when a band could not be provided. J. M. Lee, the commanding general of the Department of Texas, asked whether officers and enlisted men out of ranks and not under arms should stand at attention and uncover during the playing of *The Star-Spangled Banner*. "The uncovering is a customary mark of respect, and its omission by those in the military service is always a cause of unfavorable comment among civilians," he wrote. Army brass suggested that if men kept their hats on, observers might not notice the salute.[17]

Army Adjutant General J. T. Kerr, responsible for interpreting military code, replied in an internal memo that "it is questionable whether uncovering is a suitable military salute." To avoid the appearance of a lack of proper patriotic feeling in the eyes of civilian spectators, "it would seem that some mark of respect, in addition to standing at attention, should be shown during the playing of the 'Star Spangled Banner.'" He wrote that foreign armies stood at attention and "saluted with the hand being raised at the first note and dropped at the last note during the playing of national anthems. This is military, and, it is thought, a more appropriate way of showing respect than the civilian method of uncovering." Noting that the navy required the salute to be performed at the last note of *To the Colors* or *The Star-Spangled Banner*, Kerr wrote that "this method is believed to be preferable to uncovering, but it is not as effective as keeping the hand up in the salute during the entire" song. As soon as the music ceased, he noted, "the attitude of attention is relaxed and the salute is consequently rendered during the confusion attendant on replacing their hats by civilians or resuming seats if they have risen. As a result, the salute is perhaps not noticed and the general effect is as though no respect has been shown other than standing at attention." He also took issue with bands that repeated strains of the song. To combat musical derivations, in 1905 army officials ordered that Key's creation be played in its entirety and never as part of a medley, a policy first suggested in 1898 by a group of nine concerned citizens from Tampa, Florida, led by L. E. Lovejoy.[18]

That same year, army officials changed the policy again: "Whenever 'The Star Spangled Banner' is played by the band at a formal occasion at a military station, or at any place where persons belonging to the military service are present in their official capacity, all officers and enlisted men present will stand at attention, and if not in ranks will render the prescribed salute, the position of the salute being retained until the last note." This directive to salute throughout the entire airing of *The Star-Spangled Banner* or *To the Colors* ran counter to the practice in the navy, where personnel saluted at the last note, generating confusion among civilians and military personnel. The welter of rules and changes created chaos among midlevel officers, and letters seeking clarification filled the adjutant general's mailbox. In 1905, W. H. Simons at the Citadel in South Carolina wondered if the "salute is to be made with the hand, with no arms in hand, or whether it is considered as analogous to the salute . . . to be made by uncovering." Major E. P. Pendleton, at Fort Douglas in Utah, asked whether the salute should be held for the entire song or just for the last note. The drill requirement that army personnel remove their hats seemed to negate the idea of rendering a proper salute, wrote Pendleton, which is usually performed in full dress with hats on. In 1907, Hugh Scott, superintendent of West Point, inquired whether ordinary band concerts at the academy constituted a formal occasion that required officers and enlisted men to salute the song. The acting chief of staff replied that it is impossible to "determine in advance whether or not upon these occasions persons in the military service who are present are there in their 'official capacity.' The 'Star Spangled Banner' might be played several times a day at a military outpost or station, and whether or not any of them could be properly described as 'formal'" should be left to the decision of local commanders.[19]

After the army ordered its personnel to salute throughout the entire song, officers and enlisted men from Maine to California protested the regulations by ducking out of evening ceremonies en masse. Some arguments against the requirements bordered on the absurd, even as base commanders assured higher-ups that soldiers desired to show respect to the flag. In 1907, Major General Adolphus W. Greely, a polar explorer and Medal of Honor recipient stationed at Vancouver Barracks in Washington State, reported hearing "many unofficial complaints and expressions of opinion . . . regarding the present custom of standing at attention, facing the flag, with the hand at the visor, during the playing of 'The Star Spangled Banner,' which keeps the men in a strained attitude from 45 to 60 seconds." In the previous year and a half, he wrote, at least fifty officers had expressed unfavorable opinions toward the practice. "The statement has repeatedly been made that on the sounding of the first call for retreat, officers hasten to their houses to avoid giving the prescribed salute." Enlisted men "similarly disappear from view, as far as practicable." Greely bemoaned the "general aversion to what ought to be a patriotic and welcome duty—that of saluting the flag of our country. Certainly, any practice which tends to make such patriotic duty unpleasant or distasteful should be modified."[20]

The notion that army regulations to stand at attention and salute during one verse of *The Star-Spangled Banner* represented a burden for military personnel is comical, given the rigors of military life. When the adjutant general polled army commanders across the country, almost to a man they reported the same aversion to the practice and detailed an astonishing degree of disobedience toward flag regulations. Major H. C. Davis of Fort Andrews in Massachusetts referred to the new orders as "awkward & tiresome." Lieutenant Colonel W. H. Coffin at Fort Washington in Maryland criticized the salute for being "undignified & ridiculous" and admitted that he "avoided it when he could." At Fort Miley in California, Major E. S. Burton stated that "it is a known fact that officers and enlisted men hasten to their quarters or barracks to keep from standing at attention while 'The Star Spangled Banner' is being played." The commanding officer at Fort Monroe in Virginia referred to the current regulation as "embarrassing," and a dispatch from Fort Preble in Maine called the regimen "unpleasant in bad weather" and "at times a hardship." Lieutenant Colonel J. R. Williams, based at Fort Hamilton in Brooklyn, New York, wrote that "the present form is an awkward imitation of a foreign style and it is felt by all concerned to be not a proper salute." One commander suggested adopting the navy's practice, since it would "give uniformity where officers and men of both services are thrown together."[21]

Perhaps the mandatory nature of the rules bred contempt; the commander at Fort Baker in California reported that the current regulations did little to "increase patriotic sentiment." Colonel Cornelius Gardner at Fort Crook in Nebraska wrote: "True patriotism or true religion is not measured by ostentatious outward display of these estimable qualities. There is unanimity of opinion among all the officers of this regiment that in this case the matter has been overdone." Commanders at Fort Russell in Wyoming, Fort Des Moines in Iowa, and Fort Meade in South Dakota concurred. Lieutenant Colonel William Glassford at Fort Omaha in Nebraska reported that "the holding of the hand to the visor for so long a time is constrained," adding that "facing the flag at attention and saluting at the last note would be an improvement." In the Department of the Colorado, ten commanders also favored saluting at the final note of Key's song; two preferred standing at attention uncovered. Captain R. F. Knabenshue at Fort Ontario in upstate New York called the practice of ducking out of evening colors a disrespectful "disregard of duty that should be met with punishment."[22]

Of the fourteen officers at Fort Douglas in Utah, Captain E. W. McCaskey reported that half supported the present method, five wanted to emulate the navy, and the other two favored a return to removing hats. McCaskey claimed that the then-current method suited all weather conditions, and he ridiculed anyone who found the regulations to be onerous: "I do not believe that standing at attention, facing the flag with the hand at the visor, causes anyone to assume a more strained attitude than is required many times each day, and therefore, do not see why there is any objection to it for a minute at retreat time." The commander at Whipple Barracks in Arizona Territory explained that the custom of uncovering for *The Star-Spangled Banner* appealed to civilians, and "it became almost the universal custom to pay this tribute to the national air by all within hearing, whether soldiers or civilians. This conformity has almost entirely ceased—the prescribed position appears forced and stilted and no one who is not obliged to do so will expose himself to the ridicule of his fellows by attempting to assume it."[23]

As the issue ping-ponged around the War Department bureaucracy, army higher-ups debated the policy and finally adopted the navy's practice. The episode revealed the limitations of official edicts to enforce cultural customs, even within a regimented military setting. One correspondent, who identified himself as the holder of "a commanding position that prevents my signing my name," wrote to President Roosevelt regarding the "recognition of the National Anthem ('The Star Spangled Banner'). In 1898 the army was instructed to uncover when the hymn was played and the people were only too glad to honor it by doing the same, and it was a grand sight to see the masses respond gladly to the example set by the soldiers. Then the army were directed not to uncover, but to stand at salute. Another order since issued now directs them to stand at attention and salute the last note." Taking issue with the directive, the letter writer claimed that "this is all right as far as the army is concerned, but the people do not understand it, and at a recent encampment when a boy uncovered his chum said 'Don't do that. . . . Look at those officers, they don't do it anymore.'" He implored Roosevelt to "let us return to the religious reverence of the Anthem of our country which should represent to us what the 'Angelus' does to foreign countries."[24]

When the United States began occupying foreign territories, the armed forces exported *The Star-Spangled Banner*, triggering an inevitable backlash. In the 1800s, the kingdom of Hawaii turned into a musical battleground when entrepreneurs and missionaries from England and the United States remodeled its economy and political structure. In response to foreign encroachment, Hawaiians informally adopted the *Restoration Anthem*, written by Edward Hall in 1843, as an unofficial, influential national air. Fearful that their culture would be subsumed, the royal family tried to preserve their nation's heritage. In 1861, a group of prominent citizens in Honolulu sponsored a contest to determine "a new song for our Chief." To win the ten-dollar prize, they sought "something to please Hawaiians, the people who love the King. The new song is wanted for this race to praise the Chief and the Chefess and the Prince of Hawai'i. The British have a song, so have the French, and so also, the Americans, to make their countries famous; it is right also that there be a song with which the Hawaiians can praise their King." The contest rules required a fusion between Hawaiian-language lyrics and the music of *God Save the King*. The winning version served as the Hawaiian anthem for a few years, but, as with most national song contests, its long-term impact remained limited.[25]

With their control over the Hawaiian Islands slipping, the royal family fought back in song. Liliuokalani, the future queen, recalled the moment in 1866 when her brother, King Kamehameha V, "brought to my notice that fact that the Hawaiian people had no national air." Other nations around the world expressed "patriotism and love of country in [their] own music; but we were using for that purpose on state occasions the time-honored British anthem, 'God Save the Queen.' This he desired me to supplant by one of my own composition." In a week, she completed the Hawaiian national anthem (*He Mele Lahui Hawaii*): "Bless O Lord our nation's chiefs, grant them wisdom so to live / That our people may be saved, and You the glory give." Around twenty years later, the song *Hawaii Ponoi* (Hawaii's Own), with lyrics written by the king and music by Henri Berger, head of the Royal Hawaiian Band, supplanted the first anthem and called for "Hawaii's own true sons" to "be loyal to your chief, the country's liege and lord."[26]

The Star-Spangled Banner eventually drowned out both native Hawaiian anthems. In the 1880s, as American influence increased, annexationists maneuvered to seize political power from the royal family. Fueled by the rallying cry "Hawaii for the Hawaiian," the islands experienced a renaissance of indigenous culture after Queen Liliuokalani ascended to the throne in 1891 and composed patriotic songs, with lyrics in Hawaiian, designed to instill a will to resist the outsiders. The United States engineered a coup d'état in 1893, enforced by a contingent of U.S. Marines, and annexed the islands in August 1898.[27] At the official ceremony marking the transfer of power, the Royal Hawaiian Band remained silent. One witness reported that the "Hawaiian damsels who were to have lowered for the last time the Hawaiian flag would not lower it. The band refused to play the *ponoi* and loud weeping was the only music contributed by the natives." Under a banner headline reading "ANNEXATION!" and a subheading "Here to Stay," the *Hawaiian Gazette* printed an illustration of the American flag, along with the line: "And the star-spangled banner in triumph shall wave / O'er the Isles of Hawaii, and the homes of the brave."[28]

Music also followed the flag in 1898 during the Spanish-American War, the "splendid little war." What began as an alleged anticolonial excursion to free Cuba and avenge the sinking of the USS *Maine* in Havana's harbor ended with a lopsided United States victory after three months. American officials also controlled the future of Spain's other colonies—Puerto Rico, Guam, and the Philippines—and faced a quandary over whether to grant the islands autonomy, turn them into territories, or oversee a transition period on the way toward independence. The United States adopted a different approach for each country, but remained closely involved in their internal affairs. As natives resisted United States rule in Cuba, Puerto Rico, and the Philippines, liberal patriots and anti-imperialists charged the Republican administration of President William McKinley with empire building and claimed that taking colonies mocked the founding creed of the United States, whose foundation rested on the hallowed revolt against England's rule.

In a dangerous world, however, the decision to hold on to Guam and the Philippines made sense to militant patriots as the great naval powers jockeyed for advantage. Had the United States pulled out, Germany and Japan, countries shut out of foreign possessions during the colonial heyday, would probably have moved in. Even England, who ruled Hong Kong, eyed the Philippines as a potential colony. At the time, Holland occupied Indonesia, Portugal administered Macau, and France colonized Vietnam. As China weakened, many Western nations (and Japan) sought to carve that country into spheres of influence, and the United States promoted the Open Door Policy. Cuba, Puerto Rico, and the Philippines fought for years against Spanish rule, yet under the guise of protection and uplift, the United States exercised different degrees of control over the former Spanish colonies.

Flag ceremonies featuring *The Star-Spangled Banner* reinforced American power and competed with indigenous symbols. Long before their independence, in the 1840s Cuban rebels designed a flag consisting of a red triangle at the hoist side, with a white star in the middle and five blue and white stripes. The country's anthem dates to 1867, when Perucho Figueredo wrote the melody *El Himno de Bayamo*, known as *La Bayamesa*. The song became popular the following year, during an uprising against the Spanish in Bayamo, where Figueredo aided the rebels. When the Spaniards stormed the village of Guanabacoa, the revolutionaries asked Figueredo to write lyrics; his words celebrated blood sacrifice in the name of national honor. The song achieved iconic status after the composer, standing before a Spanish firing squad in 1870, shouted "To die for the motherland is to live," a line from the song. In the 1860s, Puerto Ricans adopted a revolutionary flag but revamped the design in the 1890s, which copied the Cuban banner but inverted the red and blue color scheme. The anthem of Puerto Rico, *La Borinquena*, originated during a period of anticolonial fervor in the late 1860s. The song took its title from the island's precolonial name, and the lyrics, written by Lola Rodriguez de Tio, exclaimed: "Arise Boricua! / The call to arms has sounded / Awake from the slumber, it is time to fight!," echoing the sentiments of *The Marseillaise*. Claiming no need to fear "the roar of the cannons," the words stated that "we want freedom, and our machetes." In 1903, Manuel Fernandez Juncos wrote new lyrics, in use today, removing the association with violence and extolling Puerto Rico's natural beauty and favorable climate.

Under pressure, Spanish authorities granted autonomy to Puerto Rico in 1897 and declared Cuba to be independent just before the United States declared war against Spain in April 1898. After defeating the colonizers in Cuba, the United States occupied the country for three years, flying the American flag and playing its patriotic songs. During the formal transfer of power from Spain to the United States on January 1, 1899, a flourish of trumpets greeted Cuban and American generals when they arrived at the governor general's palace to meet their Spanish counterparts. The Second Illinois Regiment's musicians, the "best band in the Seventh Army Corps," played *The Stars and Stripes Forever*. After the last stroke of noon, the musicians performed Spain's national anthem, and when the American flag reached the peak of the flagstaff atop the palace, "the band on the plaza played 'The Star Spangled Banner,' while the guns of the fleet and fortresses began to roar out the National salute of twenty-one guns."[29] During the United States' three-year occupation after the war, the American Flag Association reported that the Cuban press "notes the display of the American flag upside down from residences, and the hissing of the flag in the theaters of Havana."[30] In 1902, when the United States formally recognized the nation's independence, the Cuban government adopted *La Bayamesa* as the official ode.

In Puerto Rico, which had long clamored for independence, Americans routed Spanish troops on the island and held a flag ceremony at high noon on October 18, 1898, "unmarred by disorder of any kind," according to the *New York Times*. The front page of the newspaper carried an article head-lined "Puerto Rico Now Is American Soil: The Stars and Stripes Raised over San Juan, the Capital; Flag Cheered by the People; Band Plays 'The Star Spangled Banner' and Guns Thunder a Salute."[31] One eyewitness, Winfield Scott Schley, a native of Frederick, Maryland, and U.S. Navy admiral and commissioner to Puerto Rico, wrote that "amid the strains of the 'Star Spangled Banner,' rendered by the regimental bands, were mingled the loud huzzas of the populace. In a moment the islanders had pinned on the lapels of coats, or on the breasts of the ladies, miniature American flags."[32] The United States established a military government that anglicized the name of the country, calling it Porto Rico; taught English in the schools; and oversaw the rewriting of the lyrics to the national song *La Borinque-na*, which now praised the geography of the country rather than extolling revolution. The Grand Army of the Republic sent six hundred flags to the island, and education officials outlined their plans to place special emphasis "on the singing of patriotic songs, salutes to the flag, and short, interesting accounts of the essential facts in American History." Officials attempted to include locals in the decision-making process, but they exercised veto power over the legislature. After taking over, United States officials outlawed the public display of the Puerto Rican flag, though protestors waved it in defiance during independence rallies in the 1930s and also sang the original words of *La Borinquena*.[33]

When Americans first arrived in Guam, they raised the Stars and Stripes without incident. In the Philippines, however, occupation degenerated into a grueling guerilla war. In 1892, Filipino patriots organized the Katipunan, a secret society dedicated to overthrowing Spanish rule. The colonists ex-ecuted the group's guiding light, José Rizal, in 1896, creating a martyr in a country that practiced an almost medieval form of Catholicism and gen-erating a relentless uprising. After the United States declared war on Spain, Admiral Dewey and his fleet steamed into Manila Bay as the ship's band performed the song *There'll Be a Hot Time in the Old Town Tonight*, the war's top contribution to popular culture. Dewey decimated the Spanish Navy and became a hero back home. "At 5:43 I saw the Spanish flag come down and then our own float in its place," he wrote. "The guns of all our ships thundered out a national salute, while the band of one of our regiments . . . played the 'Star-Spangled Banner,' the troops saluted, officers uncovered, and for the first time over Manila, was greeted with all the honor so punctiliously given the flag on ceremonious occasions both by the army and navy."[34]

But Spain still occupied Manila, and Filipino rebels stepped up their liberation campaign, seeking to establish the outline of a representative democracy modeled on that of the United States. Prior to American involvement, Filipino revolutionary Emilio Aguinaldo commissioned a flag and an anthem. The banner's design included two equal-sized red and blue horizontal bars, broken by a white triangle on the hoist, surrounding a yellow sun. Eight rays represented the first provinces to join the uprising and three stars symbolized the main regions of the archipelago. Aguinaldo designated an anthem in 1897, but he replaced it with *La Marcha Filipina* (Philippine National March), an instrumental number by composer Julian Felipe that reflected Spain's cultural influence and first aired on June 12, 1898, when Aguinaldo formally declared the nation's independence. In December of that year, Spain ceded the country to the United States. The McKinley administration dismissed Filipino aspirations of nationhood and decided to administer the islands, rather than turn them over to Aguinaldo. A series of missteps led to a brutal war that lasted until 1902. Dewey later told Congress that he "never dreamed that they wanted independence." President McKinley claimed that God directed him to educate, uplift, and Christianize the islands' population (although Catholics dominated the middle and upper classes). Many Americans looked down on the natives, evidenced by a popular parody of the Civil War song *Tramp! Tramp! Tramp!*, reworked as *Damn, Damn, Damn the Filipinos*, which included the line "underneath the starry flag, civilize them with a Krag [a rifle]."

In August 1899, after fighting began between Filipino rebels and United States troops, patriotic newspaper reporter José Palma wrote the poem "Filipinas," which rejected American claims of sovereignty over the islands, to fit the country's anthem. Referring to the Philippine flag, he wrote: "Thy banner, dear to all our hearts / Its sun and stars alight / O never shall its shining field / Be dimmed by tyrant's might."[35] Over the three years that it took to pacify the Philippines, American forces held flag ceremonies that featured rousing renditions of *The Star-Spangled Banner* and attempted to institute economic and cultural changes. The Philippine Commission, appointed by President McKinley, undertook an ambitious project from 1907 to 1916 to Americanize the country by building roads, schools, sewers, and post offices under U.S. military rule. Policies banned the locals from playing their anthem or displaying their flag and attempted to bind the country together through the use of the English language and the teaching of American history. Providing a model and a measuring stick of assimilation, the United States Army taught Sousa marches and American patriotic songs to the Philippine Constabulary Band, the official musical ensemble of the new national police force. In April 1902, with the war almost over, the Annin Flag Company shipped 2,500 United States flags to Manila for use in the public schools and on buildings.[36] The commission recognized Washington's Birthday, Flag Day, and July 4 as official school holidays. As they did in Cuba, the American Flag Association denounced the "pollution" of the Stars and Stripes after learning that "houses of shame" in Manila and in the provinces, licensed by United States authorities, used the flag "as a decorative signboard . . . to advertise their traffic and attract soldiers to these abodes."[37]

The Philippines, consisting of more than seven thousand islands and home to around eighty widely used languages, represented a difficult place in which to create homogeneity. Headhunting tribes in northern Luzon fought to maintain their mores. Rebels in Mindanao never submitted to any external authority and remain in revolt against the Philippine government to this day. But the occupiers remained optimistic. During the 1901 Pan-American Exposition, held in Buffalo, New York, anthropologist Frederick Starr attended a theater performance at a re-created Philippine village, writing in his diary that the band "played the national anthem— The Star Spangled Banner!" At the 1904 Lewis and Clark Exposition, also known as the St. Louis World's Fair, President Theodore Roosevelt visited the Philippine Reservation and observed members of the Igorot tribe sing *My Country, 'Tis of Thee*. He touted the performance as a great sign of advancement for a group considered to be primitive, even in their home country. One anthropologist claimed that "the native music of the Filipinos will soon pass away." At the fair, she wrote, the Philippine Constabulary Band "played our own national anthem, while hundreds of Filipinos in khaki saluted the American flag as it was slowly lowered. So the sunset gun is measuring the days until all Filipino music shall be merged at last in 'The Star-Spangled Banner.'"[38]

In the Philippines, as in the United States, army regulations regarding Key's song created confusion among civilians and military personnel. During frequent band concerts held at the Luneta (now called Rizal Park), military and civil performers ended with the de facto anthem. Americans taught the Filipinos to stand and uncover during the song, but the revamped army regulations for saluting on formal occasions created confusion. In 1907, Major General John Weston wrote to the adjutant general that the concerts are "a place of recreation where hundreds, ay, thousands, of people are assembled of an evening to hear the music; but under the interpretation of the order the officers and soldiers now stand to attention, caps on, and the natives and others assembled no doubt feel much surprised, and are getting out of the habit of taking their hats off." Filipinos regarded removing their hats as a form of respect, and Weston argued that the practice should be continued. In Washington, D.C., Major General William P. Duvall agreed that uncovering on informal occasions "is a most fitting expression of patriotic sentiment and should be encouraged in every way." But since the salute "has been prescribed in the Navy for a number of years, and has the sanction of custom in the leading military and naval establishments abroad," he refused to change the regulations for formal settings. At the Luneta, wrote Duvall, military personnel should stand and uncover without rendering the salute, which "would undoubtedly conduce to a greater show of respect on the part of the civil element." *The Star-Spangled Banner* and its customs became ingrained in the Philippines. In 1935, after United States policy makers granted interim independence to the islands, Manuel Quezon, the president of the new Philippine Commonwealth, took office to the strains of *The Star-Spangled Banner* and *Hail to the Chief.* The American anthem again aired at the ceremony granting the nation full independence in 1946.[39]

The outbreak of the Spanish-American War unleashed an explosion of popular music, but no lasting patriotic songs emerged from the conflict. The 1896 minstrel number, *There'll Be a Hot Time in the Old Town Tonight*, written in phony African American dialect, served as the war's theme song. Otherwise, reported the *New York Press*, "No Real Battle Hymn for the Occasion Has Appeared." Popular topical numbers included *Remember the Maine*, which whipped up hawkish sentiments in 1898 and claimed that the North and the South had buried their differences. One verse included the line: "With 'Yankee Doodle' Dixey swells, With no discordant notes / And Northern cheers and Southern yells, Come from ten million throats." The chorus quoted a popular Civil War song, *The Battle Hymn of the Republic.* The tune *Old Glory, the Blue and Gray*, written in 1898, questioned, "Who dares to say we are divided still, 'Tis ninety-eight, not sixty-one." Sheet music publishers Howley, Haviland & Company in New York distributed numerous titles to capitalize on the war and emphasize sectional reconciliation, including *Meeting of the Blue & Gray*, *We're Brothers True from North and South*, and *We'll All Be with You Uncle Sam*. Another tune outlined the patriotic hierarchy: *Your God Comes First, Your Country Next, Then Mother Dear.* The sheet music cover for *Uncle Sam Forever* depicted that American icon standing on the North Pole, literally on top of the world (with the flag beneath his feet, for some reason), and listed the country's territories, including Puerto Rico, the Philippines, Cuba, and Alaska.[40]

Even though the official status of the nation's anthem remained unsettled, for many people around the world *The Star-Spangled Banner* signified the United States. In his 1904 opera *Madame Butterfly*, Italian composer Giacomo Puccini used snippets of the melody as a leitmotif to signify the American character, U.S. Navy Lieutenant B. F. Pinkerton. In the early 1900s, Asia became embroiled in turmoil as the Western powers sought to divide China. After Japan and Russia went to war over Korea and Manchuria in 1904, the Japanese shocked the world by gaining the upper hand over the Czar's forces. After negotiating a truce, President Theodore Roosevelt won a Nobel Peace Prize for his efforts. Flush with success, he sponsored a world tour by the Great White Fleet, sixteen massive battleships with bright white hulls. The fleet undertook four heralded journeys from 1907 to 1909, which reinforced the arrival of the United States as a formidable world power. When the ships reached Japan in 1908, local schoolchildren sang *Hail, Columbia* and *The Star-Spangled Banner* as the sailors disembarked. With the newfound stature of the United States, foreign countries remained confused about the nation's anthem; just before the fleet landed in

Australia, local authorities cabled American officials, inquiring about which song to play on the ships' arrival in Sydney. Governor Harry H. Dawson of New South Wales informed the state's premier that "in consequence of a doubt existing as to what is the recognised American National Anthem, the Governor made telegraphic enquiries." The reply from a United States Navy official read: "National Anthem is 'Star Spangled Banner' ADMIRAL."[41]

In the absence of a designated anthem, the National Song Society held a contest in 1909 and announced the winner, entitled *A New National Anthem*. When this failed to take hold, the group promoted *My Own United States* by Stanislaus Stangé and Julian Edwards. In the early 1900s, amateur songwriters and music publishers sent numerous homespun patriotic ditties and anthem alternatives to the secretary of the navy, the secretary of state, and the president for consideration, as if the federal government were running a nationwide talent search. The fleet's journey inspired several compositions, including *America's Bell of Freedom around the World*, by B. C. Tabor of Dennison, Texas; *There's a Fleet on the Sea, from the Land of the Free*, submitted by Atlas Music House in New York City; and *When Our Fleet Comes Sailing Home* by Myra Moore of Manchester, New Hampshire. High-level officials sometimes exceeded the call of duty, as with the case of Charles Banbury of Sandy Lake, Pennsylvania, who offered to distribute copies of his song *Our Old Glory* to every ship in the navy. Incredibly, Secretary of the Navy George Meyer sent Banbury a list with the names of commanding officers and their post office addresses. Pittsburgh resident Edward Napier claimed that his song, *With the Fleet*, "is already being played at Amusement centres where Musical Directors are Keen to detect its coming popularity judging by the acclaim which is accorded it—especially now that the expansion of the Navy . . . occupies a prominent position in the National eye."[42]

Many letters ended up in the hands of William H. Santelmann, director of the U.S. Marine Band from 1898 to 1927, who passed judgment on the compositions. Music publisher Charles Johnson of Kansas City, Missouri, submitted the song *Allegiance to the Navy*, offering to distribute copies free of charge. Johnson included a newspaper clipping headlined "American Sailors Embarrassed in Foreign Ports by Ignorance," which claimed that officers aboard the fleet's ships detailed a "woeful lack of knowledge of anything approaching a national anthem." When the sailors landed, the locals showed "prompt and vigorous" attention to "the delivery of an appropriate air, and such an incident was usually followed by an attempt to render the 'Star-Spangled Banner,' with the result . . . that the singers were rarely able to proceed with the song for more than three lines." Secretary of the Navy Truman H. Newberry sent Santelmann's assessment of *Allegiance to the Navy* to Johnson: "The song referred to has been duly examined and is found to possess some merit, but to be hardly of a character to become a national air."[43]

Other composers with visions of grandeur submitted anthem alternatives. John Pope Hodnett of New York City claimed that "there is now no great National Anthem in America" and criticized *The Star-Spangled Banner* over the foreign origin of its melody. His *Great, New National American Anthem: The Glorious Washington* undoubtedly "fills a vacuum in our National songs, for it is devoted to Washington alone, the one great God-inspired General who first gave freedom to all mankind. It was not the 'Star Spangled Banner' [that] gave freedom to all men, but Washington," who served as liberty's prime mover, just as "Christ founded Christianity." James Meakins of New York City sent in new lyrics to *The Star-Spangled Banner*, which he called *The Great Hurray That Makes Us Say Uncle Sam's Prayer*.[44]

As the United States flexed its muscle around the globe, popular songs reflected the country's newfound confidence. *The American Marseillaise* dismissed Old World anthems: "In old England they sing 'God Save the King,' While all Russia sounds the praises of the Czar / And the 'Watch on the Rhine' is music fine, to the Germans when they see their grand hussar / In Spain as in Italy's domain, To their monarchs they sing their song of praise." The cover illustration of *Uncle Sam's Invitation* depicted him planting a large flag on the equator as representatives of other nations hoisted smaller banners in tribute. The cover of *Salute to America* showed representatives of Japan, Turkey, Russia, China, France, Germany, and England taking off their hats and bowing before Uncle Sam. Other songs asserted that God blessed the nation's endeavors, including *The Heaven Born Banner*, published in 1905 and dedicated to the school children of America.[45]

The song *There is No Flag Like the Red, White, and Blue* by Charles K. Harris, composer of the turn-of-the-century hit *After the Ball Is Over*, stated: "All nations may have their own emblems / For which they will fight and also die . . . There's only one flag in this world / And that one's the red, white, and blue." *The Flag of Uncle Sam* boasted that while every nation took pride in its flag, "America's got them all beat with the old red, white, and blue." As it reeled off the names of other nations, the chorus quoted *God Save the Queen, Watch on the Rhine,* and *The Marseillaise.* In *You've Got to Be American to Feel That Way,* lyricist Louie Dacre wrote: "There is every nationality, from every principality / Some foreigners of quality in this man's land today . . . When they forget their cares, they sing their national airs," but "everyone knows" that the grand old flag of the United States "waves on high," a point underscored by quoting "Say can you see, by the dawn's early light" in the chorus.[46]

Stars and Stripes Forever, 1890–1920

DESPITE THE PATRIOTIC POMP of the 1890s, many Americans rejected presumptions about the unstoppable march of progress. An influx of Europe's "tired and poor" helped to double the population of the United States from thirty-one million in 1860 to sixty-two million in 1890. Some children toiled in harsh conditions, the 1873 and 1893 bank panics put people out of work, and labor strikes sometimes led to riots. Rural radicals organized buyers' cooperatives and established the Populist Party. In 1901, native-born anarchist Leon Czolgosz assassinated President William McKinley. Responding to the turmoil, idealistic elite and middle-class reformers took control of city and state governments. Known as Progressives, they put their faith in expertise and efficiency to promote social uplift and undertake public health crusades. Led at first by trust-buster Theodore Roosevelt, who ascended to the presidency after McKinley died, Progressives tackled some of the country's most entrenched issues and helped boost patriotic conformity and reverence for *The Star-Spangled Banner*, until that movement shattered after World War I.

After the Civil War, railroads stimulated unprecedented internal mobility. From Niagara Falls to the Rocky Mountains and from the Great Plains to the Grand Canyon, the United States contained seemingly boundless beauty and fertility. Stunning western landscapes, which symbolized the ideal of a shining land of promise, stirred patriotism. The cover of one "profusely illustrated" 1889 booklet with the title *The Star-Spangled Banner* featured sketches of Purgatory Chasm in Rhode Island, the Hudson River Valley in New York State, and giant sequoia trees in California's Yosemite National Park. Inside, illustrations of Minnehaha Falls in Minnesota and scenes of geysers in Wyoming's Yellowstone National Park adorned the thick pages. The booklet's only text: the lyrics of all four verses to the song.[1]

In 1893, geographic splendor inspired Katherine Lee Bates, a professor of English at Wellesley College, to write a poem, "America the Beautiful." On her way to teach summer courses at a college in Colorado, Bates visited the Columbian Exposition in Chicago ("alabaster cities" in the fourth verse), crossed the "fruited plain" (with its "amber waves of grain") and reached the top of Pikes Peak ("purple mountain majesties"), where the wonder of America spread across the horizon. Her verses achieved instant popularity in 1895, when they first appeared in print, and remained a favorite afterward, prompting composers and amateur musicians to set the lines to original music or identify a suitable existing composition, including *Auld Lang Syne* (yes, it fits).

Through the years, Bates made several revisions, polishing the imagery and altering the flow to make it easier to sing. After she submitted a revised version to the *Boston Evening Transcript* in 1904, a copy reached the hands of Rochester, New York, clergyman Clarence Barbour. Leafing through a hymnal, Barbour stumbled on the 1882 song *Materna*, by Samuel Ward, a church choirmaster and organist in Newark, New Jersey. Barbour's near-perfect pairing of music and verse, which suited soloists, quartets, and choirs, began to spread across the country. The popularity of Barbour's version increased after he published the tune and the poem for the first time together in a 1910 songbook, even though alternative pairings continued to circulate. Ward died in 1903, never knowing the fame his tune achieved. Katherine Bates displayed the same unassuming modesty as Francis Scott Key. During an era attuned to copyright protection for popular songs, she freely shared her poem and never sought a dime in royalties. Suggestions for lyrical changes and music pairings arrived at her home in Cape Cod over the course of thirty-five years, and although she refused to influence the musical debate, she insisted that her words remain intact, to forestall chaos.

At first glance, *America the Beautiful* is a semi-lightweight paean to the nation's natural beauty that celebrates God's grace and took its cue from *My Country, 'Tis of Thee*, which praised New England's "rocks and rills, Thy woods and templed hills." All four verses of *America the Beautiful* begin with the phrase "O beautiful" (the letter *O* also opens the first and last verses of *The Star-Spangled Banner*) and consist of declarations, followed by a plea to God. Bates ended the first and last verses with the famous lines "America! America! God shed His grace on thee / And crown thy good, with brotherhood, From sea to shining sea." The two middle verses, however, which juxtaposed the nation's potential and its reality, rejected the assumption that the Almighty granted unconditional approval to the United States. The first stanza of the second verse, "O beautiful for pilgrim feet, Whose stern, impassioned stress / A thoroughfare for freedom beat, Across the wilderness!" offers no offense to militant patriots, yet the reply scolds: "America! America! God mend thine every flaw / Confirm thy soul in self-control, Thy liberty in law." The third verse venerated participants in past struggles who embodied virtuous public spirit, yet railed against ill-gotten gains, echoing the rhetoric of leftist labor unions and rural activists:

O beautiful for heroes proved in liberating strife
Who more than self the country loved
And mercy more than life!
America! America! May God thy gold refine
Till all success be nobleness
And every gain divine!

The song's immediate popularity and the lasting appeal of the poem rested on Bates's ability to capture the yin and yang of American patriotism, balancing the promise provided by the past and future with the conditions of the present and using general references that allowed the song to cross generations. In her personal life, Bates supported women's suffrage, opposed the death penalty, refused to wear fur, and promoted pacifism after World War I. She lived in a domestic partnership with companion Katherine Coman, also a professor at Wellesley, an alternative lifestyle known during Victorian times as a "Boston marriage." During her lifetime, Bates achieved celebrity status in spite of her personal and political proclivities.[2]

With the 1910 songbook's combination of verses and melody, *America the Beautiful* rocketed to popularity relatively quickly in the days before radio and television, but it came along too late for serious consideration as the national anthem during the critical period from 1890 to 1910, when Americans attempted to single out and cling to one song. Well before World War I, Key's song evolved into the undisputed, yet unofficial, national anthem in the federal hierarchy and in popular culture, but *My Country, 'Tis of Thee* offered an alternative that also packed a patriotic punch and made it easier for children to fulfill their musical duties during flag-worship sessions. The fatal flaw of *My Country, 'Tis of Thee*, its borrowed melody from *God Save the Queen*, kept it from receiving any serious consideration as the national anthem, though many Americans believed it to be the official song of the nation.

Civil War songs and Stephen Foster tunes remained the main reference point for national music during this period. *The Battle Hymn of the Republic* received limited attention as a national anthem candidate after Teddy Roosevelt promoted it in 1908 and recruited author and Atlanta resident Joel Chandler Harris to help win favor for the song below the Mason-Dixon Line. Harris died soon after allying with Roosevelt, and the anthem issue generated heated editorial page debates. Southerners dismissed the song, which they still associated with the Northern cause. Activists transformed the prominent Union hits *The Battle Cry of Freedom*, *Marching through Georgia*, and *Tramp! Tramp! Tramp!*—or parodies using their melodies—into war and protest songs. Though popular nationwide, *Dixie* remained too closely identified with the Confederacy. Some topical original numbers rose to prominence as composers vied for fame. In 1881, renowned bandleader Patrick Gilmore billed his song *Columbia* as a "New National Anthem." *American Hymn*, by Matthias Keller, became popular in schools during the late 1800s.[3]

Prominent lawyer Stephen Salisbury chronicled the status of anthem candidates in an 1872 address to the American Antiquarian Society. He noted that *Yankee Doodle* "is a national property, but it is not a treasure of the highest value." *The Star-Spangled Banner*, he said, is "a favorite of our people," but he claimed that "the distinction of being the undisputed and most approved American national song is conceded to 'Hail Columbia.'"

Foreshadowing the future, however, Salisbury noted that "as time goes on, it [*Hail, Columbia*] is called for . . . with increasing infrequency." In 1897, an author affiliated with the Sons of Veterans, U.S.A., dismissed *Hail, Columbia*, claiming that "instrumental usage alone has saved it from merited extinction." Two years later, music critic Louis C. Elson wrote that "if an American were asked the name of his national anthem, he would probably pass by the rollicking 'Yankee Doodle,' and the bombastic 'Hail Columbia,' and acknowledge only the 'Star-Spangled Banner.'" Others agreed, including Colonel Nicholas Smith, a writer and state official in Wisconsin: "Of all the songs inspired by patriotism . . . 'The Star Spangled Banner' probably has the firmest hold on the American people."[4]

Yet the matter remained up for debate more than a decade later. Writing just before the outbreak of World War I, Michigan resident Henry Wood Booth reported that "it is a curious fact" that any American could assert that the country did not have a national anthem, or question "whether it is 'Hail Columbia,' 'My Country, 'Tis of Thee,' 'Yankee Doodle,' or 'The Star Spangled Banner.' The truth is that among those who know there is no doubt whatever. The source of doubt is to be found in the fact that the people of these United States have never spontaneously and of one accord chosen an anthem as the English did in 1745." Booth claimed that "the sentiment surrounding the flag has influenced the great majority to prefer 'The Star Spangled Banner' as the national hymn." In 1914, organist and composer Homer N. Bartlett reported that Americans engaged in "constantly recurring disputes and discussion as to which is the recognized and authentic national anthem of the United States," but he suggested that "we should prize even to adoration both the words and the music of our 'Star Spangled Banner.'"[5]

As various radical and reform organizations arose, they trumpeted their patriotic bona fides by co-opting familiar national songs, using musical parodies to promote their causes and add an emotional edge to their positions. The Patriots of America, a leftist labor organization in Chicago, filled their songbooks with tunes attacking capitalism. Parodists reworked *The Battle Hymn of the Republic* as *Good Times Will Come Again* and recast *The Marseillaise* as *Freemen, Reclaim the Nation*. One collection used the music of *Columbia, the Gem of the Ocean* for *The Gold Standard Must Go*. Many of this group's volumes included the four original verses of *The Star-Spangled Banner*, which their editors called a "beautiful and patriotic national song."

The biggest battles centered on *The Star-Spangled Banner*, due to its stature, and a wide range of protestors repurposed the song. One issue contained the parody *Sixteen to One*, which supported wealth redistribution and the debtor-friendly, free silver policy of the Populist and Democrat parties in the 1890s:

> When the people have learned how Wall Street rules the land
> Then they will resolve the great wrong shall be righted
> They are bound to succeed, for the time is at hand
> When the friends of free silver stand firmly united
> And thieves who by stealth have secured boundless wealth
> Must learn income taxing is good for their health
> For the wealth made by toilers the toilers shall own
> And no one shall reap what his brother has sown.

A different ending claimed that with the coinage of silver, "Our Star Spangled Banner in triumph shall wave, O'er the land that is free, with homes owned by the brave." A bleaker far-left take, *The Banner of Labor*, appeared in the first songbook issued by the radical Industrial Workers of the World (I.W.W.) union in 1908 and called for a new revolution: "The blood and the lives of children and wives / Are ground into dollars for parasites' pleasure / The children now slave, till they sink in their grave— / That robbers may fatten and add to their treasure / Will you sit idly by, unheeding their cry? / Arise! Be ye men! See, the battle draws nigh / And the Banner of Labor will surely soon wave / O'er the land that is free from the master and slave."[6]

The Woman's Christian Temperance Union continued to sustain their fervor through song. Movement leader Anna Adams Gordon compiled a songbook that included three verses of Key's original words, along with *The White Ribbon Star-Spangled Banner*, named after the organization's emblem. Lyricist Kate Lunden Sunderlin included different endings for her four-verse parody, including "Let the banner of freedom and purity wave / Like a signal of hope 'midst the perils we brave" and "this banner of world-circling love e'er shall wave / In the name of our Christ who is mighty to save." Other temperance parodies borrowed the melodies of Civil War favorites; popular hymns; *Dixie*; *Hail, Columbia*; and *My Country, 'Tis of Thee*.[7]

The movement to give women the vote, launched at the Seneca Falls Convention in 1848, battled adversity for decades. During the 1913 Woman Suffrage Procession down Pennsylvania Avenue in Washington, D.C., for example, many members of the crowd, in town for the inauguration of Woodrow Wilson the next day, taunted and assaulted some of the five thousand marchers, sending a hundred to the hospital. The police merely looked on and, in some cases, joined the abuse. Order in the streets returned after the secretary of war mustered a cavalry troop from Fort Myer, next to Arlington National Cemetery. At the end of the grueling day, on the steps of the Treasury Building across from the White House, one hundred women and children presented an elaborate historical tableau that began with *The Star-Spangled Banner*, followed by the appearance of "a commanding figure of Columbia dressed in national colors, emerging from the great columns." Newspapers denounced the "disgraceful scenes" visited on the marchers, who earned sympathy for their cause.[8]

Numerous subcultures in the United States remained independent from the mainstream and retained a degree of cultural independence. In 1890, coinciding with the end of the Indian Wars in the western part of the nation, the U.S. Census Bureau announced the disappearance of the frontier. Federal policy focused on Americanization programs on the reservations, and agents supplied band instruments to schools. Some tribes learned standard patriotic tunes and participated in flag formalities to illustrate their assimilation. At the 1898 Omaha Trans-Mississippi and International Exposition, the *Omaha Bee* reported that during a flag-raising ceremony before the start of a multitribal Indian parade and convocation, a band from the Sisseton Agency in South Dakota played *The Star-Spangled Banner* and gave three cheers for Old Glory. Such cheers "were given in as many languages and dialects as there were tribes represented, but they were given with a hearty good will, and the hundreds of whites who were standing around took up the spirit of the occasion and cheered Old Glory again and again." After the celebration wound down, an army captain "ordered the Indians to their dinner, the band playing 'Yankee Doodle' as they scampered away."[9]

The majestic composition *Lift Every Voice and Sing* is known as the anthem of African Americans. While teaching in Jacksonville, Florida, James

Weldon Johnson wrote the poem for a celebration of Lincoln's Birthday in 1900. His younger brother, John Rosamund Johnson, set the words to a haunting, complicated melody that served as a springboard for lush vocal harmonies. The brothers' publisher printed five hundred copies for the performance in Jacksonville, and James wrote that after they moved to New York, "the song passed out of our minds." He later learned that schoolchildren in Jacksonville kept singing it. When these children grew up and "went to other schools and sang it, they became teachers and taught it to other children. Within twenty years it was being sung across the South and in other parts of the country." *Lift Every Voice and Sing* spread through segregated schools and churches, and, according to accepted lore, the words could be found pasted into the back covers of hymnals across the South, where the song became popularly know as the Negro National Anthem. Johnson referred to it as the Negro National Hymn, taking pains to avoid the term "anthem," which emerged spontaneously after the National Association for the Advancement of Colored People (NAACP) designated the composition as its "official song" in the 1920s. The lyrics delivered an unflinching portrayal of African American history (including a reference to the "blood of the slaughtered"), but they ultimately embraced an optimistic outlook: "Sing a song full of the faith that the dark past has taught us / Sing a song full of the hope that the present has brought us / Facing the rising sun, of our new day begun / Let us march on till victory is won." Sometimes wrongly derided for being unpatriotic, the song instead declares, "forever stand true to our God, true to our native land."[10]

European newcomers to America, who enjoyed widespread freedom to retain their native cultural practices, preserved the music of their homelands. But they also adapted to their adopted land by consuming popular music, participating in dance fads, and absorbing patriotic influences. German singers in Baltimore, who formed the Leiderkranz Singing Society in 1836, venerated *The Star-Spangled Banner*, and German translations of the song date to the Civil War. Elaborate Saengerfests, multiple-day events featuring contests and concerts, spread to Philadelphia and New York. The grand finale of the 1888 festival, held on July 4 in Baltimore, assembled a 4,000-voice choir to perform Key's creation. In case anyone forgot the words, the program printed all four verses in English. In 1903, the event program included a full-page history of the song, calling it "by common consent the national anthem of the United States." The proceedings opened on Flag Day, when the orchestra played a translation, *Das Sternen Banner*, "sung by the entire audience, standing," according to the program notes. The following evening the festivities ended with *My Country, 'Tis of Thee* and *Hail, Columbia*, "sung by the audience," with no reference to standing. The repertoire of the American Union of Swedish Singers, based in Chicago, consisted of songs in the group's native tongue, but they picked up a few American melodies along the way. During a tour of their home country in 1910, they performed *The Star-Spangled Banner* and *My Country, 'Tis of Thee* and *Swanee River*, among other topical numbers. Czech Americans in Omaha included a translation of *The Star-Spangled Banner* in a 1909 songbook, and singer Frantisek A. Pangrac recorded a Czech-language version on the Victor label in 1918.[11]

Militant patriots responded to the tumultuous era by instituting what some historians call the cult of the flag, marked by a movement to establish reverential rituals surrounding flag worship and support legislation protecting this emblem from desecration. Their main targets consisted of advertisers and politicians, who often wrote their names and other identifying marks on the white stripes of the flags. In the early 1900s, the U.S. Copyright Office refused to trademark any design that could be construed as a flag, and thirty-three states and territories passed "clean flag" laws by 1907. That same year the Supreme Court upheld Nebraska's flag-desecration law, used to stop a brewery from putting American flag labels on its beer bottles. Flag defenders also supported the schoolhouse flag movement and attempted to decree signs of outward respect, including standing at attention and removing hats.

One group on the front lines, the American Flag Association, founded in 1898, consisted of "a union of flag committees of all patriotic societies." At its peak, the association counted twenty-three organizations—including offshoots of the Grand Army of the Republic, Sons of the American Revolution, and Daughters of the American Revolution—as members. The list of officers and executive committee members included Theodore Roosevelt (pre-presidency), General Nelson Miles, Admiral George Dewey, and Rear Admiral Winfield Schley, the latter a native of Frederick, Maryland, Francis

Scott Key's hometown. The association attempted to educate Americans about proper flag etiquette, but in his presidential address to the group in 1899, Colonel Ralph E. Prime of Yonkers, New York, disavowed any heavy-handed, top-down approach. "Without expressing any desire that the people of our Country should seek to express its patriotism in Military service," he said, "it would be an advance upon the present, if our people one and all, old and young, might be so filled with a patriotic reverence for that sacred emblem of our Country's glory, as to lead them to stop a moment, and think, and bare their heads, as they pass it." In 1907, Prime favorably reported a "greater reverence" toward the flag: "I have observed in individuals a recognition of this sentiment . . . and I have seen many a business man, standing, raising his hat, at the passing of the Flag of our country. It would be a most beautiful thing if this habit could become universal among us."[12]

In the 1890s, militant patriots instituted Flag Day, which honored the adoption of the Stars and Stripes by Congress on June 14, 1777. Early proponents of the holiday included Jonathan Flynt Morris of Hartford, Connecticut; New Yorker George Cantine; and William T. Kerr of Pennsylvania. Wisconsin schoolteacher Bernard Cigrand, who moved to Illinois and became a dentist, tirelessly promoted the anniversary, which caught on during the early 1900s. Between 1898 and 1907, the American Flag Association reported that the celebration of Flag Day evolved from "a new feature in the events of our Country" to a date that "has come to be generally observed all over the land." In Washington, D.C., prominent citizens with military and political connections organized the city's first formal Flag Day observance in 1901. William Santelmann led the U.S. Marine Band, plus a choir consisting of two hundred children from local schools, in *The Star-Spangled Banner* and other patriotic selections. In 1911, the Benevolent and Protective Order of Elks mandated that every lodge celebrate Flag Day.[13]

A major thrust of organized patriotic activity centered on the schoolhouse. Outsiders shaped the curriculum and outlined the content of assemblies, exerting considerable influence in their quest to manufacture conformity with industrial efficiency and to transcend racial, regional, and ethnic divisions. In 1892, schoolchildren first recited the Pledge of Allegiance, written by Christian Socialist Francis Bellamy to commemorate Columbus Day. Congress twice changed the original version, which initially read: "I pledge allegiance to my Flag and the Republic for which it stands, one nation indivisible, with liberty and justice for all." Many students accompanied the recitation with the Bellamy salute, which differed from region to region but included several common characteristics. In New York, for example, children stood "with the right hand lifted, palm downward to a line with the forehead and close to it." Upon uttering the words "'to my Flag' the right hand is extended gracefully, palm upwards, towards the flag and remains in this gesture to the end of the affirmation; whereupon all hands immediately drop to the side." The motion of an outstretched arm reaching toward the flag became identified with German Nazis and Italian Fascists by the 1930s.[14]

As flag worship became more ingrained into the school day, states revamped their grade-school curriculum to emphasize civics and history. Educators inculcated patriotism through pageantry. In 1901, the Rhode Island legislature designated February 12 as Grand Army Flag Day, requiring that all public schools hold an afternoon-long assembly to honor Abe Lincoln and the flag. Pamphlets containing programs to commemorate the event, sent by the state education superintendent to public schools between 1902 and 1933, included poems, songs, speeches, and readings to foster "true patriotism," defined as a "genuine love of one's country and of her typical institutions with devotion to their maintenance and perpetuity at whatever cost." The publications explicitly included *The Star-Spangled Banner* almost every year, and the song exerted an overpowering influence on the exercises.

In Rhode Island, G.A.R. veterans participated in school ceremonies, and the organization's booklets, distributed by the tens of thousands, included several works that became widespread in classrooms across the country. "The Flag Goes By," a poem by Henry Holcomb Bennett, influenced patriotic protocol: "Hats off! / Along the street there comes / A blare of bugles, a ruffle of drums, / A flash of color beneath the sky: / Hats off! / The Flag is passing by!" A gory third verse evoked past battles: "Sea-fights and land-fights, grim and great, / Fought to make and save the State / Weary marches and sinking ships; / cheers of victory on dying lips." The poem's title quoted a line from "The Old Flag," by Henry C. Bunner: "Off with your hat as the flag goes by! Uncover the youngster's head; / Teach him to hold it holy and high / For the sake of its sacred dead." Rhode Island educational officials also recommended "The Battle Flags," a graphic poem by Moses Owen that also relied on morbid imagery: "They are sacred, pure, and we see no stain, / On those dear beloved flags which came home again / Baptized in blood, our purest, best, / Tattered and torn, they are now at rest." Another reading popular in Progressive Era schools, "The American Flag" by Joseph Rodman Drake, lifted imagery from *The Star-Spangled Banner*. Writing in 1819, Drake referred to "freedom's banner," the "banner of the Free," the "flag of the brave," and the "flag of the free."

The Rhode Island Flag Day pamphlets included military regulations applicable to flag and song. In 1907, new state educational superintendent Walter E. Ranger solicited comments from public figures to share with the state's children. Congressman Adin Capron (R-R.I.), born in 1841, recalled that he never learned about the country's symbols or their meanings in school, "which largely accounts for the ignorance, often displayed in public assemblages, of the words, not to say the music set thereto, of patriotic songs." He added that, in contrast, the current generation of children were "not only taught the words and music of the 'Star-Spangled Banner' and 'My Country, 'Tis of Thee,' but also the history of our national and state flags." Mrs. Richard Jackson Barker, vice president of the General National Society, D.A.R., paraphrased the third verse of *The Star-Spangled Banner* and predicted that under the influence of patriotic education, "the day would not be distant when the national anthem would be treated with lofty respect and heads would be bared at the passing of the flag . . . that 'made and preserves us as a nation.' "[15]

In North Dakota, the Department of Public Instruction sent schools a collection of songs, primary documents, readings, and poems to help celebrate holidays, suggesting that on Memorial Day, for example, students read the Gettysburg Address and sing *The Star-Spangled Banner*. Schools in New Mexico Territory commemorated Flag Day on February 12, and officials issued a pamphlet with a suggested program for teachers to follow. In 1908, educational superintendent J. E. Clark prepared "a printed program providing for a uniform salute to the flag" and instructed teachers to "instill reverence for 'Old Glory' " and "arouse the patriotic spirit by your earnestness in telling of the flag and in preparing exercises." Clark also provided a primer on proper flag etiquette and suggested inviting the children's relatives and other community members to participate: "Possibly some ex-soldier will tell of his experiences in following the flag in battle." New Mexico's laws required every school to buy a flag and a flagstaff and fly this national emblem every school day, instructing boards of education to "establish rules and regulations for the proper care, custody, and display of the flag" and to observe Flag Day "with patriotic exercises." In 1908, ceremonies on Flag Day opened with Key's song. The superintendent also instructed children in the lower grades to recite the flag pledge, written by pioneering patriotic educator George Balch, and perform the accompanying salute, which required pupils to point to their head, then to their heart, and finally to the flag. This gesture resembled the sign of the cross and trained them for the Bellamy salute, performed by older students as they recited the Pledge of Allegiance. In 1915, the New Mexico commissioner of education issued circulars to every school in the state requiring students to memorize the words of *My Country, 'Tis of Thee* and *The Star-Spangled Banner*.[16]

Virulent patriotism also found expression in popular songs emanating from Tin Pan Alley songsmiths and theater composers. In 1906, George M. Cohan courted trouble when he called his new flag song *You're a Grand Old Rag*, even though he meant no disrespect. After the inevitable uproar, Cohan explained the origin of this odd title, saying that he had recently met a Civil War veteran who carried a carefully folded old flag and told the songwriter, "She's a grand old rag." Cohan figured this would make a fitting refrain for the musical centerpiece of his play "George Washington, Jr.," but the explanation hardly quelled the uproar over referring to the flag as a "rag." Cohan soon caved in and called his song *You're a Grand Old Flag*, though his first lyrical revision of the chorus kept the rag reference—"You're a grand old flag / tho' you're torn to a rag"—which he later changed to "You're a grand old flag, / you're a high flying flag." The words "You're the emblem of / the land I love, / The home of the free and the brave" evokes Key's famous line. The song also quotes lyrical or musical snippets of *Dixie*; *Marching through Georgia*; *Yankee Doodle*; *Auld Lang Syne*; *Columbia, the Gem of the Ocean*; and his own composition, *Yankee Doodle Dandy*, written in 1904.[17]

Though Cohan wished that the flag would wave "forever in peace," in Europe the Great War broke out in 1914. The United States tried to remain neutral at first, but President Woodrow Wilson and the Progressives eventually joined on the side of England and France in April 1917, after Germany continued to attack merchant ships. In part by decree from above, patriotic fervor reached a fevered level during what became the greatest undertaking ever mounted by the federal government to that point. The Wilson administration and Congress enforced straitjacket conformity and meted out ten-year jail sentences for anyone who publicly opposed participation in the conflict. Many composers tried to recreate the magic of Francis Scott Key. The tune *To Thee, O Country*, billed as a "National Hymn," included a message on the back cover, headlined "Forward March with Music." When "Americans sing of the love we have for our country, sing of the greatness and goodness we find in it, sing of the ideals which we are determined it shall maintain, and sing of the guidance we pray it may receive," it generates "a power which enemies of freedom cannot withstand." In 1915, a headline in the *Musical America* weekly reported on a "New National Anthem Gaining Favor: Many Musical Societies Singing George C. Turner's 'Hail, Land of Freedom.'" Turner, a journalist by day, dabbled in composition and singing, but his song soon disappeared from popular consciousness. The publisher of the song *America My Country* billed this tune as the "New National Anthem," and a note on the cover requested that "the Audience will please rise and remain standing while this Anthem is sung or played."[18]

American tunesmiths created surprisingly few original songs that survived the end of World War I. Another George M. Cohan smash, *Over There*, joined Geoffrey O'Hara's *K-K-K-Katy* (billed as "The Sensational Stammering Song Success Sung by the Soldiers and Sailors") as the country's biggest hits. Other popular numbers—*Mademoiselle from Armentieres* (also known as *Hinky Dinky Parlez Vous*), *Keep the Home Fires Burning*, *Pack Up Your Troubles in Your Old Kit Bag*, and *It's a Long Way to Tipperary*—derived from British and European sources. During the war years, imagery from *The Star-Spangled Banner* influenced many popular songs. A minor hit, *The Star-Spangled Banner (Is the Song That Reached My Heart)*, acknowledged that "ev'ry nation has its national air of which they boast and brag," yet nothing compared to "Maryland, My Maryland . . . And when the band plays Dixie grand, Way down south I want to be / My country tis for thee Home of the brave and free / But the Star Spangled Banner, from thee I'll never part." *Columbia Is Calling* pledged that "none shall dare to trample Old Glory in the dust, We'll fight once more 'neath the Stars and Stripes in God we place our trust." One modestly successful song, *Let's*

Keep the Glow in Old Glory, quoted "oh say can you see." Daisy M. Erd, who worked at the Boston Navy Yard, wrote the hit songs *We'll Carry the Star Spangled Banner thru the Trenches* and a sequel, *We Carried the Star Spangled Banner thru the Trenches*:

> We'll carry the Star Spangled Banner thru the trenches of good
> old France
> Then onward Christian soldiers forward we all advance
> Our cause is right our hearts are light we march to victory
> To France we go ever crushing the foe and we'll carry the Star
> Spangled Banner.[19]

Patriotic Americans continued to submit songs to top federal officials, including Secretary of War Newton D. Baker, Secretary of State William Jennings Bryan, Secretary of the Navy Josephus Daniels, and President Wilson. Adam Wackman of St. Louis shared his parody of the Confederate anthem, *The Bonnie Blue Flag*. Senator Kenneth McKellar of Tennessee sent Secretary Baker a copy of *Right Triumphant*, "a National Anthem" dedicated to the "Youth of America." The senator stated that "one of my warmest friends in Memphis" wrote it and asked, "Is there any way this Anthem could be used officially?" Baker replied: "It is not the policy of the War Department to disseminate or approve songs or poetry." Theodore Northrup in Denver sought Wilson's approval for a tune simply called *Star Spangled Banner*: "A New National Anthem, which subject has long been agitated. I feel confident that I have struck the right attitude of the American Public." Like many aspirants to patriotic fame, Northrup wrote that "I believe that it can be made the Nation's hymn of praise to be used in all National institutions, schools, celebrations in the Army and Navy," and at all patriotic events. Northrup's words focused on the flag: "Star Spangled Banner blow, Star Spangled Banner flow, Spread to the air / Thou art the flag we love, Blest by God above / With you a nation moves to do and dare."[20]

Owing to the country's multicultural makeup, including the absorption of millions of immigrants from Germany and its World War I allies, Americans feared potential subterfuge from within. The drive against all things German turned sauerkraut into "liberty cabbage" and the Germania Life Insurance Company into Guardian Life. Many German Americans joined to fight with Uncle Sam, and popular music pushed the great melting pot ideal—up to a point. The lyrics of *We're All Uncle Sam's Boys Now* referenced a number of countries that contributed to the American populace, including England, Ireland, France, Scotland, Russia, and Italy, but they omitted Germany. In that song, an Englishman, once true to the Union Jack, declared that "the Star Spangled Banner now is good enough for me," and a Russian referred to the United States as "the land of the free, and 'tis the homeski of the brave." The tune *America First* extended a welcome "to those who come across the sea from ev'ry land / She offers them the sacred rights of liberty / Beneath the starry emblem of the brave and free." *For the Honor of the U.S.A.* claimed: "When the Star Spangled Banner is waving. . . we'll be proud of our boys who are fighting."[21]

Along with its ability to unite, Key's song could also divide. Karl Muck, German-born conductor of the Boston Symphony Orchestra, attracted notoriety after he developed an ill-timed program of all-German works for the orchestra's fall 1917 tour. In October, a newspaperman demanded that Muck be put "to the test" and play *The Star-Spangled Banner* at the orchestra's Providence, Rhode Island, engagement. The Rhode Island Council of Defense, the Liberty Loan Committee, and several patriotic women's groups in the city echoed this request and sent a telegram to orchestra officials, but Muck received the message too late. After a disingenuous dispatch detailing the conductor's alleged disrespect and disloyalty circulated nationwide, Muck immediately offered to play the song at every concert, but protestors dogged his tour. Former president Theodore Roosevelt declared that "any man who refuses to play the 'Star-Spangled Banner' in this time of national crisis, should be forced to pack up and return to the country he came from." Baltimoreans took particular offense, and ex-governor Edwin Warfield vowed to riot rather than let the orchestra hold its scheduled concert. "I told the Police Board members that this man would not be allowed to insult the people of the birthplace of 'The Star-Spangled Banner,'" said Warfield. "I told them that mob violence would prevent it, if necessary, and that I would gladly lead the mob to prevent the insult to my country and my flag." Fearing chaos, the police cancelled the performance. Media scrutiny helped ruin the conductor's reputation and immigration authorities eventually deported him.[22]

Negative publicity over improper deference shown toward *The Star-Spangled Banner* also roiled the Chicago Symphony Orchestra. In August

1918, Assistant District Attorney Francis Borelli, suspecting that German-born conductor Frederick Stock tolerated Axis sympathizers, hauled orchestra manager Albert Ulrich and four musicians into his office to investigate "anti-American utterances." The controversy began after cellist Walter Ferner accused his mentor, Bruno Steindel, of singing "obscene words to the air of the national anthem as it was being played by the orchestra." Ferner further recalled a performance of *The Marseillaise* the previous year, when the audience and every orchestra member except Steindel stood up. Afterward, Steindel insulted his protégé in German and called him a traitor. The attorney general told Steindel, "Just think of the situation: Mr. Stock of the same frame of mind as you are, leading an orchestra including such men as you in the playing of the Star Spangled Banner; you know that under such conditions the music doesn't come from the heart." Borelli also questioned kettle drummer Joseph Zettleman, who had allegedly "shown contempt when the national anthem was played." Trumpeter William Hebs claimed to support the American war effort and averred that he always stood when the song aired. When word spread that Stock's naturalization papers had expired, loyal Americans criticized him as an "enemy alien." The celebrated conductor enjoyed the full support of the orchestra's board of trustees, but he resigned his post in October to straighten out his immigration status. He returned in February 1919 to great fanfare and resumed his career without any further taint. The day after Stock resigned, the orchestra dismissed Steindel. The noted cellist joined the Chicago Opera Company and toured as a soloist, though he aroused the ire of the American Legion in 1919 when he performed several concerts to aid German war orphans. In 1921, Steindel's wife, distraught over her husband's sullied reputation, committed suicide.[23]

By 1917, with *Hail, Columbia* "sinking into neglect" and *My Country, 'Tis of Thee* never a serious contender for anthem status, *The Star-Spangled Banner* earned "first place among our national songs." The patriotic compilation *Bugle Calls of Liberty* called Key's creation "the National Anthem" and claimed that every true American who hears its music "stands at 'attention.'"[24] As the conflict continued, militant patriots considered the song to be a convenient litmus test of loyalty. In April 1917, former Socialist newspaper reporter Frederick S. Boyd and two suffragists refused to stand for *The Star-Spangled Banner* while dining at Rector's restaurant in New York City. Patrons attacked Boyd, who protested that, as an Englishman, he did not have to rise, "but the crowd would listen to no explanation." Waiters stepped in to stop the fracas, and patrons marched the group outside, into the arms of a policeman who brought Boyd to night court. The judge told him that even though no legal obligation existed to stand for the song, "it was neither prudent nor courteous not to do so in these tense times." He found Boyd guilty of disorderly conduct and released him with a suspended sentence. In another instance, on Lincoln's Birthday in 1918, zealous patriots in Staunton, Illinois, tarred and feathered two suspected members of the radical I.W.W. labor union. Rioters dragged other alleged admirers of Germany's kaiser into the streets to undergo impromptu tests of allegiance and to kiss the flag. According to one newspaper account, those "who could play musical instruments were forced to play 'The Star Spangled Banner,'" and anyone who could not received a pummeling.[25]

President Wilson encouraged the musical mayhem. As a Princeton Glee Club member, he had enjoyed impressing audiences by hitting the high notes of *The Star-Spangled Banner*. In 1915, his daughter Margaret recorded the song to raise money for the Red Cross. Wilson remarked: "The man who disparages music as a luxury and non-essential is doing the nation an injury. Music now, more than ever before, is a national need. There is no better way to express patriotism than through music."[26] A week before declaring war on Germany and its allies, Wilson established the Committee on Public Information. This committee administered a wide-reaching propaganda program run by George Creel, a former journalist who served as police commissioner in Denver. Creel used musical groups and parades to drum up support for Liberty Loan bond drives, Loyalty League pep rallies, armed forces recruitment efforts, and other public mobilizations. In September, the committee's ubiquitous traveling speakers, the Four-Minute Men, launched a series of Four-Minute Sings to maintain a "'white-heat' of patriotism." One agency bulletin boasted that "'The Singing Army,' whether it be a fighting army or a working army, cannot be beaten." The executive branch equipped the Four-Minute Men with slides for sing-alongs to topical tunes and patriotic standards, including *The Star-Spangled Banner*.[27] To bring different ethnic groups into the fold, Creel and President Wilson declared July 4, 1918, as a day for foreign-born Americans to pledge loyalty to the United States. Representatives of thirty-three ethnic and national organizations from Washington,

D.C., sailed to Mount Vernon on the *Mayflower*, the presidential yacht, where they laid wreaths and offered prayers at George Washington's grave. It so happened that "a piano was tucked away behind a clump of cedars," Creel reported. After a round of speeches, Irish tenor John McCormack, a popular entertainer, "sang 'The Star-Spangled Banner' as it was never sung before," and the entourage returned to Washington.[28]

Military engagement on the battlefields of Europe elevated the importance and visibility of the flag, *The Star-Spangled Banner*, and other historic national songs. Two months after the United States entered the war, a front-page cartoon in the *Chicago Tribune* satirized Americans' lack of familiarity with Key's lyrics. Beneath a headline reading "Does Your Club Contain One of These?" the panels showed a father patting his boy's head, saying "My son—learn our national anthem and <u>always</u> prove your patriotism by joining in the singing of it on all occasions." The youngster replies, "Yes pop. I know it by heart." Later that evening, "father had a chance to sing the national anthem." After "Oh-ho say—can—you See-ee," he fumbled the next lines, rendering them as "Da De Da Dada D'yah! Hm-m Proudly hm—hm—m—dah de Twi-lights slass glee-ming," followed by more stumbling and bumbling. On the same day, the *Chicago Herald* implored, "If You Can't Fight, Sing! New Appeal to Citizens." The article reported on the efforts of the Civic Music Association, which planned to conduct community sings across the city during summer 1917. The association suggested that patriots "learn the old songs and sing them 'as they used to sing them,'" and that they should know by memory *The Star-Spangled Banner*; *My Country, 'Tis of Thee*; *The Battle Hymn of the Republic*; *Columbia, the Gem of the Ocean*; *Dixie*; *Illinois*; and even *Swanee River* and *Old Folks at Home*.[29]

The Star-Spangled Banner also made repeated appearances at community singing events during the war years. "One of the developments of the war was the wide use of music in interesting and stimulating the men in uniform," reported the Maryland Council of Defense. Indeed, "the government made it a policy, and at every camp there were song leaders and other agencies for the encouragement of the singing of the patriotic airs. It worked so well in the army and navy that it was decided to carry the movement into the civilian population." Volunteer preparedness groups distributed song sheets stamped with the names of local businesses. The sings derived their popularity from their inclusiveness. In Baltimore, organizers cautioned that "professional musicians are not necessarily the best leaders."[30] Through summer 1918, Americans across the country spontaneously gathered in public parks to sing patriotic songs. In Philadelphia, the site of an active movement, participants received free lyric sheets sponsored by Strawbridge & Clothier and circulated by the Philadelphia League of Women Voters and the Philadelphia Music Bureau. On Sunday afternoons in July and August, singers in Hunting Park ran through around two dozen popular, patriotic, Civil War and Stephen Foster melodies. Community song sheets often began with *The Star-Spangled Banner*, and they circulated at war training camps in Providence, Rhode Island, and Worcester, Massachusetts. One lyric sheet carried the slogan "sing together—think together—act together." Advertised in the *Saturday Evening Post*, a sixty-four-page booklet titled *Songs of Cheer for Camp, Fireside, Liberty, & Community Singing* contained "the national anthems of the Allies, the songs of long ago, the new hits of today."[31]

Activists worked to influence popular practices by codifying etiquette toward the Red, White, and Blue. One poem, a "Eulogy of Our Flag," which appeared in an Indiana songbook, encouraged public displays of patriotic fervor, suggesting that boys stand and take off their hats when they see the flag displayed. Anyone can "blaspheme in the street, and stagger drunken in public places, and the bystanders will not pay much attention to you." But "if you should get down on your knees in the street and pray to Almighty God or if you should stand bareheaded while a company of old soldiers march by with their flags to the breeze, some people will think you are showing off. But don't you mind!" When the flag passes, "salute, and let them think what they please! When you hear the band play 'The Star Spangled Banner,' while you are in a restaurant or hotel dining room, get up, even if you rise alone; stand there, and don't be ashamed of it, either!" The 1917 compilation *Our Flag and Our Songs* venerated the customs of standing at attention and saluting during flag raisings. The compiler suggested that "civilians, when the flag is passing on parade or in review, should, if walking, halt, if sitting, arise, and stand at attention, with hat in right hand held over the heart." Whenever *The Star-Spangled Banner* is played, "all persons within hearing should rise and stand uncovered during its rendition."[32]

Leaders of grassroots movements sought President Wilson's help in instituting the mores of patriotism. Edith Riggs of New York City sent a letter detailing her campaign to "interest the managers of theatres and of other places where it would be appropriate to play the National Anthem at the close of their performances or meetings." She asked: "Can you do anything to help us? Or make suggestions." Edwin L. Turnbull of Baltimore implored the president to "make a personal request that the National Anthem be played at the conclusion of all concerts by orchestras and military bands throughout the Country," calling on the "magic aid of music" to arouse patriotism. Turnbull claimed that the practice of performing *The Star-Spangled Banner* after formal gatherings "is by no means a general one, and Americans are accustomed to hear other patriotic tunes substituted for the National Anthem on public occasions"—including *My Country, 'Tis of Thee*; *Dixie*; *Columbia, the Gem of the Ocean*; *Marching through Georgia*; and *Hail, Columbia*—"at the expense of diminished enthusiasm and respect for the official National Anthem." Justine Collins of Asheville, North Carolina, requested the designation of "a National Anthem that will inspire some patriotism or at least may the public be taught through the schools, theatres, and all public gatherings just what our anthem is." She reported that at a gathering of college students, several in the crowd stood during a rendition of *The Battle Cry of Freedom*. "When the 'Star Spangled Banner' was played only a motley few rose. I have seen this on many occasions and have about decided that our people are devoid of patriotism or do not know our anthem. I think it is the latter."[33]

John Carr, general agent at Victoria Attractions in Dorchester, Massachusetts, asked Wilson to "issue a request to all theatres thru the Press to have our National anthem played at the opening or closing of all performances," to conform with the practice in Europe. New York City resident Charles Issacson, an editor of the theater periodical *Music for Everyone* and "Our Family Music," an insert in the *New York Globe*, sought support for his push to establish an "absolute rule that no audience disperse without singing the 'National Anthem.'" When "they do it—properly—they go out filled with fervor. We want to spread the plan everywhere. May we ask you to say whether you consider it worthwhile?" Issacson claimed to have deployed twenty-five thousand patriots carrying a broadside titled "Giving the National Anthem a New Meaning." Only when Americans sing the song en masse, the flyer stated, does *The Star-Spangled Banner* become "more than a song—a prayer; more than music—a consecration; more than words—an avowal." Even if audiences are "laughing, joking, careless, being entertained, amused, strike up the first notes of the anthem. People jump to their feet, no longer carelessly obeying a custom, but with the manner of soldiers at attention. And when they sing! The air throbs with the sincerity of their devotion." Afterward, everyone "goes out a better American. . . . Let us start here and now a movement. 'Sing the Anthem Every Day.' "[34]

Helen Fulton of New York City implored her congressman, Thomas F. Smith, to lobby the president on behalf of what she called an attractive "plan of propaganda" to make *The Star-Spangled Banner* into one of America's "household gods." She lamented the "ignorance among Americans as to the words of the NATIONAL ANTHEM," claiming that only one in a thousand knew even the first verse. Promoting the slogan "ONE FLAG, ONE ANTHEM, ONE COUNTRY," she proposed designating one day a week for the duration of the war as National Anthem Day, which would be recognized at "Moving Picture houses, Theatres, restaurants, Churches, Parks, and Business Corporations." To familiarize Americans with the words and music, she suggested recruiting groups of national anthem singers, akin to the Four-Minute Men, to lead public sing-alongs, show a film about the song's history, and display slides of the lyrics. Fulton also recommended that theaters print the words to *The Star-Spangled Banner* in all of their programs, that restaurants place them on each table, that shops put them in "every package bought on that day," that the song be performed in churches, and that universities open each day with the song. She also asked Wilson to designate September 14 as National Anthem Day.[35]

By World War I, just over a century since the song's inception, *The Star-Spangled Banner* experienced so many changes that it evolved like a folk tune, making it mutable to the whims of performers. The rise of the recording industry in the early 1900s, however, helped freeze common practices. The earliest documented artifacts include an 1896 wax-cylinder version by the Edison Concert Band, and a solo vocal take by Frank Stanley the following year. Many early recording artists came from the opera stage and delivered dramatic renderings on 78-rpm singles. In 1917, John McCormack enjoyed a huge hit with his version. Taking breathy, dramatic leaps in the high parts and landing firmly on each new plateau, McCormack rolled his *R*'s with particular gusto, conforming to the practice of the day.[36]

Alterations in popular performance practices initially remained subtle, but then the pace of life quickened as humans conquered flight and began to drive around in motorcars. The advent of ragtime in the 1890s and the birth of jazz in the 1910s introduced variations of *The Star-Spangled Banner* that drew immediate protests from traditionalists. Fin-de-siècle ragtime pianists, in particular, delighted in deconstructing sacred musical cows, from classical selections to show tunes to patriotic numbers. Performers amazed audiences by playing one song with the left hand while simultaneously using the right hand to render a different tune. Jay Roberts blended *Yankee Doodle* and *Dixie* in *The Entertainer's Rag*. Mike Bernard modernized *Yankee Doodle*, *Dixie*, *Marching through Georgia*, and *The Star-Spangled Banner* in a dazzling medley, and stride pianist James P. Johnson mixed *Dixie* in the bass notes with *The Star-Spangled Banner* in the treble register. Despite concerns over ragging and jazzing the song, most controversies surrounding Key's creation centered on public rituals rather than the interpretation of the music. Some notable alterations became standard practice. Though early sheet music divided the song into 6/4 or 3/4 time, marching bands in the late 1800s squared it off to 4/4 time, revealing the unique flexibility of the tune, which enhanced its allure and allowed it to endure. Singers toyed with the phrasing, stringing out certain syllables and clipping others. One of the major differences between renditions during World War I and the original melody of *To Anacreon in Heaven* centered on the very first line. Through the 1800s—including John Philip Sousa's influential version—two notes, both at the same pitch, represented the words "O say." By 1914, common practice rendered the passage with three different descending notes.[37]

Settling on one accepted musical and lyrical version proved to be difficult. For years, beginning in the late 1880s, the army and navy attempted to standardize *The Star-Spangled Banner*, distributing copies of Sousa's arrangement. Progressive Era sensibilities, the proliferation of divergent practices, and the outbreak of World War I gave military bandleaders and music teachers an incentive to devise an official rendition. In March 1917, Secretary of the Navy Josephus Daniels received a letter from the Naval Training Station in Newport suggesting that a board of musicians representing the army, navy, and marine bands hammer out a standard copy of the song for bands and orchestras. The version would be distributed to "all Government Bands, and also furnished to civilian musical organizations to the end that the National Air may be rendered uniformly." Daniels forwarded the letter to Newton D. Baker, secretary of war, who replied that the department had already investigated the matter. In 1911, "all Army bands were furnished with various scores of 'Star Spangled Banner' for trial and comparison and the consensus of the opinion of Army band leaders was that the Sousa score be adopted," he responded. That year, every one of the sixty-eight army music ensembles had received copies of Sousa's book, *National, Patriotic, and Typical Airs of All Lands for Full Bands*, and "no complaints have been received that any Army orchestra has played the Air in an unbecoming manner or with objectionable variations." Sousa's clunky arrangement suited military brass bands, wrote Joseph E. Kuhn, chief of the War College Division, but no regulations or official scores for orchestras existed. Kuhn cautioned that "it is customary for orchestras to include variations in the rendition of standard music and that the regimental and other commanders in control of Army bands can and will prevent orchestras composed of band musicians from rendering the 'Star Spangled Banner' in an unbecoming manner." He deemed "minor differences," loosely defined, "to be of little importance."[38]

Newspapers and educators also stumped for a standard arrangement. Just after President Wilson declared war on Germany and its allies, the publisher of the *New York Sunday American* sent a telegram to Secretary Baker indicating that the newspaper "is preparing to print authorized version of 'Star Spangled Banner' for free distribution. Lieutenant Santelmann has furnished corrected copy as played by Marine Band. We are holding up printing pending confirmation from you that this is correct version." The War Department responded that it had "no information" regarding Santelmann's version and that Sousa's version of *The Star-Spangled Banner* "is the arranged authorized version for Army Bands." Claiming that "nobody seems to know exactly how to sing" the song, the newspaper published the Sousa music score, accompanied by Santelmann's vocal score, under the headline "The Right Way to Sing and Play 'The Star Spangled Banner.'" James O'Shea, director of music for the Boston public schools, urged universal adoption of Sousa's arrangement. The *Boston Globe* suggested that "every American learn this version and none other, so that the expression of our patriotic sentiments may be accompanied by as much real inspiration and fervor as possible and not be marred by a condition of confusion and uncertainty."[39]

In 1917, the federal Bureau of Education organized a committee to establish a standard edition for concert bands; this committee included John Philip Sousa, renowned maestro Walter Damrosch, and Oscar Sonneck at the Library of Congress, among others. The following year they published what became known as the "education version." At the same time, another group sought to establish what would eventually be known as the "service version" of *The Star-Spangled Banner*. By chance, it ended up being almost the same as the education version. The service project germinated in 1913, when the Music Supervisors' National Conference compiled a book of eighteen songs suitable for community sings. The collection included a version of *The Star-Spangled Banner* supplied by the National Education Association, which removed every dotted—or held—note, making it stiff and devoid of passion. When the music supervisors expanded their compilation to fifty-five selections, they sought a suitable substitute, wrote committee chairman Peter W. Dykema, a music professor at the University of Wisconsin. When Dykema learned that the military attempted to include an appropriate arrangement of Key's song in the *Army Song Book*, whose print run reached three million copies, he formed the Committee of Twelve, which included representatives from music publishers, the War Department, and the National Conference of Music Supervisors.

More committee discussions focused on *The Star-Spangled Banner* than on any other national song, wrote Dykema, who also served as a music supervisor at army training camps during the war. His committee, he noted, found that "every version used today has changed greatly from the original form." In typical Progressive Era style, committee members studied renditions by soldiers and professional singers: "Army and Navy song leaders were asked to gather their men in groups of various sizes and start them singing the 'Star-Spangled Banner' and to allow them to finish without conducting and without accompaniment." Song leaders jotted down the version that "emerged from the masses" and sent their data to the committee.[40] Songwriter Geoffrey O'Hara, who scored a hit with *K-K-K-Katy*, helped conduct one of those sessions at Fort Oglethorpe in Georgia, where 3,600 officers and men read sheet music as they accompanied a band. Recognizing that the musicians and singers clashed in several instances, after the war O'Hara assembled three large groups of nonmusicians in different New York City neighborhoods and recorded them singing the song a capella. Finding the results to be nearly identical, he transcribed the performances into a version that he copyrighted.[41]

When Dykema and his committee compiled their statistics, they concluded that "the American people emphasize their rhythm by using freely the unequally divided beat," prolonging notes to color the melody (as in the first syllables of "proudly" and "ramparts" in the first verse). "Whether or not this is connected with their liking for ragtime may be a debatable question, but it seems, as one observer put it, that our people in the singing of the 'Star-Spangled Banner' at least, dot a note almost every time they have a chance." The group circulated printing plates of the music to newspapers, distributed copies to bands in the service of the United States government, and placed the solo melody in the *Army Song Book* and in collections for the navy and the marines. Sheet music and education publishers, along with the Victor and Columbia talking-machine companies, promoted the committee's handiwork. The final version would "be settled only by the real judges of all folk material—time and the people," wrote Dykema, who claimed that with official backing, his version "has a far better chance of standardization than any other version ever dreamed of." Nonetheless, he admitted, "we think it is about ninety-five to one, but it is a chance just the same!"[42]

In addition to school and military band performances, most Americans heard *The Star-Spangled Banner* at baseball games. During the 1918 World Series, after a war-shortened season, the Chicago Cubs faced the Boston Red Sox in the only September classic on record. During the seventh-inning stretch of game one, a low-scoring affair, the spectators stood up "to take their afternoon yawn, that has been the privilege and custom of baseball fans for many generations." When the band spontaneously broke into *The Star-Spangled Banner* from their station in the outfield, "the yawn was checked and heads were bared as the ball players turned quickly about and faced the music," wrote one eyewitness. At first, a limited portion of the crowd participated. Others then joined in, "and when the final notes came, a great volume of melody rolled across the field." When the music ended, the onlookers exploded into thunderous applause "and rent the air with a cheer that marked the highest point of the day's enthusiasm." The song served as "the great moment" of the game and represented something "far different from any incident that has ever occurred in the history of baseball." Key's song aired during the next two games in Chicago. Not to be outdone, Red Sox owner Harry Frazee opened each game in Boston with it. The cost of hiring bands precluded providing live music at every game, but through the 1930s, *The Star-Spangled Banner* accompanied opening day, special occasions, and World Series games.[43]

A VIEW of the BOMBARDMENT of Fort McHe

Observatory, under the Command of Admirals Cochrane, & Cockbur

thrown from 1500 to 1800 shells in the Night attempted to land by forcing

near Baltimore, by the British fleet, taken from the
the morning of the 13th of Sepr 1814 which lasted 24 hours, &
ssage up the ferry branch but were repulsed with great loss,

References.
A. Fort McHenry.
B. Lazaretto.
C. Salauave House
Admiral Ship. North Point
E. Ferry and Fort.

John Bower's circa 1814 aquatint, with hand coloring, of the Fort McHenry bombing.

Though inaccurate in its details, Edward Percy Moran's oil painting, *By Dawn's Early Light,* circa 1912, depicted the moment that Key spotted the flag fluttering above Fort McHenry.
LIBRARY OF CONGRESS

First known photo of the star-spangled banner, taken by flag historian George Preble on June 21, 1873, at the Boston Navy Yard. COURTESY OF THE AMERICAN ANTIQUARIAN SOCIETY

In San Francisco, the first monument in the country to honor Francis Scott Key—dedicated in 1888—towers over the policeman in this photo from the turn of the twentieth century.

Photo of the memorial to Francis Scott Key at Mount Olivet Cemetery, Frederick, Maryland, taken on the day of its dedication August 9, 1898.

COURTESY OF THE FRANCIS SCOTT KEY MEMORIAL FOUNDATION

Commissioned in 1907 and completed in 1911, the monument to Francis Scott Key in Baltimore serves as a gateway to the Bolton Hill neighborhood.
COURTESY OF ERIC HAGEMANN, SOLSTICEPHOTO.COM

A stern-looking Mrs. Reuben Ross Holloway holds the British and United States flags.

National anthem boosters in Frederick, Maryland, rejoiced when the U.S. Postal Service issued a stamp to honor Francis Scott Key in 1948, the fiftieth anniversary of the Key Memorial dedication.
COURTESY OF USSTAMPGALLERY.COM

This take on the inability of many Americans to remember the first verse of *The Star-Spangled Banner* appeared during World War I. *CHICAGO DAILY TRIBUNE*, MAY 12, 1917

Ripley's Believe It or Not! (November 3, 1929) portrayed the Anacreontic Society in a doubly negative light, since its members came from a higher stratum of society than depicted here. The copy reads: "America Has No National Anthem! The U.S.A. (being a dry country) has been using—without authorization--a vulgar old English drinking song—As recent as 1914, Congress has refused to indorse the 'Star Spangled Banner' (which is the air of 'To Anacreon in Heaven')."

Reproduction of the front (a) and back (b) designs of the 1964 commemorative coin issued by the Francis Scott Key Memorial Foundation and the Maryland World's Fair Commission. COURTESY OF THE FORT MCHENRY NATIONAL MONUMENT AND HISTORIC SHRINE, NATIONAL PARK SERVICE

Marching under the Banner, 1898–1931

IT TOOK 117 YEARS from the morning when Francis Scott Key wrote his poem in Baltimore to the moment President Herbert Hoover signed the national anthem bill into law in 1931. The date may suggest that the anthem measure represented a contrived response to the Great Depression, but the real story is more innocent, and complicated. By adopting a hands-off policy, Congress fostered the emergence of the true people's choice.

Interest in honoring Key and his legacy first stirred in 1866, after the Civil War, when his daughters moved the poet's remains from Baltimore to the new family plot at Mount Olivet Cemetery in Frederick, Maryland. Locals attempted to erect a suitable monument in Key's honor, but progress remained slow. Militant patriots in Maryland reeled after the July 4, 1888, dedication of the nation's first memorial honoring Key in Golden Gate Park in San Francisco. James Lick, an eccentric businessman who first brought Ghirardelli chocolate to California from South America, bequeathed his fortune to build a school, public baths, the world's largest telescope to date, and a $60,000 edifice to Francis Scott Key. According to Nathan Appleton, a relative of Fort McHenry defender George Armistead, with such a large sum, "this monument ought to be the finest in the land." Lick apparently became enchanted with *The Star-Spangled Banner* when he lived in Valparaiso, Chile, and heard it during a visit by two United States navy vessels. Sculptor William Wetmore

Story designed California's elaborate 51-foot monument, consisting of a marble pedestal topped by a life-size bronze statue of Key, which is surrounded by four Corinthian columns. A statue of Columbia holding a flagstaff caps the edifice. Curiously, one of the panels that contain lines from the second verse and wrap around the top of the monument refers to "The StarSpangled Banner," as if the designers adopted too large a font to fit the name with a space or a dash.[1]

In Frederick, the movement to construct a memorial to the city's native son gained momentum after nineteen-year-old Elkton, Maryland, native Folger McKinsey took a position at the *Frederick News* in 1886. After hearing about the monument in California, McKinsey drew attention to the issue and helped establish the Key Monument Association in 1894. With the help of a $5,000 appropriation from the Maryland legislature, the association raised a total of $10,000. Sculptor Pompeo Coppini, who had immigrated from Italy in 1896, crafted a bronze statue atop a circular granite pedestal depicting the moment Key noticed the flag. The family again moved the poet's remains (and added those of his wife) into a crypt within the base of the memorial, where a figure of Columbia sits with two children who represent war and music. At the monument's dedication on August 9, 1898, special trains transported thousands of visitors to the cemetery grounds, where Julia McHenry Howard, Key's great-granddaughter, unveiled the statue. The assemblage sang *The Star-Spangled Banner*, followed by the *Doxology*. A choir performed *Festival Te Deum* and two versions of *Gloria in Excelsis*. Clergymen led an invocation, a prayer, and a benediction. After McKinsey read a long "Ode" he had written for the occasion, another speaker alluded to Lick's statue: "The hand of Maryland stretches across the Continent to the hand of California (where, too, Key's name is writ in lasting stone) and the two clasp. North and South join theirs. The bond is complete, the circle of the country perfected. Never will it be broken, for Maryland binds it fast with 'The Star-Spangled Banner.'" McKinsey eventually went to work for the *Baltimore Sun* and became known as the Bentztown Bard.[2]

Just as Maryland patriots built the *second* memorial to Francis Scott Key, they also lagged behind Pennsylvanians in the drive to influence Congress to designate *The Star-Spangled Banner* as the national anthem. According to a prominent Baltimore patriot, in 1869, Reverend George Leakin proposed official sanction for the song by Congress, but he never acted on his suggestion. Momentum picked up after the Daughters of the American Revolution held their 1895 Congress in Atlanta. A speech by Miss Janet E. Hosmer Richards, a member of the Mary Washington Chapter of the D.A.R. in Washington, D.C., made reference to a recent concert that featured renditions of mediocre national songs performed by trained singers and the United States Marine Band. Lasting anthems, Richards claimed, resulted from "a mighty inspiration, born of a passionate desire for a nation's freedom." Comparing the origins of *The Marseillaise* with Key's experience, she concluded that "public sentiment" singled out *The Star-Spangled Banner* as the potential national anthem, due in part to its focus on the flag. "In times of peace, dear flag, we hail thee! In time of danger, inspired by this anthem, we will gladly rally to thy defense and shed our life's blood, if necessary, in order that we may proudly proclaim, after the heat and hardship of the struggle, 'Our Flag is still there!'" She implored her group to "petition the Congress of the United States to so recognize and designate it by special enactment, that henceforth it may be conceded to be, from among all rivals, the American National hymn."[3] The speech, repeated and reprinted through the end of the decade, stirred the Pennsylvania Society of the Colonial Dames of America to "petition Congress for legislation looking to the adoption of 'The Star Spangled Banner' as the National Air" in 1896. Two years later, the group requested that all music venues "order the 'Star Spangled Banner' to be played at every performance and to request the audiences to rise while the air is being played, after the manner and customs practiced in England and throughout Europe." Also in 1898, the Philadelphia Chapter of the D.A.R., claiming that the song "is generally recognized as the National Anthem," recruited other state chapters to form Star-Spangled Banner Committees and lobby Congress.[4]

Marylanders instead commemorated the song of their native son on a local level. In 1907, the Francis Scott Key Memorial Association in Washington, D.C., pledged to buy and preserve the house in Georgetown where Key had lived for most of his life. Members included Admiral George Dewey, Rear Admiral Winfield Scott Schley, and Francis Scott Key-Smith, the poet's great-grandson. One supporter wrote that Key's house had fallen "into evil ways and is now used as a home for street vendors, its outer walls employed to advertise sundry forms of refreshment dispensed from the sidewalk below." The building—covered with large letters hawking soda, cigars, jewelry, telephones, and steam laundry services—resembled a three-dimensional billboard.[5]

Tobacco titan Charles Marburg died in 1907 and left $25,000 to build a memorial to Key in Baltimore. Completed in 1911 at the entrance of the historic Bolton Hill neighborhood, the base of the elaborate fountain includes bronzes of Key and an allegorical sailor occupying a rowboat. The poet holds his manuscript aloft and gazes toward Columbia, who stands atop a marble temple. Other memorials in Baltimore include a bronze tablet at Mt. Vernon Place Episcopal Church, donated by a local D.A.R. chapter in 1913 to mark the approximate spot of Key's death, and a sculpture in Patterson Park of two children holding a scroll that commemorates the centennial of the events of 1814.

Representatives of hereditary and patriotic groups regularly corresponded with high-level officials in the federal government, requesting information about rules and regulations regarding *The Star-Spangled Banner*. In response, the War Department, in an attempt to fill the vacuum caused by congressional inaction, created a form letter explaining that their guidelines only applied internally. Yet top-ranking officials recognized the pivotal role of the military in fostering respect for the song among civilians. In 1903, an internal memo to the chief clerk of the army indicated that the army's General Staff had previously considered "the adoption of the air as the National Anthem" but concluded that only an act of Congress or an executive order by the president could determine the official song.[6] Responding to a 1904 letter from Mrs. F. A. Aiken of the Cincinnati D.A.R., inquiring about the status of the national anthem, the army's adjutant general wrote that "it is not the prerogative of the War Department to ordain what shall be the national anthem," but he acknowledged that official recognition given by the department to the song "is believed to be an important factor in the education of the people towards its universal recognition, and its possible ultimate adoption by Congress or the President as the national anthem." The navy's rule to salute the flag during the song's airing "extends the scope by requiring proper respect to be observed whenever 'The Star Spangled Banner' is played."[7]

The adoption of *The Star-Spangled Banner* by the army and navy countered the classroom popularity of *My Country, 'Tis of Thee*. In 1903, Lucy P.

Scott of New York City reported that her son learned to "stand at attention, with the hat held over the heart" for the military anthem during a tour of duty in the Philippines. She noted that "a very great many persons consider 'America' ([based on] England's National Air) our own national song, that it is so used in schools. Our public school children are so well instructed in regards to the patriotic observances of the flag that it seems a pity there should be any confusion" regarding Key's creation. The following year, an exasperated George Lancaster, principal of Everett City High School in Washington State, sent the War Department a newspaper clipping that "has caused us much uncertainty." The article recounted military rules regarding *The Star-Spangled Banner*. When Brooks' Ragtime Band played the song at a local concert, he wrote, some people in the audience stood up, although "those who arose were made to feel somewhat awkward. In the large cities it has become a fixed custom for an audience to rise whenever and wherever this air is played or sung, and mostly the hall resounds with cheers." In the past, Lancaster wrote, "we have risen en masse when 'My Country' was sung."[8]

The U.S. Marine Band experienced the confusion firsthand. In 1901, during a performance in Detroit, the musicians stood during *Hail, Columbia*, and only two boys got out of their seats when the band played *My Country, 'Tis of Thee*, but "it was not until the familiar strains of the 'Star Spangled Banner' crashed out, at the concert's very end, that the audience came to its senses and rose to its feet." On another tour by the band in 1907, a few audience members in Bangor, Maine, stood for the finale, followed by everyone else, though "apparently with small intent to do honor to the National Anthem. Most of them were looking for their hats and coats," according to the *Bangor Daily Commercial*. The following week, the *Manchester (N.H.) Union* reported that when the band stood up to play "what really is the national anthem . . . there was a noticeable movement for the door." By 1910, Loyal League member Albert Pirtle of Louisville, Kentucky, called the practice of standing for *The Star-Spangled Banner* a "growing one." G.A.R. Commander in Chief Alfred B. Beers wrote to the secretary of war in 1913 that "misunderstanding exists as to when one should stand on the playing of the 'Star Spangled Banner' and on the playing of 'America.'"[9]

Laws related to the future anthem first appeared at the state and local levels in the early 1900s. Initial legal battles over the song centered on school textbooks that included the pro-Union fifth verse, written by Oliver Wendell Holmes during the Civil War. After hearing their grandchildren sing the incendiary words at a school program, Confederate veterans in New Orleans protested to education officials, who compelled the publisher to remove books with the objectionable addendum. A similar bill against the mutilation of *The Star-Spangled Banner* stalled in Indiana's state legislature but passed in New York State.[10] In 1907, Thomas Tuite, affiliated with the Bronx, New York, chapter of the G.A.R., organized the Star-Spangled Banner Association to "preserve the exact words of 'The Star-Spangled Banner' as written by Francis Scott Key." At the time, under the guise of patriotism, Irish nationalists in the United States also pressed city and state legislatures to compel the singing of all four verses. Previously, owing to the growing Anglo-American alliance, many published versions of *The Star-Spangled Banner* omitted the third verse, which maligned England. Thomas R. Marshall, serving as Indiana's governor from 1909 to 1913, discovered that the Association for the Promotion of Truth, which lobbied the state to require the airing of every verse, really sought to give "the British lion's tail a particularly vicious and nerve-wracking twist," rather than express devotion to the United States.[11]

Reflecting popular interest in national songs, in 1907 the Librarian of Congress commissioned Oscar Sonneck, head of the institution's Music Division, to compile information about *The Star-Spangled Banner*; *Hail, Columbia*; *Yankee Doodle*; and *My Country, 'Tis of Thee* (consigning *Columbia, the Gem of the Ocean* to the dustbin of history). Sonneck's pedantic report, published in 1909, concluded that tradition and the emotional appeal of Key's song outweighed other proffered rational judgments. Focusing mainly on basic questions surrounding the origins of *The Star-Spangled Banner* and its history in print, Sonneck correctly identified John Stafford Smith as the composer of *To Anacreon in Heaven* and refuted the idea that anyone besides Key put the words and music together. In 1910, Representative William Griest (R-Pa.) introduced the first Congressional bill related to *The Star-Spangled Banner*, which authorized the publication of ten thousand copies of Sonneck's book. Sonneck then completed an expanded study of the song in time for its 1914 centennial, and his overt bias stamped it with quasi-official status. He wrote: "We took the air [Smith's tune] and we kept it. Transplanted on American soil, it thrived." Sonneck stated that

The Star-Spangled Banner, despite detractors, still "stirs the blood of every American, regardless of his origin or the origin of the air." The American people would decide the matter, he noted, "regardless of critical analysis, legislative acts, or naive efforts to create national songs by prize competitions."[12]

In the 1910s, two Baltimoreans, Representative J. Charles Linthicum (D-Md.) and indefatigable superpatriot Ella Virginia Houck Holloway (aka Mrs. Reuben Ross Holloway), emerged as the chief conduits of the crusade on behalf of *The Star-Spangled Banner*. Linthicum, a former school principal turned lawyer, represented Baltimore in Congress from 1911 until his death in 1932. His family established Linthicum Heights, a real estate development located near Baltimore-Washington International Airport, and he married another old-line Marylander. He regarded patriotism as "the great bulwark of the Republic." In an expansive country, "consisting of a large cosmopolitan population gathered from every nation of the world, it is highly essential that patriotism be instilled into the hearts and minds of the young, as well as taught to the older generations who come to our shores from foreign countries," declared Linthicum. Holloway, a local media star and arbiter of all things patriotic, displayed a distinctive dramatic flair. Although an easy target to satirize, due to her brusque style, air of certainty, and signature black hat, she, too, descended from a prominent family. In addition to the D.A.R., the Daughters of 1812, the United Daughters of the Confederacy, and the Daughters of Founders and Patriots, Holloway also supported the Red Cross and the Maryland Historical Society. In 1908, after the death of her husband, the scion of a chemical fire engine and fire extinguisher company, she began scanning newspapers to expose enemy propaganda. "When she speaks of 'The Star Spangled Banner' her face beams," reported a local newspaper, "but when the conversation turns to radicals and revolutionists her mild eyes flash."[13]

In 1912, Linthicum launched a lobbying effort on behalf of *The Star-Spangled Banner*, and to great fanfare, the Smithsonian Institution permanently acquired the giant flag that inspired Key. That same year, Representative George Foss (R-Ill.) introduced a bill to adopt Key's creation as the national air, the first of thirty-five similar resolutions proposed in Congress through 1929. Also in 1912, the army decommissioned Fort McHenry, which had lost its strategic military value. Linthicum lobbied to transfer the fort to the City of Baltimore for use as a park, a measure that passed in June

1914. In an article entitled "Why We Preserve Fort McHenry," Linthicum evoked the rampart's "almost religious sacredness" and the ability of Key's song to arouse "as if by magic every smoldering sentiment of patriotism in our country." During World War I, however, the military reappropriated the site for use as a hospital, and Congress approved $75,000 for a memorial to Key on the fort's grounds.[14]

The hundred-year anniversary of *The Star-Spangled Banner* in 1914 presented Americans with diversions from the war in Europe. Cities across the country commemorated the milestone with elaborate parades and ceremonies, including in Frederick, Maryland; Madison, Wisconsin; and Columbus, Ohio. In Baltimore, the weeklong extravaganza served as a lavish coming-out party for the city after a devastating fire leveled the heart of downtown in 1904. One centerpiece of the rebuilding effort, the Francis Scott Key Highway, connected residential neighborhoods and Baltimore's Inner Harbor with Fort McHenry, which city officials promoted as a tourist destination. Forty-five committees worked to maximize the impact of the celebration. Patriotic groups organized numerous plaque and monument unveilings across the region, including a Francis Scott Key Buoy to mark the approximate spot where the ship on which he drafted his immortal lines weighed anchor (and the buoy is still put into the water every spring by the U.S. Coast Guard). Concerts filled the air almost every night, and eight parades threaded through the streets, including an historical pageant with twenty-four floats. During the ceremony's grand finale at the fort on Defenders Day, 6,400 public school students formed a human flag chorus and sang patriotic songs, accompanied by a 250-piece band. A water carnival and fireworks display, overseen by the Pyrotechnic Committee, demonstrated the power of large-scale spectacles to intensify nationalism. President Wilson, although invited to the event, declined, due to wartime priorities. At Linthicum's prodding, Wilson signed a proclamation requiring all army posts, naval stations, and ships to participate in a special salute to Old Glory on September 12, in recognition of the start of the battle leading to the song's composition, and urging citizens to "display the flag from their residences and places of business on that day."[15]

Baltimore officials mixed patriotic and parochial aims as they promoted tourism. From 1911 to 1919, successful lawyer James Preston, a member of one chapter of the Sons of the American Revolution and two Masonic lodges, served as mayor of Baltimore and advanced the city's interests with "untiring zeal and energy." As president of the National Star-Spangled Banner Centennial Committee, Preston toured twenty-one midwestern and southern cities to drum up interest in the song's centennial. Local luminaries held a Citizens' Testimonial Dinner at the Hotel Rennert upon his return home. According to an acquaintance, historian Matthew Page Andrews, "Preston had a hobby about the 'Star Spangled Banner,' and incidentally he never lost an opportunity of advertising the city or any Star Spangled Banner dates." In 1916, Preston sponsored a contest that selected *Baltimore, Our Baltimore* as the city's anthem, and he presented the $500 prize to lyricist Folger McKinsey and composer Emma Hemberger.[16]

Centennial fervor in Baltimore generated spin-off projects, including a drive to preserve the house where Mary Pickersgill sewed the large flag that flew over Fort McHenry. Preston also organized the Star-Spangled Banner Association of the United States, which attracted 250 charter members, most of them from Baltimore. The association promoted Flag Day and sought to institute "a public ceremonial on September 14th of every year, on which occasion the 'Star-Spangled Banner' shall be sung."[17] The Maryland Society, Daughters of the American Revolution, also published the first volume of the *Patriotic Marylander*, a quarterly journal "Dedicated to the Memory of Maryland Patriots and to the Great Events in Maryland History," but the periodical lasted only three years.[18]

In 1916, as United States involvement in the European conflict increased, War Department brass approached President Woodrow Wilson to approve recognition of anthem status for *The Star-Spangled Banner* by the military. Though Wilson signed an executive order proclaiming that "the composition consisting of the words and music known as 'The Star-Spangled Banner' is designated the National Anthem of the United States of America," he considered the order to be applicable only to the armed forces. On July 3, 1916, the U.S. Marine Band inserted a notice in their concert program declaring that "the entire audience is required to stand to attention, men with their hats removed, when the National Anthem is being played," thus extending military edicts to civilians. The next year, army regulations declared that "the playing of the national anthem at any time or place shall be taken to mean 'The Star-Spangled Banner' to the exclusion of other tunes or musical compositions popularly known as national airs."[19]

That same year, the Maryland Society, Sons of the American Revolution, convinced the Baltimore city council to unanimously pass the first ordinance in the country compelling respect for the song. This law held that "the indiscriminate rendition of 'The Star-Spangled Banner,' or parts thereof in connection with other compositions tends to lower the esteem and reverence in which the National Anthem should be held by the people of our Nation." To prevent its desecration in any "public place, or at any public entertainment, or in any theatre or moving picture hall, restaurant, or café," the song must be played in its entirety, "without embellishments of national or other melodies." Presumably "in its entirety" meant at least one full verse. Following the military's lead, Baltimore's ordinance also banned performing any part of the song in a medley and directed that it never be played for dancing or as an exit march. The law required "musicians, performers, or other persons" to stand while playing or singing *The Star-Spangled Banner*, when practicable. Fines for doing otherwise ranged up to one hundred dollars, and police officers distributed informational leaflets to theaters, cafes, restaurants, moving picture halls, and the offices of musicians' unions, though the statute held business owners responsible for overseeing its provisions. Between 1917 and 1921, Colorado, Massachusetts, Michigan, Minnesota, and New Mexico passed similar laws.[20]

One local newspaper supported the endeavor, claiming that *The Star-Spangled Banner* "forms a part of our national religion which cannot occupy too high a place in our patriotic worship." Still, the Baltimore ordinance generated controversy. Opponents objected to the "folly of trying to instill patriotism by law," calling it a "dictation to individual liberty" that smacked of German militarism. Sons of the American Revolution member Laydon Smith, who first proposed the statute, claimed that it centered on performance practices desecrating what he called the "national anthem" and attempted to stop "the ragtime mutilation of 'The Star Spangled Banner.'" He added, "We do not believe that it should be set to jig time, as has been done by one popular comedian. We do not believe that a few strains from it should be introduced in an indiscriminate medley every time an American soldier or an American warship is shown on the screen in a moving-picture house." Smith vowed to lobby the Maryland statehouse, but the effort fizzled after the city gave up on enforcing the law's provisions.[21]

In 1917, at a time when governmental bodies prescribed patriotic practices and the United States prepared for war, New York City singer, lecturer, and children's performer Catharine Smiley "Kitty" Cheatham published a pamphlet decrying *The Star-Spangled Banner* as "deadly in its insidious mental poison." A devout Christian Scientist, Cheatham considered the sentiments of the song to be at odds with the spirit of Christianity and the idealism of the era, represented by President Wilson and his Progressive supporters. She argued that Americans "not only resist learning and singing 'The Star-Spangled Banner,' but, up to the present time, have refused to establish it as the national hymn." In February 1918 the *New York Times* published excerpts of her essay, and the full text appeared in the March issue of *Musical America* magazine. Militant patriots attacked her in the press.[22]

At the war's end in 1918, Congress signaled its willingness to foster patriotism by formally adopting the American's Creed. Henry Sterling Chapin, New York State's commissioner of education, proposed holding a contest to select one concise statement of the country's values. Many newspapers and magazines participated, and Baltimore Mayor James Preston offered a $1,000 award for the winning entry. The prize committee received about three thousand submissions, judging them anonymously. The winner turned out to be Frederick, Maryland, native William Tyler Page, a descendant of Declaration of Independence signer Carter Braxton and a relative of President John Tyler. Page, who had attended school in Baltimore, worked as a clerk at the House of Representatives, and Mayor Preston touted Page's local and statewide ties. In his composition, Page borrowed from the Declaration of Independence, the Federalist Papers, and the Constitution, along with the writings of Daniel Webster and Abraham Lincoln, all of which he referred to as his "American Bible." After hearing the Apostles' Creed at church, wrote Page, "the thought came to me as I walked along that a secular creed should be fashioned in form on the lines of the Christian Creed."[23]

Also in 1918, U.S. Representative Linthicum of Maryland introduced his first national anthem bill after Mrs. Holloway sent him a petition gathered by the Maryland Society, United States Daughters of 1812. That document included signatures representing fifty-one individuals and forty-nine civic, fraternal, and patriotic societies. Only a few of the supporters, including the state librarian of Vermont and the state registrar of the Arkansas chapter of the Daughters of 1812, lived outside of Maryland. Linthicum wrote to

Holloway that "it will be well to continue to secure endorsements, as large a number as possible. We must impress the Committee and the House of Representatives with the fact that the citizens of our country desire action." Help came from fraternal organizations, including the Freemasons, Moose, Elks, Knights of Columbus, and Odd Fellows (founded in Baltimore). With their membership increasing, these organizations moved beyond charitable endeavors to actively promote patriotism.[24]

The Veterans of Foreign Wars (V.F.W.), founded after the Spanish-American War in 1899, also provided pivotal support for *The Star-Spangled Banner*. In 1919, World War I veterans formed the American Legion, which grew to a position of such strength that even its enemies recognized the organization as "second to none in its influence on Capitol Hill." Both veterans' groups allied with hereditary, patriotic, and fraternal organizations to ramp up the promotion of patriotism in the schools and the designation of *The Star-Spangled Banner* as the nation's official anthem. One militant patriot reported: "During the war, many citizens began to practice simple rules of conduct denoting respect to our flag. It has been noted in the daily press that this attitude is giving way to one of indifference."[25] To enforce conformity to their patriotic vision, expressed as "100 percent Americanism," the V.F.W. and the American Legion cooperated to spread their message through print, radio, and film, but the two organizations also competed for recognition. In 1921, Walter I. Joyce served as the national patriotic instructor and director of the National Americanization Committee of the V.F.W. The following year, former Maryland state senator Garland W. Powell headed the National Americanism Commission of the American Legion. Joyce compiled *Etiquette of the Stars and Stripes* and Powell published *"Service": For God and Country*, flag handbooks that included overlapping information and instructions.[26]

The enhanced status of *The Star-Spangled Banner* among militant patriots triggered a backlash against the song during the Roaring Twenties. In general, liberal patriots favored *America the Beautiful* as the national anthem. Complaints about Key's creation centered on the wide, twelve-note range of the melody. Some objected to the English origins of the tune, while other opponents decried the anti-British sentiments in the lyrics. Moralists argued that Key's song glorified war. Polarization between militants and liberals intensified after the Communists came to power in Russia during

World War I, and the anthem controversy served as a prism for weighty concerns. In 1919, strikes and race riots across the United States stirred unrest, the economy experienced a recession, and the Justice Department's Red Scare raids routed suspected leftists and radical unionists. Popular music shifted from ragtime to the more jarring jazz, and Congress moved to limit immigration from war-torn Europe with quota laws in 1921 and 1924. After Prohibition became the law of the land in 1920, temperance forces disingenuously associated *The Star-Spangled Banner* with *To Anacreon in Heaven*: "All the perfumes of Araby cannot eliminate the taint of booze from the black past of the tune," wrote the *New York World*. "It may even be true that certain difficult intervals in the song were intended to be filled with hiccups."[27]

With the presidency in the hands of conservative Republicans through the 1920s, the National Park Service took the lead in preserving the past and presiding over its public presentation. With the hospital on the grounds of Fort McHenry shuttered, Congress again considered the future of the property. On Flag Day in 1922, U.S. Representative Linthicum and Maryland Senator Joseph France hosted President Warren Harding at the dedication of a federally funded sculpture at the fort. Many Marylanders expressed disappointment that the statue depicted Orpheus, the legendary Greek god of music, rather than Francis Scott Key. A bas-relief on the base includes a bust of Key and a dedication to the fort's defenders. The *Baltimore Sun* crowed that the city finally "received her distinguished service medal 'for valor in action.'" Public schools held special events leading up to the big day and required students to sing *The Star-Spangled Banner* during every gathering, a process designed to burn the words "into their minds with A, B, C, and the three R's." Harding's speech represented a milestone—the first national presidential radio broadcast. On hand to dedicate Fort McHenry as a "sacred shrine of American patriotism," Harding referred to the song as an "invocation" to the flag and the embodiment of "militant Americanism." Though the canon included other patriotic songs, "none has, even for a moment, threatened the throne which 'The Star Spangled Banner' occupies as the royal anthem of American patriotism."[28]

The day before the monument's unveiling, Augusta Stetson, a prominent Christian Scientist in New York City, blitzed newspapers with ads trumpeting "'The Star-Spangled Banner,' with its words breathing hatred of our

Anglo-Saxon brother, Britain, and its music borrowed from a ribald, English drinking song, 'Anacreon in Heaven,' can never become Our National Anthem." A confidante of Christian Science founder Mary Baker Eddy, Stetson, who inspired Kitty Cheatham's campaign against *The Star-Spangled Banner* in the late 1910s, objected to the allegedly violent nature of the song and the "evil influence" it exerted on children. Stetson contended that "from the pages of America's historic record, 'The Star-Spangled Banner' is today being erased, by fiat of God." Another goal included Stetson's desire to promote her own composition, *Our America*, written in 1916 with Alice Morgan Harrison: "America, on-pressing van / Of all the hopes of waking man / We love thy flag! / Thy stately flag of steadfast stars / And white, close held to heart-red bars / Which none shall drag!"[29]

Stetson's high-profile campaign attracted the wrath of Irish nationalists, who insisted on airing *The Star-Spangled Banner* whenever possible to remind Americans of English wrongdoing and rally public opinion behind their cause. In 1923, Irish activists in New York City almost turned free concerts in Central Park into riots. Bandleader Harry Barnhart refused to play the song, claiming that a group of people "with a venomous spirit . . . incited heated arguments among the people present, during and after the concert, over the political question between England and Ireland." The bandleader's position prompted a confrontation with an Irish police captain, who insisted that Barnhart perform the song. Barnhart sabotaged his cause when he called *The Star-Spangled Banner* warlike and pointed out that the tune possessed no official sanction. New York City Parks Commissioner Francis Gallatin cited a standing order that all concerts in city parks must begin with the song and denied that the pro-Irish Universal Truth Forum attempted to compel the song's airing, referring to the protestors as a "bunch of agitators." He also dismissed Barnhart as a "professional pacifist." Gallatin brought in the Seventy-First Regiment Band as a substitute. When the bandleader told Gallatin that his group typically ended concerts with *My Country, 'Tis of Thee*, which would evoke an obvious association with *God Save the King* and perhaps incite the crowd even more, the commissioner told them to proceed anyway.[30] The following year, city officials catering to the Irish vote held hearings on Stetson's campaign, and the American Association for the Recognition of the Irish Republic hauled her in front of Wood Loudon, the city's deputy commissioner of accounts. Accused of receiving assistance from England to help subvert the Irish cause, Stetson testified that she spent $16,000 of her own money to place the ads. Beginning in 1925, she resumed her campaign in the major daily newspapers in New York City, Albany, Boston, and Washington, D.C., which continued through the end of the decade.[31]

With flag worship becoming more entrenched, militant patriots, in league with commercial interests, began to influence the federal government regarding patriotic practices. During World War I, Bernard Cigrand, a primary Flag Day promoter, compiled a flag treatise published and distributed by the Marshall Field & Company department store in Chicago. In Baltimore, Mrs. Holloway, in her role as state chairman of the Daughters of 1812 Committee for the Prevention of the Desecration of the Flag, distributed over two thousand copies of a flag code. In the 1920s, the Commonwealth of Massachusetts and the John Hancock Life Insurance Company published *The Flag of the United States, with Rules for Correct Use and Proper Display*, which referenced *The Star-Spangled Banner*. To aid teachers, G.A.R. patriotic instructor Hosea W. Rood issued *A Little Flag Book*.[32]

Congress, hesitant to tackle a nonpressing emotional issue, avoided anthem legislation as long as possible, arguing that popular custom reflected the people's will. For years, Pennsylvanians and Marylanders remained active in Washington, D.C., on behalf of *The Star-Spangled Banner*, but once they finally received outside support, the campaign gained traction. In 1924, the uncertain status of Fort McHenry, coupled with pressure from well-organized interest groups, led the House Committee on the Judiciary to consider two national anthem bills, one introduced by Representative Linthicum, the other sponsored by Representative Emanuel Celler (D-N.Y.). Speakers at the hearing referred to holy sites, fallen martyrs, and reverential historical events. Though committee chairman George S. Graham (R-Pa.) handed his two colleagues the floor, Linthicum's opening appeal fell flat. Celler then asserted that the anthem aired "at all occasions—at the grave, in camp, on ships, in the lodge room, in the church, in the school room; wherever there is some patriotic inspiration its inception always is in 'The Star Spangled Banner.'"

Representative John Hill (R-Md.) argued that formal recognition would send a message that "people like this woman Stetson can not go around and try to throw mud on the national anthem, which is the same thing as throwing mud on the American Flag and mud on the memory of the men who, when they were buried, had that 'Star-Spangled Banner' in their minds when the bugle blew taps over them." As Mrs. Holloway indelicately put it, "bodies have been brought home to the strains of the 'Star-Spangled Banner.'" She urged the bill's passage, "so that all the school children to-day can sing the national anthem and have it instilled in their hearts." Emissaries from the G.A.R., the Sons of the American Revolution, the American Legion, and the United Spanish War Veterans of New York City also testified. John Martin, representing the Bureau for American Ideals, called it "sacrilegious" to defile the song: "When the 'Star-Spangled Banner' is played, spontaneously everybody rises, and if anybody does not rise, they are very soon shook up and may be knocked down and made to get up again." No one spoke against the song, yet the impassioned pleas failed to stir action and the bills died.[33]

That same year, Linthicum and Holloway turned their attention to Fort McHenry and the House Committee on Military Affairs, which held a hearing to designate the site as a national monument. By 1924, abandoned army buildings and a small immigration station occupied the grounds of the former fort. At the hearing, Linthicum claimed that the 1814 clash in Baltimore harbor represented "one of the decisive battles of the world." Fort McHenry, said Holloway, should "be preserved for all time as a patriotic shrine for all true Americans." A resolution supporting the bill and referring to the fort as "hallowed ground" sailed through the state legislature in Annapolis, Maryland. On Defenders Day, September 12, 1925, Congress designated the decommissioned fort as a national park.[34]

In another federal action, the War Department aggregated popular practices and established a set of flag recommendations that served as a blueprint for the Flag Code. At a National Flag Conference convened by the American Legion at D.A.R. headquarters in Washington, D.C., sixty-eight organizations, including the U.S. Army and U.S. Navy, adopted the code on Flag Day 1923. In addition to guidelines on handling, folding, and displaying Old Glory, along with other directives, the document recommended *The Star-Spangled Banner* for "universal recognition as the National Anthem" and directed civilians to "stand at attention, men removing the headdress" during renditions of the song. In President Harding's speech before the assembly, he asked, "Don't you think we ought to insist upon every American being able to sing 'The Star Spangled Banner'?" Harding noted that when audiences try to sing what he called "our national anthem," all but 2 percent "mumbled the words, pretending to sing." Somehow, he said, "I would like the spirit of American patriotism and devotion enabled to express itself in song."[35] Almost every major newspaper published the Flag Code on July 4, 1923. Colonel James A. Moss, who founded the United States Flag Association in 1924, distributed copies that included a history of Key's creation, along with a rundown of proper behavior and performance practices. He claimed that "paying respect to the National Anthem is becoming general amongst civilians, with whom it is now customary to rise (and uncover if covered)." Moss included strict performance guidelines, and he devised a catechism of ninety-four questions concerning the flag and thirty-six queries regarding the song in order to help children master the material. Moss also compiled another pamphlet, *The Flag: How to Respect It, How to Display It*, and patriotic organizations claimed to have distributed fourteen million copies of it.[36]

After Garland Powell left the Americanism Commission of the American Legion in 1925, Walter Joyce, the V.F.W.'s self-appointed super patriot, turned his focus toward *The Star-Spangled Banner*. Raised in Massachusetts, Joyce grew up in a military family. In his youth, he formed and commanded a school battalion. After moving to New York City, he saw active duty in the Spanish-American War and organized the first V.F.W post in Manhattan. He belonged to a range of fraternal and patriotic organizations, including the American Flag Association, the Sons of the Revolution, the Freemasons, the Knights of Pythias, and the Knights Templar.[37] Joyce cultivated Representatives Hamilton Fish III (R-N.Y.) and Emanuel Celler, both of whom allied with veterans and backed anthem legislation. At the 1925 V.F.W. national encampment in Tulsa, Oklahoma, the anthem issue became a topic of discussion. The proceedings opened with an invocation, followed by a rendition of *The Star-Spangled Banner* by Miss Dorothy Aggas. The group's platform promised a determined fight "to secure the adoption of the 'Star-Spangled Banner' by the next Congress as our national anthem in reality as well as at heart," a move "long sought by our organization." The chairman said that "the recent attack on this beautiful anthem in paid advertising by Mrs. Stetson seems to have created a reaction against her, and I intreat our national encampment at the session to again indorse the bill and lend hearty support."

As head of the Americanization Committee, Joyce borrowed the slogan "One flag, one country, one language" from patriotic education advocate George Balch's Pledge of Allegiance. Joyce, who often complained about his health and bemoaned his "entirely inadequate help," nonetheless modeled his several activities after those of the national patriotic instructor of the Grand Army of the Republic, promoting Flag Day, supporting the distribution of flags in schools, and fighting "the abridgment or mutilation of our national anthem." Joyce also sponsored essay contests and, in 1925, circulated 110,000 copies of his flag etiquette pamphlet and published it in two hundred magazines and newspapers. He also campaigned on behalf of Americanization Day, observed on April 27, the birthday of Ulysses S. Grant. Joyce designed the holiday to help eliminate the existence of "hyphenated Americans" and reverse the "appalling ignorance as to the proper respect for our national emblem" among the native born.[38]

The American Legion and the V.F.W. alienated foes in the universities and at many newspapers, attracting criticism for undertaking the "work of reaction and suppression under the mask of patriotism." The cry of "100 percent Americanism" really came to mean "100 percent agreement with the American Legion point of view." Opponents wrote that the Legion claimed to serve as "the court of last appeal in the use and interpretation of patriotic symbols" and engaged in "emotional conditioning" to fortify "their power over the American mind." Legionnaires sometimes resorted to street violence, preventing peace signs from being carried at a Boston Armistice Day parade, for example, and disrupting a 1926 conference held by the New England Fellowship of Youth for Peace in Concord, Massachusetts, with stink bombs, eggs, and stones. Such tactics invited comparisons with Italian fascists.[39]

Other supporters of *The Star-Spangled Banner* organized elaborate commemorations and publicity programs. A multistate network of D.A.R. and Colonial Dames chapters raised money to install the Star-Spangled Banner National Peace Chime at Washington Memorial Church in Valley Forge, Pennsylvania, on July 4, 1926, the 150th anniversary of the Declaration of Independence. Thirteen bells, representing the original colonies, intoned the notes of *The Star-Spangled Banner*. In part, this nod to peace deflected charges that the song glorified war. Founders of the chapel referred to it as a shrine to "God and Country," a welcoming site where "all differences are forgotten and Jew and Gentile, Roman Catholic and Protestant, worship side by side in the great American Brotherhood." In 1927, on another symbolic date, the United States Flag Association commemorated the 150th anniversary of the adoption of the Stars and Stripes with a vesper flag service on the steps of Congress. Colonel Moss, the association's director general, delivered an address entitled "The Religion of the Flag." The ceremony featured *Nearer My God to Thee* and *God of Our Fathers*—along with *My Country, 'Tis of Thee*; *The Battle Hymn of the Republic*; *America the Beautiful*; and *The Star-Spangled Banner*—followed by a benediction.[40]

Baltimore and the state of Maryland commemorated World War I by funding an elaborate War Memorial Building in Baltimore, completed in 1925—a massive neoclassical structure that served as a clubhouse for local patriotic organizations. In 1927, public financing helped establish the Star-Spangled Banner Flag House in downtown Baltimore. On the tenth anniversary of Armistice Day, November 11, 1928, the Flag House Association—which restored the building where Mary Pickersgill sewed the original star-spangled banner and turned the house into a museum—dedicated the home as a "national shrine." Congressman Linthicum served as an active member, and Mrs. Holloway sat on its board of directors. The museum encouraged the adoption of *The Star-Spangled Banner* as the national anthem and pledged to promote "true patriotism and love of Country, and education, and fraternity among its citizens." Article III of its founding document restricted membership to "any white person above the age of twenty-one of good moral character and reputation, and who is unfailing in loyalty to the United States."[41]

The battle over *The Star-Spangled Banner* also filtered into the schools. In Sioux City, Iowa, Bible lessons accompanied the state history and patriotism curriculum, developed by M. G. Clark, the schools superintendent for the state of Iowa, and a committee of teachers. Students performed the Bellamy salute during the Pledge of Allegiance, and teachers encouraged local and state pride, along with patriotic national sentiments. In addition to Key's creation and *My Country, 'Tis of Thee*, students also sang *Iowa, Beautiful Land*, the official state song, and recited the Creed of Iowa. Flag and anthem etiquette instructions suggested: "When the 'Star Spangled

Banner' is played all present should rise and stand at attention until the end. Medleys using the 'Star Spangled Banner' are in poor taste and must never be used in the Sioux City schools."[42]

The American Legion and the V.F.W., among others, supported instituting oaths of allegiance for teachers and holding patriotic exercises in the schools. In Rhode Island, education superintendent Walter Ranger continued to prepare programs to enhance public school celebrations of G.A.R. Flag Day. Teachers in the state took a loyalty pledge acknowledging their "right of personal opinion" as citizens, but whether on or off duty, the rules banned them from expressing views "that conflict with honor to country, loyalty to American ideals, and obedience to and respect for the laws of Nation and State." One assembly program included the poem "For God and Country" by Edgar A. Guest, whose title referenced the motto of the American Legion: "And who can name beneath the sky / A better cause for which to die? For God and Country!" Elmer S. Hosner, a professor at the Rhode Island College of Education, referred to proper music instruction as "national security." He claimed that "if we want to make loyal citizens of our immigrant population, sing with them 'The Star Spangled Banner' and 'America' ['My Country, 'Tis of Thee']." In 1924, for the first time, state officials included Bible citations within the Flag Day pamphlets. One poem, "The Color Guard," quoted *The Star-Spangled Banner*'s opening lines and declared: "Flag of peace or flag of battle! Children it is yours to love! / Will you honor and defend it, as the gift from God above?" One school principal in Pawtucket, Rhode Island, claimed that to remove the flag from the schools would be like taking "the cross of Christ from the Christian Church."[43]

In the mid-1920s, liberal patriots encouraged teachers and administrators to adopt less strident forms of civil religious worship. In response, the president general of the Pennsylvania D.A.R. urged the group's members to oppose school boards that disseminated "propaganda which, in the guise of so-called peace literature, is in reality dangerous and insidious pacifist dogma." She also criticized the spread of "widely distributed disarmament pamphlets, posters, placards, competitive prize essays," and other efforts to "disparage the traditional teaching of patriotism in the public schools." In Baltimore, Mrs. Holloway worked with Representative Linthicum's wife to line up "all the patriotic societies for a determined and concerted drive against the anti-Star Spangled Banner propagandists." Margaret McCluer, national president of the American War Mothers, claimed in 1926 that "the pacifists have been waging war against the 'Star-Spangled Banner,'" citing a passage in the *Young Comrade* magazine that "the first songs you are taught are the capitalist and patriotic ones, such as 'America,' 'The Star-Spangled Banner,' and 'Beautiful America.' Don't sing these songs. We shall sing the 'Internationale' and the 'Red Flag.'" In 1927, the New Jersey Federation of Women's Clubs attempted to eliminate *The Star-Spangled Banner* and all songs referencing war from the Newark public schools. Louise Westwood, the music supervisor for the school system, agreed, saying "women interested in the promotion of peace" should train "children to abhor war and enmity toward people of other nations." Militant patriots denounced the American Federation of Teachers, the Association for Peace Education, the Intercollegiate Peace Association, and the National Students Forum as communists and internationalists.[44]

Pacifists, educators, aesthetic objectors, and anti-alcohol advocates publicly endorsed *America the Beautiful* instead of *The Star-Spangled Banner* as the national anthem. The National Federation of Women's Clubs, the National Association of Organists, and the National Hymn Society claimed that *America the Beautiful* "expresses the highest and deepest emotions of patriotism, not in any spirit of militant aggression and world-conquering imperialism, but with a profound gratitude and affection for the country, the government, and the traditions that have made us what we are." The Hymn Society of America drafted a bill for Congress to consider. As the issue came closer to a vote in Congress, the faculty at Teachers College in New York City argued that *America the Beautiful* promoted "love of home, neighborliness, good citizenship." The Music Supervisors' National Conference criticized *The Star-Spangled Banner* for referring to a single historical event, promoting militarism, and being difficult for schoolchildren to perform. Yet *America the Beautiful* suffered from a limited historical legacy, and its backers remained disorganized and outnumbered. In addition, experiments with musical pairings continued to cause confusion. According to one account, "the poem [*America the Beautiful*] has been sung to various old tunes and many new ones. It has been set to music more frequently than any hymn in 100 years." Even its poet, Katherine Bates, considered the musical issue of *America the Beautiful* to be unsettled. She reportedly stood when *The Star-Spangled Banner* aired and declined to promote her creation, letting it "go as far as popular goodwill carries it. As for 'pushing' it or 'urging' it or striving to have it 'supplant' something else, nothing could be more at variance with my constant attitude toward it nor more averse to my temperament."[45]

New Englanders promoted *My Country, 'Tis of Thee* and *The Battle Hymn of the Republic*, and bashers of *The Star-Spangled Banner* sponsored song contests to undermine Key's creation. In 1926, dissatisfied with *Materna* as the musical accompaniment to the words of *America the Beautiful*, the National Federation of Music Clubs held a competition to replace it, which attracted 961 compositions from every state in the union, Alaska, Hawaii, England, France, and India. No submission conformed to the judges' high standards, however. In 1928, *Musical America* magazine awarded $3,000 to composer Ernest Bloch for winning an anthem contest, and wealthy New York City socialite Florence Brooks-Aten offered the same sum as first prize in a national anthem competition. Claiming that *The Star-Spangled Banner* "has tried men's souls," she said that if anyone asked "a banker, or a merchant, or a doctor, or almost any average American he won't be able to tell you what our national anthem is." Practically everyone looked "upon 'My Country 'Tis of Thee' as the American national anthem." The contest attracted 4,500 entries, though she declined to award a prize.[46]

In 1928, the passage of the Kellogg-Briand Pact, which attempted to eliminate war as an instrument to resolve disputes between nations, gave hope to liberal patriots who opposed militant music and supported *America the Beautiful*. A humorous article in the *Baltimore Evening Sun* lampooned the sentiment, with its headline warning that "Pacifists Would Disarm French National Anthem," one of the bloodiest anthems in the world. "No definite substitute is proposed. It is difficult to imagine fitting pacifistic words to the martial music of the 'Marseillaise.'" Satirical lyrics in the article ridiculed the drive to outlaw war and, by extension, eliminate the influence of emblematic songs born of struggle: "Come, children of international brotherhood / The day of Geneva is here / The World Court will settle our possible differences / The Anti-War Treaty will defend us against aggressors / Disarm! Disarm! / And let whoever transgresses the comity of nations / Be forever despised by all righteous people!"[47]

Mrs. Holloway, who criticized *America the Beautiful* as a "namby-pamby," though a "fairly good Harvest Home Song," continued to preach on behalf of *The Star-Spangled Banner*. In an address to the Women's Patriotic Conference on National Defense in 1928, she warned that "every custom and law held sacred by the American people is being attacked in some form by un-American Americans," a favorite phrase of hers. No composer could write a suitable substitute to Key's song on a whim, she said. "ANTHEMS ARE INSPIRED—NOT MADE TO ORDER!!!!!" Holloway also decried churches and Y.M.C.A and Y.W.C.A. summer camps as hotbeds of propaganda for using a songbook that purposely omitted *The Star-Spangled Banner* and *My Country, 'Tis of Thee*, criticizing them for substituting a new anthem whose "words will be sung by increasing thousands of America's young people to the tune of the Russian hymn."[48]

Throughout the 1920s, Representative Linthicum reported to Holloway regarding the progress of his national anthem bills. One year, he wrote that the measure "is not classed with the vital matters of Congress." The following year he blamed a short session for his inability to secure a hearing: "Nothing will be taken up except supply bills, and a very few important measures appertaining to farmers and other essential financial matters." In 1927, Linthicum's letter stated that "nothing of any great importance with the exception of appropriations bills can possibly be passed."[49] Without help, Maryland patriots would never have been able to convince Congress to pass an anthem bill. Linthicum and Holloway initially had no idea that nationwide support had arrived en masse in 1928, when Colonel Joyce of the V.F.W. decided to push the issue "to the limit." Joyce blanketed the country with blank petition forms and solicited testimonials for *The Star-Spangled Banner* with the help of the V.F.W. Ladies' Auxiliary and hundreds of other like-minded groups. He also transposed the song into four different keys, to accommodate a wider range of voices. Public relations stunts included sending a caravan of cars—festooned with red, white, and blue and filled with petitions supporting *The Star-Spangled Banner*—from New York to Washington, D.C. Always seeking money, Joyce wrote to his V.F.W. superiors in 1928: "I believe that this will be the greatest piece of patriotic publicity that the organization has ever obtained and that its value can not be counted in dollars and cents." He also reorganized the National Star-Spangled Banner Association, modeled after Baltimore Mayor James

Preston's initiative in the 1910s, and declared September 10-15, 1928, as Star-Spangled Banner Week.[50]

In April 1929, the year *America the Beautiful* poet Katherine Bates died, congressmen Linthicum of Maryland and Celler of New York introduced anthem bills in the House of Representatives. Senator Arthur Robinson (R-Ind.) introduced a similar measure in the upper chamber. In November, a panel of the syndicated cartoon strip *Ripley's Believe It or Not!* revealed that "America has no National Anthem! The U.S.A. (being a dry country) has been using—without authorization—a vulgar old British drinking song." Ripley quoted the most risqué line from *To Anacreon in Heaven* ("long may the sons of Anacreon entwine—the myrtle of Venus with Bacchus's vine") and depicted a group of red-nosed tipplers cavorting in a tavern. The cartoon's influence on Congress is debatable, but the House Judiciary Committee agreed to hold hearings in January 1930.

Until this time, Holloway and Linthicum knew nothing about Joyce's campaign. At a speech recalling the moment he found out about the V.F.W. efforts, Linthicum said that "I was astonished when I learned of the great amount of work which had been done to assist in the passage of the bill." Holloway experienced "such a shock from which I will never recover," once it became clear that Joyce and his allies had gathered the requisite nationwide support. She accused the V.F.W. of stealing the limelight and tried to downplay their impact. After reading an article that Holloway wrote omitting his contribution, Joyce sent her a pointed letter, admonishing her that "in mentioning those that made an effort to further the interests of the Star Spangled Banner Bill in Congress, you do not mention our organization." He also claimed: "I do not think the people of Maryland have done half of what they should have done. I want to ask you a question. Has any other organization done half what we have?" Joyce did add that he never intended to start an argument and assured Holloway that "we have the utmost respect for you and your sincere efforts and hope the day will come when we will have a joint celebration of every patriotic organization." Holloway, who never typed her letters and wrote in difficult-to-decipher script, replied that she never heard of the V.F.W. campaign efforts: "No one, Colonel Joyce, can detract from" the "efforts of the Daughters of 1812—1918-1929 to protect our anthem." She contended that her associates could have matched the five million signatures Joyce gathered and complained that "our field has been invaded." In full defensive mode, Holloway alerted Linthicum about an article that she interpreted as a slight to her contribution. The congressman replied that he exerted "no control over newspaper reports," adding, "I have seen to it that you have been given every credit possible in the hearings and in the report."[51]

On the eve of the proceedings, the V.F.W. arranged a conference at D.A.R. national headquarters in Washington, D.C., attended by delegates of more than eighty allied organizations.[52] The hearing by the House Committee on the Judiciary, held on January 30, 1930, represented an historic opportunity. After committee chairman Leonidas Dyer (R-Mo.) called the assembly to order, the U.S. Navy band filed in to back singer Elsie Jorss Reilley in a rendition of the song under question. Dyer, who introduced anthem legislation in 1917, tolerated a circuslike atmosphere and allowed thirty-four impassioned witnesses to testify. In his stirring opening speech, Linthicum claimed that *The Star-Spangled Banner* "united us into one great Nation, it gave us patriotism; it gave us something to center ourselves about and it meant more to the cause of freedom . . . than a thousand or ten thousand bayonets." With Holloway too ill to attend, Linthicum read her words aloud. The "anthem for the people" would help assimilate newcomers. The issue came down to education, she wrote, since many immigrants insisted on "clinging to the anthem of their country; many, even Americans, wanting to thrust upon us other anthems to supplant our beloved 'Star-Spangled Banner'! Behold the Flag!" The statement quoted the title of the verse "Behold the Flag" by Ignatius Murphy, sanctioned by the D.A.R., which called Old Glory the "purest, most potent emblem of law, order, [and] Christian civilization that ever saluted the dawn."[53]

After the applause faded, Walter Joyce hauled in crates that contained what he called the "fifty-mile petition," a compilation of five million signatures from across the country. Officials from the governor on down had signed a 70-foot-long scroll titled "How Minnesota Stands on the Star-Spangled Banner Campaign." Joyce also produced statements of support from two thousand organizations, including Americans in the Philippines; the American War Mothers of Tucson, Arizona; the housewives and teachers of Boone, Iowa; bus operators in Greenville, South Carolina; and the employees of the Department of Corrections in Albany, New York. "Previous attempts to secure this recognition have failed because Congress lacked evidence of a general desire among the people for such action," he said, and ended his presentation by calling for "divine inspiration" to guide the committee's decision. The bill's sole foe, a dejected Kitty Cheatham, testified the next day. After the hearing, *Outlook* magazine criticized Congress for showing a "profound disbelief in the ability of any future poet or composer to create something better."[54]

The House Committee unanimously approved the motion to designate *The Star-Spangled Banner* "as a method of further increasing the patriotism of the people of our country, and the continued popularity of the anthem." The sixth anthem bill introduced by Representative Linthicum during his career, H.R. 14 (symbolizing September 14, 1814), came to a vote on April 21, 1930, when the House passed it without dissent. The bill quoted President Wilson's 1916 order, declaring "that the composition consisting of the words and music known as 'The Star-Spangled Banner' is designated as the national anthem of the United States of America." The Senate's Committee on the Library shelved the matter until late January 1931, as Congress squabbled over issues related to the Depression. In the interim, Joyce revived the efforts of the National Star-Spangled Banner Association and maintained pressure on Congress. On March 3, 1931, with the legislative session scheduled to end at noon, filibusters knotted both houses. Senator Millard Tydings (D-Md.) convinced five holdouts to drop their objections and steered through a symbolic unanimous vote on behalf of the anthem measure. House members, who had arranged for the U.S. Marine Band and the Interstate Commerce Commission Male Chorus to close out the session, filled the chamber with reverie for an hour as representatives took turns singing quartets and solos. To end the proceedings, Mrs. J. Charles Linthicum "unfurled a large flag from the gallery and the assembly sang the national anthem."[55]

Sitting at a desk and surrounded by advisors in a Senate antechamber blue with cigar smoke, President Herbert Hoover awaited the various legislative measures with pen in hand. Congress eventually presented him with over four hundred bills, and, of these, the beleaguered executive signed twenty-six into law immediately, including the national anthem act. With his popularity plummeting as the Depression deepened, Hoover had attracted the venom of veterans' groups incensed over his handling of the World War I bonus issue and the restructuring of the Veterans' Department. For Hoover, a notorious tightwad, signing the anthem bill required no monetary commitment, and, with two strokes of a pen, the reelection-minded president appeased ex-soldiers and appeared to be cooperative with a contentious Congress. The *Baltimore Sun* ran a cartoon showing Uncle Sam, holding a newspaper bearing the headline "Congress Votes 'Star-Spangled Banner' National Anthem," with a question mark over his head. The caption read "I Wonder if They'll Make Me Learn the Words Now?"[56]

In June, Hoover embarked on a campaign swing through the Midwest that brought him to Indianapolis, Indiana, home base of the American Legion. An advance guard of soldiers led the president's motorcade along the flag-draped route between Union Station and the governor's mansion. Met by an American Legion drum corps, a color guard, and representatives of several patriotic organizations at War Memorial Plaza, the president paid tribute to the state's war dead. That night, Hoover attended a fried chicken dinner arranged by the Indiana Republican Editorial Association, where he called for the government to "strengthen the foundations of a better and stronger national life." After the talk, the Indiana Military Band struck the first notes of the anthem and "the audience rose to its feet as one man." Reverend V. G. Leazenby, a local Methodist minister, closed the evening with a benediction.[57]

Trials and Triumphs, 1931–1954

THE FIRST FLAG DAY after Congress passed the national anthem bill in 1931 fell on a Sunday. The date prompted the National Society, United States Daughters of 1812, to hold a "most impressive service" at War Memorial Plaza in Baltimore, with the help of fifty-two patriotic, veterans', hereditary, and fraternal organizations. Congressman J. Charles Linthicum, who died the following year, bestowed on Mrs. Ella Holloway the pen that President Herbert Hoover used to sign the legislation and a photostatic copy of the law. The stalwart dowager pledged to hand them down "to posterity to inspire patriotism in the coming generations," and the artifacts are now located at Fort McHenry. On a day set aside for celebration, controversy erupted when a boy scout participating in the flag column held aloft a Confederate banner. Several veterans' organizations and auxiliaries refused to march. Asked about the incident, Holloway replied that "it is a shame to spoil such a beautiful occasion as this with talk of friction." In a letter to the *Baltimore Sun*, she explained: "Today, there is no North, there is no South, nor East nor West. We are a sovereign nation of many sovereign states, one and inseparable. A perfect Union."[1]

Yet consensus over national icons—including the national anthem—remained elusive. The codification of *The Star-Spangled Banner* in 1931 fueled even more rancor, because the terse law avoided references to lyrics, arrangements, or performance practices, since Congress never intended to enforce a welter of regulations regarding the anthem. Without clear guidelines on any of these matters, reactions to the national anthem remained spontaneous. Militant patriots lobbied to further refine standards of worship toward the flag and the anthem, but their efforts crashed into a wall of apathy. One week after the national anthem bill became law, state representative Louis Cuvillier of New York City introduced a bill in Albany requiring that the song be played at all public assemblies and sung "in whole or in part" at least once a week in every school that received public funds.[2] The next year, "amid a few audible chuckles" in the House, Representative Claude Fuller (D-Ark.) proposed a resolution "to compel every civil service employee to prove his ability to sing, recite, or write from memory" the words of *The Star-Spangled Banner* as a condition of employment.[3]

As Congress turned its attention to Depression issues, Walter Joyce at the Veterans of Foreign Wars lamented their lack of action on flag and anthem legislation. In his report to the national encampment in 1932, he wrote that "it has been absolutely impossible to foster any patriotic bills that have 'teeth enough in them' to be worthy of being advanced by an organization such as ours." Joyce expressed optimism that "when Congress gets settled down again so that they will listen to us we have bills for the protection of our flag and other unpatriotic matters of importance."[4] That same year J. I. Billman, the V.F.W.'s national historian, cautioned that "there are in our country powerful groups of men and women who not only fought the 'Star Spangled Banner' bill at every turn, but are constantly working against adequate national preparedness." He stated that these forces attempted to make the youth international minded, destroy reverence for patriotic institutions, and belittle the achievements of the forefathers. Moreover, they "sneer openly or covertly at every effort made by veteran and patriotic bodies to keep alive that militant spirit of patriotism which has been the bulwark of our national existence."[5]

A widely circulated pamphlet entitled *The Flag of the United States: How to Display It, How to Respect It*, written and published in 1934 by Colonel James A. Moss of the United States Flag Association, suggested that readers "use and handle" the flag "as you would your Mother's picture." Religious allusions underscored his point: "As the Cross is the symbol of the Christian's faith, and the Star of David is the emblem of the Jew's religion, so is the Flag of the United States the badge of the American's political faith. And as the sign of the Cross is to the Christian a religious sacramental, so is the salute to the Flag the American's national sacramental." Yet Moss warned about adopting "a sort of 'glorified idolatry' that makes the would-be 'patriot' ridiculous," writing that "we should guard against so-called 'Flag Worship'—blind and excessive adulation of the Flag as an emblem or image."

Moss included a short section outlining national anthem rituals that offered impractical and contradictory advice. "Whether or not we should stand when 'The Star-Spangled Banner' is heard over the radio depends on circumstances," wrote Moss. "Generally speaking, if it seems natural and not forced to stand and uncover, it should be done; otherwise, it should not. For example, if sitting in a living room or elsewhere reading or talking, one should stand. On the other hand, if eating at a table, talking over the telephone, playing cards, cooking a meal, or taking a bath, it would be forced and unnatural to stand." Presumably referring to live performances or renditions heard over a radio, he wrote that the "proper thing to do" if the song is heard "when walking along the street, if the music is near, you should stop, stand at attention, and uncover. If driving in an automobile, if the music is near, the car should be stopped, all conversation cease, and the men (remaining seated) uncover." The song could also stand in for the sacred flag: "All present should stand and face toward the music. Those in uniform should salute at the first note of the Anthem, retaining this position until the last note. All others should stand at attention, men removing the headdress. When the Flag is displayed, the regular 'Salute to the Flag' should be given."[6]

Moss sold other pamphlets to veterans' and patriotic groups and partnered with established businesses to help increase the distribution of this material. The Equitable Life Insurance Company of Des Moines, Iowa, sponsored an eight-page booklet by the United States Flag Association, *Our Star Spangled Banner: It Protects Us All.*[7] Moss earmarked its profits to conduct patriotic educational work among "the youth of America." The flag pamphlet appeared in textbooks across the country, including *Our Flag and Our Schools*, a collection of patriotic readings, songs, plays, and presentations put together by Delaware's state school superintendent, Samuel Engle Burr, in 1936, with assistance from the American Legion. In addition to including Moss's flag pamphlet, the textbook also supplied all four verses of the national anthem and the words to the state song, *Our Delaware*. Education officials sent a copy to every school in the tiny state and vowed to distribute more "as funds become available." Requests for the book came from as far away as Colorado.[8]

Burr compiled the work primarily to "secure an attitude of respect for the flag on the part of every citizen of the state" and to "secure continued and more prominent display of the flag on proper occasions." He also suggested that students "learn to stand at attention, facing the flag, during the flag salute, the singing of *The Star Spangled Banner* and *America*, and during the playing of *To The Colors*," a bugle call traditionally used by the military whenever a band is unavailable.[9] In the essay "Respect the Flag," Alvin M. Owsley, past national commander of the American Legion, exhorted youngsters to participate in public displays of patriotism, while indicating that the practice of standing for the anthem remained spotty. "When you hear the band play 'The Star-Spangled Banner' while you are in a restaurant or hotel dining room, get up even if you rise alone; stand there and don't be ashamed of it either!" Owsley urged readers to honor the flag "as you would reverence the signature of the Deity. Listen, son! The band is playing the national anthem—'The Star-Spangled Banner'! They have let loose Old Glory yonder. Stand up—and others will stand with you." An Armistice Day program, held at the William Penn School in New Castle, Delaware, opened with a display of colors and a "community singing" of one verse of *My Country, 'Tis of Thee*. With representatives of the American Legion on hand, the children joined veterans to sing songs from World War I, read the Bible, recite the Lord's Prayer, and salute the flag. The event ended with another community sing featuring the first verse of the national anthem, which closed almost every ceremony outlined in the book.[10]

As the economy weakened during the Great Depression, veterans' groups suffered. V.F.W. patriotism chief Walter Joyce reported that "to a greater extent than ever before we find ourselves constantly in touch with many schools and educational institutions," and that interest in the national anthem "during the past year has been much greater than ever before." One California post sold three hundred sheet music copies of the anthem and made "a very respectable profit."[11] But Joyce's health began to deteriorate, and he came clean about the limitations of his efforts, lamenting "the same old story": the lack of cooperation by local departments.[12] In 1934, Joyce wrote that he continued to pay the bills at his office in New York City out of pocket. Though reluctant to close shop, he discontinued his annual essay contest and sent his supply of flag etiquette pamphlets to V.F.W. national headquarters in Kansas City.

Assistant Director Victor E. Devereaux of the V.F.W.'s new National Department of Americanism pledged to continue presenting flags to schools, observing patriotic holidays, and conducting flag education efforts to combat radicalism.[13] Some statewide chapters of the V.F.W. kept Joyce's flame alive. Norman J. Carey, patriotic instructor of the Department of New York, wrote that the group must imbue "the children of our Nation . . . with a sense of loyalty to our Country, love of Flag, and a patriotism, which bespeaks well for the future of our Nation." In 1935, Joyce applauded when the Chicago School Board ordered every student in the city to recite the Pledge of Allegiance and sing the anthem daily, to "instill in the minds of youth the loftiest ideals of patriotism." The next year, the anthem received a big boost when the National Broadcasting Company (NBC) announced its intention to play the song several times a day over its radio network. "It's a patriotic move," said John Royal, NBC program director. "We have decided to broadcast 'The Star-Spangled Banner' so the people will not forget about it. England does it, so why shouldn't America? The schools sing it, so why shouldn't radio?"[14]

Influential Baltimoreans continued to guard against the denigration of *The Star-Spangled Banner*. One anthem champion, Neil H. Swanson, first gained attention after publishing *The Flag Is Still There* in 1933. Growing up in Minnesota, he remained frustrated by a lack of information about the Battle of Baltimore. After visiting Fort McHenry, Swanson determined "to find out just what happened in the little red-brick-and-green-sod fort," and the results of his study solidified his reputation in Baltimore's social circles. Swanson spoke frequently at patriotic gatherings and served as president of the Flag House Association in the 1950s.[15] Francis Scott Key-Smith, great-grandson of the composer and a lawyer in Washington, D.C., joined forces with the Daughters of the American Revolution to defend the anthem. In addition to delivering speeches at patriotic events, Key-Smith supported efforts to preserve landmarks associated with his family and wrote a number of pamphlets, including *The American Flag and the National Anthem* in 1935, which recounted the events behind his forebear's inspiration.

As always, Mrs. Holloway relished a good scrap with those who would desecrate the flag or the anthem. Until her death in 1940, she became a go-to source for local reporters, though they sometimes ridiculed her more outlandish antics and fashion sensibility. She routinely toured the city to police the proper display of Old Glory and suggested that families hold a daily flag salute in their homes before breakfast. "It is quite true that Mrs. Holloway, in her patriotic zeal, sometimes goes further than her less ardent disciples are willing to follow her," according to an editorial in the *Baltimore Evening Sun*. "But that is her way. Baltimoreans understand and appreciate her little foibles. When she is most extreme, they take joy in her." Mrs. Holloway, "in short, is an institution. An institution is never perfect." The piece also referred to her as "That Hat looming in the horizon," a reference to her "towering" black bonnets, which sometimes included a plume that shook when she spoke and stood "out and above the usual run of woman's head covering as does Mount Everest above the Himalayas."[16] An article by a *Baltimore American* gossip columnist, entitled "Mrs. Holloway Tells 'Inside'—Ssh!—Story of Her Famous Hats," revealed that "she wears them on purpose, as they enable everyone to recognize her immediately."[17]

Holloway enjoyed her status as a local celebrity. An article in the *Evening Sun* commended her for sparing "neither time nor money in her crusade" and for working "laboriously to keep the 'Star-Spangled Banner' as the National Anthem." But the reporter also had fun with her. Referring to Colonel James A. Moss's confusing instructions for when to stand during the playing of the anthem, Holloway, "Baltimore's No. 1 patriot," said that she stood for the anthem regardless of the situation, whether eating, playing cards, lying in bed, or when telephoning. Even when in the bath? "*Absolutely*! Many's the time I've done that! I didn't work thirteen years for that national anthem without learning how to respect it." She also flashed a sense of humor. The newspaper article centered on Elizabeth Faff, wife of the "No. 1 patriot" in Glendale, New York, whose husband inquired if he should wake her when the anthem played over the radio during the station's sign-off, so they could stand for the song together. Holloway sympathized with Mrs. Faff: "If Mr. Faff had been standing at attention properly and attending to its own patriotic business he wouldn't have had time to bother his wife. One cannot respect the national anthem and bother one's wife at the same time."[18]

A friend recalled the time when a business owner painted an American flag on the side of his van. "Mrs. Holloway hauled the hapless mover into court, and after the magistrate listened to both sides, he ruled: 'If Mrs. Holloway says that it is against the law to use a painting of the American flag in an advertisement, then it's against the law.' She was the undisputed arbiter in such matters."[19] In her capacity as president of the National Society, Daughters of 1812, Holloway sent a letter to the *Baltimore Evening Sun* after Walter Joyce died in 1937, protesting the paper's recognition of his work on behalf of the national anthem bill. "Yes, the V.F.W., with numerous societies, organizations, etc., supported this bill," she wrote. And "Mr. Joyce undoubtedly did an excellent piece of work in assisting, with other organizations, to put the bill through, but it should not be overlooked that the bill was originally introduced through Representative Linthicum and Senator Tydings by the Daughters of 1812. To this organization, I think, should go the credit for its passage as we did the majority of the work. Yours in love of true history, Mrs. Ella V. Holloway."[20]

Several key developments threatened the national anthem in the 1930s. When top Philadelphia ear, nose, and throat specialist Dr. Leon Felderman presented a paper to the otolaryngological section of the Baltimore City Medical Society, he unwittingly strolled into the lion's den. "Asserting that probably more schoolchildren's voices are ruined by singing 'The Star-Spangled Banner' than any other song," Felderman "suggested that two national songs be composed, one for children, and the other for adults." Though paying due deference to the anthem, he claimed that the "abrupt alteration of pitch" placed a "great strain" on undeveloped children and made them avoid a duty they "should tenderly embrace." He also criticized the words as being so difficult that in later years, youngsters forget them. Felderman reminisced about attending a celebration in France where participants sang their anthems with gusto, but when it came to *The Star-Spangled Banner*, voices trailed off. He circulated sheet music to prove his point. Felderman repeated an old argument, of course, but his standing in the medical community lent gravitas to his opinion.[21]

In 1938, popular New York City bandleader Vincent Lopez caused a tempest after he copyrighted and publicized an arrangement of *The Star-Spangled Banner* that eliminated the high notes, making it easier for amateur musicians to sing. In a telegram sent to President Franklin Roosevelt, Lopez explained his intentions, arguing that his revisions streamlined the song and subjected it to "neither swing nor syncopation." The anthem, he wrote, "is now singable, not swingable," a reference to the controversial practice where big bands arranged jazz versions of classic songs. Bandleader Kay Kyser, among others, protested, claiming that "we don't want any jitterbugs and swing artists changing this patriotic song. . . . Call it 'Tiger Rag' or anything else, but don't change it." That same year, a New Jersey lawyer revived the Star Spangled Banner Association to safeguard the anthem and "prevent dance orchestras from 'swinging and jazzing'" the song. Lopez attracted an ally, Representative Emanuel Celler, who helped pass the 1931 anthem law. Addressing the House, Celler, a "publicity-loving Congressman," according to *Time* magazine, recounted how the melody underpinned many tunes "hardly fit for Aunt Sarah's ears," but that strong emotions toward the historic song would remain. Americans, he said, "should be encouraged to sing the anthem with a new enthusiasm and vigor, sing lustily and loudly with smiling and unworried expressions, and even learn the words." Lopez introduced his version in New York City and announced that he would perform it at the opulent Hippodrome Theater in Baltimore. That, the *Baltimore News-American* wrote, "was tantamount to a fight" with Mrs. Holloway, a "formidable one-woman army who arose to such attacks with a fervor to match those who kept the flag flying over Fort McHenry."[22]

The following year, in 1939, Metropolitan Opera tenor Frederick Jagel filed a federal lawsuit in New York to overturn the national anthem act because, he claimed, the Depression had sapped the people's will to resist. Jagel stated, "I have never seen an audience really stirred by the music or the words of Francis Scott Key's amateurish poem." He claimed that Maryland patriots railroaded the song through Congress and placed "greater emphasis on honoring a native son than they did in helping to select an anthem expressive of the hopes and aspirations of country." Jagel offered $1,000 if a replacement for what he called a "vindictive and hodge-podgy" fifth-rate composition could be found. Francis Scott Key-Smith dismissed the ploy as "tomfoolery" and said: "One of the chief troubles of this country is that is contains too many people who have too little to do. Anyone can sing the 'Star-Spangled Banner.'"[23]

None of these efforts generated staying power, but the media coverage rattled national anthem boosters. An even more serious, long-term threat emerged when Irving Berlin dusted off a twenty-year-old song called *God Bless America* and presented it to radio personality Kate Smith in 1938. Her version created an instant sensation among the American population, selling 500,000 music sheets by the end of 1939 and staying on *Billboard* magazine's hit-music charts for fifteen weeks. *God Bless America* joined *America the Beautiful* as the most viable anthem alternative to emerge in the twentieth century, but Berlin explicitly disavowed intending the song as a replacement for *The Star-Spangled Banner*. Already tired of hearing it by February 1940, singer-songwriter Woody Guthrie wrote a response initially entitled *God Blessed America*. The folk icon crafted lyrics that echoed *America the Beautiful* as a love letter to the nation's natural splendors but also delivered pointed commentary, including a controversial verse (omitted in various recordings) condemning private property. He later renamed his song *This Land Is Your Land*.[24]

Kate Smith's exuberance on behalf of *God Bless America* found a counterbalance in rival Lucy Monroe, referred to as the "Star-Spangled Soprano." A New York City native, Monroe first sang the song in 1937 at an American Legion gathering and became a favorite of veterans. After regularly singing the tune on the radio, she landed a gig at the 1939 New York World's Fair, where she starred in the final act of all 650 performances of the Oscar Hammerstein and Arthur Schwartz spectacle, "The American Jubilee."[25] During World War II, Monroe achieved a measure of fame after appearing at war bond rallies. In 1945, she claimed to have performed *The Star-Spangled Banner* 1,500 times. Monroe, a staple of every opening day and World Series game at Yankee Stadium from 1945 to 1960, also sang the anthem at countless charity events and government functions. In a 1954 article, "The Star-Spangled Girl," comedian Bennett Cerf joked at her expense: "Try to open a convention or championship prizefight without her!" Monroe had "become so identified" with the anthem, Cerf wrote, "that every time she appears with a new male escort wits immediately presume his name is Francis Scott Key." Monroe refused to sing the tune for the troops, however, since they lived the song. Asked about her "most exciting rendition," she recalled a July 4 performance attended by three hundred thousand people at the Washington Monument. "The audience kept time by waving lighted matches," she said, and at the end of the song everyone joined in the chorus. "It was the kind of moment when you could cry with pride and joy at being an American."[26] In 1961, Monroe married a Manhattan lawyer and retired from her singing career.

As *God Bless America* catapulted onto the national music scene, a new publicist for Francis Scott Key emerged in Frederick, Maryland. Edward S. Delaplaine, who rose to a judgeship on the Court of Appeals, Maryland's highest court, grew up in a newspaper family with deep ties to the town. An avid speaker and historian, Delaplaine followed his biography of Maryland's first governor, Thomas Johnson, with *Francis Scott Key: Life and Times* in 1937. The dust jacket touted the author's credentials, including his lifetime membership in the Star-Spangled Banner Flag House Association. "This thrilling life of a great son of Frederick Town could only have been written by another son of Key's birthplace. A son whose forefather . . . *built the first Frederick House.*" The blurb also carried a provocative teaser about Key's impish youth: "At one moment we see the author of the 'Star-Spangled Banner' devising tricks against unpopular college ushers; or—we find him composing pasquinades on odd characters of the town, sending shafts among the prim, starch ladies of Annapolis; suddenly we discover him galloping round the college green on the back of an unfortunate cow."[27]

With this biography, Delaplaine embarked on a lifelong public relations campaign to elevate the stature of Key and his song. Delaplaine regularly promoted the cause at home and in Annapolis and Baltimore, as well as in Washington, D.C., where he circulated in powerful circles and distributed copies of his books to dignitaries from around the world. In response to the rise of *God Bless America*, Delaplaine solicited favorable comments about *The Star-Spangled Banner* from luminaries, including Irving Berlin, who staunchly supported Key's song as the national anthem. Delaplaine and Berlin, who lived a combined 196 years and died in the same year, corresponded for decades. Delaplaine routinely fed stories about Key and the anthem to his family's daily newspaper, the *Frederick News-Post*, and also embraced the power of radio to spread the word. His main goals, however, focused on generating commemorative action on the federal level. Delaplaine supported the Baltimore Philatelic Society in their quest for a Francis Scott Key postage stamp, for example, which came to fruition in 1948.

For the 125th anniversary of *The Star-Spangled Banner* in 1939, Marylanders celebrated in grand style. State officials approved a sanitized version of the state song, *Maryland, My Maryland*, which dropped the pro-

Confederate verses. The National Park Service promoted Fort McHenry as a tourist destination and officially designated the site as a "National Monument and Historic Shrine" that same year, the only one identified as such in the entire national park system. Congress created a national committee to celebrate the milestone, ceremonially helmed by President Franklin Roosevelt, Vice President John Garner, Speaker of the House William B. Bankhead, several senators (led by Millard Tydings of Maryland), and Baltimore Mayor Howard W. Jackson. Mrs. Holloway served as chair of the Star-Spangled Banner Committee, and James E. Hancock, president of the Society of the War of 1812 and known as the "patron saint of Fort McHenry," lent his efforts.[28] The September 14th afternoon program at Fort McHenry, to which Congress contributed $5,000, featured the U.S. Marine Band, a ten-minute "community sing," and a flag-raising ceremony. After a military parade and a flyover, onetime Metropolitan Opera mezzo-soprano Cecil Arden sang the anthem over a nationwide radio broadcast. Mrs. Holloway presented the fort with a painting by George Gray, depicting Key writing his famous verses, that she had bought from the Hotel Rennert, razed in 1941. A benediction closed the proceedings. Evening ceremonies, held at Municipal Stadium, opened with an invocation by Rabbi Morris Lazaron and a benediction by Reverend H. N. Arrowsmith. The spectacle featured a "Parade of Civilians," including school children, veterans' associations, representatives of foreign nations, and fireworks. A "Military Sham Battle" showcased weapons of warfare unavailable during 1814, including an "Aeroplane Attack" with "Infantry, Artillery, Machine Guns, tanks, Armored Cars, Trench Mortars, Anti-aircraft guns, Searchlights," and airplanes. The evening ended with a "Flag Celebration" and fireworks.[29]

The anthem's anniversary coincided with the 1939 New York World's Fair, and Maryland spent $35,000 to outfit a two-room exhibit at the event. The display showcased a replica of the original star-spangled banner, an aquatint of the Fort McHenry bombardment, and a picture of Francis Scott Key, flanked by photostatic copies of his anthem manuscripts. On Maryland Day, held on July 28, the Naval Academy Band "arrived on a special train from Annapolis—acquired by a special act of Congress." By the time the B & O Glee Club climbed aboard in Baltimore, a thousand passengers jammed the cars. During his speech at the ceremony in New York, Governor Herbert R. O'Conor of Maryland referenced the song's special place in his state's historical legacy: "Three wars have been fought over our land, but we are much more likely to remind our visitors that it was a Marylander who wrote the 'Star Spangled Banner.'" In all, 764,340 visitors snapped up 51,550 booklets promoting tourism, including 21,000 "Visit Baltimore" pamphlets published by the city's Association of Commerce, 700 copies of "Visit Maryland This Fall," and 300 illustrated fish and game maps issued by the state's Conservation Department.[30]

Nationwide, anthem proponents grew restless as the country lurched toward World War II. Representative Fred L. Crawford (R-Mich.) decried any "streamlining or tampering" with the national anthem and its "sacred words," which serve as a "testimony to bravery, a testimony to freedom, and testimony that in God in Heaven do we place our trust." The song "carries American ideas, history and feelings," he wrote, inculcating a "love of flag and love of national anthem," sentiments "among the keystones of a strong union of people." Agitators, who worked "with beehive industry to reduce the fires of patriotism in America" by removing the flag from public buildings and gatherings, "would eliminate the singing of the national anthem from schools and public gatherings," due to its alleged difficulty and because "it is a 'war song.'" These movements to sabotage the anthem, Crawford wrote, "emanate from the cesspools of un-Americanism. Unfortunately, well-meaning citizens are taken in by these palavering false prophets of patriotism and unconsciously weaken their support of those things so dearly purchased by our forefathers."[31]

The results of a 1939 Gallup Poll gauging Americans' knowledge of the song cast a pall over supporters of the anthem. Only 52 percent of the survey's respondents favored playing *The Star-Spangled Banner* at the end of movie performances and radio sign-offs. Those voting against the proposal "frequently say that it means more if it isn't played too often." Others said that "patriotism should be spontaneous and not drilled into you," adding, "Americans don't like to be reminded of their loyalty." One participant stated that repetition of the anthem "would help patriotic spirit, help people learn the words, and make our customs more like those of other countries." Nine out of ten people polled approved of standing in public when the anthem aired, but only one out of eight reported knowing the words to even three verses. Half knew some words, and 32 percent could not identify the anthem's title.

In response, Mrs. John L. Whitehurst, national vice president of the General Federation of Women's Clubs and a Baltimore native, proposed a three-point campaign to put the two million members of her organization to work teaching the public the words to *The Star-Spangled Banner*. "If we are going to instill [patriotism] into the nation at this time when democracy is being threatened in all parts of the world we must do everything we can" to increase knowledge about the song, she said. "Having people know the national anthem is one of the main activities we women can carry on to help" the war effort.[32] The Gallup Poll results also elicited an alarming, provincial headline in the *Baltimore Sun*: "Concern of Mrs. Holloway over Anthem Upheld by Poll." Holloway said that "everyone knows that you only have to sing one verse," adding that it should be performed "in joyous voice. Too many people sing it as though they had rigor mortis." Arrangements, which too often "plod along," should be played "with vim."[33]

In Frederick, Judge Delaplaine compiled several statements about *The Star-Spangled Banner* attributed to John Philip Sousa and sent them to the "March King" for his approval. The bandleader acknowledged that some Americans had trouble remembering the words, but "in reply let me ask how many Nations know more than the first few lines of their National song? And what does it matter? It is the spirit of the music that inspires." The "soul-stirring" song "makes splendid march music," Sousa wrote, and served as "a very satisfactory anthem during the World War," when it "played an enormous part in arousing enthusiasm and patriotism." Sousa recalled entering a national anthem contest during World War I, which he lost. In later years, he met the author of the winning poem, "and he told me that he hadn't sold a copy of his song." Sousa added: "It would be as easy to make a stream run uphill as to secure a new National anthem as the result of a prize contest. The only possible chance that we might have a new National anthem would be when the eyes of all Americans are directed toward some particular cause and another genius captures the spirit of the moment." Until then, "I do not believe the veneration for Francis Scott Key's anthem will ever be displaced."[34]

When Canada entered World War II in 1939, after Germany invaded Poland, its hockey teams began to play their nation's unofficial anthem, *O Canada*, before every game, a practice that filtered south of the border. By 1941, when the United States declared war, *The Star-Spangled Banner* became a mainstay at movie houses and sporting events, achieving "nearly universal status" at baseball games. Some professional baseball teams also included a recitation of the Pledge of Allegiance and held popular "I Am an American Day" events. One scholar argued that repeated performances of the anthem represented publicity stunts to ensure that "there would be no questioning of the patriotism of athletes who played games while others went off to serve their country," a criticism raised during World War I.[35]

The song aired incessantly during the war years. In 1942, the *New York Times* reported that *The Star-Spangled Banner* had never "been played and sung more often in so brief a period," or been "heard by more people at once. Orchestras and bands in New York City alone are said to play it twenty thousand times a week. It opens every public gathering: the opera and the football game, the play, the fight and the dance, the banquet and the town meeting. Easily forgotten in days of peace . . . it now becomes, all of a sudden, a tremendously precious and important thing."[36] The anthem also influenced popular culture. In 1941, DC Comics introduced the Star-Spangled Kid, the alter ego of fifteen-year-old Sylvester Pemberton. Along with auto mechanic Pat Dugan, also known as Stripesy, the Kid battled Nazi spies in the United States. Nicknamed "America's Comrades in Combat," the pair lacked superpowers and fought their face-to-face battles with acrobatics and fisticuffs. Pemberton, the first adolescent comic book character with an adult sidekick, provided nimble moves; Dugan brought the brawn and maintained their flying car, the Star Rocket Racer. The duo adorned the covers of six monthly issues of the Star-Spangled Comics series but then fell out of favor, appearing periodically through the late 1940s when, according to the storyline, they became lost in time.[37]

Baltimore patriots attended a somber memorial service, marking the centennial of Francis Scott Key's death, at St. Paul's Church in 1943. After the processional hymn *Onward Christian Soldiers*, "the flag bearer proceeds to top of chancel steps." The musicians then played all four verses of the anthem, and participants heard the Apostles' Creed prayer and Ephesians 6:10-20, the latter widely recited as a commentary relevant to then-current events. The chorus also sang two hymns that Key contributed to the Episcopal Church hymnal: *Lord with Glowing Heart I'd Praise Thee*, matched to the tune *Glenhill*, and *Before the Lord We Bow*, mated with *Darwell's 148th*. The ceremony ended with a recessional hymn, *God of Our Fathers*.[38]

In the absence of an official version of the anthem, several interest groups attempted to standardize the song. In 1942, the Music Educators National Conference formed a broad-based National Anthem Committee, which issued "The Code for the National Anthem of the United States of America." The project included two War Department representatives: Major Howard C. Bronson, music officer in the Special Service Branch, and Major Harold W. Kent, education liaison officer in the Radio Branch of the Bureau of Public Relations. The committee also represented school bandleaders, radio interests, music publishers, parents, music teachers, the Music Industries War Council, the Music Teachers National Association, the National Association of Band Instrument Manufacturers, the National Association of Schools of Music, the National Education Association, and the National Federation of Music Clubs. The committee concluded that the anthem should be played "only on a program and in ceremonies and other situations where its message can be projected effectively," suggesting that emphasis "be placed upon the *singing* of 'The Star-Spangled Banner'" and encouraging song leaders to invite audience participation. During performances, the audience should face the flag or, in its absence, the song leader, "in an attitude of respectful attention. Outdoors, men should remove their hats." If possible, musicians should also stand. In addition, the document prescribed detailed performance practices. "It is not good taste to make or use sophisticated concert versions of the National Anthem," which "should be sung at a moderate tempo." Metronome markings helped ensure rhythmic accuracy, and the committee stated that "the slighting of note values in the playing or singing of the National Anthem seriously impairs the beauty and effectiveness of both music and lyric. Conductors should rehearse painstakingly both instrumental and vocal groups in the meticulous observance of correct note values." The code suggested the 1918 service version of *The Star-Spangled Banner* for all civilian performances, not just school events. The committee also took the liberty of lowering the key for singability and changing "a few" words and punctuation marks "to make it more authentic."[39]

Despite the adoption of a flag code by multiple organizations at a national flag conference in the 1920s, militant patriots sought to publicize the practices even more widely and lobbied Congress to approve its contents.

In 1942, after many struggles to refine proper flag and anthem etiquette in the courts and in society, Congress passed a joint resolution approving the United States Flag Code, known as the Federal Flag Code, to "emphasize existing rules and customs pertaining to the display and use of the flag" by civilians. This code maintained the provision that the flag should wave "during school days in or near every schoolhouse" and discouraged the use of Old Glory in "advertising purposes in any manner whatsoever," though it imposed no penalties for doing so. Congress promoted the anthem, directing military personnel to salute the flag for the duration of the song and instructing civilians to stand at attention with their hats removed. To dispense with any vestige of the controversial Bellamy salute, the code emphasized that civilians place their right hand over their heart during the Pledge of Allegiance.[40]

In 1943, leaders of American military bands reevaluated their approach to the national anthem after a version by the U.S. Navy Band rankled President Roosevelt at an official state function. As they moved to scrap the trumpet and cymbal flourishes that had offended the president, the chief of naval personnel instructed that commanding officers "take steps to see that the National Anthem is played in the accepted and traditional way, and that no effort is made to jazz or modernize this Anthem." W. F. Loventhal, a retired navy commander, discovered that the navy, army, and marine corps bands used different arrangements, so he referred the matter to an Interdepartmental Committee on Music, charged with "selecting an arrangement which meets with the approval of the President and which could then be promulgated as the Official Arrangement of the National Anthem." The committee met at the Library of Congress and agreed to adopt the marine band version, but, "due to the intricate procedure necessary to give official recognition to such a melodic line nothing so far has been established," and the initiative faded.[41]

Defying the desires of music teachers, military musicians, and Congress, Americans continued to tinker with the song, and composers stretched the bounds of acceptability. After an article appeared in the *Rotarian*, the national magazine of the Rotary Club, members "in numerous cities" took "new interest in the national anthem." B. F. Affleck, a cement manufacturer in Chicago, urged the singing of the fourth verse instead of the first. It is "easier to memorize," he said, and contains "a positive statement instead of an interrogation." He convinced a local club chapter to sing the last verse at a gathering, but the initiative had little impact. A Rotary chapter in Toledo, Ohio, adopted the key of G, as opposed to B-flat, to encourage more singing.[42] In 1934, composer Aaron Copland incorporated distorted phrases from the anthem into the score for his ballet "Hear Ye! Hear Ye!," which he referred to as "a satire on justice and how she functions." Due in part to the work's limited popularity, few people noticed Copland's irreverent use of the song.

In contrast, after immigrating to the United States in 1939, Russian-born composer Igor Stravinsky completed a symphonic arrangement of the anthem that drew negative attention. On July 4, 1941, the composer donated a copy of his "caviar-spangled" version to the Library of Congress, writing that to "best express my gratitude at the prospect of becoming an American citizen, I chose to harmonize and orchestrate 'The Star-Spangled Banner.'" To Stravinsky's surprise, a 1944 performance of the arrangement at Symphony Hall in Boston caused an uproar. The objections centered on a few mildly dissonant chords. In theory, Stravinsky had violated a state statute declaring that "whoever plays, sings, or renders the 'Star Spangled Banner' in any public place, theatre, motion picture hall, restaurant, or café, or at any public entertainment," must play the song "without embellishment or addition in the way of national or other melodies." Folklore holds that the police arrested the composer, but the officers merely informed him of the law and then left the concert hall.[43]

As with past conflicts, interest in the anthem increased during World War II. Richard Hill, a librarian in the Music Division of the Library of Congress, reported that he usually received one letter a month inquiring about the song, a number that grew in the war years to around two dozen letters per week from "private individuals, schoolchildren, teachers, and official organizations."[44] In August 1944, conductor Arturo Toscanini led the NBC Symphony Orchestra, the Westminster Choir, and tenor soloist Jan Peerce in a version of composer Giuseppe Verdi's *Hymn of the Nations*, written in 1862, which stitched together a medley of European national anthems. Produced by the Overseas Bureau of the Office of War Information and broadcast on NBC, Toscanini attempted to present a united front for the Allied powers by adding *The Star-Spangled Banner* and *The Internationale*, at that time the Russian anthem, to Verdi's score.

And just as it did during previous wars, imagery from the anthem influenced temporal compositions. *There's a Star Spangled Banner Waving Somewhere*, carried abroad by American soldiers, became a big hit during and after the war. The young narrator in the song, though unable to fight due to an unspecified disability, longed to be included in the pantheon of martyrs: "God gave me the right to be a free American / And for that precious right I'd gladly die. . . . There's a Star Spangled Banner waving somewhere / In that heaven there should be a place for me." Toward the war's end, popular performer Eddie Cantor, in *There's a New Flag on Iwo Jima*, sang "there's a Star-Spangled Banner flying there."[45]

Lesser compositions fusing God, flag, and country flooded the marketplace. *American Anthem* hailed "that sacred obligation" to preserve intact the blessings bestowed by the country's founders: "O ye who gave your all for us, Legions praise and honor thee / Your vow we keep—Oh sacred trust / Our Flag still waves o'er the free!" Another song, *The Ramparts We Watch*, culminated with "God keep America / Now, and evermore! For freedom and for right / Always we will fight. And we will never surrender / The Ramparts We Watch." A key lyric in *Our Flag*, by Merrick Fifeld McCarthy and Geoffrey O'Hara, stated: "This flag is made in God's design / This flag of yours / This flag of mine! / For with this flag He clearly gives / A sign for all the world to see / That in this Nation moves and lives / The Will of God that Men be free!"[46] The compilation *Army Hit Kit of Popular Songs* included the patriotic Big Five from the 1800s, along with several Civil War tunes that "come to our hearts and minds when spontaneous expressions of patriotism are stirred within us. We are Americans—and Americans sing!"[47] The music collection *Songs of Freedom for Schools, Clubs, Homes, Service Gatherings, and Community Singing*, published in Philadelphia, included the service version of the anthem and illustrated the continuation of the communal and participatory role of music in the lives of ordinary Americans.[48]

Increased exposure to *The Star-Spangled Banner* once again stimulated controversy. In an unsigned editorial, the *New York Times* stated: "Pleas for a more singable national anthem continue to be heard. That is to phrase it mildly." The writer noted the proliferation of homespun compositions attempting to unseat the song. "Sometimes the proposed substitute is little known, not particularly impressive, and in other ways an unpromising candidate." The article acknowledged the futility of replacing *The Star-Spangled Banner* by committee or by contest: "National anthems are like national languages. They cannot be created by fiat or propaganda. They grow, they happen, they strike the public fancy, but unlike so many other things that strike popular fancy, they remain rooted . . . over great stretches of time." The anthem "has seen the American people through two world wars for the defense of great causes ending in victory. Functionally, it has been an enormous success. It has inspired countless multitudes who cannot sing it aloud. They have hummed it or whistled it, whispered it to themselves or silently replicated the words; but they have whole-heartedly subscribed to its contents." The song, "compared with some of its rival streamlined competitors," reflected the nation's messy political system, according to the writer, who found it "in some ways fitting that the national anthem of a democracy should be hard to sing. . . . Ever so many people fall hopeless-ly short of the high C at 'the rocket's red glare,' but love the anthem just the same. Democracy, too, can fall short of the very highest ideal without forfeiting its claim on our affections."[49]

Almost three months later, William C. White, the U.S. Army bandleader, revisited the topic in "Oh, Say, Can You Sing It?" an article published in the *New York Times Magazine*. "With the song essentially unchanged in words and music . . . it is enjoying the greatest popularity in its history." Its ability to inspire "rose steadily as the world edged closer to war in the late Nineteen Thirties and reached an all-time peak immediately after Pearl Harbor." Wide interest in the song "is indicated by the fact that 35 to 50 percent more recordings are sold annually now than in normal peacetime years," though White noted that "opinions still differ" about its appropri-ateness as a national song. Some "critics fail to see real patriotic value in the inspired verses. Others look upon the words merely as a flag song—not as a nation anthem." Summarizing the music's durability, White wrote that the "spirited" melody and bold, forceful finale "remains a stirring inspiration to fighting America."[50]

In the mid-1940s, Washington, D.C., officials proposed expanding the Francis Scott Key Bridge, nicknamed the "Car-Strangled Spanner," built in 1923 near Key's former residence in Georgetown. In 1931 the National Cap-itol Board and Planning Commission bought Key's house, located at 3516 M Street, and by 1947 F. Regis Noel, president of the Columbia Historical

Society, reported that this building had been "totally neglected." Few activists realized that little of the original structure remained after an extensive renovation in 1913, except for two walls and the original foundation. Judge Delaplaine of Frederick, Maryland, proposed turning the home into the historical society's headquarters. Noel wrote that for want of raising $10,000, the house had become expendable. Almost a dozen local patriotic, legal, and historical organizations prevailed upon Senator Robert Taft (R-Ohio) to attempt to remedy the situation, and he introduced a preservation bill, which included several lines from the anthem, on Flag Day 1947.[51] When President Harry Truman rejected the bill, preservationists aired their disappointment. During a radio appearance in 1948 with Judge Delaplaine, Noel said that although he had lined up a long list of supporters and the House and Senate unanimously passed the measure, Truman "subjected it to an ignominious pocket veto, the statement first being made that 'He did not like the Bill, or anyone connected with it.'" The president also claimed that the bridge itself memorialized Key and that the upkeep of the restored residence would cost too much. Noel lamented that all the work to save "a symbol which will enthrall millions" remained in vain.[52] In 1949, the federal government dismantled the residence and stored it for safekeeping. Over the years, however, the wood, stone, and brick remnants disappeared, prompting wags to quip that anyone could lose a house key but only the government could lose Key's house. The Francis Scott Key Foundation eventually built a park at the site, including a large tablet and a bust of Key, and bequeathed it to the National Park Service. Other memorials to Key in the nation's capital are a marker placed by the National Society United States Daughters of 1812 on the Key Bridge; three stained glass windows at Christ Church in Georgetown; and a brass tablet at Washington National Cathedral, donated by the Daughters of 1812 and dedicated in the "faith of Jesus Christ" at a solemn religious ceremony.[53]

Despite the defeat over Key's homestead, Judge Delaplaine and his allies celebrated in 1948. In June, local luminaries observed the 200th anniversary of Frederick County at a ceremonial dinner that opened with an invocation and the national anthem, performed by a local orchestra. Delaplaine delivered an address, and the program ended with a group rendition of *Maryland, My Maryland* and a benediction.[54] Also in 1948, the U.S. Postal Service issued a Francis Scott Key stamp to coincide with the fiftieth

anniversary of the Francis Scott Key Monument in Mount Olivet Cemetery. Judge Delaplaine joined Representative J. Glenn Beall (R-Md.) at the
Frederick Post Office for the cancellation ceremony honoring the first issue
of the three-cent stamp. The design featured a bust of Key, flanked by two
flags—the original star-spangled banner and a forty-eight-star version—
along with a depiction of Fort McHenry and the "Old Key Home."[55] Guests
gathered at the Francis Scott Key Hotel in Frederick for cocktails and a
luncheon, then traveled to the cemetery, where the United States Marine
Band of Quantico Barracks serenaded the crowd and Frederick bigwigs
rededicated the memorial.[56]

Like Mrs. Holloway in Baltimore, Delaplaine revered his forebears,
relished his self-appointed stewardship of Key's legacy, and cherished the
ideal of historical accuracy. He could also be a bit of a scold, but, unlike
"Baltimore's No. 1 patriot," he usually displayed more tact. For example,
after *Chicago Tribune* editor Robert R. McCormick published an article
entitled "The Vision of Francis Scott Key" in July 1950, Delaplaine sent the
newspaperman a copy of his Key biography and a thank-you note. Yet the
judge also admonished McCormick for two errors. "I have never seen in
any of the records or books that the British officers were intoxicated and
that they were singing 'To Anacreon in Heaven' at the time of the bombardment of Fort McHenry, although such may be possible." Delaplaine also
took great offense with another of McCormick's assertions, noting—and
underlining—the fact that "the statement that Key was a lawyer of Baltimore is incorrect." Still, Delaplaine praised the article for its "fine patriotic
tone."[57] In a contrite response, sent eight days after Delaplaine typed his
letter, McCormick pleaded guilty and wrote, "PS I have been surprised at
the number of letters I have received from descendants of Key."[58]

Beginning in the 1930s, militant patriots across the country encouraged
communities to celebrate National Flag Week. On the federal level, in
1916 President Woodrow Wilson had issued a proclamation requesting
Americans to observe the date. Yet among the states, Pennsylvania became
the only one to recognize Flag Day as a holiday, in 1937. James A. Moss, of
the United States Flag Association, first raised the idea for a flag week in
1939, outlining his vision for instituting a National Flag Week (leading up
to Flag Day). Moss died in 1941, and "American's Creed" author William
Tyler Page took over the effort, but Page passed away the following year

and the Flag Association disbanded. In 1944, the Star Spangled Banner Flag House Association in Baltimore began spearheading the initiative. In the early 1950s, the organization prepared a series of speeches, a pageant called "The Flag Grows," and "dramas on the historic events suitable for radio, television, and school use." In addition to distributing instructions codifying "the correct use of the flag," these Flag Week promoters suggested that movie houses show patriotic short films, and they exhorted stores, hotels, and "everyone in the Community" to display the flag every day during that week, "from sunrise to sunset." They also urged patriots to hold Flag Day programs in churches and other houses of worship on Sunday.[59] In 1953, Flag House Association president Neil Swanson tried to boost support for this extended commemoration by appointing President Dwight Eisenhower as honorary chairman of the National Flag Week Committee. "We all know that the kind of world we live in attaches to our flag a meaning perhaps more significant for us and others than ever before in our history," wrote Eisenhower, framing his words about this national symbol in stark Cold War imagery.[60]

In addition, militant patriots attempted to institute National Anthem Day on September 14, and Pennsylvania observed the country's first state-wide National Anthem Day on that date in 1947. Pennsylvanian troops had helped repel the British during the Battle of Baltimore, and a replica fifteen-star plus fifteen-stripe flag flew above the opulent Union Club in Philadelphia to honor the Pennsylvania Society of the War of 1812, whose "long list of notables making up its membership" prevailed on the state's House of Representatives to single out the anniversary. Members of the society in other states began to work for similar local and national adoption and planned celebrations for schools, clubs, and various civic bodies. "The Society is not trying to create another national holiday," wrote a newspaper reporter in 1947. "It simply wants to have this day set aside for remembrance and recognition of the deep patriotism which the Anthem so well symbolizes."[61] Marylanders began to push for National Anthem Week, though they debated whether to celebrate the event in March, when President Hoover had signed the anthem bill into law, or in September, when Key wrote the song. Annual rituals surrounding National Anthem Day lasted for several years, but then faded. In 1954, Governor Theodore R. McKeldin of Maryland delivered an address at the National Anthem

Commemorative Service, held at Christ Church in Philadelphia, to "freely acknowledge our debt to Pennsylvania" during the Battle of Baltimore. "It was not our victory, it was an American victory, just as the song that came out of it is not a Maryland song, but the National Anthem." McKeldin acknowledged that many Americans regarded the battle as inconsequential. "A cynic might argue that the blood was spilled to no purpose, since all we got out of it was a song," he said. "But—what a song! After five generations it still has power to lift the hearts of men." Exhorting Americans to confront the Russians—America's Cold War enemies—with confidence, McKeldin claimed that it is impossible "for any nation to be the land of the free unless it is the home of the brave." The words "then conquer we must, in God is our Trust," he stated, are "only the repetition of what the Psalmist said more than two thousand years ago; 'Through God we shall do valiantly; for He it is that shall tread down our enemies.' "[62]

During the Cold War, many Americans turned to comforting symbols and rituals. The America Heritage Foundation sponsored the Freedom Train exhibition, which the National Archives called "the finest collection of documents and artifacts ever assembled in one place." From 1947 through 1949, the traveling archive visited three hundred and twenty cities across the country. The treasure included the working draft of the Bill of Rights, the Gettysburg Address, the thirty-one-star flag flown by Matthew Perry on his trip to Japan in 1854, and the flag that flew over Iwo Jima. Ephemera representing the War of 1812 included the original "Star-Spangled Banner" manuscript, Andrew Jackson's letter to the secretary of war describing the Battle of New Orleans, and the logbook of the USS *Constitution*, nicknamed "Old Ironsides."[63]

Even if the star-spangled banner that inspired the song could have fit into a train car display, the old flag remained in too fragile a state to make the trip. Baltimoreans lamented the artifact's condition and called for the return of the historic cloth to Fort McHenry, the site that made it famous. In 1954, Earle R. Poorbaugh, director of the Maryland Department of Information and the director at WBAL radio, wrote a newspaper article entitled "The Flag is NOT There," relating his profound disappointment during a visit to the Smithsonian Institution. Finding the flag "virtually invisible," he located the artifact through its number, 76023, making it "an item, more or less." The experience left him "hurt" and "astonished." Dr. Benjamin Buckner, commander of the Maryland Department of the American Legion, also lamented the flag's "half-hidden, dusty showcase tomb." Buckner, who was also a member of the Americanization Convention Committee in Washington, D.C., encouraged colleagues to help find a "suitable shrine" for the flag. But the Smithsonian never entertained the notion of giving it up and eventually recognized it as one of the most prized items in its collection.[64]

In 1954, the Maryland Historical Society heralded the arrival of what instantly became its premier possession, the original manuscript draft of *The Star-Spangled Banner*, written in Key's hand. The document ended up in the hands of Key's brother-in-law, Judge Joseph H. Nicholson, and eventually passed down to Nicholson's granddaughter, Mrs. Edward Shippen. After she died in 1907, it went on the auction block, with the stipulation that it remain in Maryland. Henry Walters, one of Baltimore's leading art collectors, bought it for $2,500; when he passed away in 1931, the trustees of the Walters Art Gallery in Baltimore acquired it for $26,400.[65] The gallery focused on fine arts, and the document constituted an anomaly within its collection, so they put it up for sale in 1953. Influential Baltimoreans, fearing that it might leave the city, scrambled into action. Catherine Key Jenkins, a descendant of Francis Scott Key, provided the money to purchase it from the gallery, with a provision that the manuscript be donated to the Maryland Historical Society in Baltimore. Jenkins paid the same price as Walters, though experts contended that if offered on the open market, it might have commanded double or triple that sum.[66]

The historical society worked with consultants from Johns Hopkins University to create an exhibition case similar to the ones used for the Declaration of Independence and the Constitution. Built into the wall of a fireproof room, the niche, lined with Tennessee marble, includes a chamber "hermetically sealed in a glass container filled with helium gas" and a yellow filter to keep out ultraviolet rays.[67] In September 1954, three hundred people attended the dedication ceremony, including many of Key's descendants. The Maryland Historical Society's president, former senator George L. Radcliffe, referred to the occasion as the most important event in the institution's (then) 110-year existence and predicted "that people would come for the next 25,000 years to see the symbol of American freedom." Local author Gerald W. Johnson, in his speech, noted that *The Star-Spangled Banner* is the only national anthem born from a single military skirmish and written on the "wrong side of a battle line." Dynamic Jesuit preacher Reverend William Driscoll delivered a prayer: "Lord of Hosts, let us do for our country something even finer than the thing that was done by Francis Scott Key," by living "our lives as true Americans. Yet more, O Lord: this Star-Spangled Banner and all it stands for we love with our whole hearts. Protect it with Thy omnipotent power, cherish it with Thy infinite love; give peace and security to this land so precious to us."[68]

Star-Spangled Conflict, 1954–1963

DUE IN PART to wholesome black-and-white television sit-coms like "Father Knows Best" and "Leave It to Beaver," the 1950s are often portrayed as a bland era in the United States. In that myth, cohesion and conformity dominated. Unprecedented prosperity spurred suburban sprawl, consumer culture, and the Space Age, undercut with the fear that Communists angled to subvert the American way of life. Though the 1960s are credited with changing American society forever, the previous decade served as a more buttoned-down dress rehearsal for the tie-dyed times to follow. In addition to the beginnings of the Civil Rights movement and the war in Vietnam, the 1950s counterculture contradicted the staid stereotype. Bebop jazz musicians and Beatnik writers experimented with free-form styles. Drip-painter Jackson Pollock and the abstract expressionists adopted unorthodox techniques to create seemingly formless works of art. Soul music, rockabilly, and Elvis Presley injected rebellious sexuality into pop music. The folk craze, led by Woody Guthrie and Pete Seeger, presaged the protest movements of the 1960s. Hollywood released edgy films, including "Rebel without a Cause," starring James Dean, and "The Wild One," with Marlon Brando. From 1957 to 1959, independent filmmaker Ken Jacobs shot "Star Spangled to Death" in the streets of New York City. He described the film as an avant-garde work that portrays a "stolen and dangerously sold-out America, allowing examples of popular culture to self-indict. Racial and religious insanity, monopolization of wealth and the purposeful dumbing down of citizens and addiction to war oppose a Beat playfulness."[1]

Militant patriots viewed the national anthem as a barometer to measure the nation's adherence to its cherished traditions. With the rise of wars hot and cold in the 1940s, the federal government continued to regulate patriotic rituals. In 1949, Congress recognized Flag Day as an unofficial holiday and approved a resolution allowing Old Glory to fly around the clock at the Key Memorial in Frederick, Maryland. In 1954, legislators extended the practice to Fort McHenry and another law that year added the words "under God" to the Pledge of Allegiance. Two years later, the national motto changed from "E Pluribus Unum" to "In God We Trust," a line adapted from the last verse of *The Star-Spangled Banner*. The slogan first appeared on the nation's paper currency in 1957. Legislators designated May 1, 1958, as Loyalty Day to counter International Workers' Day, alternatively known (since the late 1800s) as the leftist holiday May Day.

The House of Representatives also revisited the anthem issue during the 1950s. Representative Joel T. Broyhill (R-Va.) introduced a bill to designate an official version of *The Star-Spangled Banner* in 1955. Broyhill first became involved that year after a group of high school students requested copies of the exact words and music to the anthem. "To me, at the time, it was just one of hundreds of requests from constituents that every Member of Congress receives every week," he said. "However, upon painstaking investigation which covered virtually every Government Department, I discovered that there was no official version in existence. There was not even a commonly accepted version of the words or the music." On Flag Day 1955, Broyhill helped introduce House Joint Resolution 341, to adopt a specific version of *The Star-Spangled Banner*, yet several tactical blunders undermined his position. For one thing, he promoted the 1918 education version of the anthem without researching the issue. This arrangement only included three verses and failed to credit Key or music composer John Stafford Smith. After Broyhill's 1955 bill stalled in Congress, he worked with the Library of Congress, Defense Department bandleaders, and thirty-six patriotic organizations and resubmitted his bill in 1957, with the education version of the song still included in it.[2]

Broyhill's persistence resulted in a controversial Congressional hearing in 1958. According to an article in the *Veterans of Foreign Wars Magazine*, "'The Star-Spangled Banner' is in the news headlines again." The magazine contended that "one would not think that getting Congress to approve such a measure would be much of a task." The article encapsulated the arguments of the opposition: "Some of these people are international minded and object to anything nationalistic. Some are pacifists and feel that the song is too militant. Others feel that, deriving from an old English waltz ('To Anacreon in Heaven'), the music is not militant enough. Some—as the news headlines prove—just don't like the song."[3] The *Baltimore Evening Sun* expressed surprise that anyone would revisit the issue, since Congress already decided on *The Star-Spangled Banner* as the national anthem in 1931: "The only argument would be whether the song's so familiar as to be stale."[4]

Leading up to these hearings, Broyhill's office received five thousand letters from around the country, most opposing the measure. The outpouring of negativity from the Daughters of the American Revolution and their allies puzzled the congressman. A concerted effort to stymie the bill featured breathless updates circulated by the U.S. Flag Committee, founded and run by patriotic watchdog Helen P. Lasell of Jackson Heights, New York. Lasell adopted a unique approach to punctuation, often ending sentences with a dash and relying on exclamation marks and underlined words in her mimeographed screeds. Writing to James W. Foster, director of the Maryland Historical Society, Lasell contended that if the nation continued "with the present international One Worldism—and grandiose give-away programs, soon, we will become a has-been country—We have to look behind the 'lace curtains' today of every bill, to determine who and what is behind the issue—So many in our country are working to undermine and destroy any nationalism that is left."[5] In her *Be Alert Bulletin*, Lasell contended that "all good patriotic minded people are satisfied completely with our NATIONAL ANTHEM as it is now—and as we have always known it—To tamper with it with the idea of changing or destroying it seems almost sacrilegious and certainly unnecessary and UN-AMERICAN." Lasell complained that Broyhill used the *Richmond News-Leader*, edited by James J. Kilpatrick, as a propaganda vehicle.

As a testament to her influence, in the 1958 Congressional hearing the House subcommittee raised many of the issues Lasell highlighted in her newsletter. She objected to what she called the "most drastic and sinister change," using a lowercase *p* in the word "power," which appears in the final verse during the phrase "Praise the power that hath made and preserved us a nation." Lasell took the term to signify God, though Key might have referred to military might or the ideals of democracy. None of the five surviving manuscripts attributed to Key capitalizes the word, though the first printer took the liberty of doing so on his own. Lasell also overlooked the explicit phrase "in God is our Trust" from the same verse, yet she shaped the rhetoric surrounding the issue by declaring "HANDS OFF OUR NATIONAL ANTHEM . . . NOW AND FOR ALL TIME."[6]

In a letter to the Maryland Historical Society, Lasell's ally, Helen B. Krippendorf of Keene, New Hampshire, reported that she had contacted officials at the American Legion, the D.A.R., the V.F.W., the Catholic Daughters of America, the Knights of Columbus, and other influential individuals: "No one knew anything about this, but it has stirred them all."[7] Hinting at Broyhill's troubles to come, a *Baltimore News-Post* editorial quoted a local musician, who referred to all proposed musical changes as "sacrilege." The statement caught Broyhill off guard. He intended to "prevent any changes to our national anthem. We want to merely state what this national anthem is and we do not want it changed in the future."[8] But Broyhill's message never connected, and he remained a step behind his opponents in the public relations battle. Though often misunderstood, Broyhill did receive support from the American Legion and the V.F.W., causing a rare split between veterans' and hereditary groups over the anthem.

Broyhill also won over the board of trustees of the Maryland Federation of Music Clubs and former senator George L. Radcliffe, president of the Maryland Historical Society, a potentially powerful ally. "I believe it is most important that we establish the most fitting words and music in order that we may all enjoy without controversy the wonderful stirring message of our National Anthem," Radcliffe wrote.[9] In a speech before the National Society Daughters of the American Revolution, Radcliffe suggested that an official version would merely serve as a "directive—an aid, a guide."[10] In a letter to Radcliffe, James Foster, director of the Maryland Historical Society, noted the changes that affect folk or popular songs over the years: "And our national anthem is no different, in fact the different ways in which it is published by various music houses is so bewildering that stabilizing it.

.. seems almost imperative—if it can be accomplished."[11] Foster also stated that "this matter of the National Anthem has great publicity possibilities."[12]

Broyhill undermined his position with the bluebloods by seeking help from the forty-six-member National Music Council, a group that belonged to the United Nations Educational, Scientific, and Cultural Organization (UNESCO), an entity despised by militant patriots. Broyhill also allied with Richard Hill, a librarian in the Music Division of the Library of Congress, who convened an ad hoc committee to investigate the song's evolution. The group tracked dozens of minute punctuation changes, based on historic documents, including an investigation of "whether there should be more than one 'bomb bursting in air' or many bombs busting in air or more than one 'foul footstep's pollution' since various versions have 'bombs' and 'footsteps.'"[13] Many Americans expressed shock when they discovered that variations to the lyrics and melody had crept into popular practices and that the words most people sang differed from the ones Key wrote in his first manuscript draft. Representatives and reporters also revealed that the Library of Congress maintained registrations for 262 copyrighted versions of the anthem.[14]

In May 1958, Broyhill's bill received a hearing before a subcommittee of the House Judiciary Committee, chaired by anthem ally Emanuel Celler. The subcommittee considered four other bills in addition to Broyhill's; his curiously continued to omit the third verse, spurring conspiracy theories and eliciting opposition from purists. Representative Herbert Zelenko (D-N.Y.) introduced a rendition that eliminated the song's high notes. Other bills included readings with detailed punctuation variations. Newspapers in Baltimore and Washington, D.C., publicized features of the proposed versions and, according to the *Washington News*, letters and resolutions from patriotic organizations and school children "flooded" Capitol Hill. Murray Drabkin, chief counsel of the subcommittee, considered bringing in the U.S. Marine Band or the Air Force Singing Sergeants to perform at the hearings. "The members have no special competence in reading music and we're all a little leery of handling this particular song," he said. "It's like legislating on religion or motherhood."[15] The hearings, held over three days, for a total of eight hours, evoked often-intangible feelings held by Americans toward their national song and provided a fascinating exploration of the history of the anthem and its role in public life. Only one lawmaker professed any expertise in music, and the subcommittee viewed the issue through a legalistic framework, a line of inquiry that raised a number of provocative perspectives.

At 10:00 a.m. on May 21, 1958, subcommittee chair Elijah Forrester (D-Ga.) brought down the gavel in Room 346 of the House Office Building. "After 140 years there is still no single standard authorized version of our national anthem," he said. The assembly proposed "to determine whether a single version should be adopted, and, if so, what it will be," as well as "to consider suggestions concerning whether any change in the musical score or range will be helpful and conducive to a wider use of our anthem."[16] During his testimony, Broyhill portrayed the matter as an attempt to "end our national embarrassment over the confusion in our anthem." Broyhill played several recordings, prompting subcommittee member Basil Whitener (D-N.C.) to question if Congress would be required to consider versions for symphony, brass band, a mixed chorus, a male chorus, and first-year piano students. Whitener also commented that on a recent trip to his hometown, Gastonia, North Carolina, he had mentioned the upcoming anthem hearing. "My barber says, 'We have had one [for] over a hundred years, haven't we not?'" said Whitener. "The average person does not realize there is no official version."[17] Broyhill replied that if left unchecked, the anthem's words could change in the future, and that the subcommittee should try to eliminate confusion and ambiguity. The 1931 anthem legislation failed to designate an official version, but Broyhill noted that a band played the song for Congress during the proceedings. Referring to his personal motivation for introducing his bill, Broyhill stated that "it was rather embarrassing to me when I told the high school class I could not get the copy of the national anthem." Forrester replied that no official version of the Lord's Prayer existed, either. When it came to the anthem, "there is a controversy and no matter what we do we will not settle that controversy."[18]

During the hearing, Congressman Francis E. Dorn (R-N.Y.), the sponsor of one of the other bills under consideration, sparred with Whitener over the scope of federal power. Dorn addressed the capital *P* matter at length and mentioned the deluge of letters received by his office. Whitener claimed that everyone present knew that military regulations and common customs dictated certain courtesies when the anthem aired. But "suppose that an orchestra plays what we might refer to as a 'clandestine version' of 'The

Star-Spangled Banner,' assuming that we have adopted an official version."
Are Americans "able to distinguish between the clandestine version and
the official version the Congress might adopt and remain seated instead
of standing if it is a clandestine version?"[19] The reason for the bills, said
Dorn, is to create "just one and distinct 'Star-Spangled Banner,'" arguing
that a band could play the national anthem of some foreign country and
call it "The Star-Spangled Banner" unless Congress designated the words
and music for an official version. Whitener replied that "a lot of us get all
thrilled when we play 'Dixie,' but we do not think it is 'The Star-Spangled
Banner.'" Dorn admitted that even though bands had the freedom to call
any song the national anthem, Americans performed *The Star-Spangled
Banner* without "serious diversions," undermining his argument. Whitener
joked that "if somebody would start playing, well, 'Hound Dog,' and call it
'The Star-Spangled Banner,' the revulsion of the public would be so great
that that fellow would probably never want to hear either tune again."
Hinting at his reluctance to act, Whitener asked, "As we are situated now,
who is being hurt?"[20]

Dorn and Whitener exchanged barbs after the latter asked if the F.B.I.
would be loosed on the public to police renditions of the anthem. Whitener,
a southerner and a staunch segregationist, referred to the occupation of Little Rock High School by federal troops in 1957 to enforce racial integration.
The North Carolinian said: "Suppose there is a band leader in Big Stone,
Tenn., who just says, 'I am not going to play that and my students in this
school are not going to play this official version,' and some President says,
'By golly, he is going to play it. We will regulate the schools. We will send the
airborne down there.'" New Yorker Dorn replied that there would never be
penalties for playing an unauthorized version. Whitener then asked if there
should be freedom of music, akin to freedom of speech. Dorn responded:
"Is there a freedom of saying what the Ten Commandments are? I think
the Ten Commandments are pretty well set." Whitener reminded him
that Americans regulated their behavior when it came to the anthem and
recalled a time when a radio station used the notes corresponding to "O
say can you see" for their tone signal and signal breaks. After three weeks,
suddenly they stopped doing so. "I'm sure many folks felt as I did, that they
were misusing the national anthem. Apparently it was the pressure of the
public that caused them to change."[21]

With Broyhill's bill unlikely to pass, due to the number of patriotic groups amassed against it, the hearings devolved into political grandstanding. During the testimony of Edwin Hughes, executive secretary of the Paris-based International Music Council, Chairman Forrester asked if the organization had ties "with other national music organizations of international scope," meaning UNESCO. Forrester grilled Hughes about the council's activities in Paris and asked if they did the bidding of any foreign country. After Hughes responded that the group helped spread the knowledge of American music to other countries, Forrester asked if Russia belonged to UNESCO and then dismissed Hughes. As the subcommittee considered the changes to the lyrics that occurred over time, they zeroed in on the original version by Francis Scott Key and pointed to the document held by the Maryland Historical Society as the template of the author's true intentions.[22]

At this point in the proceedings, with the House of Representatives ready to convene and consider Alaskan statehood, Forrester announced his plans to resume the hearing in the afternoon. Before adjourning, he introduced "Star-Spangled Soprano" Lucy Monroe, there to support Representative Zelenko's bill, which attempted to make the melody easier to sing. Monroe stood as spectators applauded.[23] In the short window of time remaining before the recess, Forrester let Zelenko begin his statement, which eloquently captured the average person's relationship with the anthem. Zelenko counted seventy-five newspaper editorials about the anthem bills and noted, "I have received some mail, and I am sure that the chairman has, which, in effect, says, 'Why do we waste time on this when we have such other important things to do?'" Zelenko responded that "one of the things that puts our Americanism together is our inner feeling, our patriotism, our symbol, and our flag, among other things. The anthem is one of them." A singable version is a national necessity, Zelenko said, since patriotism is usually sparked by emotion. "The average person goes about his citizenship in a most inarticulate way," spending "daily life doing his chores as a good citizen. How can he express himself? Very rarely does he get called upon to make a speech but when the 'Star-Spangled Banner' comes along he wants to sing it and shout it as loud as the next one. He finds he cannot do it."[24]

Business on the House floor canceled the afternoon session of the hearing. The next day, the subcommittee met at 10:00 a.m. Zelenko again introduced Lucy Monroe, who stated that she performed the national anthem over five thousand times at baseball games, public events, and government functions. Monroe called the song "difficult for an untrained voice." She always asked people to join her, but audiences often struggled: "The people want to sing 'our song' well."[25] Congressman Zelenko also recruited Paul Taubman, musical director for both the NBC and CBS television stations, who supervised seventeen network programs each week. While serving in the army from 1943 to 1946, Taubman noticed that soldiers sang military or popular songs "with great enthusiasm and abandon." But when they tried to sing the national anthem, "just the reverse held true. Those men who happened to remember the words invariably would lower their voices, perhaps sing an octave lower . . . or hum quietly to themselves. Others would remain mute, some just move their lips looking sheepishly ahead, while others would stop singing entirely after a few moments." It happened everywhere, he said. After watching spectators at baseball games ridicule professional singers who failed to reach the high notes, Taubman lowered them for the phrases "rocket's red glare" and "land of the free."[26]

Another representative with a bill before the subcommittee, Carroll D. Kearns (R-Penn.), a former public school music teacher, decried the national anthem situation. Other countries have "hymn type" music that is easy to sing, he argued. *The Star-Spangled Banner* is a "challenging, dashing song that is characteristic of a new republic such as ours." He cringed when he attended "different nationalistic banquets and they put the spotlight on the Stars and Stripes and we all stand there mute. Then they play the anthem of their nation . . . and they all burst forth and sing. To me it is rather embarrassing that we do not take a more active part in singing our 'Star-Spangled Banner.'" Kearns sought an official version so that "when the anthem is played" at any official function or ball game, "we should adhere to that version and not deviate from it whatsoever." Just before that day's recess, Esther Linkins of Washington, D.C., made enough of a commotion to be recognized by the chairman. Linkins claimed that she had led *The Star-Spangled Banner* thousands of times, beginning with community sings during World War I. She also toured military camps and hospitals in the capital region and recalled an instance when one band, performing before an audience of ten thousand, "galloped through it" and another "played it like a funeral dirge. I nearly lost my mind. It isn't so much version. It is interpretation." Her remedy echoed the approach urged by Mrs. Holloway in Baltimore: "You have got to have pep in it."[27]

The subcommittee met again on May 28, a session that Maryland Historical Society director James Foster, in his memorandum on the hearings, wrote would be given over to "the main guns of the opposition, chiefly patriotic organizations led by certain ardent ladies." Foster reported that radio and television interests backed Zelenko's bill to make the anthem easier to sing. The American Federation of Musicians union got behind Broyhill's bill, but their support backfired because the subcommittee considered them to "be too international."[28] Mrs. Charles Carroll Haig, who represented the National Society of the Daughters of the American Revolution, praised the stirring high notes and cautioned that any changes or "further legislation might result in weakening or liberalizing amendments, the result of which could be a lessening of reverence in performance."[29] Chairman Forrester turned the subcommittee's focus toward *To Anacreon in Heaven* and the differences between Key's handwritten manuscript and subsequent versions. Whitener asked, "If we have struggled along ungrammatically for all these many years, we might do it a little while longer without injury; is that right?"

Francis J. McNamara, assistant director of the National Legislative Service of the Veterans of Foreign Wars, supported "an official text," based on the manuscript at the Maryland Historical Society. He also endorsed a law to penalize jazz or popular arrangements of the song. Militant patriots had long targeted attempts to "jazz up" *The Star-Spangled Banner*, dismissing almost any ambitious pop or instrumental arrangement with that four-letter word. McNamara stated that some musicians "object to our anthem because they cannot 'swing' it and it is not adaptable to a 'jazzed-up' rendition. We [the V.F.W.] believe that any swinging or jazzing up of the national anthem of this country is disrespectful, inappropriate, and abusive, and should be barred." Any bill should be worded "so as to forbid . . . any 'jazzed-up,' 'swing,' or any other form of temporarily popular, fad music treatment of 'The Star-Spangled Banner.' " Whitener replied that an African American quartet might sing the anthem in a different manner than the Air Force Male Chorus. "They would sing it with as much feeling and with as much love of country, and perhaps with more beauty, than any others," he said. But "some F.B.I. man sitting out there might say that that is a strange and bizarre rendition." Whitener joked that "if I stood up here now and sang

'The Star-Spangled Banner,' we could all agree that [it] would be a strange and bizarre rendition . . . [but] I may be perfectly sincere in trying to sing it." McNamara replied that an individual may not intend to be "disrespectful if he tears down that flag over there, but that does not mean that he should be permitted to do so."[30]

Mrs. William D. Leetch, secretary of the American Coalition of Patriotic Societies, took issue with the jazz magazine *Downbeat*, which "carried two articles, saying they are campaigning for a NEW Anthem—because they cannot SWING ours, and it no longer represents America." One of the *Downbeat* editorials, written by its chief editor, Jack Tracy, asked, "Why is it that ours, the most free-swinging of democracies, has the most non-swinging, constricted of national anthems?" Tracy argued that "it don't mean a thing if it don't have that" and it "don't mean a thing to crowds at ball games, at prize fights, at Fourth of July gatherings, or at conventions." Calling the song a two-minute stage wait, he wrote that "as a band attacks it, or as Lucy Monroe sings, Americans shift from foot to foot." Lasell's *Be Alert Bulletin* also referred to these editorials, which called for *The Battle Hymn of the Republic* to replace the anthem. "A musical trade magazine is campaigning for a new national anthem because 'you cannot swing *The Star-Spangled Banner*,' and they write ungrammatically and thoughtlessly, 'it don't mean a thing,' which in itself is a sad commentary on our educational system," said Leetch, who probably did not know the 1932 Duke Ellington song, *It Don't Mean a Thing (if It Ain't Got That Swing)*.[31]

With so many other important national issues dominating the headlines, Mrs. Leetch expressed concern that "our office has been swamped with mail on this subject." Chairman Forrester agreed: "That is also the experience of this subcommittee. We have Alaska statehood, we have mutual security, we have the most controversial problems before this Congress that we have had in many, many years. But so far as my mail is concerned I have had more letters on this particular thing." Leetch claimed that the push behind the anthem proposals originated with the Department of Health, Education, and Welfare, which she stated "is the chief channel of UNESCO propaganda into the Nation's schools." She also cast aspersion on Broyhill's endorsement of the education version of the song, blaming Richard Hill, Broyhill's supporter at the Library of Congress, who graduated from Oxford University in England: "This perhaps accounts for his purported concern lest the third stanza of our national anthem offend the British and so left it out."

Subcommittee member H. Allen Smith (R-Cal.) asked Leetch what edition of *The Star-Spangled Banner* she would send if her organization received a request to provide a version of the song. She contended that every American knows when he or she hears it played correctly. When pressed, she flipped the question, putting the onus on the schools to "teach respect and the meaning of this anthem. I think we fall down right there. We have to re-educate a whole generation of young people in an appreciation of things American because they have been brainwashed through the new educationists and frontier thinkers away from Americanism." Whitener noted the impossibility of legislating "respect for the flag or the national anthem or anything else." Leetch agreed: "It is a matter of education that begins right in the home and the schools."

Mrs. Raymond D. MacCart of Stamford, Connecticut, who represented the National Society Congress of States, Inc., and the National Society of Colonial Dames XVII Century, assigned malicious intent to the high school students who solicited Broyhill in 1955: "We feel these things that happen today such as this writing by school people to Mr. Broyhill to do something about an authorized official version is part of a trend. It might become a habit to attack our history and our traditions." Juliet Brooke Ballard of Ilchester, Maryland, a descendant of Francis Scott Key, told the panel that altering the poem would be "precedent making," since "writers all over the country would be very much disturbed if they thought that it was going to be possible to correct an author's work." Forrester asked if "the lady knows that they changed 'Old Black Joe' and 'Swanee River,'" two Stephen Foster songs that emerged from the minstrel tradition and originally mentioned "darkies."[32]

Tacitly acknowledging that the subcommittee would be unlikely to move on any of the bills, the chairman allowed librarian Richard Hill to plead his case again. Hill said that the Library of Congress regularly received requests for an official version of the anthem and shared a letter from William Hillcourt, a member of the National Council of the Boy Scouts of America, who sought an approved copy of the song for use in the organization's handbook. "In the first line of the first verse," for instance, Hillcourt found "'O say can you see,' 'O! say, can you see,' [and] 'Oh; say, can you see.'" He also listed discrepancies in six other lines of the first verse alone. Hillcourt then stated: "We would appreciate it greatly if you will be kind enough to send us a copy of the official version of the 'Star-Spangled Banner'—as approved as our national anthem. Also kindly inform us of the official choice of the following: 'the flag of the United States,' 'The Flag of the United States,' 'our flag,' 'our Flag' . . ." The inquiry, said Hill, represented "merely a sample of what the library receives in quantity." After responding to many similar requests, Hill unintentionally became an expert on the subject and admitted that it "got to be fascinating." When answering such inquiries, he referred the letter writers to the document at the Maryland Historical Society and suggested the arrangements of either the education version or the service version for the music. When it came to the melody, there's "no such thing as a right reading" unless Congress weighed in, Hill said, arguing that establishing official editions of important creeds is the "sort of norm." He noted that even the Bible appeared in authorized versions that vary between different denominations. Committee member F. Jay Nimitz (R-Ind.) concluded that no matter what decision the committee made, the only result would be more dissension. All five bills under consideration died without further consideration.[33]

Despite his defeat, Representative Broyhill continued to consult experts and perfect his bill. In 1959 he solicited support from President Dwight Eisenhower, who replied that variations in the song did nothing to "affect the spirit of our national anthem," yet the president agreed to support an official version, "just as a standard pattern of stars in the flag itself is desirable. I would gladly sign a bill containing such a version."[34] Broyhill then wrote to Forrester, stressing that "our desire is not to change 'The Star-Spangled Banner.' It is to state exactly the words and music for the anthem so as to prevent for the future the inconsistencies and changes which abound today."[35] In his next bill, presented to Congress in 1962, Broyhill included an adaptation with all four verses. He advocated for a "traditional series of chords" and included a clause that "strange and bizarre harmonizations should certainly be avoided." Still, "there will be those who wish to embellish the basic harmonization," and he recognized that "reasonable latitude must be allowed." Rather than "risk the implication of specific restrictions, it has seemed best not to give an exact working out of the chord progressions." According to this version of the bill, the anthem should always be played with "due honor and respect. It should never be performed as part of a medley or in circumstances where its importance as a national symbol is in any way cheapened. Its use to build dramatic effects, wholly subsidiary to its fundamental purpose, should be discouraged."[36]

Helen Lasell again vowed to thwart Broyhill's anthem initiative and taunted the congressman over the defeat of his previous effort in 1958. After studying the 1931 law designating *The Star-Spangled Banner* as the national anthem, which predated the formation of the United Nations, she concluded that the version played before the House Judiciary Committee in 1930 represented the official version. She also examined Broyhill's voting record and found it to be lacking. His main transgression consisted of supporting the Trade Expansion Act of 1962, which Lasell considered to be the first step in the creation of a Common Market and regional world government. She fretted that the defensive alliance of the North Atlantic Treaty Organization would be placed within the framework of the United Nations, which planned a world federation that threatened United States sovereignty.[37] In February 1962, her *Be Alert Bulletin* warned about insidious forces "who constantly strive to destroy our heritage and all we have cherished." She concluded that Broyhill, "for want of something to do," is working as a front for "INTERNATIONALISTS AMONG US" who had already changed the teaching of history in the schools, which influenced the outlook of young people. "Naturally, they want TO CHANGE THE SYMBOLS WHICH REPRESENT OUR HERITAGE to correspond." In 1963, she expanded her theories in a book, *Power behind the Government Today*, which warned against lax moral standards, communist infiltrators, and, especially, the Council on Foreign Relations, the real rulers of the nation.[38]

Broyhill tried to control the public relations message by sponsoring a March 1962 concert at Constitution Hall in Washington, D.C., featuring the 100-piece U.S. Army Band, "with their herald trumpet group." Broyhill expected representatives from two hundred patriotic, veterans', and musical societies to attend. He promised that the event would be "unique in our patriotic history."[39] In an open letter, Broyhill urged attendance at the concert to help eliminate the "widespread abuse and misuse of words and music" to *The Star-Spangled Banner*. On some occasions, he wrote, "the abuse has been intentional, carried out by those who dislike national patriotism."[40] Unfortunately for the congressman, an elderly attendee stole his thunder. After the performance of Broyhill's rousing version of the anthem, which featured fourteen long-stemmed herald trumpets on the high notes at the song's end, the *Washington News* reported that "Miss Ottile Sutro, 90, of Baltimore, stood up and shouted . . . 'It's fine for brass bands, but you can't sing it.'"[41] The *Washington Star* called her "fighting Otilie Sutro" and reported that she waved around what she called the correct version of the anthem, which she learned from Key's kin. Sutro, a renowned pianist who spelled her name Ottilie and claimed that she once played piano for President Grover Cleveland, held a "private press conference after the program."[42] Sutro's friend, Dena Cohen, attending on behalf of the Maryland Historical Society, recounted the event. Clutching a copy of *To Anacreon in Heaven*, Sutro stood and asked Broyhill to consider the melody and time signature on the music sheet. "I also called attention to Miss Sutro, telling him that she had known Mr. Key's grandchildren and they had taught her how to sing the anthem as their grandfather had sung," wrote Cohen. "The reporters flocked to Miss Sutro's side when they heard this." As Broyhill began to leave the hall, Cohen showed him the music, but "he did not seem to want any argument about it. I also went to the conductor and tried to show him the original music but he had no time for me." Cohen speculated that Broyhill "was evidently seeking publicity for himself as a politician."[43]

Though Broyhill set up the event to plug his version, with added dramatic effect, he lost yet another battle over public opinion. In a *Baltimore Sun* article that appeared after the concert, Broyhill reflected on his seven-year quest. In 1955, "all hell broke loose and I think it proved our point better than anything else we could have done," he said. As letters poured in from around the country, "the office file grew so fat one man could barely lift it." Broyhill also spoke about other suggested changes to the anthem, including the line "then conquer we must, when our cause it is just." He recalled that "apparently some would not admit the possibility of our cause being anything but just" and wanted the phrase changed to "for our cause it is just." The newspaper concluded that Broyhill's new bill most likely would face a similar procedural fate as his previous ones, even though the congressman tried to rally support among patriotic groups by offering to educate them on the matter.[44] Through 1963, Broyhill continued to attract press attention, but reporters recognized the futility of his endeavor. "One would be hard-pressed to imagine anything that could possibly be less controversial, but

curiously enough, Mr. Broyhill has found the going very rough indeed,"
wrote the *Washington Star*. Despite being consistently misunderstood,
"the Congressman is persistent indeed in this cause—eight fruitless years
of work in its behalf do not seem to have shaken his determination to solve
this little problem."[45]

Broyhill believed he had earned an effective endorsement when bandleader Guy Lombardo sent the congressman an unsolicited letter indicating
Lombardo's support for "this most worthwhile effort." Lombardo wrote
that he, too, recoiled in horror "at sometimes hearing 'The Star-Spangled
Banner' played or sung in rock 'n roll tempo, swing tempo, and in many
other ways that indicate a lack of respect for something so meaningful to
our American heritage." The bandleader favored renditions that "reflect its
elegance, its stateliness, its importance" and lauded Broyhill's latest proposal
for setting "a policy for respectful treatment of the anthem whenever it is
played." A press release issued by Broyhill's office claimed that Lombardo
would adopt the melody in the Broyhill bill for his arrangements and present the congressman with a musical score.[46] Nothing significant came of
this, however, and Broyhill's anthem bills became less focused over time.
In 1969, for example, he sought an official declaration recognizing Rossell
G. O'Brien, former mayor of Olympia, Washington, for originating the
customs of standing and uncovering one's head during renditions of the
national anthem. In all, Broyhill introduced nine anthem bills during his
tenure in Congress, which ended when he lost the 1974 election. Broyhill's
fears of a changing national anthem eventually came to fruition as moder-
nity inevitably caught up with *The Star-Spangled Banner*.

In 1964, Marylanders worked to commemorate the 150th anniversary
of the anthem by promoting the song, its author, and the state's role in the
saga. With core members of old-line fraternal, hereditary, and patriotic
organizations growing older and a new generation turning to other pursuits, this occasion served as a last hurrah for militant patriots and their
supporters. As with the 125th anniversary of the song, the 1964 milestone
happened to coincide with another world's fair, located once more in New
York, and Maryland officials again concentrated on promoting tourism.
Getting a jump on the anniversary proceedings, Judge Delaplaine and
his supporters in Frederick, Maryland, joined Postmaster General Arthur
Summerfield to celebrate the release of a new four-cent Francis Scott Key

stamp in Baltimore on September 14, 1960. With a print run of 120 million, the issue represented one of six stamps in the American Credo series, which also included portraits and quotes from George Washington, Ben Franklin, Thomas Jefferson, Patrick Henry, and Abe Lincoln. For Key, postal officials chose the line "And this be our motto, in GOD is our TRUST," with emphasis added by them.[47] In 1962, a mailing sent by state officials in Maryland depicted the Fort McHenry bombardment and offered help to recipients seeking information about "Baltimore's Historic Inheritance and Its Preservation," along with "Accommodations, Sightseeing, and Recreation."[48] In 1963, officials redesigned the state highway map and issued four hundred thousand copies identifying Maryland as the "Star-Spangled Banner State" and Baltimore as "National Anthem City."[49]

The city of Frederick, whose minor league baseball team is called the Keys, also asserted its stake in the anthem's legacy. In 1963, Delaplaine retired from the bench to devote more time to publicizing Key and his song. At one of his first presentations, held at the Historical Society of Frederick County, a capacity crowd heard Delaplaine outline a fourteen-point program to promote the anniversary of the anthem's creation. His plan included appeals for official government recognition and for historic preservation efforts, all framed within grandiose goals. One objective centered on instituting the observance of National Anthem Day. In 1963, the D.A.R. lobbied every state governor to proclaim September 14 as National Anthem Day, but only Maryland Governor Millard Tawes acceded. The following year, the Maryland Assembly proclaimed September 14, 1964, "and every year thereafter," as National Anthem Day, but this effort generated little lasting interest. Other initiatives suggested by Delaplaine included petitioning Congress and the president to issue another commemorative postage stamp, and promoting Key's gravesite and birthplace, though the house where the poet grew up had been demolished in the mid-1800s. Delaplaine's presentation motivated the local Daughters of the American Revolution chapter to announce the launch of a nationwide movement to increase appreciation toward the anthem and its author. Their main goal required gathering and preserving Key's documents and papers, which would serve as the nucleus of a museum dedicated to the anthem author and to William Tyler Page, who wrote the American's Creed in 1918. Chapter regent Frances Thomas Bussard opined that the institution "will be visited by tourists from all over the land."[50] The group pledged to establish the museum's headquarters in Frederick after the Civil War Centennial ended in 1965. They also vowed to preserve former Chief Justice Roger B. Taney's home and fill a room on the second floor with Key memorabilia.

To raise money for the proposed museum, Delaplaine, along with Bussard's husband, C. Lease Bussard, founded the Francis Scott Key Memorial Foundation in 1963. Their first task consisted of minting and selling Francis Scott Key Sesquicentennial Souvenir half dollar coins, which sold for fifty cents each and depicted the Key monument at Mount Olivet Cemetery on one side and Fort McHenry on the other. First issued in December 1963, the coin became the official medal at the Maryland Pavilion during the New York World's Fair and circulated widely. Buyers also received a free souvenir pamphlet.[51] The Maryland Economic Development Commission sold the "pocket souvenir of Maryland" at the fair and dedicated the proceeds to the proposed Key memorial and museum in Frederick.[52] The foundation attempted to sign up five hundred charter members at twenty-five dollars apiece, offering each a special sterling silver Francis Scott Key charter medal. Early adopters also received a certificate on a colored parchment scroll and a promise that each person's name would "be placed on a memorial tablet, when [the] memorial is erected." By 1964, the foundation amassed almost $66,000, due mainly to the coin sales.[53]

Anthem enthusiasts received a morale boost in January 1964, when the Smithsonian Institution opened the new $36 million Museum of History and Technology (now called the National Museum of American History), which featured a permanent and prominent exhibition spot near the main entrance built specifically to house the massive flag that inspired Key.[54] Just before the New York World's Fair began, about seventy-five women associated with the Star-Spangled Banner Flag House in Baltimore decided to create a 75-pound replica of the original 42 by 30 foot star-spangled banner. For seven weeks, they followed the same sewing method used by Mary Pickersgill in 1813, which required half a million hand stitches. The project began in participants' homes, and the women first assembled the pieces in the lobby of the State Office Building in Baltimore, subsequently moving to the Fifth Regiment Armory. Working from 10:00 a.m. to 8:00 p.m. every day, "the women are strangely silent," reported the *Baltimore Sun*. "Theirs has been an attitude of reverence toward the flag, and they regard their participation in the sewing as a distinct privilege."[55] When they shipped their creation to the Maryland Pavilion at the fair in New York, however, it proved to be too large, since officials had designed the exhibit before the flag project got underway. Delaplaine reported distinct "disappointment in Maryland because of the lack of space."[56]

Maryland officials spent $1 million on the state's pavilion at the New York World's Fair. Located just inside the main entrance to the fair and across from the national United States exhibition hall, which displayed the replica star-spangled banner flag, the state's hall showcased Maryland attractions and included a 450-seat restaurant and 300-seat snack bar that served local food, crab cakes in particular.[57] A twelve-minute film about Key and the anthem, "O'er the Ramparts We Watched," looped repeatedly, around forty times a day. In cooperation with the Department of Defense and the United States Army, the U.S. Rubber Company picked up the film's $40,000 production costs. Radio and television personality Arthur Godfrey served as the narrator, and the producers commissioned watercolors to depict the historic scenes. Major Samuel Loboda, director of the U.S. Army Band, contributed original music, and the U.S. Army Chorus sang *The Star-Spangled Banner*. According to the *Baltimore Sun*, the movie vied with the seafood wharf as the pavilion's most popular attraction.[58]

Judge Delaplaine continued to promote Key's creation. A relative, Francis A. Hyde, who published the *Builder's Weekly Guide* in Baltimore, arranged for two newspapers to run an article written by Delaplaine about the song's anniversary and the establishment of the Key Foundation. Promising to distribute the piece to the Kiwanis, Rotary, and Optimists clubs, Hyde also touted his connections with public relations officials at the Department of the Interior, which administered Fort McHenry. "After using our story in the local papers, they plan to distribute it nation-wide through their Information Department," Hyde wrote. In his article, Delaplaine detailed his drive to elect Key to the Hall of Fame for Great Americans—a largely forgotten landmark on what is now the Bronx Community College campus in New York City. Every five years over a thirty-year span, Delaplaine and his allies pushed for Key's induction, but the poet never received more than 11 out of 150 votes; in 1945 and 1950, no one voted for him. Delaplaine resented the slight, attributing these failures to the nature of Key's achievements, which came in the field of patriotism and fell outside of the hall's established categories. Delaplaine looked forward to the 1965 vote. "I am certain that our celebration will increase Key's fame," he wrote in his letter to Hyde. "It is possible that an outcome of the Sesquicentennial may be the election of Key to the Hall of Fame."[59]

Building up to the anniversary day, Baltimore played host to a nearly three-month-long Star-Spangled Banner Festival. Throughout the baseball season, the Baltimore Orioles team wore commemorative patches on their uniforms, and home games opened with the national anthem and *Maryland, My Maryland*. Organizers, including the Tourist Division of the Maryland Department of Economic Development, the Maryland Travel Association, and the Travel Bureau of the Baltimore Association of Commerce, promoted the Star-Spangled Banner Festival. Sponsors expected 750,000 visitors to the city between July 2 and September 14. The event's highlight, "So Proudly We Hail," presented an historic reenactment performed by 1,500 Marylanders, recruited to dramatize events from the birth of the United States to the early 1960s. "The gigantic production will be fully staged in an area the size of three football fields. Horse, wagons, antique automobiles, and fire works will be set against a background of period costumes and elaborately designed sets," according to a press release. In spite of the production's logistic complexity, it shared more in common with historical tableaux from the 1920s than a Space Age spectacle. On Defenders Day, September 12, visitors attended the "Story of the Flag," a presentation by the Old Guard Fife and Drum Corps and the U.S. Army Chorus. For the reenactment of the Fort McHenry battle on September 13, "drill troops and other selected military units" presented productions entitled "Prelude to Taps" and "History of the Flag." Judge Delaplaine wrote that "every effort will be made to make the occasion one of the most inspiring programs ever presented there."[60]

The official program for the Star-Spangled Banner Sesquicentennial Commemoration included letters from President Lyndon Johnson and the surviving former presidents. Herbert Hoover, who signed the anthem bill into law, wrote that it is "right and fitting that we commemorate the anniversary of the writing of the stirring words of our national anthem." During an interview with journalist Edward R. Murrow, former president Harry Truman said that he considered the *Missouri Waltz*, the official state song, to be "as bad as 'The Star-Spangled Banner' as far as music is concerned."

In the commemorative program, Truman wrote: "Of course, I have always been interested in our National Anthem. I believe I have stood at attention while it was being played, on more occasions that I can recount, and never failed to be deeply moved by its call." Dwight Eisenhower claimed that the song "brings to mind pictures of my past; of my home and upbringing, of the unique opportunities that have come to me because I am a citizen of the United States of America." Whenever any American at home or abroad hears the song, Eisenhower continued, "he stands straighter, his chin goes up, and he tingles with pride as he says to himself, 'I am an American.' These are the normal, almost universal, reactions to the words and music of our national anthem." President Johnson trumpeted his political program, paying lip service to the anthem and playing up "the Great Society of tomorrow."[61]

The hullabaloo over the anniversary could not disguise the reality: Baltimore faced pressing issues. In the official program, Eugene F. Petty, assistant executive director of the Greater Baltimore Committee, delivered a candid rundown of the city's problems, including "blighted residential areas, the stagnation of business in the heart of the city, [an] inadequate system of mass transportation, and growing traffic congestion." Stuck in a "downward spiral," Baltimore lagged far behind Boston, Philadelphia, Cleveland, Detroit, and Pittsburgh.[62] Turning to tourism, the Chamber of Commerce of Metropolitan Baltimore announced the establishment of the city's Star-Spangled Banner Trail in 1965, a string of ten sites billed as the "answer to Boston's Freedom Trail." Though the actual route remained unmarked, the city installed two hundred red, white, and blue signs pointing to Fort McHenry, located in a desolate neighborhood almost two miles from downtown. Baltimore provided "at least as much history to display to the American public in general as any city in the United States," said Maurice P. Freedlander, chair of the Star Spangled Banner Trail Committee, which distributed one hundred thousand copies of its *Visitor's Handbook*.[63]

Mirroring Baltimore's decline in the mid-1960s, militant patriots in Maryland and beyond saw their power and cohesion dwindle. Membership plummeted in once-thriving fraternal organizations, including the Freemasons, Elks, Knights of Columbus, V.F.W., and American Legion. For hereditary associations, the culture shift hit even harder. A remarkable document, *1812 in '58*, the annual report of the Society of the War of 1812 in Maryland, chronicled declining zeal within the group from the late

1950s through the mid-1960s. Nonetheless, the document noted that each year the organization hosted a dinner in January commemorating General Andrew Jackson's victory at the Battle of New Orleans. In May, they held a Mint Julep Party to recognize the society's original Organization Day in 1842. They also looked forward to re-creating the Battle of Baltimore on Defenders Day, along with a dinner and dance held around September 14 to celebrate the anthem. In 1958, after their banquet at the sumptuous Lord Baltimore Hotel, members and guests made their "annual pilgrimage to the historic and patriotic shrines of the battle of North Point." Accompanied by distinguished compatriots from one of their sister State Societies, Maryland's governor and Baltimore's mayor laid wreaths at monuments marking critical locations in the defense of the city. After a gathering at the Battle Monument downtown, the celebration moved to Fort McHenry and reenacted the bombardment with fireworks.[64]

In September 1959, the society's president, C. Elliott Baldwin, reported that a cavalcade of a dozen cars proceeded to Fort McHenry, and Mayor Harold J. Grady and Governor J. Millard Tawes laid wreaths there. The next evening at the Defenders Day Dinner, society member and retired Marine Corps Major Nicholas A. Canzona delivered an address entitled "Patriotism," which suggested ways to stem the decline of the organization's influence. The descendants of the War of 1812, he said, inherited the responsibility "to lead and inspire, by exemplary conduct, other Americans who are perhaps less conscious of sacred traditions," but he noted the "tendency among some members of historical patriotic societies to regard themselves as exclusive heirs to some particular facet of Americana or Americanism." Canzona warned against making "ritual an end in itself, something strangely remote and forbidden." Like the three wise kings of old, "they should bear their gifts publicly and humbly for all to behold and venerate."[65]

Public flag rituals had fallen out of vogue, even with this patriotic crowd. In 1962, the president of the Society of the War of 1812 in Maryland, Herbert Lee Trueheart, decried "the lack of support by members of the Society of the patriotic celebrations at Defenders Day," which "caused great concern to the Executive Committee and to the Mayor of Baltimore." Several branches of government designated the organization as the official sponsor of Defenders Day celebrations, including the City of Baltimore, which paid the memorial cavalcade's expenses. State officials, along with the army, the navy, the Department of the Interior, and other federal agencies, cosponsored the society's program at Fort McHenry. Trueheart also admonished members for their uninspiring Flag Day appearance at the Star-Spangled Banner Flag House the previous year, which "was so lacking that it was mentioned by the Mayor." In 1964, society president Robert Emory Michel tried to muster troops for the anthem's anniversary, but he estimated that only 25 percent of the enrolled members remained active in the organization. "I cannot help feeling disappointed," he wrote.[66]

After the 150th anniversary of *The Star-Spangled Banner*, enthusiasm among patriots in the city of Frederick and the county also waned. In April 1965, the Francis Scott Key Memorial Foundation shuttered its office in the Francis Scott Key Hotel, located in the heart of downtown. Bylaws requiring that trustees be residents of Frederick County limited the foundation's scope and impact. With Mr. Bussard at the helm and Delaplaine as vice president, the net worth of the foundation peaked at $75,000 in 1966, but neither the planned museum nor the memorial to Key ever came to fruition. Instead, the members tackled less lofty issues, such as deciding what to do with the gift of a chair that once belonged to Governor Thomas Johnson of Maryland and other donated historical artifacts. In the end, the group loaned them to the Historical Society of Frederick County: "The President appointed Judge Delaplaine a committee of one to execute this directive." The foundation got a boost when they took over the administration of the Roger Taney House—and received a hundred dollars, curiously—from the Historical Society of Frederick County. Over time, administration of the Taney home, along with Key's papers and other possessions, reverted to the historical society. The Key Foundation currently operates from an office at Mount Olivet Cemetery, where it maintains Francis Scott Key's memorial and tomb.[67]

As *The Star-Spangled Banner*'s traditional defenders lost their influence, a new generation arose, which came to both berate and venerate the sacred symbol on its own terms.

Postmodern Patriotism, 1964–2014

IN THE MID-1960s, the growing counterculture movement supplied a watershed moment for the national anthem. Rock and soul musicians dared to experiment with the song, left-leaning activists exploited it to underscore their opposition to the status quo, and hardhat construction workers supported a hard line against any change whatsoever. *The Star-Spangled Banner* features an ambiguous, adaptable chord pattern for voice and instruments, and many musicians in the last half century have tried, with varying results, to make the song their own, leading to widespread acceptance of creative interpretations. While ragtime pianists in the 1890s, big bands in the 1930s, and bebop combos in the 1950s altered the approach to the anthem, they nonetheless lacked the luxury of taking too many chances, because a swing or free-form jazz version by African Americans would probably have generated an uproar. The audience's positive response to the no-frills rendition by the Duke Ellington Orchestra at Carnegie Hall in 1943 contrasted with the reaction of proper Bostonians to Stravinsky's arrangement the following year. The evolution of the song-as-spectacle at sporting events and other high-profile occasions, along with the encroachment of social issues onto the playing fields, created indelible popular images. Anthem performances evolved into closely watched minidramas preceding big games, leading many performers merely to mouth the words to a backing track. Executed live,

The Star-Spangled Banner offered "the same possibilities for tragedy and defeat and glorious triumph in the playing of the song as there are in the playing of the game that follows it," commented one sportswriter.[1]

In January 1965, one year after the 150th anniversary of the song, *Fact* magazine ran an article, based on a celebrity poll, entitled "Let's Waive the 'The Star Spangled Banner.'" A press release promoting the issue revealed that "Right-winger Westbrook Pegler and Communist Party leader Gus Hall are agreed on at least one thing: America should get a new national anthem." Literary figures Fannie Hurst and Marya Mannes; composers Igor Stravinsky, Morton Gould, Hoagy Carmichael, Meredith Willson, and Elmer Bernstein; folk musicians Joan Baez and Pete Seeger; and music critics Alan Rich and Harold Schoenberg lined up against the anthem. Comedian Phyllis Diller joined the list of those who, in previous years, suggested a contest to find a replacement. Bernstein, an Academy-Award-winning movie composer, criticized the song's "warlike" qualities, and Carmichael submitted a more singable version, published for the first time with the *Fact* article. Willson, of *The Music Man* fame, said *The Star-Spangled Banner* "violates every single principle of song writing that possibly could be violated." Author LeRoi Jones (Amiri Baraka) called the song "pompous, hypocritical, vapid, and sterile, and [reflecting] the kind of minds that have canonized themselves into some kind of Chosen People. For me, it's as fake as anything else in America." Reverend Billy J. Hargis, founder of the "right-wing Christian Crusade," supported the anthem. Other defenders included music figures Irving Berlin, Richard Rodgers, Roberta Peters, Leopold Stokowski, Sophie Tucker, Marian Anderson, and Duke Ellington, as well as illustrator Norman Rockwell and General Lucius Clay. Berlin called the anthem "a comfortable chair; you pick it out over some new highfalutin' chair because you know you want to sit in it."[2] The following year, the *Saturday Review* published an irreverent article entitled "The Case for A New National Anthem," that also called for a contest to find a replacement.[3]

In May 1965, Robert Goulet, a staple performer in the major Las Vegas clubs from the 1970s to the 1990s, became the first entertainer to earn the wrath and ridicule of virtually the entire nation when he publicly flubbed the anthem at the heavyweight boxing title rematch between Muhammad Ali and Sonny Liston at the St. Dominic Arena in Lewiston, Maine. Other singers and musicians had muffed the words and tripped over the notes before Goulet, but they elicited a less intense reaction. One professional vocalist attracted attention in 1947, during the radio broadcast of a speech delivered by President Harry Truman in Kansas City. "Listeners all over the world heard the singer's voice crack on one of the high notes" and the incident awakened "sleeping foes." At the 1956 Democratic National Convention in Chicago, crooner Johnny Desmond, who rose to fame with the Glenn Miller band, forgot the words and drew "some self-conscious tittering" from those present, but his mistake went largely overlooked. Later, at a party, Desmond joked that "there is no truth in the rumor that I was paid by the Republicans to blow the lyrics to our national anthem."[4]

In contrast, the public never forgot Goulet's transgression. Performing before the fight, Goulet tripped over the song in front of 2,434 spectators and a national television audience. Though he carried a crib sheet in hand, which he glanced at twice, Goulet sang the "dawn's early night" and "perilous night." His voice also quavered on the high note at the end. One attendee reported that in addition to being off-key and out of sync with the organ, Goulet mangled some of the words yet "finally managed to slur his way through it." After the song ended, Goulet walked toward a corner of the ring, slumping his shoulders and covering his face in mock shame. Goulet explained that having been raised in Canada, he didn't know the song well. No one bought his excuses, however, and the gaffe dogged him throughout his career. After he died in 2007, even obituaries recounted his moment of shame.[5]

Goulet's trials stirred a renewed debate over the tune's merit and suitability as the national anthem. His performance also left a legacy that continues to haunt almost anyone who tackles the tune. "I'm more nervous when I'm out in center field singing than I am center stage at the Met," said the "Star-Spangled Baritone," opera star Robert Merrill. "The words aren't that difficult, it's the fear of forgetting them. Robert Goulet created a monster."[6] From the 1960s through the 1990s, Merrill, a longtime opera and radio star in New York, regularly performed the anthem at baseball games in Yankee Stadium. His forceful recording, done in the quasi-bombastic style of John McCormack, became a popular option at many major league ballparks.[7] Merrill proclaimed his opposition to any "distortions" and "different interpretations" of the song, and he remained an island in the sea of musical change that first inundated the anthem in 1968, a tumultuous year in

United States history, marked by assassinations, the quagmire in Vietnam, urban riots, and a more strident turn in the Civil Rights movement. War protestors and longhaired iconoclasts burned the flag with such regularity that Congress passed the Flag Protection Act, outlawing the practice (though the Supreme Court overturned the statute in 1989). As the counter-culture exerted its influence, a growing coterie of Americans championed individualism when paying musical homage to the nation. Yet to militant patriots, taking liberties with the anthem demonstrated that the country had become unglued.

In August 1968, soul singer Aretha Franklin chose to make an artistic statement in her interpretation of *The Star-Spangled Banner* at the Democratic National Convention in Chicago. Franklin's rendition elicited outraged comments, but national attention mainly focused on other events during this particular presidential nominating process, which became a free-for-all that included shocking violence in the streets outside the convention hall. Gene Callahan, then working for the governor of Illinois, remembered the entire convention as a "debacle," including the anthem, broadcast live on national television. Franklin and the band never rehearsed in advance and "were completely out of kilter," said Callahan. According to the Sunday newspaper magazine *This Week*, Franklin "made even bigger news" than Goulet when she "stumbled over a few difficult words during an unusual arrangement." One television critic claimed that she sang "what to many ears, notably those of a thoroughly rattled orchestra, was the first soul version of 'The Star-Spangled Banner.' Musically, the generation gap was never so wide." Letters condemning Franklin's interpretation poured into many newspapers. In the *Washington Evening Star*, one contributor, under the signature "Union Musician," called it "a new low in musical taste and an affront to all Americans. It was a sacrilege to hear the jazzed-up version of our National Anthem and any instrumentalist would probably be called before the National Board of the American Federation of Musicians for such conduct." A letter in the *Chicago Tribune* contended that her "low-key spiritual" reflected "very poor taste" and suggested that "Miss Franklin should have learned the words . . . long ago."[8]

Little more than a month later, during the televised 1968 World Series baseball championship between the Detroit Tigers and the St. Louis Cardinals, *The Star-Spangled Banner* changed forever. Tiger Stadium hosted games three, four, and five of the contest and team announcer Ernie Harwell booked the anthem performers. At the first game, local singer and actress Margaret Whiting delivered a "straight ballad" version, he said. Harwell tapped pop singer Marvin Gaye for the second game, recalling a "little irony" when team officials told him to ask Gaye "not to give too much of a soul rendition, a Motown tone, to the national anthem, so I did and he said 'Yeah, I'll sing it straight.'" From his perch in center field, Gaye, backed by a horn section, made good on his promise.

For game five, on the advice of a friend, Harwell booked twenty-three-year-old singer and guitarist José Feliciano. Born in Puerto Rico and raised in New York City's Spanish Harlem, Feliciano had scored a hit with a cover version of *Light My Fire* and played an engagement in Las Vegas with Frank Sinatra. After arriving on a red-eye flight and serenading Tigers' stars Al Kaline and Dennis McLain in the clubhouse, the blind musician, accompanied by his guide dog Trudy, walked out to center field with Harwell. Sitting in a chair in front of the Merle Alvey Detroit Tigers Dixieland Band, Feliciano launched into an acoustic guitar and vocal version of *The Star-Spangled Banner*. Most band members, appearing onscreen to television audiences for a few seconds, held their horns to their sides. One mouthed the words, another laughed, and the rest tried to look straight ahead as Feliciano strummed his way into history. The broadcast then cut to a shot of the flag, the color guard, the teams, and the stadium—anything to avoid showing the singer delivering arguably the most important performance of the national anthem since its very first airing in Baltimore. Adding a folk flair to his stripped-down approach, Feliciano crafted an original chord arrangement, overlain by a plaintive, pleading lyric line injected with several soaring, blues-inspired passages that departed from the song's familiar melody, phrasing, and cadence. This version remains one of the most heartfelt and original interpretations ever recorded, yet offended listeners expressed outrage over the singer's nonchalance and his seemingly casual inclusion of "yeah, yeah" at the end, an innocent flourish to a flawless performance.[9] Feliciano's rendition, to a greater degree than his predecessors over the decades, turned the song into a vehicle for individual expression.

Harwell, who considered the adaptation to be "beautiful," heard a mixture of cheers and catcalls as he and Feliciano walked off the field. The singer, oblivious to all this, looked forward to spending a few innings in the press box before taking the next flight back to Las Vegas. Feliciano recalled that during a break in the game's action, announcer Tony Kubek asked him, " 'Do you realize what you've just done?' And I said 'No.' He said 'You have created a commotion here, veterans were throwing their shoes at the television, and the switchboard really got deluged by calls.' " Feliciano expressed surprise. Kubek then patted the musician on the back and said: " 'Don't worry, kid, you didn't do anything wrong. I really enjoyed the way you did 'The Star-Spangled Banner.' " When Harwell heard about the objections to Feliciano's performance, he realized that the singer cut a controversial figure for many by growing his hair a tad long, wearing dark sunglasses due to his blindness, and playing the "instrument of the hippies."[10]

Feliciano meant no disrespect with his "soul-spangled" banner. "A man can express a love for his country any way he feels," he told a newspaper at the time. "The song had practically passed into oblivion. Now it's back in every home as it should be. . . . I don't think the kids dig it. So I changed it to suit the new generation."[11] Almost a decade later, Feliciano commented: "All I did was try to make it contemporary enough so that young kids would listen. And have respect for the country. America's been good to me, and I wanted to say thanks."[12] Harwell partially blamed the media for the controversy: "NBC had someone going through the stands saying 'Wasn't that awful?'—and everyone agreed with him." Local headlines that accompanied the syndicated Associated Press write-up stated: "Fans Protest Soul Singer's Anthem Version" and " 'Soul' Anthem Raises Furor." The article included quotes claiming that the disgraceful, insulting, and "unpatriotic" version "stunk" and "ignited a storm of protest" as the crowd howled. "A lot of people got anxious and took it the wrong way," said Harwell, who almost lost his job. "The American Legion wanted to pass a resolution that everybody had to sing it on note."

Harwell also referred to coverage of the controversy in the *New York Times* as an example of undue attention. A negative news item about Feliciano's interpretation appeared in the sports section, but the paper's editorial board and its chief music critic supported the singer. "Hearing our national anthem sung to an unfamiliar tune should not make that anthem any less meaningful," exhorted the editorial, which criticized detractors and praised diversity in expression. "Thank God for people like José Feliciano." *New York Times* critic Donal Henahan questioned why anyone would be disturbed: "He does, certainly, distort the melody somewhat, but only a bit more than most singers . . . in public places. Feliciano's distortion is at least on purpose." In its "scar-spangled history, our National Anthem has been put through a 1,001 transfigurations. It has been edited and improved, arranged and deranged, revised and juggled until it is a wonder that it survives in any recognizable form, let alone in its pristine, sanctified, original unsingability."[13] Others liked Feliciano's version, too. Just over a week after his World Series performance, RCA records released the rendition as a single, which reached number 50 on the charts. The Associated Press quoted one person at the game who expressed admiration for the singular interpretation: "It seems to bring out a little more than the regular versions." Later, on a National Public Radio program, the singer commented that for about three years after the incident, disc jockeys blacklisted him, but his career rebounded after he wrote *Feliz Navidad* in 1970, one of the most popular Christmas songs of all time. "I opened the doors for anybody who wants to do the Anthem . . . in their own way," Feliciano said. "I was the first one and usually pioneers get the stones and everybody else gets the accolades. So I'm happy to get the stones."[14]

Rock guitarist and singer Jimi Hendrix first performed his flamboyant live version of the anthem a month before Feliciano's rendition in Detroit. According to one music critic, Hendrix's distorted, feedback-drenched instrumental rendition of *The Star-Spangled Banner* "made those of Aretha and José sound like a Sunday class sing-a-long." Hendrix introduced the anthem into his concerts in September 1968, when he debuted it in his hometown of Seattle, Washington. By April 1969, word of Hendrix's take on the anthem spread to Texas, where five thugs stood outside his dressing room at Memorial Auditorium and threatened him. "No one does that in Dallas, Texas, and lives to tell about it," one of them said. Hendrix played *The Star-Spangled Banner* anyway, without incident.

Hendrix's most famous performance—at Woodstock in August 1969 during the height of the Vietnam War—featured battle-like noises and free-form-jazz drum rolls that sounded like rumbling artillery. Hendrix also inserted a few notes from *Taps*, the bugle tune that accompanies military funerals. Reaction to his Woodstock performance, included in the feature film and on the separate soundtrack, both released in 1970, further polarized the generations and "freaked out" America's Silent Majority, who fretted that public desecrations of the national anthem signaled the end of the world as they knew it. The *Los Angeles Times* called it "the cheapest form of sensationalism." During his short career, Hendrix performed the anthem live about two dozen times, and he included a snippet as part of a medley he recorded at Olympic Studios in London in February 1969. The electric guitar guru also recorded a complete solo studio version in March 1969, included on his *Rainbow Bridge* album. Radically different from his approach at Woodstock, this four-minute take, augmented with sound effects, layered numerous overdubs that provided a power-chord underpinning to the high-pitched melody line that remained faithful to the original tune. Engineer Eddie Kramer likened the sound to a guitar synthesizer. The track brooded toward its conclusion, and then descended into sonic chaos as an echo of guitars washed into a muddle of noise.[15]

Hendrix defended his version. Soon after Woodstock, he said: "When it was written it was played in a very beautiful state, you know? Nice and inspiring, you know? Your heart throbs and you say 'Great, I'm American,' but nowadays, we play it the way the air is in America today. The air is slightly static, isn't it? You know what I mean?" Hendrix, honorably discharged from the army, attracted criticism for supporting the Cold War's domino theory, used to justify American involvement in Vietnam. On "The Dick Cavett Show," when the host asked about Woodstock, Hendrix shook his head and said: "I don't know, man. All I did was play it. I'm American, so I played it. I used to have to sing it in school—they made me sing it in school, so it's a flashback, you know." Cavett turned to the camera and said, "This man was in the 101st Airborne, so when you write your nasty letters in . . ." As he paused, Hendrix scrunched his face, saying: "Nasty letters? Why? You're really trying hard, aren't you?" Cavett replied, "When you mention the national anthem and talk about playing it in any unorthodox way, you immediately get a guaranteed percentage of hate mail from people who say 'How dare anyone.'" The guitarist disagreed. "That's not unorthodox," he said, tugging on his upper lip. "I thought it was beautiful. There you go." As the audience applauded, Hendrix flashed the peace sign right side up and upside down and then clowned around with the host.[16]

Hendrix delivered an even more incendiary version at the Berkeley Community Theatre in California on May 30, 1970, ten weeks before he died at age twenty-seven. After the notes corresponding with the line "ramparts we watched," he simulated a wolf whistle, used in old films and cartoons when males spied an attractive female. When Hendrix played the melody for the passage "our flag was still there," he paused and muttered, "Big deal."[17] Hendrix's innovations—and the reactions to them—scared off other performers, who opted to adopt conservative arrangements or turned down opportunities to sing the anthem. "Never in our history has one song caused so much bother to so many people as 'The Star-Spangled Banner,'" wrote the *Baltimore News-American*. After a bad experience performing the song at a Los Angeles Dodgers baseball game, Nat King Cole said, "If you do nothing else in your life, don't ever sing the national anthem at a ballgame." Frank Sinatra hated the song. "It's a terrible piece of music," he said. The words "have no relation to what this country is all about. In this time of trouble and misunderstanding, they talk about guns and bombs and all that jazz."[18]

Shockwaves emanating from the music world influenced the realm of sports, which generally tried to shield itself from political and social turmoil. The infamous black power salute at the 1968 Summer Games, arguably the most iconic Olympic image of all time, occurred ten days after Feliciano's rendition of *The Star-Spangled Banner* at Detroit's Tiger Stadium and subtly influenced anthem ceremonies for years. Tommie Smith, favored to medal in the 200-meter dash at the 1968 Olympics, finished first, in world-record time, and John Carlos took bronze. While attending San Jose State University, the two black sprinters fell in with the Olympic Project for Human Rights, which proposed the idea of organizing a boycott of the games by African American athletes. For their symbolic, premeditated podium protest, both runners carried their shoes behind their backs as they approached the podium, wearing black socks to represent "black poverty in racist America." Smith wore a black leather glove on his right hand, which stood for "the power in black America." The glove on Carlos's left hand signified "the unity of black America." Smith wore a black scarf and bowed his head to simulate prayer. Carlos's unzipped jacket symbolized solidarity with blue-collar workers and his beaded necklace paid homage to victims of lynching. Along with Peter Norman of Australia, who won the silver, the three medalists affixed round Olympic Project for Human Rights patches on the left breasts of their clothing. When the first notes of *The Star-Spangled Banner* echoed through the stadium, Smith and Carlos turned their backs to the flag, bowed their heads, and each raised a gloved fist, transforming the medal podium into a political platform. Smith called it a "statement about the conditions in which my people and I were living in the greatest country in the world. I never said a word as the national anthem was playing. My silent gesture was designed to speak volumes." As they walked off the victory stand, the two Americans raised their fists again. Though they later backed off on their militant talk, calling their Olympic actions a human rights protest, the sprinters received hate mail and death threats. Nonetheless, in 2005 San Jose State University erected a statue of the two athletes standing on the medal podium, leaving Norman's spot empty.[19]

The media continued to generate controversy over the national anthem. In a 1969 feature recycling several quotes from the *Fact* magazine piece in 1965, *This Week*, a widely circulated Sunday newspaper supplement, held a reader referendum on the matter: "'The Star-Spangled Banner' has a difficult tune and the words are controversial—if you think we should change it, here's your chance to vote." The publication printed two tabs to cut out and mail in—one to keep the anthem, the other to replace it—along with a space in which to write an alternative. It urged, "Our national anthem is a good deal like the weather: everybody talks about it, but nobody does anything about it." Congress took "117 years just to recognize 'The Star-Spangled Banner' as the national anthem." Even then, they "didn't bother to specify which of a dozen or more conflicting versions was the official tune." At a time "when TV brings 'The Star-Spangled Banner' into our living rooms with every telecast of a ball game or public event, we tend to talk even more about it." Thus *This Week* proposed that readers "stop just 'talking' and start 'doing.'" The magazine claimed that the voting results "should give a really valuable idea of what we Americans think about our own anthem." The accompanying derogatory article emphasized the anthem's unusual range along with its awkward words, which "often come in tongue twisting masses, and the breaths don't fall in the right places." It cited confusion over the song: "Many people take for granted that the anthem is of revolutionary origin." The article also claimed that "the history of the music is not entirely respectable." And, in addition to being anti-British, the anthem glorified bloodshed. "The pros are fewer than the cons."

The magazine suggested holding a competition or substituting an alternative, among them *My Country, 'Tis of Thee*; *The Battle Hymn of the*

Republic; *God Bless America*; *Columbia, the Gem of the Ocean*; *America the Beautiful*; and *Hail, Columbia*. Bandleader Mitch Miller called the anthem "a joke." Jazz giant Benny Goodman said: "I'd like to declare a truce on those bombs bursting in air. That's just not the image that best reflects the basic ideals for which we stand." Folk singer Joan Baez said that she refused to sing *The Star-Spangled Banner* in high school, "because I knew it was just so much trash." On the other hand, celebrated pianist Van Cliburn applauded it as "the most beautiful national anthem in the world. The critics who don't like 'The Star-Spangled Banner' are the kind of people who don't like anything." Broadway composer Richard Rodgers called it "impossible to sing. But—as far as I'm concerned—tradition is more important than simplicity." Ease of singing "is unimportant," said renowned bandleader Duke Ellington. "It's the symbol of our great nation—and that's all there is to it." Composer Aaron Copland appealed to sentiment, which "far outweighs any musical consideration. The national anthem is not like an auto tire that you change when it goes flat. You don't change brands as if it were so much toothpaste."[20]

After tallying the results, 50,000 to keep it and 20,000 to change it, *This Week* ran the headline "Most Readers Love Our Anthem." Thousands of people "sent letters, notes, music, poetry—and suggested more than 200 other songs." R. C. Carrigan of Westfield, New Jersey, argued, "We have enough unrest and attempts to change the American tradition without bringing this latest question to the surface." Dedham, Massachusetts, resident Charlotte N. Noyes claimed that "if the Bible can be revised," why not the anthem? "These young upstarts don't know music and most of them never will," wrote Mrs. E. McCoy of Fort Lauderdale, Florida. "All they know is how to yell their heads off and stamp their feet and shake their bodies like nuts." Another reader, Clara L. Emerson, from Powhatan, Virginia, claimed that "plenty [of] people can't sing period—so what will we do for them?"[21]

The medal-stand protest in 1968 at the allegedly apolitical Olympic games, along with the advent of idiosyncratic renditions, influenced subsequent anthem rituals and performances. From the 1940s on, professional sports served as an incubator for racial integration in the United States. In 1964, when promising Kentucky-born boxer Cassius Clay changed his name to Muhammad Ali, he embodied a new outspokenness and an individual orientation that influenced team sports, where lopsided contracts long favored the owners. In the late 1960s, St. Louis Cardinals baseball player Curt Flood, and Dave Meggyesy, who played for the St. Louis Cardinals football team, took the first steps toward organizing players' unions, which led to free agency and ever-more-lucrative contracts for athletes. Meggyesy further elicited the wrath of team officials and the National Football League (NFL) by circulating a petition in the locker room opposing the Vietnam War, which numerous teammates signed. Responding to the Olympics imbroglio, the league's commissioner, Pete Rozelle, required players to hold their helmets in their left hands and salute the flag during the anthem. Meggyesy took offense and responded by pulling "a low-key Tommy Smith," referring to the controversial sprinter, and "held my helmet in front of me and bowed my head." After getting benched the next year, Meggyesy left football and wrote *Out of Their League*, a 1970 exposé that competed with *Ball Four*, written by baseball pitcher Jim Bouton in 1969, as the era's most scandalous sports book. Anthem controversies helped institute an increased analysis of sports, which turned into the primary battleground over the beleaguered national anthem and its meaning. "Football fields and basketball courts and boxing rings are not the playgrounds of gods but of men who are finding it increasingly difficult to play the role of heroes," wrote one reporter in 1972. Performances of *The Star-Spangled Banner* gave "athletes the opportunity to express their feelings about the institution of sports and the conditions in the country," but the tradeoff came in a higher level of scrutiny on aspects such as gambling on professional sports, drug abuse among athletes, brutality, and "the unabashed commercialism that television feeds constantly."[22]

As conservatives feared, demonstrations against Vietnam and the status quo rippled through the nation's heartland. In 1970, Forrest Byram, a football player at Niles North High School in Skokie, Illinois, refused to remove his helmet during the playing of *The Star-Spangled Banner*, as "his way of protesting American foreign policy." The coach suspended Byram, but school principal Gilbert Weldy urged his reinstatement. "People talk while it [the anthem] is being played, eat hot dogs and drink Cokes, visit friends and pay no attention whatsoever to it," said Weldy. Others "stand there with their hats on and with their hands in their pockets. So why bother at all? The only thing the National Anthem accomplishes before a sports event is that it helps numb the crowd for a minute or two." According to one reporter, "the youth's political act, the principal's candid views, the coach's stand, and the reaction of the students and parents set off community turmoil. Those on both sides were threatened, although the youth and the principal got the worst of it."[23]

The Star-Spangled Banner became politicized long before the 1960s, of course, but never with such emotional intensity. "Liberal whites and blacks don't feel as if it is their National Anthem," said Jack Scott, director of the Institute for the Study of Sports at the University of California at Berkeley, who argued that the song should be dropped from games altogether. "It represents to them a powerful ruling elite from Pete Rozelle to President Nixon who seem to expect athletes to give up some of their civil liberties on the playing field. Athletes are expected to dress and act in a certain way and are not supposed to be critical of their country." The anthem, Scott said, "is not the cause of anything, just a symptom." In a nation that values freedom, popular pressure enforced conformity to somewhat arbitrary rituals surrounding the anthem, ensuring that The Star-Spangled Banner exerted a subtle influence on the lives of almost all Americans. "Any display of disrespect for the song—even a variation in the musical rendition—became tantamount to an act of treason," wrote the Washington Star. "Sensitivity has been especially keen at sporting events which Americans like to think of as endowed with all the virtues and spirit of the nation." Airing the anthem as a prelude to games, the article continued, inevitably became a "time for individuals to give socio-political views as well." At the 1972 Olympics in Munich, two black American sprinters, Wayne Collett and Vince Matthews, turned their backs to the flag during the playing of The Star-Spangled Banner and "stood casually, hands on hips, their jackets unzipped. They chatted and fidgeted," prompting the International Olympic Committee to bar them for life. Justifying his action, Collett said, "I couldn't stand there and sing the words because I don't believe they're true." An act of Palestinian terrorism during the games, however, overshadowed this anthem incident.[24]

Among all sports, The Star-Spangled Banner is most closely associated with baseball. After World War II, the song continued to air before almost every game, due in part to improved amplification technology and the installation of organs and public address systems. After the war, the Chicago Cubs stopped playing the anthem at every home game, reserving its airing for opening day and holidays. During the inaugural season of the Baltimore Orioles in 1954, general manager Arthur Ehlers announced his decision to not play *The Star-Spangled Banner* before each game. Frequent repetition at sports events "tends to cheapen the song and lessen the thrill of response," said Ehlers, a onetime American Legion post commander and World War I veteran with impeccable patriotic credentials. "I remember the old days of vaudeville when the management would bring out the flag to win applause for a poor act," Ehlers said. "Crowds at stadiums and other sports arenas have a way of continuing to laugh and talk and move about while the anthem is being played. That applies to fights, wrestling matches, stock-car races—and baseball games. To me it is very distasteful." He planned to play the national anthem on special occasions, such as Memorial Day, when the team proposed showcasing veterans' groups, a color guard, and a drum and bugle corps. Responding to the ensuing general uproar, Baltimore's city council passed a unanimous measure to encourage the playing of the anthem before every game. Within a month, Ehlers relented.[25]

Public pressure also influenced other professional sports teams. On opening day in 1966, the Chicago White Sox decided to substitute *God Bless America*, expressing "no hard feelings toward" the anthem. " 'God Bless America' is a patriotic song and we think perhaps it's better tailored for fan participation," said Ed Short, the baseball team's general manager. "This is an experiment and the consensus after the three games is that 'God Bless America' brings more response than 'The Star Spangled Banner.' " When White Sox officials conducted a poll, 395 fans voted for the anthem, 251 for *God Bless America*, and 51 for *America the Beautiful*; three respondents suggested no song at all. Irving Berlin wrote to the team, urging them to restore *The Star-Spangled Banner*, leading *Chicago Tribune* columnist Herb Lyon to refer to the situation as "a new Berlin crisis." Bowing to pressure by militant patriots to honor the troops fighting in Vietnam, the White Sox reverted to the anthem by the end of May. Uptown, despite pressure, the Chicago Cubs continued their practice of not playing the anthem before every baseball game. Longtime owner Philip K. Wrigley said that the song "shouldn't be cheapened by routine renditions in athletic arenas," adding that "during wartime, we always played the national anthem before a game was started." In 1967, recognizing the growing conflict in Vietnam, Wrigley relented and resumed the practice of airing *The Star-Spangled Banner* before every home game. In 1972, with defeat in Vietnam almost certain, Kansas City Royals owner Ewing Kauffman decided midseason to drop the anthem, except on Sundays and holidays, due to "the apathetic attitude of many fans during the song." Kansas City is home to the national headquarters of the V.F.W., and after an immediate outpouring of complaints—"almost all expressing indignant and emotional opposition," said Kauffman—the team reinstituted the anthem ritual after two games. Several basketball clubs successfully tinkered with the formula in the 1970s. Perhaps reflecting the pioneering spirit of the West, Oakland, California's Golden State Warriors conducted the Pledge of Allegiance before games, and Oregon's Portland Trail Blazers switched to *God Bless America*. Another West Coast team, the Seattle Supersonics, substituted *America the Beautiful*, *God Bless America*, and Francis Scott Key's third verse.[26]

In the mid-1970s, fans and officials of the Philadelphia Flyers hockey team claimed that Kate Smith's rendition of *God Bless America* delivered before games—instead of the national anthem—brought them good luck, especially after they won the National Hockey League's Stanley Cup championship in 1974 and 1975. In the late 1970s, the New York Knicks basketball team dropped the anthem in favor of *America the Beautiful*. Even the tradition-bound New York Yankees baseball team experimented with alternatives. The practice of "playing the anthem before sporting events has created an insatiable market for bigger, better, or hipper versions" of the song, wrote the blue-collar *New York Daily News*. "In the past, the Yankees have invited [Robert] Merrill, Janis Ian, Yul Brynner, Ray Charles, Pearl Bailey, and Charlie Pride and all performed for a couple of free tickets on the first base side. Once, for variation, George C. Scott talked the words to 'America the Beautiful.'" Bernie Landers, the team's director of promotions, said: "It doesn't always have to be the anthem. But you have to be careful. You don't mess with the *Banner*. It gets people very upset."[27] With the regular seasons for baseball, basketball, and hockey being so long, anthem duties usually reverted to a house singer. Some celebrities charged for their services (Kate Smith reportedly earned $5,000 per game for appearances in Philadelphia), but most performers settled for two tickets to the game. "The biggies among house singers also get free parking, but that is definitely not a trend," said one basketball executive. Notable local stars at baseball games included Fat Bob the Singing Plumber (Bob Taylor), a regular at Detroit Tigers games, and Cleveland Indians singer Rocco Scotti.[28]

Beginning in World War II, the National Hockey League played the United States and Canadian anthems when teams from the two countries faced off. During the Vietnam War, however, the Montreal Canadians ceased playing *The Star-Spangled Banner* before games with teams from across the border in the "Lower 48," to avoid incidents. A team official cited the strong sentiment against the war in Canada, including from the large number of "Americans who came here to escape the draft." In January 1973, track and field officials in New York City generated a backlash after announcing their intention to drop the anthem during a major event. The issue emerged during a Knights of Columbus track meet held at Nassau Veterans Memorial Coliseum on Long Island in New York State, when runners on the mile team from Eastern Michigan University did warmup stretches during the national anthem instead of standing at attention. Some fans became unruly, which led to the team's disqualification. "I don't think this is the time or place for the national anthem," said one competitor afterward, not realizing that in addition to the facility being an arena memorializing veterans, at that time a large portion of Long Island's economy depended on military contractors.

Two days later, the *New York Times* reported that "amid growing controversy over whether the National Anthem should be played at sports events—and how the public and competitors should act during the song—'The Star-Spangled Banner' Monday was dropped from the prestigious Olympic Invitational track and field meet at Madison Square Garden." The anthem typically aired before the mile race, held at or near the end of track competitions, and event officials at Madison Square Garden said it would be pointless to change and play it at the beginning of the meet, when few spectators occupied the stands. Still, according to the reporter, "it was apparent that the fear of an incident, by fans or players, was a major factor in the [officials'] decision." Edwin H. Mosler Jr., chairman of the Garden's meet committee, admitted: "Sure, the black factor crossed our minds. One doesn't relish incidents that disrupt an event. It entered into our decision, but it wasn't the key factor." Although "most of the controversy surrounding the playing of the anthem at sports events has cropped up following incidents with black competitors," the *New York Times* reporter wrote, "there appears to be no national organization that is making a concerted effort to prevent black athletes from standing or appearing in front of fans while the anthem is being played." Roy Wilkins, executive director of the NAACP, issued a statement insisting that "there is no national anthem for Negroes. There is only one National Anthem. The National Anthem is for all Americans." The next day, facing public pressure, race officials reinstated the song.[29]

The Star-Spangled Banner achieved even greater significance in the 1970s, when pregame ceremonies grew from quaint, utilitarian rituals into spectacles. The military occasionally began providing jet fighter flyovers at taxpayer expense, timed to coincide with the anthem's final notes. The U.S. Air Force, seeking recruits, focused most of its attention on college athletics. "We do it for the national publicity and exposure and to remind the public that there are still POW's in Vietnam," said Pentagon information officer Colonel Mark D. Secord. In 1971, air force jets buzzed overhead at eleven college football games, including the Rose and Orange bowls, along with the NFL's American, Super, and Pro bowls. Liberal patriots took issue with the display of militarism surrounding *The Star-Spangled Banner*, but Jim Kensil, executive director of the NFL, defended the anthem ritual in sports, claiming that the games offered a "forum for people to honor the flag." One professional baseball player said that "we are able to hold games because our country has provided us with a place where people can live peacefully together." According to New York baseball icon Gil Hodges, the anthem provided a moment to reflect on "how fortunate we are in this country." Baseball Hall of Famer Reggie Jackson once told a reporter: "When I'm in the outfield facing the flag, I see kids messing around—laughing and wrestling—when the song is being played. Afterward I go over and tell them 'Either you stand at attention for our national anthem or you go over to China and see how you like it. You don't stand at attention over there, they shoot you.'" Yet the athletes themselves sometimes lacked decorum. "Basketball players slouch, spring up on their toes, shake their arms, and roll their necks as if the *Banner* were part of a precisely choreographed Chinese warm-up ritual," wrote one commentator. In response to the lackadaisical attitude in his league, NFL commissioner Pete Rozelle "issued orders against talking, nervous footwork, gum chewing, and shoulder-pad slamming during the *Banner*."[30]

As opponents continued to attack the anthem, pundits directed unprecedented sarcasm and contempt toward the song. A whimsical article in *Stereo Review* called it "low camp" that should have died out decades ago. "Few Americans escape exposure to 'The Star-Spangled Banner' in some form for more than a week at a time in their daily lives." Mentioning the memorable performances by Goulet, Franklin, and Feliciano, the writer argued that the United States is "lively, industrious, optimistic, irreverent, careless, tender, cantankerous, and friendly." The melody is "somber, pompous, and cumbersome, three properties seldom found in the American spirit." Blaming the Great Depression for the 1931 anthem law and inaccurately calling the choice "purely arbitrary," he argued that if the country successfully repealed Prohibition, instituted by a constitutional amendment, then surely the anthem could be revoked. The writer also recommended that *The Star-Spangled Banner* be replaced "with some more accurate description, something about a big-hearted, hard-working nation with its share of bungling father figures and crabgrass problems, a nation that is showing signs of putting aside its violent past and taking up sex and computer programming."[31]

Marylanders tried to reverse the troubling trend, especially after George London, onetime singer with the Metropolitan Opera in New York City, took over as artistic director at the John F. Kennedy Center for the Performing Arts in Washington, D.C. "The difficulties of our national anthem awe me," London told *Life* magazine in 1968. "I prepare for it as I would a major opera role. If you want to know the truth, most singers avoid singing it in public. It is just too hard." One newspaper article quoted another remark by London: "We are stuck with a pretty bad anthem. I have always wished that we had another national anthem." In 1971, Senator Charles Mathias Jr. (R-Md.), a native of Frederick, Maryland, Key's hometown, issued a pun-filled press release declaring that he was "not in harmony" with replacing the anthem. According to the senator, George London "is out of tune with the rest of the Nation. . . . 'The Star-Spangled Banner' is more than just a song. It is an epic of the courage of our ancestors during troubled times."[32]

In Frederick, Judge Delaplaine also confronted the critics. In 1972, Senator Mathias placed an article, written by Delaplaine, into the *Congressional Record* about the efforts in Maryland to celebrate the 158th anniversary of the anthem. Delaplaine recounted the modest movement to institute National Anthem Day around the country in honor of the song's 150th birthday in 1964. Since that time, "National Anthem Day has not received much public attention. On the contrary, there have been some individuals who have criticized 'The Star-Spangled Banner' and have urged that it be replaced by an anthem easier to sing."[33] In addition to keeping a file of people who attacked the song, Delaplaine continued to solicit the opinions of prominent musical figures. In 1973, Irving Berlin wrote: "No song could replace our National Anthem. . . . Nobody has to sing it. All they have to do is stand up when it's played." The composer dismissed the folly of conducting contests to concoct a different anthem, which would be "the same as asking someone to make a new Liberty Bell."[34]

An emboldened media magnified anthem controversies with straw polls and person-on-the-street interviews. In a revealing article published in 1973, the *National Tattler* reported that eight out of ten respondents (78 percent) to a reader's poll could not recite the song's first verse, and that two-thirds of them could not recall its title. Yet even ambivalent Americans wanted to keep it. "That is the rather paradoxical result of an extensive survey conducted by TATTLER on what Americans really think (and know) about their national anthem." The tabloid initiated the survey "because of a growing debate in the United States over how, when, and where the national anthem should be played." Almost three-quarters of the survey participants (72 percent) agreed that *The Star-Spangled Banner* should precede athletic competitions. Reporting other "rather shocking results," the *Tattler* found that 82 percent favored no change "under any circumstances." Asked if "every American should show respect for the national anthem whenever and wherever it is played," 86 percent agreed. The same percentage of respondents under age twenty-five wanted to keep the anthem, versus 79 percent of those older than twenty-five. The article included responses from ordinary Americans, who "are not bashful about expressing an opinion on their ideas of patriotism." Jerry Sather of Seattle, Washington, said: "I'm an American and I'm damn proud of it. Of course, it should be played." Law student Eldon Spenser noted: "The whole idea of the national anthem was to foster unity. But ironically, it is causing division." Another respondent stated: "I believe everyone should show respect for the national anthem if it means something to them. But it should not be required. After all, it's a free country." The article concluded that "while Americans do not know very much about 'The Star-Spangled Banner,' they have a great deal of patriotic respect for Francis Scott Key's timeless composition."[35]

Many articles carried the same headline, "Oh Say Can You Sing?," that mocked the song and tacitly blamed it for the debacle in Vietnam. Advocates for *America the Beautiful* hinted that adopting their favored hymn would somehow cleanse the nation of its sins. In 1975, a Boston-based Unitarian minister published a piece in *Atlantic* magazine that called the upcoming bicentennial of the adoption of the Declaration of Independence the perfect time to correct the mistake of choosing *The Star-Spangled Banner*, which celebrated a "minor incident in a minor war," as the national anthem. Unintentionally undermining his weak position, the writer stated that "except for the vote of the 1974 annual conference of the Minnesota United Methodist Church, there has been neither a ground swell nor a ripple of public opinion indicating any desire for a new anthem." The country would be ready for a new anthem, however, "when we realize that if the bombs once more burst in the air, the flag will not still be there in the morning because nothing will be there," a reference to the earth's nuclear threat. Understanding that a move to replace the song would trigger widespread disagreement over any potential successor, the writer suggested that Congress "disestablish" the anthem for ten years and "declare an open season on national anthems," during which "annual anthem contests can be held." Polls would "take weekly readings of the nation's lyric pulse" and "ministers, editors, and commentators can whoop for their favorites." Then, after a national referendum in 1986, the issue would finally be settled.[36]

Newspaper editorials also pilloried the anthem. Criticizing the "exotic rendering" at Super Bowl X in 1976 by Tom Sullivan and Up With People, a favorite group of NFL commissioner Rozelle's wife, the *Washington Star* wrote: "We thought the Democratic Party had wrung Mr. Key's song dry of schmaltz at the 1972 convention, when a succession of crooners negotiated those craggy musical intervals like somewhat tone-deaf mountain goats." Calling the tune "one of the great American vulgarities," the paper nonetheless admitted that "there would be quite a row over its replacement."[37] The following year, the magazine *Sports Illustrated* examined the topic, since the song is "bellowed, bebopped, blown, or just plain botched before virtually every game." Given the enormous "amount of time, emotion, and money devoted to presenting the *Banner* at sports events," the anthem "probably will always be with us. Attempts to do away with it have almost invariably met with resistance from fans, owners, and players. The song has come to be equated with sports, as if the game could not proceed if the anthem were not played."[38]

Calls for a new anthem edged toward critical mass during the bicentennial of the Declaration of Independence in 1976. The nation reeled after the last helicopter lifted off from the roof of the United States Embassy in Saigon—following the capture of the city by the communist North Vietnamese, which ended the war. Seeking to rally around something positive, Americans turned to the bicentennial, which featured fireworks across the country, a parade of tall ships up the Hudson River in New York City, and self-congratulatory pats on the back. The flip side consisted of soul-searching, centered on the nation's recent history and its future direction. Detractors lumped Francis Scott Key with other "dead white males" whose work and legacy attracted criticism. A press release issued by the American Revolution Bicentennial Commission (ARBC), which Congress created in 1966, announced that it received a deluge of correspondence about the anthem. "Suggestions have ranged from rescoring the National Anthem to changing it entirely. The major dialogue in these debates has been about a 'singable' National Anthem vs. the historic and traditional values of the current one." The commission recommended "that Congress not change or rescore the National Anthem on the basis that it would be inappropriate for anyone to use the Bicentennial to change the National Anthem, since 'The Star Spangled Banner' is so associated and ingrained as our National theme." Any changes lie "within the purview of Congress, to whom the ARBC can make a recommendation."[39]

Televised bicentennial celebrations across the country featured disappointing renditions of *The Star-Spangled Banner*, further tarnishing its reputation. The words of the song "should have been on millions of American lips," wrote the *New York Times*. "Instead, there seemed to be a lot of humming." The *Boston Globe* reported that when the Boston Symphony Orchestra, under the direction of Arthur Fiedler, presented a July 4 concert on the banks of the Charles River, thousands joined in to sing a medley of *America the Beautiful*, *This Land is Your Land*, and *The Battle Hymn of the Republic*. "It was an unabashed display of patriotism, a symbol that, after a decade of war and Watergate, the nation's wounds were healing and the mostly under-thirty crowd didn't feel self-conscious about singing their country's praise." When the orchestra struck up *The Star-Spangled Banner*, however, "thousands mouthed the lyrics, or stood mute."[40]

In 1977, representatives James M. Collins (R-Tex.) and Guy Vander Jagt (R-Mich.) blustered about repealing the anthem. Collins remarked on "America's dismal singing performance last July Fourth." Watching televised celebrations of the bicentennial throughout the day, he saw various groups "either mouthing it, or just not singing at all." Collins agreed with the results of a poll taken in his Dallas district favoring *God Bless America*. Vander Jagt preferred *America the Beautiful*. Anthem opponents amassed even more ammunition after radio station WMAL-AM in Washington, D.C., aired an editorial supporting *America the Beautiful*, which would "better symbolize the new change in our national mood." Quiet strength, the editorial argued, "can be more powerful than exploding force." Though the station's management prepared for a backlash, a majority of its listeners favored the change, placing 276 votes for *America the Beautiful*, 238 for the anthem, 33 for "other," and 18 for *God Bless America*. Opponents of *The Star-Spangled Banner* publicized the results and tried to create a tipping point.[41]

In response, many voices rallied around the anthem. In July 1977, Maryland native James M. Cain, author of *The Postman Always Rings Twice*, published an op-ed piece in the *Washington Post* dismissing "the same old brouhaha, a move to junk the 'Star-Spangled Banner.'" He recalled a revealing incident. Working as a school principal on the Eastern Shore of Maryland, Cain assembled his students to sing *The Star-Spangled Banner* together. When the time came, only his voice could be heard. The next day, after he dropped out from singing, only the pianist remained audible. To Cain's amazement, when he attended the 1960 Democratic National Convention in Los Angeles, where a friend served as its musical director, all fifteen thousand people in attendance sang along, because the band played the song in the key of A-flat, whereas Cain had used the key of C, four steps higher in pitch.[42]

As Cain's experience illustrated, a big problem plaguing the anthem throughout much of its history centered on rigid musical customs that hindered listeners' participation. The keys of B-flat and C are ideal for many wind instruments, and since brass and military bands helped etch the song into the minds of listeners from the 1880s on, these keys became a default of sorts for musicians and educators, even though they could strain vocal chords. One article in 1942 claimed that although "the people of this free country play it and sing it as they like . . . the only rule generally observed is to do the song in B-flat." Yet every composition is transposable and can be performed with the same melody at any pitch. In the 1960s, musicians stopped paying slavish devotion to the dictates of sheet music and set the song in keys that kept the infamous high notes from hovering too far out of reach. The key of G seems to suit many singers, and a good tip for performing the tune is to place the first notes as low as possible in an individual's or a group's vocal range and let the melody blossom from there.[43]

In 1977, less than a decade after José Feliciano's pioneering performance, one reporter wrote that blues, pop, and soul versions of *The Star-Spangled Banner* "received wider acceptance" as popular tastes and tolerances changed. A tidal shift can be dated to the powerful anthem performance delivered by jazz singer (and Democrat) Ethel Ennis during the presidential inauguration of Richard Nixon, a Republican, in January 1973. A fan of the singer, Vice President Spiro Agnew, who hailed from Maryland, arranged to book Ennis for the event. In full command of her voice, the Baltimore native declined offers of an instrumental accompaniment. Sounding as clear and cutting as a horn, Ennis took one- or two-note liberties with about a half dozen words, adding just enough innovation and blues hues to give her deliberate version a distinctive flair, yet she surrounded her more adventurous passages with the familiar melody. Ennis later recalled receiving criticism for the version's jazz and blues influences, which added dramatic tension to her slow-paced singing. Not long afterward, one observer wrote that Aretha Franklin, Lou Rawls, "and many others have done soul versions of the song with little or no adverse reaction from fans, the American Legion, or anthem cultists," and these variations became more commonplace on the anthem circuit.[44] In 1977, even though his career rebounded, Feliciano declined an invitation to perform the song at a Los Angeles Lakers basketball game, saying that "it brought back too many bitter memories."[45]

In addition to the serious stakes surrounding the national anthem for performers and political activists, its repetition at games sometimes bothered cynical sportswriters. *New York Post* reporter Paul Zimmerman earned some renown on the local newspaper beat for timing the duration of the song at events he attended, in an attempt to shorten the performances. Through 1977, the longest version he clocked, by the Christy Minstrels at the 1973 World Series, lasted two minutes and thirteen seconds. Once, after the Princeton University band completed the song in 53 seconds, he stated: "I was so excited I went up to the bandleader and told him that if he really moved through 'the rocket's red glare,' he could go under 50 seconds. It's never been done. He said he once tried it but got in trouble with the alumni."[46] In 1977, John Kiley, the organist at baseball's Fenway Park in Boston, "became an anthem legend for coming in at a snappy 51 seconds," reported *Time* magazine. "But that is still not fast enough for [the] ABC Sports [broadcast network]. 'The goal,' says former producer Dorrance Smith, 'is to cut away to a commercial.' "[47] Nowadays, star-spangled bookies and casinos float an over/under wager on the length of the anthem performed at big games, timed from the utterance of the first "O" to the final note in "brave." During almost every regular-season and playoff game in all major sports, television and radio stations break away from the anthem for a word from the sponsors.

Around the time of the bicentennial, a grassroots groundswell began to build around adopting *America the Beautiful* as the signature national song. Soul music icon Ray Charles released his powerful studio version of *America the Beautiful* in 1972 and remained associated with the composition throughout his career, promoting it as the national anthem.[48] Though countered by the presence of *God Bless America* as a popular alternative, this movement to change the national anthem eventually posed the most serious challenge to *The Star-Spangled Banner* in the twentieth century. Liberal patriots, religious groups, and New Englanders had long championed *America the Beautiful*, which never achieved official recognition on even the local level until Julie Rosegrant, a seventy-two-year-old grandmother in Putney, Vermont, promoted the song. Rosegrant, a former teacher of English who held a number of posts in local government and established the state's first credit union, claimed a longstanding hatred of the anthem. On March 1, 1977, she convinced town meeting participants to approve a measure in favor of recognizing *America the Beautiful* as the national anthem, which passed by a vote of 87 to 64. When a group of local farmers heard about the results, which they contended took place after most of the town's one thousand registered voters left the meeting, they formed the Committee to

Save Our National Anthem.[49] Spurred by the controversy, the *Boston Globe* conducted a poll: 493 readers voted for *America the Beautiful*, 220 supported the anthem, 141 chose *The Battle Hymn of the Republic*, 98 selected *God Bless America*, and of the 94 votes for a different composition, most opted for *This Land Is Your Land*. Some *Globe* readers admitted, however, that *America the Beautiful* "lacks pizazz," and Arthur Fiedler, conductor of the Boston Pops Orchestra, backed the anthem. "It's not the most comfortable thing in the world to sing, but it has a certain character to it that expresses the country," he said. "It has zip to it. I guess I'm conventional."[50]

By the month's end, the national networks came knocking on Rosegrant's door. Charles Kuralt devoted a segment of his long-running "On the Road" television series to the issue. According to a reporter from the *Brattleboro [Vt.] Reformer*, who shadowed the television crew, "a somewhat nervous Julie Rosegrant smiled to a most relaxed Charles Kuralt in the living room of her home Thursday" as the two spoke about her crusade. At one point, she loosened up enough to blurt: "Lead me in the paths of television . . . for the cause!" She joked about the lineage of the anthem as a former drinking song: "I've heard that you have to have a few under your belt to reach 'the rocket's red glare.'" She also criticized the song for being warlike and inappropriate for the optimism embodied by the Jimmy Carter administration, extolling *America the Beautiful* as a more singable alternative, one, moreover, written by two Americans. The local reporter opined that "some network somewhere was bound to sense the snowballing attention being given the lady of Putney." Rosegrant told Kuralt that "letters—most of them supportive—began to flow in from all over the nation almost immediately," yet none of Vermont's three congressional representatives in Washington, D.C., agreed to sponsor her measure. Undeterred, she sent petition forms to everyone who wrote to her, asking them to lobby their representatives. She also vowed to contact music educators, symphony orchestra conductors, and President Carter. "I represent a town, and I've gotten a heck of a lot of publicity," she said. Asked by Kuralt if the drive would ultimately be successful, Rosegrant "paused and stared off past [the] television lights. 'I'm going to hedge on that one,' she said. 'But maybe this is the right time. I think we've hit a responsive chord.'"[51]

During the taping, Rosegrant credited her cohorts, Edward J. Sherry of Falmouth, Massachusetts; Madeleine Rushton of Waltham, Massachusetts; and Alfred Stevens of Old Lyme, Connecticut—sturdy New Englanders all—who worked "for years" to get the anthem changed and operated under the guise of the Committee for *America the Beautiful* and the Committee to Change the Anthem, names that puffed up the groups' modest membership. Stevens, a retired Yale University Press copyeditor, criticized the "blatantly militaristic" anthem: "It's about an old battle. It's an English drinking tune that says reprehensible things about the British." His choice, however, "speaks of peace and brotherhood. It describes the breadth of the country in terms that we can understand, and almost everyone knows the words and can sing the melody."[52] Though this quartet tried to generate a national movement on behalf of *America the Beautiful*, their influence waned as the nation turned its attention toward the death of Elvis Presley, the oil crisis, and the Iran hostage drama. Rosegrant claimed to be "looking for a groundswell—a campaign of the voice of the people." By July 1977, she received only a thousand letters from forty-eight states. Of the fifteen correspondents who resisted change, most were "American Legionnaires who feel 'America the Beautiful' is too sweet and we have to put up a tough stance against the Russians and the Chinese," she said.[53]

Within a year, Rosegrant's campaign collapsed, though ultimately she collected thirteen thousand signatures from across the country. In March 1978, the Committee to Save Our National Anthem called for a paper-ballot referendum among all 977 registered voters in Putney to repeal the earlier town-meeting vote and support *The Star-Spangled Banner*. The results came back 252 to 168 in favor of the anthem, but a crestfallen Rosegrant vowed to fight on: "If I quit, I'd be letting an awful lot of people down." Donald Harlow, cochair of the anthem committee, claimed to represent a Silent Majority that only spoke up "when it begins to look like our national anthem really will be changed." The group disbanded after the vote, and Harlow's committee cochair, Leslie Switzer, said: "Right now, it's enough that Julie can't use Putney's name to endorse her position."[54]

Publicity on behalf of *America the Beautiful* elicited a backlash in Maryland as well. The statewide department of the American Legion vowed to fight any anthem change.[55] Judge Delaplaine recirculated John Philip Sousa's pro-anthem statements and reached out to Boston Pops conductor Arthur Fiedler. "I am with you and Irving Berlin," Fiedler wrote in August

1978. "Many times a national anthem has been changed, and not always for the best. I, for one, am very, very pleased that we have not changed our national anthem because it is a very stirring piece of music. Though it has its difficulties vocally, I still think it is a great piece of music." When Delaplaine died in 1989, the anthem lost a diligent, longstanding advocate who helped solidify its stature in the face of numerous attacks.[56]

Like any oft-repeated canonical song, *The Star-Spangled Banner* grated on the nerves of a percentage of the population, and it faced new challenges as events kept the anthem in the news. Efforts to replace it rippled through the 1980s, due partly to the spread of experimental versions of the song, and also to a concerted campaign on behalf of *America the Beautiful*. Motown star Marvin Gaye deviated from his 1968 World Series performance and delivered a singular rendition of the anthem at the 1983 National Basketball Association All-Star Game in Los Angeles. Accompanied by a spare beat-box and synthesizer track, Gaye riveted the crowd with a laid-back groove that drew out certain words and added unfamiliar accents. People shouted their approval at the end of several passages, since he left a lot of space between the notes in his nearly three-minute take. Toward the end, during the line "O say does thy star-spangled banner," after the audience's initial bewilderment at his approach wore off, the entire arena clapped in unison and erupted after the final note. "I did it the way I thought Mahalia Jackson might have sung it with a little bit of my style, but borrowing a bit of her, and I put it to a march beat with a slight reggae undertone; very, very slight," he told an interviewer. "While singing it, while practicing it . . . I felt it from my soul, you know. I felt that singing it with that kind of music as the background gave me an inspiration and I asked God that when I sang it would he let it move men's souls and, um, I decided to go with it."[57]

Gaye's rendition attracted attention to the efforts of Congresswoman Marjorie Holt (R-Md.) of Baltimore, who replaced Joel Broyhill as the House member most preoccupied with the song. Beginning in 1974, at the behest of the local American Legion post and other veterans' groups, Holt revisited the standardization issue and introduced legislation proposing that the official version of the anthem "consists of the words and music as composed by Francis Scott Key and arranged by Thomas Carr," the Baltimore music publisher who first set the lyrics and music together in print. Carr's version from 1814 would probably have sounded woefully outmoded to an

American in the 1970s, and Holt said she sponsored her locally focused bill "because both [men] were from Maryland." Though she received an "amazing" amount of letters on the subject from around the country, the congresswoman "tackles her anthem proposal with something less than wild-eyed enthusiasm," wrote the *Chicago Tribune*. The article's headline referred to a "rocket red flare-up in Congress," yet its text reported that although José Feliciano, Aretha Franklin, Jimi Hendrix, and Marvin Gaye stirred up anger, "America's musical patriots can't seem to get Congress as hot under the collar as they are." One "less than chagrined House committee aide" predicted that the bill would die quietly, but "the extremists, the God, country, and flag faction, will at least be able to say they tried."[58]

The anthem issue resurfaced in the mid-1980s when Representative Andy Jacobs Jr. (D-Ind.) attracted attention with a bill to designate *America the Beautiful* as the national anthem. The House of Representatives subsequently referred his bill to the Committee on the Post Office and Civil Service. Jacobs had introduced similar proposals at every session of Congress, beginning with his first term in the mid-1960s. He later studied the issue and published several articles in favor of the switch, but he professed fealty to the anthem, writing that *The Star-Spangled Banner* "can do wondrously chilling things to our innermost feeling." Still, he contended that "the anthem should be about the entire nation and not just one battle over in Baltimore." Changing the national anthem "is not the burning issue of my congressional service," Jacobs wrote in 1986. "I simply ran it up the flagpole after numerous constituents argued [that] we should have a national anthem the nation can sing. Participatory democracy implies participation in the singing of the anthem," a duty and pleasure that "should not be left only to budding opera singers."[59]

In the mid-1980s, Jacobs galvanized "talking heads"—self-professed experts armed with prepared commentary—who unleashed what appeared to be a coordinated volley of articles and appearances on television shows and radio programs, timing their efforts to generate enthusiasm for the bill. The first salvo in what turned into a yearlong media campaign against the anthem came from theater critic and Brandeis University music professor Caldwell Titcomb. His piece in the *Baltimore Sun* took issue with the anthem's wide melodic range and "low quality as poetry." He promoted *America the Beautiful* as a song not only written by Americans, but also half written by a woman, which would help "overcome the notion that this is mainly a man's world." He suggested arranging the tune for an a capella quartet and noted that it is the "official song of the American Federation of Women's Clubs." Titcomb suggested that the 200th anniversary of the Constitution in 1987 represented a prime time to make a change.[60] That same month, he published another article in the *New Republic* that repeated part of the *Sun* headline, "What So Loudly We Wail."[61]

Another piece of the seemingly synchronized attack on the anthem arrived within a week, when the Universal Press newspaper syndicate distributed a column written by James J. Kilpatrick, who allied with Congressman Joel Broyhill in the 1960s. Kilpatrick lauded Titcomb by name and repeated the same points raised by the professor's article, but switched around the introduction and the conclusion. Kilpatrick also noted that "the National Federation of Music Clubs long ago took a strong stand" in favor of *America the Beautiful*. Congressman Jacobs, he wrote, would let things "germinate under the winter snows, but come next spring" the bill would get a good push. "Every ballpark basso who has reached for the high C in 'The Star-Spangled Banner,' and fumbled the note disgracefully, will wish the congressman well."[62] Another anti-anthem article admitted that with neither momentum nor big money behind the measure, "some members of Congress may feel skittish about voting against a national symbol, however flawed." Some of the "awkward and embarrassing" words in *The Star-Spangled Banner* included the line about bombs bursting in air, which the article's writer considered to be an inappropriate turn of phrase for the nuclear age. *America the Beautiful,* by contrast, contained lofty and lovely urban and rural imagery, points raised in other publications that supported changing the national anthem. "We should have an anthem written by Americans, not an old English drinking song." Related opinion pieces ended with the premise that "any legislator can go to a baseball game this spring, count on one hand the number of fans who can sing their way through 'The Star-Spangled Banner,' and get a good idea of how many other voters would welcome the switch."[63] Titcomb and his allies later served as panelists on an episode of "This Week with David Brinkley," where all present supported the Jacobs bill. "I was surprised when Brinkley chimed in with the rest of them," said Jacobs. "They disagreed about everything else."[64]

Defenders of the anthem responded, "Since when did Americans shrink from something merely because it was difficult?" The *Wall Street Journal* attested to the longevity of *The Star-Spangled Banner* and intimated that changing it would be a waste of time. From Fort McHenry to Fort Sumter to Iwo Jima, "the flag flying under hostile fire has been a symbol of American determination and ideals. Words paying homage to that very sight are the most appropriate ones to serve as our national anthem. Now that that's settled, Congress can concentrate on controlling spending."[65] In July 1986, *Atlantic* magazine acknowledged that even though the song had become subjected to the type of scrutiny typically reserved for presidential candidates, by 1931, when President Hoover signed the national anthem into law, *The Star-Spangled Banner* had long served as the country's de facto anthem. But "Americans don't like to be told what to eat or drink or sing. Though they have eaten hot dogs and drunk beer and sung 'The Star-Spangled Banner' in baseball parks for generations, try to pass a law requiring them to do so and Congress will never hear the end of it. It is the American way, and a good way." The writer contended that in spite of the "vocal challenges, unmarchability, and checkered past" of the song, the 1931 vote remained "a gesture of affection with few parallels." Lauding the anthem as "one of the purest examples of unpremeditated, inspired genius in American history," he quoted an old editorial from the *New York World* by James M. Cain that praised the tune in spite of its difficult melody. In 1986, the *New York Times* concluded that "many Americans are not wholeheartedly happy with 'The Star-Spangled Banner,' but they won't stand for anything else."[66]

The controversy stimulated a sustained period of analysis and headline writers devised clever anthem puns. *USA Today* devoted its entire July 18, 1986, opinion-page spread—which included five articles, a poll, and comments from celebrities—to the row kicked up by Congressman Jacobs and his supporters. An editorial cartoon showed a childlike Francis Scott Key on a ship, quill pen and parchment in hand, staring up at the skies beneath a full moon as a bomb burst over Fort McHenry. The bubble by his head read, "When th' moon hits your eye, like a big pizza pie, that's amore," lyrics from a 1950s hit song by crooner Dean Martin. The newspaper's editorial promoted "a national debate about our national anthem," which it claimed stirred the heart, but "also strains the vocal chords." *The Star-Spangled Banner* reminded Americans that freedom is worth fighting for, "and a verse about 'bombs bursting in air' written in 1814 doesn't mean we're encouraging a holocaust." According to the newspaper's editorial board, *America the Beautiful*, which is "more soothing than stirring," also contained lyrical shortcomings. A list of potential replacements for *The Star-Spangled Banner* mentioned *Born in the U.S.A.* by rock legend Bruce Springsteen, one of many baffling calls for this bleak anti–Vietnam War song to be considered as the country's anthem. Other suggestions included *God Bless America*; *Lift Every Voice and Sing*; *Columbia, the Gem of the Ocean*; and *You're a Grand Old Flag*. "Let's see if we can find a song that better reflects the resonance, scope, and grandeur of our great nation. Maybe we can't, but let's find out." The opinion-page spread included a coupon with checkboxes to designate keeping the anthem, replacing it with *America the Beautiful*, suggesting a write-in candidate, or holding a competition to find a new anthem. The paper invited readers to call their toll-free telephone number "and leave a brief message on our tape."[67]

For Marylanders, Jacobs had another strike against him. In addition to casting aspersion on the anthem, the congressman hailed from Indianapolis, Indiana, where Baltimore's beloved National Football League franchise, the Colts, relocated in 1984. Baltimore Mayor William Donald Schaefer quipped: "First they steal our Colts; now they want to steal our anthem." In his article in *USA Today*, Schaefer ridiculed the idea of decommissioning the song and wondered, if Congress seriously considered such a thing, why not change the colors of the flag or junk the eagle as the national symbol? The anthem represented "generations of our ancestors, people brave enough to want to be free, people courageous enough to settle a vast wilderness." The song served as a "symbol of everything for which the U.S.A. stands. That special piece of music that brings tears to the eyes of patriotic people of the U.S.A. when the flag is raised and *The Star-Spangled Banner* is sung."[68]

Jacobs, on the other hand, quoted portions of the anti-English third verse and argued that because Britain evolved into a trusted ally, the United States should jettison *The Star-Spangled Banner* in favor of *America the Beautiful*. Indulging in name-dropping, Jacobs cited supporters of his position, including entertainer Danny Thomas and media figures George Will, James J. Kilpatrick, Sam Donaldson, and David Brinkley. He also pointed to an article in the *Arizona Republic* and the results of a poll taken by the *Clearwater [Fla.] Sun*. Jacobs contended that "it isn't terribly important what politicians in Washington decide our national anthem should be," because "in recent years, an enormous number of citizens are voting with their voices for *America the Beautiful.*" As evidence, he cited the 1985 memorial service for the victims of the space shuttle *Challenger*'s postlaunch breakup and the centennial celebration of the Statue of Liberty, a patriotic showcase akin to the bicentennial, where *America the Beautiful* played a central role. Genuine patriotism, Jacobs wrote, is "an abiding thing," not a boisterous matter. "*America the Beautiful* is not about an American war. It is not about the American flag. It is about *America*, which we have a duty to make ever more beautiful, not necessarily in the eyes of Hollywood cameras, but in the eyes of God."[69]

USA Today's feature spread also included quotes from celebrities. Singer Melissa Manchester favored *America the Beautiful*, but she also singled out *You've Got a Friend* as a suitable anthem. Soprano Beverly Sills, at that time the general manager of the New York City Opera, called the anthem difficult for children to master and supported *America the Beautiful.* The *Star-Spangled Banner*, said country singer Eddie Rabbitt, represented a "time-honored tradition, and changing it would be like changing the colors of our flag." Key's creation "is better structured for singing" and is "symbolic of our country," said Aretha Franklin. Yet she added: "From a sentimental standpoint, I like *America the Beautiful* because the lyrics are more touching. But they are both wonderful songs." Legendary bandleader Cab Calloway called *The Star-Spangled Banner* the "theme of the U.S.A.," adding that it's "not hard to sing. The range is rather difficult, but you cannot satisfy everyone. We have been singing it since the 1930s, and we should keep on singing it with respect, as we should respect our country." That same year, however, at a Golden State Warriors home game, Calloway, then in his late seventies, delivered a perfunctory performance akin to parody, singing: "Whose bright stripes and bright stars and the heavenly light / Oh, the ramparts we watched, were so allan-ly fleeing."[70]

In 1989, the 175th anniversary of Key's creation passed largely unnoticed. One Baltimore humorist, Neil Grauer, wrote an op-ed piece revealing that local jazz vocalist Ethel Ennis and Edward Polochick, director of the Baltimore Symphony Chorus, joined with Ray Charles to try and replace the "unsingable" anthem, a stance tantamount to treason in Monument City. With *The Star-Spangled Banner* "under siege," Grauer wrote, "pressure may be mounting to replace it with 'America the Beautiful.' " If every American could sing the anthem together, said Ennis, "maybe something positive would come out of it." Grauer attacked the generic lyrics of *America the Beautiful*, since every country has "spacious skies," Switzerland has "purple mountains' majesties," and Canada has "shining seas" on its coasts. "Even Russia has 'amber waves of grain' in good years. And almost every nation pays lip service to the concept of brotherhood."[71] The controversy prompted a 1989 poll in *Parade* magazine, another Sunday supplement, and the results revealed that most Americans favored changing the anthem.[72] Offering a contrary viewpoint, a joint *Time* magazine and Cable News Network poll reported that 53 percent of the respondents "feel the anthem is easy to sing," 28 percent "think it should be replaced by *America the Beautiful*," and 64 percent "claim to know all the words." Representative Jacobs continued to introduce bills favoring *America the Beautiful* until he left Congress in 1997, but his later proposals died, in large part because Tip O'Neill, longstanding speaker of the House of Representatives, never got on board.[73]

In 1990, comedienne Roseanne Barr's crass take on the anthem at a San Diego Padres baseball game set a new low standard. After screeching the song at a rapid pace, she compounded the problem by grabbing her crotch and spitting on the ground at the end. Spectators expressed extreme disapproval, and critics referred to it as the "Barr-Mangled Banner." "I figured everybody knew I wasn't the world's greatest singer," she said at a Beverly Hills press conference two days later. "I thought it was going to be very well received." Tom Werner, the owner of the Padres and producer of Barr's hit television sitcom, had invited her to sing as a publicity stunt. Unlike Hollywood, however, San Diego is a more conservative California military town. During her rendition of the anthem, "I went into this panic thing and I thought, 'Can I get out of here? Can I quit?' " Barr said. "But I couldn't. It took all the guts in my life to finish that song." Before the performance, several Padres players encouraged her to mimic ballplayer behavior when she finished singing. "I thought it would be really funny," she said. Afterward, the team decided that for the time being, all "home games will be preceded by a rendition of 'The Star-Spangled Banner' as performed by the U.S. Marine Corps Band—in a prerecorded version."[74]

In 1991, award-winning singer Whitney Houston illustrated the anthem's power and appeal by delivering a riveting performance at the Super Bowl—

played in 4/4 time to give it extra oomph. Three weeks after the game, her record label released this version as a CD single (along with *America the Beautiful*). Never mind that she lip-synched to a prerecorded track during her performance. The Gulf War and Operation Desert Storm had broken out ten days before the game, and the emotional context helped elevate Houston's rendition into one of her iconic moments.[75] But *The Star-Spangled Banner* is more than just a gauge of patriotic fervor; it also measures musical acuity. Not every singer or instrumentalist is inspired by the song, but if a professional musician is booked for the gig, he or she is expected to perform a creditable version, despite the intense audience scrutiny, knowing that any flub or differentiation could conceivably be construed as being disrespectful to the country and to patriots of yore. Audiences are quick to turn their thumbs down if they dislike a vocalist's version of *The Star-Spangled Banner*. Amateurs are often given leeway, but not Olympian Carl Lewis, who bludgeoned the song so badly at a New Jersey Nets home basketball game in 1993 that he apologized to fans midway through, saying, "Uh oh, I'll make up for it now." Replays of the most tortuous passages in Lewis's version prompted the anchormen on television sports network ESPN to laugh uncontrollably on camera and joke about "Francis Scott Off-Key."

Sports devotees often display hypocrisy toward the nation's official song. John Amirante—a regular anthem performer at New York Rangers hockey games, New York Knicks basketball games, and New York Yankees baseball games since 1980—sang "o'er the land of Wayne Gretzky, and the home of the brave" at the hockey star's final game, held at Madison Square Garden in 1999. The pop band Huey Lewis and the News once changed the anthem's lyrics in tribute to San Francisco 49ers quarterback Joe Montana. Rock star Steven Tyler of Aerosmith warbled overexaggerated, faux-blues scat passages at auto racing's Indianapolis 500 in 2001, ending with "and the home of the Indianapolis 500." Headline writers again criticized Tyler for his screechy interpretation at the 2012 American Football Conference's championship game. In December 2010, when country singer Eli Young went blank after "twilight's last gleaming" and stopped the tune cold at a Kansas City Chiefs home football game against the Denver Broncos, the crowd pounced. After a pause, he started over from the beginning, but skipped a few passages. Then, "as Chiefs fans always do, they paused their booing to howl 'And the home of the Chiefs' at the song's conclusion," wrote one sports blogger, identifying an obvious discontinuity. Altering the anthem "to support a sports team is perfectly acceptable" to fans, "but accidentally blowing a verse or two is a major sin."[76] In Baltimore, of all places, crowds at the city's Camden Yards ballpark also put team devotion above patriotic decorum by screaming out the "O"—for Orioles—during the line, "O say does that star-spangled banner yet wave." The custom also spread to supporters of the Baltimore Ravens football team. In Atlanta, crowds at baseball's Turner Field predictably shout their team's name in "home of the Braves" at the song's end. Houston Rockets basketball fans yell the words "rocket's red glare" and audiences at Dallas Stars hockey games scream the team name during the line "broad stripes and bright stars." At Chicago Blackhawks home hockey games, the crowd tries to drown out the anthem with cheers, a so-called tradition that dates to 1985.

From the 1970s on, stadium and arena officials, well aware of the controversies over *The Star-Spangled Banner*, responded by playing no-frills recordings. These straight-arrow selections, which lasted through the 1990s, included renditions by operatic baritone Robert Merrill, vocalist Jerry Vale, the Mormon Tabernacle Choir, and the Johnny Mann Singers. The grandest sports spectacle of them all, American football's Super Bowl, has long attempted to avoid anthem-related controversies. University marching bands performed the anthem at the first two Super Bowls and National Symphony Orchestra trumpeter Lloyd Geisler (not Anita Bryant, as the official histories have it) played it at Super Bowl III. At Super Bowls III, IV, and VII, the Pledge of Allegiance preceded *The Star-Spangled Banner*. Before singing the anthem at Super Bowl VIII, held in 1974, country music singer Charley Pride performed *America the Beautiful*. Other notable renditions in the 1970s included those by the U.S Air Force Academy chorale; the Little Angels, a children's choir from the Holy Angels Church in Chicago; and a choir from Colgate University in upstate New York. In 1977, just after the bicentennial year, Vikki Carr sang an elaborate version of *America the Beautiful* instead of the anthem, without incident. In the 1980s, the NFL began booking established pop stars to sing *The Star-Spangled Banner*, including Diana Ross, Barry Manilow, Neil Diamond, and Billy Joel, except for 1985, when two children's choruses from San Francisco performed in nearby Stanford, California. The first significant Super Bowl anthem controversy centered on singer Jewel's lip-synched version in 1998.

That development should have come as no surprise, since event producers, attempting to avoid mishaps and maximize predictability, recommend that performers leave nothing to chance. In 2003, the three women forming the country band the Dixie Chicks created controversy by singing to a backing track. Aretha Franklin again found herself at the center of an anthem spat in 2006, when she, Aaron Neville, and Doctor John delivered a languid gospel version. Franklin punctuated the rendition with dramatic vocal flourishes, including a long riff after the line "land of the free," and attracted criticism for singing the word "yes" as she drew out the ending.

Athletes continued to stir up trouble. While playing for the Denver Nuggets basketball team in 1996, point guard Mahmoud Abdul-Rauf (formerly Chris Johnson) refused to stand during the anthem, claiming that doing so would clash with his Islamic beliefs. This led to a standoff with the National Basketball Association (NBA). After a one-game suspension, Rauf gave in and decided that he would pray as he stood with the rest of the team. The brouhaha prompted media mogul Ted Turner to promote *America the Beautiful* as a replacement for the anthem during a July 4, 1997, speaking appearance at Independence Hall in Philadelphia. In 2003, as the United States moved to invade Iraq, Toni Smith, captain of the Manhattanville College women's basketball team, caused a tempest by turning her back to the flag during the anthem. At a subsequent home game, a Vietnam War veteran ran onto the court and held up a flag in front of her face. Smith's stance ignited a debate over her constitutionally protected, free-speech right to protest versus her duty to avoid making waves before every game.

Under certain circumstances, *The Star-Spangled Banner* brings Americans together. Before a 2003 NBA playoff game between the Dallas Mavericks and the Portland Trail Blazers, thirteen-year-old Natalie Gilbert, who had won a contest to sing the anthem at that game, strolled onto the floor of the Rose Garden Arena in Portland and promptly forgot the words after the phrase "twilight's last gleaming." Clearly flustered and unable to regain her lyrical footing, she began to glance around for help. Just then, Blazers coach Maurice Cheeks stepped forward, putting his hand on her shoulder and whispering the words in her ear. Still lost, her voice quavering, Gilbert froze, so Cheeks—who is no Sam Cooke, the fluid gospel and soul singer—took over and led the entire arena to the song's conclusion, including players and the opposing coach, who spontaneously joined in after Cheeks began directing them.

The anthem paradox continued as Americans showed little interest in the song until controversy ignited a counterattack in defense of its importance. After a 2004 Harris Interactive Survey revealed that almost two-thirds of the respondents expressed unfamiliarity with the words of the first verse to *The Star-Spangled Banner* and 38 percent could not name the title of the song, the National Association for Music Education sponsored "The National Anthem Project: Restoring America's Voice," designed to reintroduce Americans to their anthem. In June 2007, the festivities culminated in several performances at various landmarks in Washington, D.C., and environs.[77] In 2006, just as the Senate began a debate on the immigration issue, British music producer Adam Kidron assembled an all-star cast of Latino musicians to create *Nuestro Himno* (Our Anthem), with loosely translated words, a fairly faithful melody, and a march beat with a hint of hip hop. About halfway through, it turned into a rap song that included the lines "these kids have no parents because of the mean laws" and "let's not start a war, all these hard workers they can't help where they were born."

Immigrant groups had set *The Star-Spangled Banner* to foreign languages in the past, but those versions retained a degree of deference that could readily be interpreted as a sign of assimilation and honor toward the United States. The federal government twice commissioned Spanish translations of the national anthem, the first time in 1919, when the Bureau of Education published a sheet music version of *La Bandera de las Estrellas*, with lyrics by Francis Haffkine Snow. In 1945, the State Department sponsored a competition to bolster the government's Good Neighbor Policy toward Latin America. The winner, Peruvian immigrant Clotilde Arias, titled her translation *El Pendón Estrellada*. The State Department also approved of a version in Portuguese. But the attempt by *Nuestro Himno* to equate love for country with a sympathetic view toward illegal immigrants irked militant patriots. The following year, as the ultimately unsuccessful immigration bill continued to float around Congress, Philadelphia talk show host and song parodist Steve Bryant, along with Tony Polito, penned *Jose Can You See?*, which carried the subtitle "New National Anthem":

Jose can you see, there is no fence in sight?
Once we get there, I hear, they will never send us back.
We won't pay any tax; they won't put up a fight.
Send all our kids to school, even though it's just not right.
We can go on welfare, we'll have money to spare.
Cause Congress is blind, and George Bush doesn't care.
We walked across the border, we didn't need any boats.
Now the Liberals love us, politicians want our votes.[78]

As irreverence toward many sacred national symbols crept into popular culture, controversies over the anthem began to lose their edge and staying power, as a form of outrage fatigue took hold. In 2008, jazz singer Rene Marie generated a minor controversy when she opened the mayor's State of the City address in Denver with the melody of the anthem, but substituted the words of *Lift Every Voice and Sing*. As she sang, Marie received strange looks, but no one raised a ruckus until the media started asking questions afterward. That same year, at a celebrity flag football game in Baltimore hosted by basketball player Allen Iverson, then-Dallas Maverick Josh Howard looked into a cell phone and said "'The Star-Spangled Banner' is going on. I don't celebrate that [bleep], cause I'm black. [Bleep] Obama and all that [bleep]."[79] For Super Bowls in the years leading up the 200th anniversary of the song, NFL officials clearly chose anthem singers Jordin Sparks, Jennifer Hudson, Carrie Underwood, Kelly Clarkson, Alicia Keys, and Renee Fleming, an opera star, to minimize controversy. In 2011, Christina Aguilera, another seemingly benign choice, performed *The Star-Spangled Banner* live and forgot the words midway through. Aguilera repeated lines and made up others (including a spot where she seemed to sing "twilight's last reaming"), until she somehow reached the end on fairly solid ground. Fans at the stadium barely seemed to notice, though the cameras caught the bemused reactions of several players. After the pundits dissected the tape, her blunders looped continuously over the next 24-hour news cycle and prompted *Parade* magazine to run a poll in July 2011 gauging readers' opinions about changing the anthem to *America the Beautiful* (63 percent voted to keep *The Star-Spangled Banner*).

Beyond the song's persistent joke value, Americans have become inured to anthem controversies. In 2013, pop star Lady Gaga appeared at the kickoff rally for the New York City Gay Pride Parade holding a small rainbow flag, a symbol of the gay rights movement, aloft in her right hand. During her rendition of Key's fabled song, she elicited loud applause after singing the lines "through the perilous fight" and "our flag was still there." The audience exploded when she changed the final lyrics to "O say does that star-spangled flag of pride yet wave, o'er the land of the free and the home for the gay." Most commentators shrugged the incident off, due to the pop star's outrageous persona and outspoken support of gay rights. At a minor league baseball game in Sacramento, California, held in August 2013, moreover, the audience showed uncommon forgiveness toward human imperfection, or perhaps just displayed near-complete indifference to *The Star-Spangled Banner*. When alternative rocker Jonny Craig forgot the lyrics after the line "o'er the ramparts we watched," some people in the crowd tittered and others cheered. Remarkably, no one within earshot of a video taken in the left-field stands booed. Then, after softly muttering the lines "so proudly we hailed" and "twilights last gleaming," Craig lost track of the melody. He paused for around seven seconds, then picked up the last two lines in full voice, offering multiple-note flourishes on a couple of words and earning a wild ovation, albeit with a tinge of sarcasm. Afterward, he tweeted the same excuse that Robert Goulet used almost a half century earlier, only with updated, social media–influenced jargon: "I messed up the national anthem lol give me a break lol I'm Canadian lol." The incident went virtually unnoticed, due to his status as a minor celebrity and the splintering of media outlets in the Internet age, which relegated the video of his anthem performance to a few alternative music sites, but the crowd reaction represented a telling nonchalance toward the song.[80]

Epilogue

SOMEHOW, THROUGHOUT TWO centuries of change, *The Star-Spangled Banner* captivated the American spirit. But why? It is somewhat miraculous that an allegedly hard-to-sing, anachronistic composition born of a long-forgotten conflict that seems to glorify war and consists of unmemorable poetry remains the official anthem of the United States of America. For one thing, the dramatic and inspired creation of the song, forged in the heat of battle, helped it achieve instant popularity. Written behind enemy lines, the anthem owes its existence to a gentlemanly approach toward war that allowed Francis Scott Key to tell the tale. Though considered to be relatively insignificant in the historical record, the War of 1812 included humiliating military defeats and an uncertain outcome for the United States. With victory and independence achieved, the nation turned from fear and self-preservation toward a focus on the future, an orientation reflected in the song.

The staying power of *The Star-Spangled Banner* in the face of nearly two centuries of disparagement partly rested on its adaptability and on the acceptance of modern, creative interpretations. Changes to its lyrics, meter, and melody began in the early 1800s. Ragtime artists distorted the familiar tune, and trained opera singers recorded stylized signature versions in the early 1900s. Even military bands and choral ensembles produced modern variations of the song. In the mid-1970s, no one noticed that the main marching ensemble at Butler University performed an adaptation of Stravinsky's version of the anthem, which had caused an uproar thirty years earlier. And on May 5, 2010, the day after Detroit Tigers announcer Ernie Harwell died, José Feliciano reprised his individualistic version of the anthem at the new home of the baseball club, Comerica Park, and received an enthusiastic ovation.

In the 1990s, musicians (re)discovered that the anthem's melody, based on an old British drinking song, suits a capella arrangements for solos, quartets, and choruses. Sometimes even performers in conservative genres have taken surprising liberties with the harmonies. Bluegrass groups, including Doyle Lawson & Quicksilver and Dailey & Vincent, perform surprising harmonic and note-bending changes during certain passages. A St. Louis–based barbershop quartet, the Gas House Gang, introduced flourishes that are associated with an old-fashioned musical style but are hardly traditional. Popular singing groups Take 6 and Boyz II Men created acclaimed arrangements featuring atonal, jazz-influenced chords. Take 6 steered *The Star-Spangled Banner* in a divergent direction, beginning with "the rocket's red glare" line. Boyz II Men inserted several bars of *My Country, 'Tis of Thee* into their 1996 rendition. More country-music artists have scored a hit with the anthem than singers in any other genre. The band Ricochet recorded a six-part a capella version in 1996, and Faith Hill's performance at the 2001 Super Bowl also appeared on the music charts. In 2012, a version by The Band Perry, which altered the melody at times and clipped several phrases, peaked at number 59 on *Billboard* magazine's "Hot Country Songs" chart. Country stars have also bungled the song. In addition to Eli Young's error-filled rendition in Kansas City, at an Atlanta Falcons football game in 1975, Johnny Paycheck sang: "O say can you see, it's cloudy at night / What so loudly we sang as the daylight's last cleaning."

The spirit of experimentation also influenced instrumentalists who came after Jimi Hendrix and *The Star-Spangled Banner* remains a composition that almost every musician must consider at some point. Bass guitarist Stu Hamm arranged it as a melodic four-string electric bass solo, with a gorgeous flourish at the end, highlighting the myriad harmonic possibilities of the tune. Among the strangest arrangements, Béla Fleck and the Flecktones recorded a mutant-jazz banjo version in 1991 that riffed on some of the recognizable themes but otherwise shared little in common with the familiar melody until a harmonica joined in during the "rocket's red glare" part. Ukulele master Jake Shimabukuro's spirited rendition, which blended steel drums and a rock band, built to a crescendo at the end.

Musically, the anthem features a bold, memorable melody. Nonetheless, it is notorious for straining vocal chords, and Robert Goulet's multiple mistakes in its rendition in 1965 scared off even professional vocalists. Yet Americans once knew all the words to *The Star-Spangled Banner* and performed it en masse. As one congressman wrote just before the outbreak of World War II: "Tunes difficult to sing do not gain the heights of popularity."[1] A case could be made that most of the proposed alternatives to *The Star-Spangled Banner* are also challenging. *America the Beautiful* may not include as many high notes, but the words "above the fruited plane" are pitched far above the previous line, and the phrase is rendered by a melodic sequence as outmoded as any passage in the anthem. The next two notes, especially on the second syllable of the word "America," represent another awkward leap. Katherine Bates also used apostrophes to fit the lyrics to the music, along with the stilted word "thine" instead of "thy."

God Bless America can also test amateur musicians. The song consists of two distinct parts, though the second portion, which starts with the words "God bless America, land that I love," is more widely known. The melody line, beginning with "from the mountains" and rising through the phrase "white with foam," is difficult to execute with precision. The climactic lyric "God bless America" continues climbing in pitch. Many Americans also seem to have trouble remembering the words.[2] Though well written, *Lift Every Voice and Sing* presents technical challenges, even for professional musicians. *This Land Is Your Land* is accessible on a lyrical and musical level, but its focus on geographic imagery, and its author's leftist politics, relegated it to being a school and campfire staple.

One of the most notable renditions of *The Star-Spangled Banner* in recent times occurred just before the start of the first Boston Bruins home hockey game that took place after the bombing at the Boston Marathon in 2013. When anthem singer Rene Rancourt finished the phrase "what so proudly we hailed," he dropped the microphone, stopped singing, and waved his arms like a conductor. The crowd bellowed the song without musical accompaniment, defying the critics who harp on its alleged difficulty.

The early popular appeal of *The Star-Spangled Banner* allowed it to develop into a true tradition that germinated from "the people" in a spontaneous fashion. During the late 1800s, the military sought a musical badge to represent the United States, and the song materially contributed to a sense of national identity as other countries also adopted emblematic musical compositions. Of the century's Big Five, Key's tune outlasted its flawed rivals. The chief contender for the nation's affections in the 1900s, *America the Beautiful*, arrived too late. Patriotic conformity during World War I—along with President Wilson's executive order transforming *The Star-Spangled Banner* into the national anthem for the armed forces—gave the song official standing. The emergence of *God Bless America* before World War II diluted the stature of *America the Beautiful* as an alternative, since anthem opponents disagreed over possible choices.

The proximity between Baltimore and Frederick in Maryland and Washington, D.C., facilitated the ability of *Star-Spangled Banner* proponents to lobby Congress and other federal officials. But Marylanders could not have achieved their goal alone, and they received backing by powerful veterans' groups at exactly the time when World War I bonuses and veterans' affairs reverberated in the headlines. The bill to anoint the *Star-Spangled Banner* as the nation's official anthem in 1931 sailed through Congress during a time of social turmoil and cost almost nothing to implement. It also helped that *America the Beautiful* lyricist Katherine Lee Bates, who died in 1929, and preeminent musical figures John Philip Sousa and Irving Berlin, who unwittingly wrote competing anthem candidates, never lobbied against *The Star-Spangled Banner*. In the late 1800s, Sousa might have been able to singlehandedly determine the country's anthem, but his ambiguous public stance and refusal to promote his own composition, *The Stars and Stripes Forever*, threw the decision back to the court of public opinion. By the time Berlin's *God Bless America* achieved popular favor, Congress had already made its choice, and overturning that decision would have brought negative publicity to the composer, who already suffered from an anti-Semitic backlash against his work.

Over the long history of *The Star-Spangled Banner*, generations of teachers, military bandleaders, politicians, sports leagues, and civic organizations hammered the anthem into the consciousness of virtually every American, and the song almost always appears on the naturalization exam for U.S.

citizenship. Improvements in the construction of wind instruments, the mass production of pianos, and the development of recording and playback technology helped spread the tune to ever-wider audiences. Beginning with print in the 1800s, radio in the 1920s, television in the 1950s, and the Internet in the 1990s, ever-more-powerful methods of mass communication helped the anthem saturate the country. Previously broadcast before every ballgame, by the 1990s the song took up valuable air time, and television and radio producers almost always cut to commercials during renditions of *The Star-Spangled Banner* at professional football, baseball, basketball, and hockey contests, signaling the triumph of commerce over patriotism. When the anthem is played during especially significant games, big-name artists enhance its cachet, and the song is still a staple for live audiences at stadium and arena events. When *The Star-Spangled Banner* is broadcast nowadays, at some point the camera usually cuts to the flag waving in the breeze (or, if the venue is indoors, to a facsimile shown on a big screen), highlighting a major reason why the song endured: its focus on the flag, the most recognizable and respected national symbol among all nations, not just the United States. No matter the controversies over competing visions of the true character of this revered and reviled song, it is "still there" and will remain so for a long time.

Appendix

The Original Words
of *The Star-Spangled Banner*

Based on the manuscript at the Maryland Historical Society

O say can you see, by the dawn's early light,
What so proudly we hail'd at the twilight's last gleaming,
Whose broad stripes & bright stars through the perilous fight
O'er the ramparts we watch'd, were so gallantly streaming?
And the rocket's red glare, the bomb bursting in air,
Gave proof through the night that our flag was still there,
O say does that star-spangled banner yet wave
O'er the land of the free & the home of the brave?

On the shore dimly seen through the mists of the deep,
Where the foe's haughty host in dread silence reposes,
What is that which the breeze, o'er the towering steep,
As it fitfully blows, half conceals, half discloses?
Now it catches the gleam of the morning's first beam,
In full glory reflected now shines in the stream,
'Tis the star-spangled banner—O long may it wave
O'er the land of the free & the home of the brave!

And where is that band who so vauntingly swore,
That the havoc of war & the battle's confusion

A home & a Country should leave us no more?
Their blood has wash'd out their foul footstep's pollution.
No refuge could save the hireling & slave
From the terror of flight or the gloom of the grave,
And the star-spangled banner in triumph doth wave
O'er the land of the free & the home of the brave.

O thus be it ever when freemen shall stand
Between their lov'd home & the war's desolation;
Blest with vict'ry & peace, may the heav'n rescued land
Praise the power that hath made & preserv'd us a nation!
Then conquer we must, when our cause it is just,
And this be our motto—"In God is our trust,"
And the star-spangled banner in triumph shall wave
O'er the land of the free & the home of the brave.

Notes

1. ANTHEM BEFORE A NATION, 1814–1860

1. Paul Nettl, *National Anthems* (1952; 2nd ed., New York, 1967), pp. 40, 47, 49.

2. Percy A. Scholes, *God Save the Queen! The History and Romance of the World's First National Anthem* (London, 1954), p. 6.

3. Scholes, *God Save the Queen*, p. v.

4. Robert James Branham and Stephen J. Harnett, *Sweet Freedom's Song: "My Country, 'Tis of Thee" and Democracy in America* (New York, 2002), p. 26.

5. Scholes, *God Save the Queen*, p. 111.

6. Oscar Brand, *Songs of '76: A Folksinger's History of the Revolution* (New York, 1972), p. 166.

7. Nettl, *National Anthems*, pp. 111–112.

8. Jean-Jacques Rousseau, *The Social Contract*, trans. and intro. by G. D. H. Cole (1950; reprint, New York, 1968), pp. 110–111.

9. Robert Bellah, "Civil Religion," in Robert Bellah, ed., *Beyond Belief: Essays on Religion in a Post-Traditional World* (New York, 1970), p. 170.

10. Scholes, *God Save the Queen*, p. 20.

11. Oscar Sonneck, *Report on "The Star-Spangled Banner," "Hail Columbia," "America," "Yankee Doodle"* (Washington, DC, 1909), pp. 79–156.

12. Nettl, *National Anthems*, pp. 68–69; Michel Vovelle, "La Marseillaise: War or Peace," in Pierre Nora, ed., *Realms of Memory: The Construction of the French Past*, Vol. 3, *Symbols* (New York, 1998), pp. 29–76.

13. Sonneck, *Report*, pp. 43–72.

14. George J. Svejda, *The History of the Star-Spangled Banner from 1814 to the Present* (Washington, DC, 1969), p. 26.

15. Steve Vogel, *Through the Perilous Fight: Six Weeks That Saved the Nation* (New York, 2013), p. 329.

16. A portion of Key's letter to his friend John Randolph is quoted in Irvin Molotsky, *The Flag, the Poet, & the Song: The Story of the Star-Spangled Banner* (New York, 2001), pp. 86–89; Lonn Taylor, *The Star-Spangled Banner: The Flag That Inspired the National Anthem* (New York, 2000), p. 21.

17. William Lichtenwanger, "The Music of 'The Star-Spangled Banner': From Ludgate Hill to Capitol Hill," *Quarterly Journal of the Library of Congress* (July 1977; reprint, Washington, DC, 1977), no pagination.

18. Richard S. Hill, "The Melody of 'The Star Spangled Banner' in the United States before 1818," offprint from Frederick R. Goff, *Essays Honoring Lawrence C. Wroth* (Washington, DC, 1951).

19. Oscar Sonneck, *The Star Spangled Banner* (1914; reprint, New York, 1969), p. 79.

20. Vogel, *Through the Perilous Fight*, p. 352.

21. Richard S. Hill, "A Proposed Official Version of 'The Star Spangled Banner,'" *Bulletin— National Music Council* (Fall 1957), pp. 33–42, an adaptation of a report delivered at a meeting of the National Music Council on May 23, 1957; Svejda, *History*, pp. 83–88.

22. Lichtenwanger, "Music of 'The Star Spangled-Banner.'"

23. Svejda, *History*, pp. 138–139.

24. Branham and Harnett, *Sweet Freedom's Song*, p. 58.

25. John R. Kenly, *Memoirs of a Maryland Volunteer—War with Mexico in the Years 1846– 7-8*, (Philadelphia, 1873), p. 470.

26. Branham and Hartnett, *Sweet Freedom's Song*, p. 46.

27. *Star-Spangled Banner* [Philadelphia], February 22, 1834; *Star Spangled Banner* [Nashville], April 8, 1844.

28. *Star Spangled Banner* [Boston], July 7, 1849; Harry Hazel [Justin Jones], *Big Dick, the King of the Negroes, or Virtue and Vice Contrasted: A Romance of High & Low Life in Boston* (Boston, 1846); Harry Hazel, *The Nun of St. Ursula, or the Burning of the Convent* (Boston, 1845); Tyler Anbinder, *Nativism and Slavery: Northern Know-Nothings and the Politics of the 1850s* (New York, 1992), pp. 20–21.

29. Marshall Pike and L. V. H. Crosby, *The Grave of Washington* (Boston, 1846); C. Jefferys and G. H. Rodwell James, *Land of the Free* (New York, n.d.); Svejda, *History*, p. 159.

30. Vicki L. Eaklor, *American Anti-Slavery Songs: A Collection and Analysis* (New York, 1988).

31. P. William Filby and Edward G. Howard, *Star-Spangled Books: Books, Sheet Music, Newspapers, Manuscripts and Persons Associated with The Star-Spangled Banner* (Baltimore, 1972), pp. 141–144; Joseph Muller, *The Star Spangled Banner: Words and Music Issued between 1814–1864* (1935; reprint, New York, 1973), p. 31; Bryan Lindsey, "Anacreon on the Wagon: 'The Star-Spangled Banner' in the Service of the Cold Water Army," *Journal of Popular Culture* (September 1971), pp. 595–603.

32. Svejda, *History*, pp. 130–131.

33. Filby and Howard, *Star-Spangled Books*, p. 143.

34. Svejda, *History*, pp. 124–129; William McCarty, comp., *National Songs, Ballads, and Other Patriotic Poetry, Chiefly Relating to the War of 1846* (Philadelphia, 1846), pp. 110–111.

35. National Committee for the Preservation of Existing Records of the National Society of the Colonial Dames of America, comp., *American War Songs* (1915; reprint, Detroit, 1974), p. 56.

36. Francis Scott Key, *Poems of the Late Francis S. Key, Esq., Author of "The Star Spangled Banner," with an Introductory Letter by Chief Justice Taney* (New York, 1857), pp. vii, 13.

2. AMERICAN DISCHORD, 1860–1865

1. Vogel, *Through the Perilous Fight*, pp. 13, 411; Francis Scott Key, "Will," 1837, Edward S. Delaplaine Collection, Historical Society of Frederick County, Frederick, Maryland.

2. William Howard Russell, *My Diary North and South* (Philadelphia, 1988), p. 76.

3. McHenry Howard, *Recollections of a Maryland Confederate Soldier and Staff Officer under Johnston, Jackson, and Lee* (Baltimore, 1914), p. 3.

4. James R. Randall, *Maryland! My Maryland!: A Patriotic Song* (New Orleans, 1862).

5. *Maryland, My Maryland!*, Union words adapted and music arranged by Septimus Winner (Philadelphia, 1862).

6. Frank Key Howard, *Fourteen Months in American Bastiles* (Baltimore, 1863), p. 9.

7. George Henry Preble, *History of the Flag of the United States* (Boston, 1880), pp. 494, 498; Richard B. Harwell, *Confederate Music* (Chapel Hill, NC, 1950), p. 62; National Music, *Medley, including the Marseilles Hymn* (Boston, 1861).

8. Frank Moore, ed., *Rebel Rhymes and Rhapsodies* (New York, 1864), p. 191.

9. *Six Military and Patriotic Illustrated Songs* (New York, n.d.).

10. *Dwight's Journal of Music* (January 12, 1861), p. 335.

11. Moore, *Rebel Rhymes and Rhapsodies*, p. 112.

12. Harwell, *Confederate Music*, p. 111; Kate E. Staton, comp., *Old Southern Songs of the Period of the Confederacy: The Dixie Trophy Collection* (London, 1926), p. 11.

13. Preble, *History of the Flag*, pp. 503, 505.

14. Russell, *My Diary*, p. 76; Staton, *Old Southern Songs*, pp. 35–36; Filby and Howard, *Star-Spangled Books*, pp. 146–147.

15. John M. Coskin, *The Confederate Flag: America's Most Embattled Emblem* (Cambridge, MA, 2005), p. 8.

16. Staton, *Old Southern Songs*, p. 124.

17. Harwell, *Confederate Music*, pp. 101, 114; P. E. Collins, Newton Fitz, and J. H. Snow, *The Banner of the South* (Mobile, AL, 1861).

18. "The Stars and Bars," broadside, New York Historical Society library.

19. C. D. Elder and G. George, *Confederate Flag* (New Orleans, 1861).

20. Allan Nevins and Milton Halsey Thomas, eds., *The Diary of George Templeton Strong: The Civil War, 1860–1865* (New York, 1952), pp. 142–143; Vera Brodsky Lawrence,

Strong on Music: The New York Music Scene in the Days of George Templeton Strong, Vol. 3, *Repercussions, 1857–1862* (Chicago, 1999), pp. 422–424.

21. Richard Grant White, *National Hymns: How They Are Written and How They Are not Written; A Lyric and National Study for the Times* (New York, 1861), pp. 17–19.

22. White, *National Hymns,* pp. 19, 21–22, 65, 75, 11.

23. White, *National Hymns,* pp. 67, 8.

24. White, *National Hymns,* pp. 68, 81, 102, 115, 96–97.

25. Harwell, *Confederate Music,* pp. 56–59, 130; Christian McWhirter, *Battle Hymns: The Power and Popularity of Music in the Civil War* (Chapel Hill, NC, 2012), pp. 73–77; Coskin, *Confederate Flag,* p. 4.

26. Howard L. Sacks and Judith Rose Sacks, *Way Up North in Dixie: A Black Family's Claim to the Confederate Anthem* (Urbana, IL, 1993); McWhirter, *Battle Hymns,* pp. 68, 70.

27. Harwell, *Confederate Music,* p. 43.

28. Harwell, *Confederate Music,* pp. 44, 50–51; Drew Gilpin Faust, *The Creation of Confederate Nationalism: Ideology and Identity in the Civil War South* (Baton Rouge, LA, 1972), p. 48; George M. Neese, *Three Years in the Confederate Horse Artillery* (1911; reprint, Dayton, OH, 1988), p. 352.

29. McWhirter, *Battle Hymns,* p. 34.

30. *Exercises at a Consecration of the Flag of the Union by the Old South Society in Boston, May 1st, 1861* (Boston, 1861).

31. *Opening, Initiatory, and Closing Ceremonies for Union Leagues: To Which is Appended Forms for Instituting Leagues and the Installation of Officers; Adopted by the Grand League of Maryland, August 1862* (Baltimore, 1862), pp. 4, 15; "Grand Union Concert, for the Benefit of the Ladies 'Union Relief' Association of Baltimore at the Maryland Institute, Thursday, May 22, 1862," program, Maryland Historical Society, Baltimore; Svejda, *History,* p. 188.

32. "The Flag of Fort Sumter," broadside, New York Historical Society library.

33. Svejda, *History,* p. 188.

34. Mrs. C. A. Mason and Asa B. Hutchinson, *The Triple Hued Banner* (Boston, 1864).

35. F. O. C. Darley, illus., *The Star Spangled Banner* (New York, 1861); *The Boy's Banner Book* (New York, [ca. 1861]).

36. J. L. Geddes and Henry Werner, *The Bonnie Blue Flag with the Stripes and Stars* (St. Louis, 1863); John Tasker Howard, *Our American Music: A Comprehensive History from 1620 to the Present,* 4th ed. (New York, 1965), p. 257.

37. Faust, *Creation of Confederate Nationalism,* p. 50.

38. George F. Root, *On, On, On, the Boys Came Marching! or the Prisoner Free* (Chicago, 1865).

39. John Stauffer and Benjamin Soskis, *The Battle Hymn of the Republic: A Biography of the Song that Marches On* (New York, 2013).

40. Staton, *Old Southern Songs,* pp. 39, 70, 98, 112, 130; Harwell, *Confederate Music,* p. 22.

41. Staton, *Old Southern Songs*, p. 96.

42. Raphael Semmes, *Memoirs of Service Afloat during the War between the States* (1868; reprint, Baton Rouge, 1996), p. 561.

43. Charles Hamm, *Yesterdays: Popular Song in America* (New York, 1979); McWhirter, *Battle Hymns*, pp. 131, 107; Joseph Ferguson, *Life-Struggles in Rebel Prisons: A Record of the Sufferings, Escapes, Adventures, and Starvation of the Union Prisoners* (Philadelphia, 1865), p. 108.

44. Svejda, *History*, p. 194.

45. Adin B. Underwood, *The Three Years' Service of the Thirty-Third Mass. Infantry Regiment 1862–1865* (Boston, 1881), pp. 254–255.

46. Sallie Putnam, *Richmond during the Civil War*, quoted in Richard Wheeler, *Witness to Appomattox* (New York, 1989), p. 107.

47. Nevins and Thomas, *Diary of George Templeton Strong*, pp. 574–575.

48. M. A. Kidder and E. A. Parkhurst, *The Peace Jubilee: A National Song with Grand Chorus* (New York, 1865); W. H. W. and A. B. Clarke, *The Nation's Jubilee* (New York, 1865).

49. Lichtenwanger, "Music of 'The Star-Spangled Banner.'"

50. Richard Wentworth Browne, "Union War Songs and Confederate Officers," *Century Magazine* (January 1888), p. 478.

3. STRIVING TO REUNIFY, 1865–1900

1. John Lair, *Songs Lincoln Loved* (New York, 1954), p. 39.

2. *Columbia Daily Phoenix* [Charleston, S.C.], June 22, 1865; *Fayetteville [Tenn.] Observer*, June 13, 1867; "The Democracy," *Memphis Daily Appeal*, August 28, 1868.

3. Merle Curti, *The Roots of American Loyalty* (1946; reprint, New York, 1967), chapter 8; John Higham, *Strangers in the Land: Patterns of American Nativism, 1860–1925* (New Brunswick, NJ, 1955), chapter 10; Hugh Cunningham, "The Language of Patriotism, 1750–1914," *History Workshop Journal* (Autumn 1981), pp. 8–33; Ernest Gellner, *Nations and Nationalism* (Ithaca, NY, 1983); John Bodnar, *Remaking America: Public Memory, Commemoration, and Patriotism in the Twentieth Century* (Princeton, NJ, 1992).

4. James Homer Kennedy, *Star-Spangled Banner Poems, Consecrated to Union and Liberty* (Lenni, PA, 1862), pp. i, ii, 6, 52; *Patriotic Songs, Distributed in Heck's Champion Prize Package*, broadside (Chicago, 1864).

5. Jack Sullivan, "Piso's Trio: One Step Ahead of the Law," *Bottles and Extras* (September–October 2007), pp. 18–22; Piso's patriotic song cards, Warshaw Collection.

6. Frederick. J. Nelson, "The Man and the Voice," handwritten manuscript, Historical Society of Frederick County.

7. Union Forever, *The Star Spangled Banner* (New York, 1876); Margaret H. Hazen and Robert Hazen, *The Music Men: An Illustrated History of Brass Bands in America, 1800–1920* (Washington, DC, 1987), pp. 2, 8, 136; Robert E. Eliason, *Keyed Bugles in the United States* (Washington, DC, 1972), p. 27; Dominic Gill, ed., *The Book of the*

Piano (Ithaca, NY, 1981), p. 183; David S. Grover, *The Piano: Its Story from Zither to Grand* (New York, 1976), p. 146.

8. Patrick S. Gilmore, *History of the National Peace Jubilee* (Boston, 1871), pp. 464–465; Louis C. Elson, *The National Music of America and Its Sources* (Boston, 1899), p. 310.

9. Elson, *National Music of America*, p. 310; Svejda, *History*, p. 211.

10. *Centennial Music: Groton, 1781–1881; For the Centennial Celebration of the Battle of Groton Heights Fought September 6, 1781* (New London, CT, 1881).

11. *Official Programme with Words and Music of the Semi-Centennial Anniversary of the State of Michigan Held at Lansing, June 15, 1886* (East Saginaw, MI, 1886).

12. *Report of the Board of World's Fair Managers of Maryland* (n.p., n.d.), pp. 6–81.

13. John V. L. Findlay, *Address Delivered at Chicago, in Music Hall, on the 12th of September, 1893, the Day Set Apart as "Maryland Day" at the World's Columbian Exposition* (Baltimore, 1896), pp. 10, 11, 68; *Board of World's Fair Managers*, pp. 67–77.

14. Robert B. Beath, *History of the Grand Army of the Republic* (New York, 1889), p. 652.

15. James Henry Brownlee, ed., *The Patriotic Speaker, consisting of Heroic, Pathetic, and Humorous Pieces That Inspire Patriotism* (New York, n.d.).

16. Rev. Dr. Pollard and A. B. Winch, *To the G.A.R.: Memorial Hymn* (Taunton, MA, 1870).

17. Samuel S. Peters, ed., *Odes, Hymns, and Songs of the Grand Army of the Republic* (Columbus, OH, 1883), pp. 1–9; *Our National War Songs* (Chicago, 1885); Wilson Smith, ed., *Grand Army War Songs: A Collection of War Songs, Battle Songs, Camp Songs, National Songs, Marching Songs, etc., as Sung by Our Boys in Blue in Camp and Field; To Which Is Added a Selection of Memorial Songs and Hymns for Use on Decoration Day and Other Special Occasions* (New York, 1886).

18. *40 Rounds from the Cartridge Box of the Fighting Chaplain: Embracing the "Cream" of the "Old War Songs" and Recitations, and the Odes of the W.R.C., G.A.R., S. of V.* (Mt. Vernon, IA, n.d.); John Hogarth Lozier, *The Old Union Wagon* (Cincinnati, 1863).

19. John H. Lozier and Horace Lozier, *O, Guard That Banner while We Sleep: A Song for the Patriotic Sons and Daughters of America* (Mt. Vernon, IA, 1891).

20. John Hogarth Lozier and Horace Lozier, *My Father's Flag and Mine* (Mt. Vernon, IA, 1890).

21. J. C. O. Redington, comp., *Old War Songs and G.A.R. and Patriotic Songs* (Syracuse, NY, [ca. 1894]), p. 107.

22. *Official Program of the Eighteenth Annual Encampment, Department of Michigan, G.A.R., and Thirteenth Annual Convention, Department of Michigan, W.R.C., Saginaw, Mich., March 31 and April 1 and 2, 1896* (n.p., n.d.).

23. Merle Curti, *Roots of American Loyalty*, p. 191; Wilbur Zelinsky, *Nation into State: The Shifting Symbolic Foundations of American Nationalism* (Chapel Hill, NC, 1988), p. 106; Scot Guenter, *The American Flag, 1777–1924: Cultural Shifts from Creation to Codification* (Rutherford, NJ, 1990), p. 142.

24. *The Constitution and By-Laws of the Society of the Sons of the Revolution in the State of Maryland* (Baltimore, 1894), p. 7.

25. Curti, *Roots of American Loyalty*, pp. 191–193; Guenter, *American Flag*, pp. 142, 151.

26. Willis Fletcher Johnson, *The National Flag: A History* (Boston, 1930), p. 95; Henry H. Carrington, ed., *Columbian Selections: American Patriotism for Home and School* (Philadelphia, 1892), pp. 350–353.

27. Beath, *History of the Grand Army*, p. 690.

28. Burnside Post [No. 47], *Souvenir to the Pupils of Auburn, Maine, Public Schools* (Auburn, ME, 1896).

29. George T. Balch, *Methods of Teaching Patriotism in the Public Schools* (New York, 1890), pp. viii, xxxvii, 32, 34, 97, 63–64.

30. Svejda, *History*, p. 451; Charles R. Skinner, *Manual of Patriotism: For Use in the Public Schools of the State of New York* (Albany, NY, 1904), pp. ii, vii, ix, xi, xii, 28–29, 32.

31. George F. Root and Lydia Avey Coonley, *Our Flag with the Stars and Stripes: A Patriotic Cantata for School and Choir* (New York, 1896), pp. 2, 8–9, 78.

32. Curti, *Roots of American Loyalty*, p. 191; Walter H. Jones, ed., *Songs of Flag and Nation* (New York, 1904), p. iii.

33. John Carroll Randolph, arr., *Patriotic Songs for School and Home* (Boston, 1899).

34. Charles K Langley and T. Martin Towne, eds., *Uncle Sam's School Songs: Nos. 1 and 2 Combined for Use by Schools, Colleges, Institutes, and the Home Circle* (Chicago, 1897), pp. 45, 61, 86, 191–192.

35. Carrington, *Columbian Selections*, pp. 217–218, 260, 340, 405.

36. C. Herb Williams, "Star-Spangled Patriot," *American Legion Magazine* (January 1976), p. 12; Bessie Thompson Stephens, "They Stood Up for Him," *Daughters of the American Revolution Magazine* (November 1971), pp. 796–798, 844.

37. Eleanor Wood, "What So Proudly: Flag Day, a Time for Contemplation of Our National Emblem and Others," *New York Times*, June 14, 1952; Nevins and Thomas, *Diary of George Templeton Strong*, p. 121; Semmes, *Memoirs*, pp. 409–410; Lillie de Hegermann-Lindencrone, *In the Courts of Memory, 1858–1875: From Contemporary Letters* (New York, 1912), www.gutenberg.org/cache/epub/7044/pg7044.html.

38. Liliuokalani, *Hawaii's Story, by Hawaii's Queen* (1898; reprint, Rutland, VT, 1964), pp. 124–125.

39. Balch, *Methods*, pp. 34, 104; Carrington, *Columbian Selections*, p. 407.

40. Redington, *Old War Songs*, p. 107.

41. W. J. Henderson, "Honors to the Flag," *St. Nicholas* (December 1891), pp. 139–141; Charles Sydney Clark, "Honors to the Flag in Camp and Armory," *St. Nicholas* (January 1897), pp. 760–762.

42. "The Star Spangled Banner," *New York Sun*, reprinted in the *Los Angeles Times*, December 17, 1899.

43. "Out Door Sports: Inauguration of the Union Base Ball and Cricket Grounds," *Brooklyn Daily Eagle*, May 16, 1862; the incident is mentioned, without citation, in Peter Morris, *A Game of Inches: The Game behind the Scenes* (Chicago, 2006), p. 332; James L. Terry, *Long Before the Dodgers* (Jefferson, NC, 2002), p. 37; Ed Maher and Frederick Ivor-Campbell, "William Henry Cammeyer," in Frederick Ivor-Campbell, ed., *Baseball's*

First Stars: The Second Volume of Biographies of the Greatest Nineteenth Century Players, Managers, Umpires, Executives, and Writers (Cleveland, 1996), p. 21; Harold Seymour, *Baseball: The Early Years* (New York, 1960), p. 49.

44. "Baseball Season Opened," *New York Times*, April 23, 1897.

45. "On the Baseball Field: Opening Game at the Polo Grounds Called on Account of Rain," *New York Times*, April 16, 1898.

46. "On the Baseball Field: Brooklyn Defeated by Philadelphia in the Opening Game at Washington Park," *New York Times*, May 1, 1898.

47. "Mighty Struggle: Boston Wins Opening Game 1 to 0 in 11 Innings," *Boston Globe*, April 16, 1899.

48. "Crowds Witness Unfurling of American League Pennant," *Chicago Tribune*, April 25, 1901.

49. "Pittsburgh, 4; Cincinnati, 3," *New York Tribune*, April 23, 1902; "Big Day for Baseball," *New York Times*, April 18, 1902; "Boston Wins Again, 7 to 3: Old Cy Young Does It; Makes a Show of Pirates," *Boston Globe*, October 11, 1903.

50. Our Country's Defenders, "Our Country's Defenders: Established March 15, 1879, at Amboy, Ill., Revised April 29th, 1880" (Amboy, IL, 1880).

51. T. Brigham Bishop, *A Knot of Blue and Gray* (Boston, 1876); Ida Scott Taylor and Henry Butler, *The Blue & the Gray* (St. Joseph, MO, 1886).

52. George Schleiffarth, *Harrison's Victory March* (Cleveland, 1888), back cover.

53. *G.A.R. Songs for Memorial Day* (New York, 1896).

54. " 'Star-Spangled Banner' Is Better Thought Of in the South Now," *Atlanta Constitution*, republished in the *Chicago Tribune*, August 20, 1898; *The Blue and the Gray March, introducing the Star Spangled Banner and Dixey* (St. Louis, 1899); *Musical Leader and Concertgoer* (July 16, 1903), p. 19.

55. Randolph, *Patriotic Songs*, p. 12.

56. Edward M. Wickes and Ben Jansen, *He Laid Away a Suit of Gray to Wear the Union Blue* (New York, 1901).

57. W. C. Parker, *The Boys in Blue Are Turning Gray* (New York, 1908).

4. DUTIES AND CUSTOMS, 1880–1910

1. Nettl, *National Anthems*; Martin Shaw, Henry Coleman, and T. M. Cartledge, eds., *National Anthems of the World* (1960; rev. ed., Dorset, England, 1975), p. 229.

2. George Dewey, *Autobiography of George Dewey, Admiral of the Navy* (1913; reprint, New York 1969), pp. 182–184.

3. *The Maritime Flags and Standards of All Nations* (New York, 1856); Haddock's Cards, "Cards of the Nations"; *Carter's Forty Flags, Emblematical Colors, representing Banners and Ensigns of FORTY CHIEF NATIONS OF THE WORLD* (Haverhill, MA, 1879); *Allen & Ginter's Flags of All Nations* (Richmond, VA, [ca.1880s]); *The Flags of All Nations* (Lowell, MA, 1899) all in the Warshaw Collection, National Museum of American History.

4. *Songs of All Nations* (n.p., 1890); "Eight National Anthems," *Boston Journal of Sheet Music* (December 23, 1896); "National Songs of America," *Boston Journal of Sheet Music* (April 8, 1903); *Flags of the Principal Nations* (Philadelphia, 1906).

5. *Report of the Maryland Commission to the Louisiana Purchase Exposition, St. Louis, Missouri, 1904, to the General Assembly of Maryland Session, 1906* (Baltimore, 1906), p. 32; "Catalogue of Exhibits, Maryland Building, Panama-Pacific International Exposition 1915" (n.p., n.d.); George Schleiffarth, arr., *A Trip through the Midway Plaisance: Grand Medley* (Chicago, 1893).

6. C. Neale Ronning, ed., *Intervention in Latin America* (New York, 1970), pp. 25–32.

7. Sonneck, *The Star Spangled Banner*, pp. 95–96; E. K. Ide, *The Star Spangled Banner and a Sketch of the Life of the Author, Francis Scott Key* (Boston, 1914), no pagination.

8. Gus Edwards and Will Cobb, *When Tommy Atkins Marries Dolly Gray* (New York, 1906).

9. Benjamin Franklin Cooling, *Benjamin Franklin Tracy: Father of the Modern American Fighting Navy* (Hamden, CT, 1973), p. x.

10. Svejda, *History*, pp. 218, 470–472.

11. John Philip Sousa, ed., *National, Patriotic, and Typical Airs of All Lands* (Washington, DC, 1890), p. xi.

12. John Philip Sousa, *Marching Along: Recollections of Men, Women, and Music* (Boston, 1928), p. 107; Svejda, *History*, pp. 218–219; Sousa, *National, Patriotic, and Typical Airs*, p. xi.

13. *Daily Nebraska State Journal*, April 22, 1891, p. 4; Svejda, *History*, pp. 221–222; Louis C. Elson, *The National Music of America and Its Sources* (1899; rev. ed., Boston, 1924), pp. 155–156.

14. *Omaha World-Herald*, June 7, 1898, p. 4; Sousa, *Marching Along*, pp. 236, 252, 305.

15. "Must Sing National Anthem: Captain R. P. Leary Takes Measures to Make His Men Familiar with 'The Star Spangled Banner,'" *New York Times*, October 4, 1901.

16. Svejda, *History*, pp. 232, 236.

17. H. Roberts, Major, 26th Infantry Commanding Post, to Military Secretary, Department of Texas, San Antonio, Texas, September 1, 1905, typewritten letter; Brigadier General J. M. Lee, "1st Indorsement, HEADQUARTERS DEPT. OF TEXAS, San Antonio," September 5, 1905; J. T. Kerr, "MEMORANDUM REPORT—Subject: 441 A.R.," October 11, 1905, typewritten manuscript; cited manuscripts in Army Adjutant General's Papers, War Department, National Archives, Washington, D.C.; Svejda, *History*, pp. 232, 239, 240.

18. Svejda, *History*, p. 245; Kerr, "MEMORANDUM REPORT"; L. E. Lovejoy, Tampa, Florida, to Secretary of War, May 19, 1898, typewritten letter; Assistant Adjutant General, "Army General Order," May 26, 1898. Cited manuscripts in Army Adjutant General's Papers.

19. Svejda, *History*, p. 245; J. T. Kerr, "Memorandum Report," January 13, 1906, typewritten manuscript; "MEMORANDUM FOR THE ACTING SECRETARY OF WAR—Subject:

Rendition of the Prescribed Salute When 'The Star Spangled Banner' Is Played," August 5, 1907, typewritten manuscript. Cited manuscripts in Army Adjutant General's Papers.

20. Major General A. W. Greely to the Adjutant General, September 18, 1907, typewritten letter, Army Adjutant General's Papers.

21. "SYNOPSIS of Views of Post Commanders in Dept. of the East, on Subject of Advisability of Amending A.R. 383 (as Amended by G.O. 170, War Department, 1905)," Army Adjutant General's Papers.

22. "Memorandum of the Views Expressed by Commanding Officers of Post in the Department of the Missouri on the Subject of Amendment to Paragraph 383, Army Regulations . . ." and other documents, Army Adjutant General's Papers.

23. E. W. McCaskey to the Adjutant General, Department of the Colorado, October 25, 1907, typewritten letter; "1st Indorsement: Post of Whipple Barracks, A. T.," October 21, 1907, typewritten document. Cited manuscripts in Army Adjutant General's Papers.

24. Veteran to the President of the United States, September 14, 1908, typewritten letter, Army Adjutant General's Papers.

25. John Charlot, *The Hawaiian Poetry of Religion and Politics: Some Religio-Political Concepts in Postcontact Literature* (Hawaii, 1985), pp. 15, 45–47.

26. Liliuokalani, *Hawaii's Story*, p. 31.

27. *Hawaiian Star*, August 12, 1898, p. 1.

28. Noel J. Kent, *Hawaii: Islands Under the Influence* (New York, 1983), p. 68; *Hawaiian Gazette*, July 15, 1898, p. 1.

29. "Spain Hauls Down Her Flag in Cuba," *New York Times*, January 2, 1899.

30. Nettl, *National Anthems*, p. 187; American Flag Association, *The United States Flag Dishonored and Disgraced in America, Cuba, and the Philippine Islands*, Flag Pamphlet No. 34 (n.p., n.d.), p. 2.

31. *New York Times*, October 19, 1898.

32. Winfield Scott Schley, *Forty-Five Years under the Flag* (New York, 1904).

33. Arthur Garfield Hays, "Defending Justice in Puerto Rico," *Nation*, June 5, 1937, reprinted in Kal Wagenheim and Olga Jiménez de Wagenheim, eds., *The Puerto Ricans: A Documentary History* (Princeton, NJ, 1994), pp. 180–182.

34. Dewey, *Autobiography*, p. 280.

35. Nettl, *National Anthems*, pp. 168–170.

36. Annin & Company, *Annin Flag Co. Brochure* (New York, 1931), p. 44.

37. *Report of the United States Philippine Commission to the Secretary of War for the Period from December 1, 1900, to October 15, 1901*, Part 2 (Washington, DC, 1901), p. 563; American Flag Association, *United States Flag Dishonored*, p. 3.

38. Quoted in Robert Rydell, *All the World's a Fair* (Chicago, 1984), pp. 143, 176; Frances Densmore, "The Music of the Filipinos," *American Anthropologist* (October–December 1906), pp. 631–632.

39. Stanley Karnow, *In Our Image: America's Empire in the Philippines* (New York, 1989), pp. 3–256; "MEMORANDUM FOR THE SECRETARY OF WAR—Subject: Honors

to Be Paid to the National Air on Informal Occasions," August 22, 1908, typewritten document, Army Adjutant General's Papers.

40. "Here's the Kind of Music Which Inspires Men to Do, Dare, and Die—Our Newest and Most Effective War Song Appears to Be Our Old Friend, 'There'll Be a Hot Time in the Old Town Tonight,' Put to New Uses—No Real Battle Hymn for the Occasion Has Appeared," *New York Press*, July 17, 1898; N. A. Jennings and W. A. Phillips, *Remember the Maine* (New York, 1898); Con T. Murphy, *Old Glory, The Blue and the Gray* (Chicago, 1898); Paul Branes, *For I Want to Be a Soldier* (New York, 1898); Sam'l Hirschfield, *Uncle Sam Forever* (Chicago, 1900).

41. www.thiscircularparade.com/2011/11/16/the-great-white-fleet-visits-australia-1908/ [no longer available]; Mike McKinley, "The Cruise of the Great White Fleet," *All Hands* (April 1987), pp. 4–15.

42. Glenn Watkins, *Proof through the Night: Music and the Great War* (Berkeley, 2003), pp. 289–290; B. C. Tabor to George von L. Meyer, Hon. Secretary, U.S. Navy, April 26, 1909, handwritten letter; Max K. Kahn to the Secretary of the Navy, February 20, 1909, typewritten letter; Myra B. Moore to Thomas H. Newberry, Secretary of the Navy, February 6, 1909, handwritten letter; Charles Banbury to the Hon. Secretary of the U.S. Navy, April 11, 1911, handwritten letter; George Meyer to Charles Banbury, May 2, 1911, typewritten letter; Edward Napier to Assistant Secretary Newberry, Navy Department, September 4, 1908, handwritten letter. Cited manuscripts in General Records of the Department of the Navy, National Archives.

43. CHAS. L. JOHNSON & CO. to the Navy Department, December 19, 1908, typewritten letter; Truman H. Newberry to Charles L. Johnson & Co., January 11, 1909, typewritten letter. Cited manuscripts in General Records of the Department of the Navy.

44. John Pope Hodnett, *The Great, New National American Anthem: The Glorious Washington*, lyric sheet (Brooklyn, NY, n.d.); George Meyer to John P. Hodnett, October 8, 1909, typewritten letter, General Records of the Department of the Navy; James Meakins, *The Great Hurray That Makes Us Say Uncle Sam's Prayer* (New York, 1909).

45. William Richard Goodall and H. Sylvester Krause, *The American Marseillaise* (Chicago, 1902); W. L. Neeham, *Uncle Sam's Invitation* (Chicago, 1903); Harry J. Lincoln, *Salute to America* (Williamsport, PA, 1904); Vincent Bryan and Gertrude Hoffman, *The Heaven Born Banner* (New York, 1905).

46. Charles K. Harris, *There is No Flag Like the Red, White, and Blue* (New York, 1898); Charles K. Champlin, *The Flag of Uncle Sam* (Williamsport, PA, 1910); Louis Dacre and Hampton Durand, *You've Got to Be American to Feel That Way* (Chicago, 1906).

5. STARS AND STRIPES FOREVER, 1890–1920

1. Francis Scott Key, *The Star-Spangled Banner* (New York, 1889).

2. Lynn Sherr, *America the Beautiful: The Stirring True Story behind Our Nation's Favorite Song* (New York, 2001).

3. Stauffer and Soskis, *Battle Hymn of the Republic*, pp. 146–147.

4. Stephen Salisbury, *An Essay on the Star Spangled Banner and National Songs* (Worcester, MA, 1873); Mrs. J. V. Cooke, ed., *National Hymns: Souvenir Edition* (Tipton, IN, 1897), p. 23; Elson, *National Music of America* (rev. ed.), p. 155; Nicholas Smith, *Stories of the Great National Songs* (Milwaukee, 1899), p. 44.

5. Henry Ward Booth, *The New Star Spangled Banner, with a Brief History of American National Airs* (Birmingham, MI, [ca. 1913]); Homer N. Bartlett, *The Star Spangled Banner, Harmonized as a Folk Song* (New York, 1914).

6. *The Patriots' Song Book of One Hundred Popular and Patriotic Airs* (Chicago, 1897), pp. 23–28; *The Patriots' Song Book of Popular and Patriotic Airs, with Music and Many Original Songs for the Patriots of America* (Chicago, September 1897), p. 8; Joyce L. Kornbluh, ed., *Rebel Voices: An I.W.W. Anthology* (2nd printing, Ann Arbor, MI, 1972), pp. 13–14.

7. Anna Adams Gordon, comp., *Popular Campaign Songs* (Evanston, IL, [ca. 1918]), pp. 26–30; *Responsive Scripture Reading, Lincoln-Lee Legion, Westerville, Ohio, Supplement No. 1 to the National Prohibition Lincoln-Lee Legion Program Book* (n.p., n.d.); *Sunday School Songs for Ohio Dry Campaign* (n.p., n.d.).

8. Sheridan Harvey, "Marching for the Vote: Remembering the Woman Suffrage Parade of 1913," *Library of Congress Information Bulletin* (March 1998), p. 55.

9. "Indian Congress Is Open: First Great Gathering of the Different Tribes in Close Communion," *Omaha Bee*, August 5, 1898.

10. Julian Bond and Sondra Kathryn Wilson, eds., *Lift Every Voice and Sing: A Celebration of the Negro National Anthem* (New York, 2000), pp. xvii, xix, xx, 3.

11. *Official Program of the Fifteenth National Saengerfest, Baltimore, June 30th to July 4th, 1888* (Baltimore, 1888); *Baltimore and the Saengerfest: Official Program & Souvenir* (Baltimore, 1903); *American Union of Swedish Singers Song Album* (Chicago, 1909); Svejda, *History*, pp. 285, 469.

12. *The American Flag Association Circular of Information* (n.p., n.d.); *The American Flag Association Fifth Circular of Information* (n.p., n.d.).

13. Johnson, *National Flag*, pp. 96–97; James R. Nicholson, *History of the Order of Elks, 1868–1952* (New York, 1953), pp. 9, 209.

14. Skinner, *Manual of Patriotism*, p. 35.

15. *Grand Army Flag Day, Rhode Island, 1902–1909*, pamphlets (Providence, RI, 1902–1909).

16. *North Dakota Special Day Programs, 1909, Issued by Department of Public Instruction* (Bismarck, ND, 1909), p. 92; Department of Public Instruction, *Flag Day Program: Lincoln Exercises, 1908* (Santa Fe, NM, 1908); John Watson Van Deman, *Story of the Writing of the Star-Spangled Banner* (n.p., 1921), p. 8.

17. John McCabe, *George M. Cohan: The Man Who Owned Broadway* (New York, 1973), p. 75; George M. Cohan, *You're a Grand Old Flag* (New York, 1906).

18. Mrs. John Lane and Julius Eichberg, *To Thee, O Country* (n.p., 1914); "New National Anthem Gaining Favor," *Musical America* (October 9, 1915), p. 10; Jens K. Grondahl and E. F. Maetzold, *America My Country* (Red Wing, MN, 1917).

19. M. T. Bohannon, *The Star-Spangled Banner (Is the Song That Reached My Heart)* (New York, 1914); Florence Bryant, *Columbia Is Calling* (Chicago, 1917); Robert Speroy and Wilbur D. Nesbit, *Let's Keep the Glow in Old Glory and the Free in Freedom Too* (Chicago, 1918); Daisy M. Erd, *We'll Carry the Star Spangled Banner thru the Trenches* (Boston, 1917); Daisy M. Erd, *We Carried the Star Spangled Banner thru the Trenches* (Boston, 1918).

20. Josephus Daniels to Mr. Adam Wackman, St. Louis, Mo., January 11, 1916, typewritten letter; Kenneth McKellar to Honorable N. D. Baker, Secretary of War, May 24, 1917, typewritten letter; H. P. McCain to Hon. Kenneth D. McKellar, United States Senate, May 31, 1917, typewritten letter; Annah Robinson Watson, *Right Triumphant! A National Anthem Dedicated to the Youth of America* (n.p., n.d.); Theodore H. Northrup to President Woodrow Wilson, received July 22, 1914, typewritten letter, Series 4, Case File 1424, "National Anthem," Woodrow Wilson Papers [cited hereafter as "Woodrow Wilson Papers"], Library of Congress. Other cited manuscripts within this note in General Records of the Navy, National Archives.

21. Dr. J. B. Herbert, *We're All Uncle Sam's Boys Now* (Chicago, 1917); J. Will Callahan and Eddie Gray, *America First* (Chicago, 1916); Martin F. Schram and Leo Friedman, *For the Honor of the U.S.A.* (Grand Rapids, MI, 1918).

22. M. A. DeWolfe Howe, *The Boston Symphony Orchestra: 1881–1931* (Boston, 1931), pp. 132–136; Glenn Watkins, *Proof through the Night: Music and the Great War* (Berkeley, 2003), p. 300; "Send Dr. Muck Back, Roosevelt Advises: Would Have Those Who Refuse to Play Our Anthem Pack Up and Go Away," *New York Times*, November 3, 1917; "Ex-Governor Warfield Would Mob Muck: Volunteers to Head Baltimore Citizens to Prevent Concert Conducted by German," *New York Times*, November 5, 1917; "Baltimore Forbids Dr. Muck's Concert: Boston Symphony Is Barred for Leader's Antipathy to Our National Anthem," *New York Times*, November 6, 1917.

23. "Americanized Symphony to Be Asked of Stock: Conductor Will Be Questioned on Loyalty of Members," *Chicago Tribune*, August 11, 1918; "Mr. Stock Quits Orchestra Till Made a Citizen: Trustees Meet Conductor's Views and Name Eric DeLamarter," *Chicago Tribune*, October 2, 1918; "Bruno Steindel Gives Up His Job with Orchestra," *Chicago Tribune*, October 3, 1918; "Musicians Turn Down Steindel; Mercy to Others," *Chicago Tribune*, February 14, 1919; "Bruno Karl Steindel," *New York Times*, May 6, 1949; "Wife of Bruno Steindel Kills Self in Lake: Grieved over War Taint on Husband," *Chicago Tribune*, March 7, 1921.

24. *Songs of America: A Collection of Patriotic and National Airs* (Fort Wayne, IN, 1909), p. 15; National Committee on Patriotic Literature, *Songs of Our Country* (New York, 1917); Gertrude Van Duyn Southworth and Paul Mayo Paine, eds., *Bugle Calls of Liberty: Our National Reader of Patriotism* (Syracuse, NY, 1917), p. 56.

25. "Diners Resent Slight to the Anthem," *New York Times*, April 7, 1917; James R. Mock, *Censorship 1917* (Princeton, NJ, 1941), pp. 34–35.

26. Wilson, quoted in Guillermo Tomas, *Invincible America: The National Music of the United States in Peace and War* (Havana, Cuba, 1919), p. 125, and in C. M. Tremaine,

History of National Music Week (New York, 1925), p. 8; Doron K. Antrim, "Our Musical Presidents," *Etude* (May 1940), p. 299.

27. James R. Mock and Cedric Larson, *Words That Won the War* (Princeton, NJ, 1939), p. 124.

28. George Creel, *How We Advertised America* (New York, 1920), pp. 200–206.

29. *Chicago Tribune*, May 12, 1917, reprinted in Red Cross Songbooks, *Do You Know Our National Songs?* (n.p., [ca. 1917]).

30. *General Meeting of the Maryland Council of Defense and Joint Meeting of the Maryland Council of Defense and the Women's Section, Held at Hotel Belvedere, Baltimore, Maryland, February 19, 1919* (n.p., n.d.); Kenneth S. Clark, *Baltimore: Cradle of Municipal Music* (Baltimore, 1932), pp. 7–8.

31. *Sing! Song Sheet* (Philadelphia, 1918); *War Camp Community Service* (Providence, RI, 1918); *Worcester War Camp Community Service Song Sheet* (Worcester, MA, 1918); "Reduced reproduction of a full page $5,000.00 Advertisement in the *Saturday Evening Post*" (1919), DeVincent Collection.

32. *Songs of America* (Fort Wayne, IN, 1917), pp. 28–30; H. A. Ogden, comp., *Our Flag and Our Songs: A Brief Story of the Life of the United States Flag, with a Selection of the Songs That Have Inspired the Nation in War and Peace* (New York, 1917), pp. 22–25.

33. Edith Riggs to Woodrow Wilson, February 20, 1915, handwritten letter; Edwin L. Turnbull, Baltimore, Maryland, to Woodrow Wilson, October 20, 1915, typewritten letter; Mrs. Justine Collins, Asheville, North Carolina, to Woodrow Wilson, November 28, 1915, typewritten letter. Cited manuscripts in Woodrow Wilson Papers.

34. John J. Carr, Dorchester, Massachusetts, to Woodrow Wilson, January 23, 1917, typewritten letter; Charles D. Isaacson, New York City, to Woodrow Wilson, April 3, 1918, typewritten letter, with "Giving the National Anthem New Meaning," a broadside from the *New York Globe*, attached. Cited manuscripts in Woodrow Wilson Papers.

35. Helen Fulton, New York City, to the Hon. Thomas F. Smith, August 2, 1918, typewritten letter; Thomas F. Smith, New York City, to Hon. Joseph P. Tumulty, Secretary to the President, August 5, 1918, typewritten letter; Helen Fulton, "PLAN OF PROPAGANDA for the NATIONAL ANTHEM," typewritten document. Cited manuscripts in Woodrow Wilson Papers.

36. Svejda, *History*, p. 357.

37. Terry Waldo, *This Is Ragtime* (New York, 1976), pp. 87, 89; Rudi Blesh and Harriet Janis, *They All Played Ragtime* (1950; 4th ed., New York, 1971), pp. 216–218.

38. Secretary of the Navy Josephus Daniels to Newton D. Baker, Secretary of War, March 12, 1917, typewritten letter; Secretary of War to Secretary of the Navy, April 3, 1917, typewritten memo; Joseph E. Kuhn, Chief of War College Division, "MEMORANDUM FOR THE CHIEF OF STAFF," April 3, 1917, typewritten document. Cited manuscripts in General Records of the Department of the Navy.

39. W. P. Anderson, Circulation Manager, *New York American*, to Hon. Newton D. Baker, Secretary of War, April 20, 1917, telegram; Quartermaster General William E. Hor-

ton to the Adjutant General of the Army, April 25, 1917, memo; "The Right Way to Sing and Play 'The Star Spangled Banner,'" *New York Sunday American*, June 3, 1917; "Standard Version Urged of 'The Star Spangled Banner,'" *Boston Globe*, April 28, 1917. Cited manuscripts in Army Adjutant General's Papers.

40. Peter W. Dykema, "Report of the Committee on the Community Songbook," *Journal of Proceedings of the Twelfth Annual Music Supervisors' National Conference, Held at St. Louis, Missouri, March 31–April 4, 1919* (n.p., n.d.), pp. 144–147.

41. Ann Young, "The Man Who Owned 'The Star-Spangled Banner,'" *Christian Herald* (July 1964), pp. 34–37.

42. Dykema, "Report of the Committee."

43. "Red Sox Beat Cubs in Initial Battle of World's Series," *New York Times*, September 6, 1918; Robert W. Creamer, *Babe: The Legend Comes to Life* (New York, 1992), p. 173; Richard Crepeau, "March 21, 1996: Sport and the National Anthem," *Aethlon: The Journal of Sport Literature* (Fall 2002), pp. 69–71.

6. MARCHING UNDER THE BANNER, 1898–1931

1. Arthur B. Bibbins, "The Evolution of Our National Anthem," reprinted from the *Federation of Music Clubs Annual Bulletin of 1931* (Baltimore, 1931); Nathan Appleton, *The Star Spangled Banner: An Address Delivered by Nathan Appleton at the Old South Meeting House, Boston, Massachusetts, in Aid of the Fund for the Preservation of the Building, on June 14, 1877* (Boston, 1877), p. 23.

2. Edward S. Delaplaine, "Francis Scott Key . . . and his Paradox of Fame," *Valleys of History* (Spring 1967), pp. 3–5; T. J. C. Williams and Folger McKinsey, *History of Frederick County, Maryland* (1910; reprint, Baltimore, 1979) pp. 303–313; "Official Program of the Unveiling Ceremonies of the Monument Erected to the Memory of Francis Scott Key, Author of 'The Star Spangled Banner,' August 9, 1898, Frederick, Maryland," Delaplaine Collection.

3. "The National Hymn: Address by Miss Janet E. Hosmer Richards," *American Monthly Magazine* (December 1895), pp. 536–540.

4. Mrs. Francis Howard Williams, "Origin of the Movement Regarding 'The Star Spangled Banner,'" typewritten document, Library of Congress; Svejda, *History*, pp. 223–224; Mrs. John Edward Duker, comp., *A Half Century of the Ann Arundel Chapter, Daughters of the American Revolution, 1911–1961* (n.p., 1961).

5. Susan Hunter Walker, "'The Star Spangled Banner': How the Great Song Came to Be Written and Memories of the Author," *People's Popular Monthly* (July 1907).

6. Navy Papers, National Archives; "Memorandum for the Chief Clerk," December 19, 1903, Army Adjutant General's Papers.

7. Mrs. F. A. Aiken, handwritten letter to the Hon. Sec. of War, May 26, 1904; Assistant Adjutant Secretary, War Department, to Mrs. F. A. Aiken, June 6, 1904, typewritten letter. Cited manuscripts in Army Adjutant General's Papers.

8. Lucy P. Scott to The Hon. P. C. Knox, Attorney General, January 11, 1903, handwritten letter; Assistant Adjutant General to Mrs. Lucy P. Scott, January 16, 1903, typewritten

letter; George Lancaster to the War Department, March 18, 1904, handwritten letter with newspaper clipping attached. Cited manuscripts in Army Adjutant General's Papers.

9. Quoted in Svejda, *History*, pp. 268, 281–282; Guenter, *American Flag*, p. 158; Alfred B. Beers to Secretary of War, May 25, 1913, telegram, Army Adjutant General's Papers.

10. "Mutilating 'The Star-Spangled Banner,'" *Literary Digest* (April 22, 1905), p. 582; Svejda, *History*, pp. 275–278.

11. Thomas Tuite, quoted in the *Baltimore Evening Sun*, January 26, 1927; Thomas R. Marshall, *Recollections of Thomas R. Marshall, Vice President and Hoosier Philosopher* (Indianapolis, IN, 1925), pp. 126–128.

12. Svejda, *History*, p. 322; Sonneck, *The Star Spangled Banner*, pp. 4, 8; Sonneck, *Report*, p. 7.

13. *Memorial Services Held in the House of Representatives of the United States, together with Remarks Presented in Eulogy of J. Charles Linthicum, Late a Representative from Maryland, Seventy-Second Congress, Second Session* (Washington, DC, 1933); Hon. J. Chas. Linthicum, speech on "The Star Spangled Banner," Baltimore, June 14, 1931, typewritten document, Holloway Collection, Fort McHenry National Monument and Historic Shrine, Baltimore, Maryland; Margie H. Luckett, *Maryland Women, Baltimore, Maryland*, Vol. 1 (Baltimore, 1931), pp. 196–197; "Mrs. Reuben R. Holloway: Patriotic Daughter," *Baltimore Evening Sun*, October 20, 1932; "Our Yesterdays: News of 1932 from the *Evening Sun* and How It Looks Now," *Baltimore Evening Sun*, March 19, 1957.

14. Svejda, *History*, pp. 322–338; Frank O'Connell and Wilbur Coyle, *National Star-Spangled Banner Centennial* (Baltimore, 1914), p. 47; J. Charles Linthicum, "Why We Preserve Fort McHenry," *Patriotic Marylander* (September 1914), p. 19.

15. Ethel T. Rockwell, *Star-Spangled Banner Pageant Staged in the Capitol Park at Madison, Wisconsin, in Celebration of the One-Hundredth Anniversary of the Writing of This National Song by Francis Scott Key* (Madison, 1914); Sons of the American Revolution, Ohio State Society, Columbus Chapter, *Centennial Celebration of the Bombardment of Fort McHenry, Maryland* (Columbus, OH, 1914); O'Connell and Coyne, *National Star-Spangled Banner Centennial*, pp. 97, 111; "Memorandum for Representative Linthicum and Committee," n.d., Woodrow Wilson Papers.

16. *Baltimore: Its History and Its People*, Vol. 1, *History* (New York, 1912), pp. 327–330; *Citizens' Testimonial Dinner to Honorable James Harry Preston, Mayor of Baltimore* (Baltimore, 1914); Matthew Page Andrews to Edward S. Delaplaine, Frederick, Md., June 13, 1929, typewritten letter, Delaplaine Collection; Folger McKinsey and Emma Hemberger, *Baltimore, Our Baltimore* (Baltimore, 1916).

17. Mrs. Arthur B. Bibbins, "Teachers Making New Flag Like the One Key Gazed Upon," *Baltimore Sun*, September 14, 1914; *Ritual of the Star-Spangled Banner Association of the United States of America, together with Charter, Constitution, By-Laws, and List of Charter Members* (Baltimore, [ca. 1916]).

18. The Bentztown Bard [Folger McKinsey], "The Spirit of 1812," *Patriotic Marylander* (September, 1914), pp. 24–25.

19. "Report No. 627: To Make 'The Star-Spangled Banner' the National Anthem," February 6, 1930, Star-Spangled Banner Clipping File, Library of Congress; Watkins, *Proof through the Night*, p. 307.

20. Layton F. Smith, Baltimore, Maryland, to His Excellency, the President, May 12, 1916, typewritten letter, Woodrow Wilson Papers; Svejda, *History*, p. 259; "State Laws Regulating the Rendition of the 'Star Spangled Banner,'" typewritten document, Star-Spangled Banner Clipping File, Library of Congress.

21. "Baltimore's Star-Spangled Banner Ordinance Unpopular," *New York Times*, September 3, 1916.

22. Kitty Cheatham, *Words and Music of "The Star-Spangled Banner" Oppose the Spirit of Democracy which the Declaration of Independence Embodies: A Protest by Kitty Cheatham* (New York, 1917), p. 10; "Cheatham, Catharine Smiley ('Kitty Cheatham')," *The Cyclopedia of American Biography* (enlarged ed., New York, [ca. 1926]), p. 5; Kitty Cheatham, *Correspondence Resulting from the Circulation of the Pamphlet Entitled "A Protest"* (New York, 1918), p. 11.

23. Myrtle Cheney Murdock, *The American's Creed and William Tyler Page* (Washington, DC, 1958), pp. 15–20, 55; Ethel A. Moffett, "America Needed a Creed and Mr. Page Wrote It," *Valleys of History* (Spring 1967), pp. 13–16.

24. J. Charles Linthicum, Washington, D.C., to Mrs. Reuben Ross Holloway, Baltimore, April 11, 1918, typewritten letter; handwritten petition, [ca. 1918]. Cited manuscripts in the Holloway Collection.

25. Margaret H. Lyons, "Flag Etiquette," *Grand Army Flag Day, Rhode Island 1921*, pamphlet (Providence, RI, 1921), p. 32.

26. Dorothy Culp, "The American Legion: A Study in Pressure Politics," PhD diss., University of Chicago, 1939, p. 9; Richard S. Jones, *A History of the American Legion* (Indianapolis, IN, 1946), pp. 238–239.

27. "Wet Origin of 'STAR-SPANGLED BANNER,'" *New York World*, May 12, 1921.

28. "Key Memorial Is Dedicated as Nation's Shrine" and "Public Schools Keep Day," *Baltimore Sun*, June 15, 1922; "Harding Dedicates Key Memorial as National Shrine: Declares Nation Has Kept Faith in Spirit of Anthem; Extols Poet and Defenders of Historic Fort M'Henry," *Baltimore American*, June 15, 1922; *Address of the President of the United States at the Dedication of the Francis Scott Key Memorial at Fort McHenry, Baltimore, June 14, 1922* (Washington, DC, 1922), pp. 1–2.

29. Augusta E. Stetson, advertisement beginning "'The Star-Spangled Banner,' with its words breathing hatred . . ." (New York, n.p., n.d.), appeared in the *Washington Star*, the *New York World*, and the *New York Tribune*, June 13, 1922; Augusta Stetson and Alice Morgan Harrison, *Our America: National Hymn*, sheet music (New York, 1916).

30. "Stop Band Concert When Leader Balks at Playing Anthem," *New York Times*, August 24, 1923; "Engage New Band for Anthem in the Park," *New York Times*, August 25, 1923; "Gallatin Denies Barnhart Charge," *New York Times*, August 26, 1923.

31. "No Propagandist, Says Mrs. Stetson: Defends Attack on 'The Star-Spangled Banner' at Hearing by Hirshfeld Aid," *New York Times*, March 6, 1924; Svejda, *History*, pp. 362, 368.

32. Bernard J. Cigrand, *Laws and Customs Regulating the Use of the Flag of the United States* (Chicago, 1917); *History of the General Smallwood Chapter, D.A.R., of Baltimore, Maryland, from Its Organization, November 7, 1907, to January 1, 1934* (n.p., 1932); *Our Flag: Its History and Its Anniversaries* (Boston, n.d.); *The Flag of the United States, with Rules for Correct Use and Proper Display* (Boston, 1927); Hosea W. Rood, comp., *A Little Flag Book*, 3rd ed. (Madison, WI, 1921).

33. *Hearings Before the Committee on the Judiciary, House of Representatives, 68th Congress, First Session, on H.R. 6429 and H.J. Res. 69* (Washington, DC, 1924), pp. 15, 18, 26–29.

34. *Hearings Before the Committee on Military Affairs, House of Representatives, 68th Congress, First Session, H.R. 5261* (Washington, DC, 1924), pp. 5, 11–13.

35. William Gellermann, *The American Legion as Educator*, Columbia University Contributions to Education No. 743 (1938; reprint, New York, 1972), pp. 200, 206, 212–214, 236; Guenter, *American Flag*, pp. 175–177, 211.

36. James Alfred Moss, comp., *The Flag of the United States: How to Display It, How to Respect It, and the Story of "The Star Spangled Banner"* (Menasha, WI, 1923), pp. 21–33; Moss, *The Flag: How to Respect It, How to Display It* (n.p., [ca. 1924]).

37. "Biography of Walter Joyce," *Alden Kindred Quarterly* (January 1928), pp. 492–495.

38. *Journal of the Fifty-Fifth Encampment, Grand Army of the Republic, Indianapolis, September 25 to 29, 1921* (Washington, DC, 1922), p. 222; *Journal of the Fifty-Sixth Encampment, Grand Army of the Republic, Des Moines, September 24 to 29, 1922* (Washington, DC, 1923), pp. 157–161; *Proceedings of the 26th Annual Encampment of the Veterans of Foreign Wars of the United States (Tulsa, Ok., August 31–Sept. 4, 1925)* (Washington, DC, 1926), pp. 1, 50, 61–63.

39. Gellermann, *American Legion as Educator*, pp. 85–86, 238; Norman Hapgood, ed. *Professional Patriots* (New York, 1927), pp. 3, 6, 60–61.

40. *The National Washington Memorial Church* (n.p., n.d.); *Second Annual Report, War Memorial Commission, State of Maryland, City of Baltimore* (n.p., 1926), p. 4; "Vesper Flag Service on the Steps of the Capitol of the Nation, Sunday Afternoon, June 12, 1927," Holloway Collection.

41. Mrs. Arthur B. Bibbins, *The Baltimore Book: Flag House Guide to Historic Landmarks of Baltimore*, 2nd ed. (Baltimore, 1929), p. 59; *Star-Spangled Banner Flag House Association, Inc., Certificate of Incorporation and Constitution* (n.p., n.d.), pp. 12–13.

42. M. G. Clark, *Progress and Patriotism: A Course of Study in History Problems for the Primary and Intermediate Grades and the Junior High School* (Bloomington, IL, 1923), pp. 54–55, 119, 337–361, 392.

43. Hapgood, *Professional Patriots*, p. 123; Commissioner of Public Schools, Department of Education, State of Rhode Island, "19th Annual Program for Patriotic Exercises on Grand Army Flag Day . . .," *Rhode Island Education Circulars* (n.p., 1920), pp. 23–24, 17; Commissioner, "23rd Annual Program for Patriotic Exercises on Grand Army Flag Day

. . .," *Rhode Island Education Circulars* (n.p., 1924), 24; Commissioner, "24th Annual Program for Patriotic Exercises on Grand Army Flag Day . . .," *Rhode Island Education Circulars* (n.p., 1925), p. 23; Commissioner, "28th Annual Program for Patriotic Exercises on Grand Army Flag Day . . .," *Rhode Island Education Circulars* (n.p., 1929), pp. 8–9, 24; Commissioner, "30th Annual Program for Patriotic Exercises on Grand Army Flag Day . . .," *Rhode Island Education Circulars* (n.p., 1931), p. 5; Commissioner, "32nd Annual Program for Patriotic Exercises on Grand Army Flag Day . . .," *Rhode Island Education Circulars* (n.p., 1933), p. 4–6.

44. "Fight on Anthem Flayed Here," *Baltimore News*, December 13, 1926; *Proceedings of the 27th Annual Encampment of the Veterans of Foreign Wars of the United States* (Washington, DC, 1926), pp. 13–14; Svejda, *History*, p. 375.

45. William W. Reid, *Sing with Spirit and Understanding: The Story of the American Hymn Society* (New York, 1962), p. 11; "Want Peace Ideal in National Anthem," *New York Times*, February 9, 1930; " 'Star-Spangled Banner' Opposed as Anthem: Music Supervisors Vote Protest to Congress," *New York Times*, March 30, 1930; Sherr, *America the Beautiful*, p. 88; Svejda, *History*, p. 370.

46. "Singable National Anthem Is Sought in Prize Contest Sponsored by New Yorker," *Virginia Pilot* [Norfolk, Va.], July 22, 1928; Svejda, *History*, pp. 373, 376, 378, 381.

47. William Ivy, "Pacifists Would Disarm French National Anthem," *Baltimore Evening Sun*, March 1, 1929.

48. "Patriot Raps Anthem Foes," *Baltimore News*, December 14, 1926; "Address of Mrs. Reuben Ross Holloway of Baltimore, Maryland, on 'The Star-Spangled Banner' before the Women's Patriotic Conference on National Defense, Thursday Afternoon, February 10," typewritten speech, Holloway Collection.

49. J. Charles Linthicum to Mrs. Reuben Ross Holloway, Baltimore, Maryland, March 30, 1922, typewritten letter; Linthicum to Holloway, January 25, 1923, typewritten letter; Linthicum to Thomas Tuite, Bronx, New York, January 10, 1927, typewritten letter. Cited manuscripts in Holloway Collection.

50. Gellermann, *American Legion as Educator*, p. x; *Proceedings of the 29th Annual Encampment of the Veterans of Foreign Wars of the United States* (Washington, DC, 1928), pp. 281–283.

51. Linthicum, "The Star-Spangled Banner"; Walter I. Joyce, New York City, to Mrs. Reuben Ross Holloway, Baltimore, June 18, 1929, typewritten letter; Mrs. Reuben Ross Holloway to Walter I. Joyce, n.d. (in reply to June 18, 1929, letter from Joyce), handwritten letter; Mrs. Reuben Ross Holloway, Baltimore, to J. Charles Linthicum, January 30, 1930, handwritten letter; J. Charles Linthicum, Washington, D.C., to Mrs. Reuben Ross Holloway, Baltimore, Md., February 8, 1930, typewritten letter. Cited manuscripts in Holloway Collection.

52. J. I. Billman, *The Star Spangled Banner: A Brief Story of the Song, Its Growth in Popularity, and the Campaign Conducted by the VETERANS OF FOREIGN WARS OF THE UNITED STATES which Resulted in Its Adoption as Our National Anthem by Act of Congress*, pamphlet (Kansas City, MO, 1932), p. 6.

53. *Legislation to Make "The Star-Spangled Banner" the National Anthem: Hearings Before the Committee on the Judiciary, House of Representatives, Seventy-First Congress, Second Session, on H.R. 14 and H.R. 47* (Washington, DC, 1930), pp. 2, 4.

54. *Legislation to Make "The Star-Spangled Banner,"* pp. 5, 7–9, 12–14; Marshall Kernochan, "Our National Anthem," *Outlook* (March 9, 1930).

55. "Report No. 627," Star-Spangled Banner Clipping File, Library of Congress; Walter I. Joyce, New York City, to "Dear Friend," ca. October 1930, typewritten form letter, Holloway Collection; *Congressional Record* 74, part 7 (1931), pp. 6972–6974; "President Signs after Session: Sets Precedent" and "Relief Acts Lead Long List Voted in 71st Congress," *New York Herald Tribune*, March 5, 1931; Edward S. Delaplaine, *John Philip Sousa and the National Anthem* (Frederick, MD, 1983), pp. 74–75, 80–83.

56. "President Signs after Session" and "Relief Acts"; political cartoon, *Baltimore Sun*, March 5, 1931.

57. Horace M. Coats, "5,000 Dine with President: Feast of 'Fries' Biggest Banquet Ever Attempted," *Indianapolis Star*, June 16, 1931.

7. TRIALS AND TRIUMPHS, 1931–1954

1. Walter F. Richardson, comp., *History: Department of Maryland, the American Legion 1919–1934* (Baltimore, 1934); "Flag Day, Sunday, June 14, 1931, Memorial Plaza, Baltimore," program, Holloway Collection; Svejda, *History*, pp. 432–433.

2. "Presents Star Spangled Banner Bill," *New York Times*, March 10, 1931.

3. "Star-Spangled Banner Words Made Test for Federal Jobs by Proposal in House," *New York Times*, May 20, 1932.

4. *Thirty-Third Annual Encampment, Veterans of Foreign Wars* (Washington, DC, 1932), p. 178.

5. Billman, *The Star Spangled Banner.*

6. Moss, *Flag of the United States.*

7. United States Flag Association, *Our Star Spangled Banner: It Protects Us All* (Washington, DC, 1935).

8. Samuel Engle Burr, comp., *Our Flag and Our Schools* (New Castle, DE, 1936).

9. Burr, *Our Flag and Our Schools*, p. 13.

10. Burr, *Our Flag and Our Schools*, pp. 18, 33.

11. *Thirty-Third Annual Encampment*, pp. 176–180.

12. *Thirty-Third Annual Encampment*, p. 177.

13. *35th National Encampment, Veterans of Foreign Wars* (Washington, DC, 1934), pp. 210–219.

14. "Flag Salute Is Ordered: Chicago School Board also Decrees Anthem to Be Sung Daily," *New York Times*, November 1, 1935; "NBC to Broadcast Daily 'Star-Spangled Banner,' " *New York Times*, April 19, 1936.

15. Neil V. Swanson, *The Flag Is Still There* (New York, 1933), p. vii–viii.

16. "Our Yesterdays"; "Come, Come, Arthur!," *Baltimore Evening Sun*, October 7, 1937.

17. Madison Calvert, "Mrs. Holloway Tells 'Inside' —Ssh!—Story of Her Famous Hats," *Baltimore American*, August 6, 1939.

18. "Mrs. Holloway STANDS for Anthem, Regardless: She Even Gets Up in the Bathtub, She Says, but Adds Glendale (N.Y.) Patriot Needn't Have Awakened Wife," *Baltimore Evening Sun*, October 11, 1938.

19. J. William Joynes, ""Oh! Say, Can You Sing?," *Baltimore News-American*, January 5, 1969.

20. "Most of the Credit for Making 'The Star-Spangled Banner' the National Anthem Is Claimed for the Daughters of 1812," *Baltimore Evening Sun*, December 1, 1937.

21. "2 National Anthems Urged—One for Young, Other for Old: 'Star-Spangled Banner' Probably Ruins More Children's Voices Than Any Other Song, Philadelphia Throat Specialist Explains in Speech Here," *Baltimore Sun*, March 24, 1934.

22. "Protest Revised Anthem: Musicians Oppose New Version," *New York Times*, May 13, 1938; "Oh, Say, Can You Sing?," *New York Times*, June 26, 1938; Joynes, "Oh! Say, Can You Sing?"; "Group to Fight Jazzing of the National Anthem," *New York Times*, December 21, 1938; "Squeakless Hallelujah," *Time* (June 27, 1938).

23. "Our National Anthem: Critic Renews Protest That Air and Words Are Unsuitable," *New York Times*, April 23, 1939; "War Jitters Felt in South America," *New York Times*, October 4, 1939; "Key's Descendant Ready to Defend National Anthem," *Times-Herald*, July 19, 1939.

24. Sheryl Kaskowitz, *God Bless America: The Surprising Story of an Iconic Song* (New York, 2013), pp. 16, 58, 61.

25. Lisa Belkin, "Lucy Monroe Dies: A Celebrated Singer of National Anthem," *New York Times*, October 16, 1987.

26. Bennett Cerf, "The Star-Spangled Girl," [unknown periodical] (1954), clipping in Frederick County Historical Society.

27. Edward S. Delaplaine, *Francis Scott Key, Life and Times* (Brooklyn, NY, 1937).

28. *Baltimore Evening Sun*, July 11, 1940.

29. *125th Anniversary Star Spangled Banner Committee, September 14, 1939*, (n.p., [1939]), pamphlet; Calvert, "Mrs. Holloway."

30. *Report on the Maryland Exhibit New York World's Fair, 1939* (n.p, n.d.), pamphlet.

31. Fred L. Crawford, "No Sabotage for Our Anthem!," *National Republic: A Magazine of Fundamental Americanism* (April 1939), pp. 1–2.

32. "Backs Scheme to Teach Everybody Our Anthem: Mrs. Whitehurst, National Head of Women's Clubs, Gives Full Indorsement to 3-Point Campaign of Mrs. Sadie Orr Dunbar," *Baltimore Evening Sun*, March 6, 1939.

33. "Concern of Mrs. Holloway Over Anthem Upheld by Poll: Gallup Survey Reveals Timeliness of Women's Clubs' Plan to Teach 'Star-Spangled Banner,'" *Baltimore Sun*, March 7, 1939.

34. "Key's Flag Song Championed by Sousa, Interview Shows," *Baltimore Sun*, February 23, 1939; broadside, Delaplaine Collection, also included in Delaplaine, *John Philip Sousa*.

35. Richard Crepeau, "March 21, 1996: Sport and the National Anthem," *Aethlon: The Journal of Sport Literature* (Fall 2002), pp. 70–71.

36. L. H. Robbins, "And the Song Is Still Here," *New York Times*, January 4, 1942.

37. Alan Cowsill, *DC Comics, Year by Year: A Visual Chronicle* (New York, 2010), pp. 36–37, 169; Scott Beatty and Daniel Wallace, *The DC Comics Encyclopedia: The Definitive Guide to the Characters in the DC Universe* (New York, 2008), pp. 287, 294.

38. "Memorial Service: Marking the One Hundredth Anniversary of the Death of Francis Scott Key, St. Paul's Church, Baltimore, January 17, 1843," Maryland Historical Society.

39. National Anthem Committee, "The Code for the National Anthem of the United States of America" ([1942]), reprinted from the *Music Educators Journal* (n.p., n.d.).

40. John R. Luckey, *The United States Flag: Federal Law Relating to Display and Associated Questions*, CRS Report for Congress RL 30243 (Washington, DC, updated April 14, 2008), p. 2, regarding Public Law 77–829, 56 Stat. 1074, Chapter 806, 77th Congress, 2nd Session, H.J. Res. 359, enacted December 22, 1942, "JOINT RESOLUTION: To amend Public Law Numbered 623, approved June 22, 1942, entitled 'Joint resolution to codify and emphasize existing rules and customs pertaining to the display and use of the flag of the United States of America.'"

41. Svejda, *History*, pp. 401–403.

42. "Club Sings Fourth Verse of Anthem for the First," *Frederick News*, May 1, 1942.

43. Julia Smith, *Aaron Copland: His Work and Contribution to American Music* (New York, 1955), p. 187; Arthur Berger, *Aaron Copland* (New York, 1953), p. 30; Richard Kostelanetz, *Aaron Copland: A Reader; Selected Writings 1923–1972* (New York, 2004), p. 334; "Not Even Stravinsky," *Time* (February 2, 1942).

44. *The Star-Spangled Banner: Hearings Before Subcommittee No. 4 of the Committee on the Judiciary, House of Representatives, Eighty Fifth Congress, Second Session, on H.J. Res. 17, H.J. Res. 517, H.R. 10542, H.J. Res. 558, and H.R. 12231, May 21, 22, and 28, 1958* (Washington, DC, 1958), p. 160.

45. Paul Roberts and Shelby Darnell, *There's a Star Spangled Banner Waving Somewhere* (New York, 1942); Harold Adamson and Jimmy McHugh, *There's a New Flag on Iwo Jima* (New York, 1945).

46. Milton Yeats, *American Anthem* (New York, 1942); Lt. Commander Gordon Becker and J. S. Tolder, *The Ramparts We Watch* (New York, 1940); Merrick Fifeld McCarthy and Geoffrey O'Hara, *Our Flag* (New York, 1944).

47. *Army Hit Kit of Popular Songs: Issued Monthly by Special Service Division, Services of Supply, U.S. Army, for Use by the U.S. Armed Forces Only* (New York, 1942).

48. Rob Roy Perry, comp., *Songs of Freedom for Schools, Clubs, Homes, Service Gatherings, and Community Singing* (Philadelphia, 1942).

49. "Topics of the Times," *New York Times*, June 3, 1945.

50. William C. White, "Oh, Say, Can You Sing It?," *New York Times Magazine*, August 26, 1945.

51. F. Regis Noel, "Preservation of the Residence of Francis Scott Key," *Records of the Columbia Historical Society, Washington, D.C., 1944–47* (1947), pp. 4–12; Sam Meyer,

"Francis Scott Key: He Gave Us the National Anthem," *Journal of the Council on America's Military Past* (April 1987), pp. 35–47.

52. "Radio Talk by F. Regis Noel, LL.B., Ph.D., President of the Columbia Historical Society, on Station WFMD, Frederick, Maryland, Sunday, August 8th, 1948, 2:30 P.M," typescript, Frederick County Historical Society.

53. "Oh, Say, Have You Seen the Now-Missing House of Francis Scott Key?," *People* (September 16, 1985), www.people.com/people/archive/article/0,,20091720,00.html; Sam Meyer, "Francis Scott Key: He Gave the Nation Its Anthem," in "Order of Service for the Dedication of a Tablet in Memory of Francis Scott Key Churchman, Patriot, and Poet, . . . Sunday, April Twenty-Sixth, A.D. 1931," Holloway Collection.

54. "Dinner Commemorating 200th Anniversary of the Establishment of Frederick County, Maryland," Delaplaine Collection.

55. J. Glenn Beall, Washington, D.C., to Edward S. Delaplaine, Frederick, Maryland, March 1, 1948, typewritten letter, Delaplaine Collection.

56. "Guests of Honor Luncheon, First Day Issue of the Commemorative Stamp Celebrating the Rededication of the Francis Scott Key Monument, Francis Scott Key Hotel, Frederick, Md., Monday, August 9, 1948," Delaplaine Collection.

57. Edward S. Delaplaine, Frederick, Maryland, to Robert R. McCormick, Chicago, August 21, 1950, typewritten letter, Delaplaine Collection.

58. McCormick to Delaplaine, August 29, 1950, typewritten letter, Delaplaine Collection.

59. Col. James. A. Moss, *Origin and Purpose of Flag Week* (Washington, DC, 1939–1943); Star-Spangled Banner Flag House Association, Inc., *National Flag Week, June 8–14* (n.p., 1953), pamphlet.

60. Star-Spangled Banner Flag House Association, Inc., *National Flag Week, June 8th–14th, 1958* (n.p., May 1, 1958), pamphlet.

61. Hugh Scott, "National Anthem Day: Observance in Pennsylvania Tomorrow Is First in the Nation," *Philadelphia Inquirer*, September 14, 1947; Jeff Gammage, "Flag Day Loses Importance but Lives On in Philadelphia," *Philadelphia Inquirer*, June 14, 2008.

62. "Theodore R. McKeldin, Governor of Maryland: Made before National Anthem Commemorative Service in Christ Church, Philadelphia, Penna., Sunday, September 12th, 1954," reprinted from the *Baltimore Daily Record*, September 14, 1954.

63. National Archives, General Services Administration, *Freedom Train Exhibit, September 1949–January 1950*, National Archives Publication No. 50–4 (n.p., n.d.).

64. Earle R. Poorbaugh, "The Flag is NOT There," *Baltimore Evening Sun*, September 7, 1954; Peter J. Kumpa, "State Legion Acts to Save Original Flag," *Baltimore Evening Sun*, September 1, 1954.

65. George L. Radcliffe, foreword to Harold R. Manakee and Beta K. Manakee, *The Star-Spangled Banner: The Story of Its Writing by Francis Scott Key at Baltimore, September 13–14, 1814* (Baltimore, 1954).

66. Radcliffe, foreword to Manakee and Manakee, *Star-Spangled Banner*; "The Star-Spangled Banner Manuscript Presented to the Society," *Maryland History Notes: Quarterly News Bulletin of the Maryland Historical Society* (August 1954), p. 1.

67. Manakee and Manakee, *Star-Spangled Banner*, p. 23.

68. "Star-Spangled Banner Manuscript"; *The Unveiling of the Original Manuscript of the Star-Spangled Banner*, pamphlet, reprinted from the *Maryland Historical Magazine* (December 1954); Jacques Kelly, "Rev. William Driscoll, 81, Jesuit Priest and Loyola College Chaplain," *Baltimore Sun*, February 1, 2000.

8. STAR-SPANGLED CONFLICT, 1954–1963

1. "Film Info," Star Spangled to Death, www.starspangledtodeath.com.

2. *The Star-Spangled Banner: Hearings*, p. 21.

3. *Congressional Record* (July 9, 1958), pp. A6165–A6166.

4. *Baltimore Evening Sun*, March 5, 1956, quoted in *The Star-Spangled Banner: Hearings*, p. 131.

5. Helen Parks Lasell, Jackson Heights, New York, to Mr. James W. Foster, Director, Maryland Historical Society, January 31, 1958, typewritten letter, Maryland Historical Society.

6. U.S. Flag Committee, *Be Alert Bulletin* (January 10, 1958); Helen Lasell to George Radcliff, President, Maryland Historical Society, undated, typewritten letter. Cited manuscripts in Maryland Historical Society.

7. Helen B. Krippendorf, Keene, New Hampshire, to Members of the Maryland Historical Society, February 14, 1958, typewritten letter, Maryland Historical Society.

8. *Baltimore News-Post*, 1957; *The Star-Spangled Banner: Hearings*, pp. 162, 166.

9. Elizabeth R. Davis, Chairman, American Composition, Maryland Federation of Music Clubs, to Broyhill, April 16, 1958, typewritten letter; Senator George Radcliffe, President of Maryland Historical Society, to Joel T. Broyhill, U.S. Representative, February 19, 1958, typewritten letter. Cited manuscripts in Maryland Historical Society.

10. "6 Resolutions," *Proceedings of the Sixty-Seventh Continental Congress, National Society of the Daughters of the American Revolution, April 14–18, 1958* (Washington, DC, 1958).

11. James Foster to Senator [Radcliffe], April 7, 1958, typewritten letter, Maryland Historical Society.

12. Foster to Broyhill, April 7, 1958, typewritten letter, Maryland Historical Society.

13. Svejda, *History*, p. 433.

14. Hill, "Proposed Official Version."

15. Walter Wingo, "A Star Spangled Banner Year for Words and Music," *Washington Daily News*, May 13, 1958.

16. *The Star-Spangled Banner: Hearings*, p. 12.

17. *The Star-Spangled Banner: Hearings*, pp. 17–35.

18. *The Star-Spangled Banner: Hearings*, pp. 36–40.

19. *The Star-Spangled Banner: Hearings*, p. 42.

20. *The Star-Spangled Banner: Hearings*, pp. 49–50.

21. *The Star-Spangled Banner: Hearings*, p. 50.

22. *The Star-Spangled Banner: Hearings*, pp. 52–54, 56.

23. *The Star-Spangled Banner: Hearings*, p. 56.

24. *The Star-Spangled Banner: Hearings*, pp. 58–61.

25. *The Star-Spangled Banner: Hearings*, pp. 63–66.

26. *The Star-Spangled Banner: Hearings*, pp. 73–74.

27. *The Star-Spangled Banner: Hearings*, pp. 79–93.

28. James W. Foster, "Memorandum report on hearings on the 'Star-Spangled Banner' before House Judiciary Subcommittee No. 4, May 21–22, 1958," Maryland Historical Society.

29. *The Star-Spangled Banner: Hearings*, pp. 111–112.

30. *The Star-Spangled Banner: Hearings*, pp. 112–120.

31. *The Star-Spangled Banner: Hearings*, pp. 126–127; Jack Tracy, "The First Chorus," *Downbeat* (July 11, 1957), 5.

32. *The Star-Spangled Banner: Hearings*, pp. 127–142.

33. *The Star-Spangled Banner: Hearings*, pp. 145–161.

34. Dwight D. Eisenhower to Broyhill, June 4, 1959, copy of typewritten letter, Delaplaine Collection.

35. Broyhill to Hon. E. L. Forrester, Chair, Subcommittee on the Judiciary, June 10, 1959, typewritten letter, Maryland Historical Society.

36. Copy of Broyhill's bill, Star-Spangled Banner Clipping File, Library of Congress.

37. Lasell to Broyhill, June 30, 1962, typewritten letter, Star-Spangled Banner Clipping File.

38. U.S. Flag Committee, *Be Alert Bulletin* (February 27, 1962), Star-Spangled Banner Clipping File; Helen P. Lasell, comp., *Power behind the Government Today* (New York, 1963).

39. Broyhill to William Lichtenwanger, February 21, 1962, typewritten letter, Star-Spangled Banner Clipping File, Library of Congress.

40. Broyhill to "Dear Friends," March 2, 1962, typewritten letter, Maryland Historical Society.

41. Dan Hoik, "There Are Them What Sings Anthem What Can't," *Washington News*, March 16, 1962.

42. Myra MacPherson, "Broyhill Gives 'Star Spangled Banner' a Hearing," *Washington Star*, March 15, 1962.

43. Dena Cohen, "On March 15th Miss Ottilie Sutro joined trip to Constitution Hall, representing the Maryland Historical Society," typewritten document, Maryland Historical Society.

44. John C. Schmidt, "Our Anthem—What Is It?: Congressman Seeking Halt to Wandering Course of Key's Song," *Baltimore Sun*, September 9, 1962.

45. Irving Lowens, "Making 'Star-Spangled Banner' Official," *Washington Star*, March 31, 1963.

46. Broyhill, press release, May 24, 1963, which included a typewritten letter from Guy Lombardo to Broyhill, May 6, 1963.

47. "Francis Scott Key," American Credo stamp ceremony, September 14, 1960, Delaplaine Collection.

48. "Star-Spangled Banner Landmarks" mailer, Star-Spangled Banner Clipping File, Enoch Pratt Free Library, Baltimore, Maryland.

49. Maryland Department of Economic Development, Tourist Division, *Welcome to Historic Maryland* (n.p., 1963); "Official State Highway Map Honors the National Anthem," *Frederick News*, December 23, 1963.

50. "Anniversary of 'The Star-Spangled Banner,'" *Congressional Record* (September 19, 1972), pp. S15220–S15223; "14-Point Program Presented for Sesquicentennial of Key's Writing of 'The Star Spangled Banner,'" *Frederick News*, March 29, 1963; Frances Thomas Bussard, "'The Star-Spangled Banner': A D.A.R. Program for Greater Appreciation of Our National Anthem," *Daughters of the American Revolution Magazine* (August–September 1963), no pagination.

51. Francis Scott Key Memorial Foundation, typescript press release, Delaplaine Collection.

52. "Another C.W. Coin to Be Issued Here," *Frederick News*, July 13, 1963.

53. "Report of the Treasurer," Francis Scott Key Memorial Foundation; C. Lease Bussard, President, "To The Descendants of Francis Scott Key," December 1, 1965, typewritten letter. Cited manuscripts in Delaplaine Collection.

54. *After the Smoke Had Cleared, Wednesday Morning, September 14th, 1814* (Baltimore, 1964), pamphlet, Maryland Historical Society.

55. Robert G. Breen, "Star-Spangled Banner," *Baltimore Sun*, March 13, 1964.

56. *Transmitter* (May–June 1964), a publication for employees of the Chesapeake and Potomac Telephone Company of Virginia; Edward S. Delaplaine, "The Star-Spangled Banner'—Its 150th Anniversary," *Optimist Magazine* (July 1964), pp. 25–26.

57. "Plans Move Step Closer for Showing Francis Scott Key Emblem at World's Fair," *Frederick News*, July 13, 1963.

58. David C. Goeller, "Historical Film for the Fair," *Baltimore Sun*, June 6, 1964; Delaplaine, "Its 150th Anniversary"; "So Proudly We Hail," *Star Spangled Banner Flag House Patriot* (July 1964), no pagination.

59. Delaplaine, "His Paradox of Fame"; Francis A. Hyde to Edward Delaplaine, February 18, 1964, typewritten letter, Delaplaine Collection.

60. Goodman Agency, press release, "Three-Month 'Star-Spangled Banner Festival' to Be Held in Baltimore: 'So Proudly We Hail' Spectacle to be Highlight," vertical file, Maryland Historical Society.

61. *"Star-Spangled Banner" Sesquicentennial Commemoration, 1814–1964*, official program, copy in the author's possession.

62. *Sesquicentennial Commemoration*, p. 89; Svejda, *History*, p. 436.

63. "Star-Spangled Banner Trail Includes 10 Historical Spots," *Baltimore Evening Sun*, December 7, 1965.

64. Charles F. Stern, "The President Reports [1958]," *1812 in '58: The Annual Report of the Society of the War of 1812 in Maryland* (n.p., n.d.), book, Maryland Historical Society.

65. C. Elliott Baldwin, "The President's Backward Glance [1959]," *1812 in '58*.

66. Herbert Lee Trueheart, president's report [1962], *1812 in '58*; Robert Emory Michel, "The President Looks Back [1964]," *1812 in '58*.

67. "Minutes of the Annual Meeting of the Francis Scott Key Memorial Foundation, Inc.," March 1, 1965; C. Lease Bussard to "Dear Trustee," February 9, 1966, typewritten letter; "Minutes of a Meeting of the Trustees of the Francis Scott Key Memorial Foundation, Inc.," May 17, 1968; "Treasurer Report," October 1, 1973. Cited manuscripts in Delaplaine Collection.

9. POSTMODERN PATRIOTISM, 1964–2014

1. J. D. Reed, "Gallantly Screaming," *Sports Illustrated* (January 3, 1977), pp. 54–60.

2. *Fact* magazine, press release, "Poll of Famous Americans Shows That Many Want a New National Anthem," January 18, 1965, Star-Spangled Banner Clipping File, Library of Congress.

3. Renee B. Fisher, "The Case for a New National Anthem," *Saturday Review* (June 25, 1966), pp. 45–46, 57.

4. Joseph Schott, "Francis Scott Key and 'The Star-Spangled Banner,'" *American Legion Magazine* (April 1964), 49; Tracy, "First Chorus"; John O. Jonassen, "Did I Ever Tell You How I Crashed Perle's Party?," *Chicago Tribune*, February 12, 1967.

5. "Robert Goulet Is Remembered in Lewiston, Maine, for Anthem Rendition at Ali-Liston Title Fight," *USA Today*, October 31, 2007.

6. Dave Hirshey, "Oh, Say Can You Sing It?," *New York Daily News*, July 3, 1977.

7. Elizabeth Lesure, "Opera Baritone Robert Merrill Dies," *Houston Chronicle*, October 27, 2004.

8. "More Memories of the 1968 DNC [Democratic National Convention]," *State Journal Register* [Springfield, IL], August 18, 2008; "Oh Say Can You Sing It?," *This Week*, February 9, 1969; Jack Gould, "TV: Calif. Gets 3 Candidates on Air Together; Unruh Solves Problem Networks Could Not," *New York Times*, August 28, 1968; Svejda, *History*, p. 446; "The National Anthem," *Chicago Tribune*, August 28, 1968.

9. "Ernie Harwell Recalls Choosing José to Sing the Anthem," José Feliciano website, www.josefeliciano.com/index.php?page=anthem/.

10. "Reflections: José Shares His Experience with You . . .," José Feliciano website, www.josefeliciano.com/index.php?page=anthem/.

11. Nancy Ball, "O Say Can You See Any End To It?," *Baltimore News-American*, January 15, 1969.

12. Hirshey, "Can You Sing It?"

13. "Unfamiliar Anthem," *New York Times*, October 27, 1968; Donal Henahan, "Soul-Spangled Banner," *New York Times*, October 27, 1968.

14. Tom Goldman, "Anthem Singers Test 'the Land of the Free,'" National Public Radio transcript, October 27, 2006, www.npr.org/templates/story/story.php?storyId=6394213/.

15. Johnny Black, *Jimi Hendrix: The Ultimate Experience* (New York, 1999), pp. 167, 185; David Stubbs, *Jimi Hendrix: The Stories behind Every Song* (New York, 2003), pp. 123–124; John McDermott, *Jimi Hendrix Sessions: The Complete Studio Recording Sessions* (Boston, 1995), p. 94; John McDermott, *Ultimate Hendrix: An Illustrated Encyclopedia of Live Concerts and Sessions* (Milwaukee, 2009), pp. 141, 201–202.

16. Black, *Jimi Hendrix*, p. 201; Stubbs, *Jimi Hendrix*, p. 123.

17. "American Icons: Jimi Hendrix's Star-Spangled Banner," Studio 360, November 19, 2010, www.studio360.org/story/96239-jimi-hendrixs-star-spangled-banner/.

18. Bob Baker, "Oh, Say Can You Sing?," *Los Angeles Times*, November 4, 2002; Ball, "Can You See Any End?"

19. Tommie Smith, with David Steele, *Silent Gesture: The Autobiography of Tommie Smith* (Philadelphia, 2007), pp. 2, 139, 173.

20. "Oh Say Can You Sing It?"

21. "Most Readers Love Our Anthem," *This Week* [ca. February 1969].

22. Kiki Levathes, "The Anthem and Sports," *Washington Star*, February 6, 1972.

23. Levathes, "Anthem and Sports."

24. Levathes, "Anthem and Sports"; "Wayne Collett, Track Medalist, Barred because of Protest, Dies at 60," *New York Times*, March 18, 2010.

25. "Playing Anthem at Games Urged," *Baltimore Sun*, May 18, 1954; "Play before Every Game Cheapens Anthem—Ehlers," *Baltimore Sun*, May 20, 1954; C. M. Gibbs, "Gibberish," *Baltimore Sun*, June 22, 1954.

26. "Singalong with Sox," *Chicago Tribune*, April 17, 1966; "'Star Spangled Banner' Still Out for Sox," *Chicago Tribune*, May 3, 1966; Herb Lyon, "Tower Ticker," *Chicago Tribune*, May 4, 1966; "'Star-Spangled Banner' Leads the Hit Parade," *Chicago Tribune*, May 4, 1966; "In the Wake of the News . . ." *Chicago Tribune*, May 31, 1967; "Cubs Add Organ Music . . . and Bertell," *Chicago Tribune*, February 3, 1967; Gerald Eskenazi, "Garden Track Meet Will Drop U.S. Anthem to Avoid Incidents," *New York Times*, January 16, 1973; Carl Scovel, "O Say Can You Sing?," *Atlantic Monthly* (February 1975), pp. 54–55; Levathes, "Anthem and Sports."

27. Hirshey, "Can You Sing It?"

28. Donal Henahan, "O, Say, What Have They Done to 'The Star-Spangled Banner'?" *New York Times*, January 9, 1978; Reed, "Gallantly Screaming."

29. Eskenazi, "Garden Track Meet"; Tom Ayres, "8 of 10 Americans Don't Know National Anthem," *National Tattler*, March 25, 1973.

30. Levathes, "Anthem and Sports"; Reed, "Gallantly Screaming."

31. Noel Coppage, "Oh Say! Can You Sing 'The Star-Spangled Banner'?," *Stereo Review* (February 1970), pp. 78–80.

32. Scovel, "Can You Sing?"; "FROM THE OFFICE OF SENATOR CHARLES MCC. MATHIAS, JR., (R-MD.), FOR RELEASE: Wednesday PMS, January 6, 1971," Vertical File, Delaplaine Collection.

33. "Anniversary of 'The Star-Spangled Banner.'"

34. Irving Berlin to Edward S. Delaplaine, September 21, 1973, typewritten letter, Delaplaine Collection.

35. Ayres, "8 of 10 Americans."

36. Scovel, "Can You Sing?"

37. Editorial, *Washington Star*, January 20, 1976.

38. Reed, "Gallantly Screaming."

39. American Revolution Bicentennial Commission, "Bicentennial News," press release ([ca. 1975]).

40. Georgia Dullea, "'O, Say, Can . . .' How Does It Go Again?," *New York Times*, July 6, 1976; Lise Bang-Jensen, "The National Anthem: Ditch It for Another?," *Boston Globe*, March 7, 1977.

41. Ruth Dean, "Oh, Say Can You See What the Outcome Will Be?," *Washington Star*, February 2, 1977.

42. James M. Cain, "O Say Can You Sing It?," *Washington Post*, July 3, 1977.

43. Cain, "Can You Sing It?"; L. H. Robbins, "And the Song Is Still Here," *New York Times*, January 4, 1942.

44. Bret McCabe, "Against the Grain: Ethel Ennis Cuts Her Own Path between Her Life and Music," *Baltimore City Paper*, October 14, 2009; Hirshey, "Can You Sing It?"; Reed, "Gallantly Screaming."

45. Hirshey, "Can You Sing It?"

46. Hirshey, "Can You Sing It?"

47. Margaret Carlson, "Oh, Say, Can You Sing It?," *Time* (February 12, 1990).

48. Neil A. Grauer, "It's Ours—So What If We Can't Sing It?," *Baltimore Evening Sun*, August 18, 1989.

49. Norman Runnion, "Anthem Won't Play in Putney," *Boston Globe*, March 2, 1977; Carol Oppenheim, "Oh Say, Can You See a New Anthem?," *Chicago Tribune*, September 18, 1977.

50. Lise Bang-Jensen, "Readers Favor Adopting a New National Anthem," *Boston Globe*, March 4, 1977; Bang-Jensen, "Ditch It For Another?"

51. Pete Taft, "'On the Road' Visits," *Brattleboro [Vt.] Reformer*, March 25, 1977.

52. Reed, "Gallantly Screaming."

53. Carol Oppenheim, "All Is Not Quiet in Putney, Vt." *Boston Globe*, October 10, 1978; Hirshey, "Can You Sing It?"

54. Carol Oppenheim, "Town Votes Allegiance to Old Anthem," *Chicago Tribune*, March 9, 1978; Oppenheim, "New Anthem?"

55. "Legion Opposes Anthem Change," *Frederick News-Post*, May 12, 1978.

56. Arthur Fiedler to Edward S. Delaplaine, August 15, 1978, typewritten letter, Delaplaine Collection.

57. "Marvin Gaye Interview, 1983," YouTube, www.youtube.com/watch?v=tfIjkcCE _lU&playnext=1&list=PL411C3A0EF767F286&feature=results_video/.

58. Associated Press, "Holt Wants Anthem in Original Key," April 29, 1983; Linda Sarrio, "Off-Key Renditions of National Anthem Spark Rocket-Red Flare-Up in Congress," *Chicago Tribune*, May 31, 1983.

59. Andy Jacobs Jr., *Slander and Sweet Judgment: The Memoir of an Indiana Congressman* (Zionsville, IN, 2000), pp. 380, 382; Jacobs, "Instead of Fireworks, Some Quiet Courage," *USA Today*, July 18, 1986.

60. Caldwell Titcomb, "What So Loudly We Wail," *Baltimore Sun*, December 4, 1985.

61. "Star-Spangled Earache: What So Loudly We Wail," *New Republic* (December 15, 1985).

62. James J. Kilpatrick, "On Key or Off, It's a Poor Anthem," *Baltimore Sun*, December 12, 1985.

63. Joan Beck, "A Bill to Change the National Anthem? Oh, Beautiful!," *Miami Herald*, January 16, 1986.

64. Author's interview with Andrew Jacobs Jr., August 8, 2013.

65. Maury R. Wolff, "Say, I Can't See Changing the Anthem," *Wall Street Journal*, July 3, 1986.

66. Daniel Mark Epstein, "America's No. 1 Song," *Atlantic* (July 1986); Dullea, "How Does It Go Again?"

67. "Let's Have a Debate on National Anthem," *USA Today*, July 18, 1986.

68. Jacobs, *Slander and Sweet Judgment*, p. 383; William Donald Schaefer, "No Need for Debate: Keep This Great Song," *USA Today*, July 18, 1986.

69. Jacobs, "Instead of Fireworks."

70. "Voices from across the USA: Do You Think We Should Change Our National Anthem?," *USA Today*, July 18, 1986.

71. Grauer, "It's Ours."

72. Doug Birch, "Hands Off Anthem, Schaefer Tells Hoosier," *Baltimore Sun*, December 9, 1989.

73. Carlson, "Can You Sing It?"; author's interview with Andrew Jacobs Jr., August 8, 2013.

74. "Roseanne Pitches Apologies after Throwing Fans a Curve with a Barr-Mangled *Banner*," *People* (August 13, 1990), www.people.com/people/archive/article/0,,20118450,00.html.

75. Chris Cuomo and Andrew Paparella, "Whitney Houston's Star-Spangled Secret," ABC News, February 16, 2012.

76. Ben Palosaari, "Kansas City Chiefs Fans Give Eli Young Band Hell for Botching the National Anthem," December 7, 2010, Pitch, http://www.pitch.com/FastPitch/archives/2010/12/07/kansas-city-chiefs-fans-give-eli-young-band-hell-for-botching-the-national-anthem/.

77. Samantha L. Quigley, "Project to Rekindle Singing of National Anthem," Armed Forces Press Service, November 5, 2004.

78. Francis Scott Key, John Stafford Smith, Walter Damrosch, and Francis Haffkine Snow, *La Bandera de las Estrellas* (New York, 1919); Clotilde Arias Papers, 1920–1956, National Museum of American History, Smithsonian Institution; Steve Bryant, "Jose Can

You See—New National Anthem," May 23, 2007, Philly Talk, www.phillytalk.com/funny-stuff/steve-bryant/166-jose-can-you-see-new-national-anthem/.

79. Dave McKenna, "The Other National Anthem: At Howard Football Games, 'The Star-Spangled Banner' Isn't the Only Sacred Song," *Washington City Paper*, September 26, 2008.

80. "Jonny Craig Messes Up National Anthem at Baseball Game," August 20, 2013, Lambgoat, http://lambgoat.com/blog/368/Jonny-Craig-messes-up-National-Anthem-at-baseball-game/.

EPILOGUE

1. Crawford, "No Sabotage."

2. Kaskowitz, *God Bless America*, p. 103.

Further Reading

DESPITE THE LONG HISTORY of *The Star-Spangled Banner* and its impact on American popular culture, the song has never previously received a broad narrative treatment. Past publications, including sheet music compilations, are *Star-Spangled Books* (Maryland Historical Society, 1972) by P. William Filby and Edward G. Howard, and *The Star Spangled Banner: Words and Music Issued between 1814-1864* (New York, 1935) by Joseph Muller. Other notable titles are *The Star Spangled Banner* by Oscar Sonneck (Washington, D.C., 1914), which established basic facts abut the historical record, and George J. Svejda, *The History of the Star-Spangled Banner from 1814 to the Present* (Washington, D.C., 1969). Commissioned by the National Park Service in anticipation of the bicentennial, Svejda's work reflects impressive archival archaeology.

Index